Keywords

for American Cultural Studies

D0572377

Keywords

for American Cultural Studies

Edited by

Bruce Burgett and Glenn Hendler

NEW YORK UNIVERSITY

New York and London

Frontis: Anselm Kiefer, *Book with Wings*, 1992–94, lead, tin, and steel, 74 ¾ x 208 ⅜ x 43 ⅜ inches. Collection of the Modern Art Museum of Fort Worth, Texas, Museum Purchase, Sid W. Richardson Foundation Endowment Fund.

NEW YORK UNIVERSITY PRESS
New York and London
www.nyupress.org

© 2007 by New York University
All rights reserved

Library of Congress Cataloging-in-Publication Data
Keywords for American cultural studies /
edited by Bruce Burgett and Glenn Hendler.
p. cm.
Includes bibliographical references.
ISBN–13: 978–0–8147–9947–5 (alk. paper)
ISBN–10: 0–8147–9947–7 (alk. paper)
ISBN–13: 978–0–8147–9948–2 (pbk. : alk. paper)
ISBN–10: 0–8147–9948–5 (pbk. : alk. paper)
1. Vocabulary.   2. United States—Civilization.
3. Social structure—Terminology.   4. Culture—Terminology.
I. Burgett, Bruce, 1963–   II. Hendler, Glenn, 1962–
PE1449.K49   2007
428.1—dc22   2007015067

New York University Press books are printed on acid-free paper, and their binding materials are chosen for strength and durability.

Manufactured in the United States of America

Contents

Contents

Acknowledgments

Writing the acknowledgments for a project like this one is a particularly daunting task, in no small part because we should begin by, once again, listing the names of our contributors. All of them have demonstrated immense patience and produced marvelous intellectual work, after enduring what must have seemed endless requests for revision. We thank them all for putting up with us.

The idea for this volume emerged, developed, and was tested through interactions with a series of interlocutors and audiences, including the American Cultures workshop at the University of Chicago, the American Studies Association, the Americanist workshop at the University of Notre Dame, the Columbia American Studies Seminar, the Modern Language Association, and the Simpson Center for the Humanities at the University of Washington. Thanks to everyone who participated in and attended those events, and specifically to Carla Peterson and Sandy Zagarell for sharing their concept for a "Keywords" conference panel, and to Chandan Reddy and Nikhil Singh for offering advice at various points along the way. We also want to thank the University of Notre Dame's Institute for Scholarship in the Liberal Arts for support.

Brooke Cameron has been absolutely central to this project. She has worked tirelessly to correspond with our contributors, to maintain files on all of the entries, to organize the manuscript, to check and recheck bibliographical citations, and to generate an increasingly baroque spreadsheet of deadlines, revisions, and addresses. Eric Zinner deserves credit for looking at a list of words and names in a conference program and seeing in it the idea for a book; he also deserves thanks for allowing us to run with the idea and for bearing with us as we executed it. Thanks to Joanna Glickler for editing from time to time and asking good questions, and to Brenda Majercin for putting up with all of those stoopidacademics, a keyword if we've ever heard one. Thanks as well go to Nina Rowe for drawing Glenn to New York, for tolerating sweet and expensive cocktails, and for reading the *New York Times*. Thanks finally to our readers who treat the volume not as summative of past work, but as generative of future projects. You are the reason we undertook it.

Keywords An Introduction

What is a keyword? The *Oxford English Dictionary*'s primary definition is "a word serving as a key to a cipher or the like." In this usage, a keyword solves a puzzle, breaks a code, or unlocks a mystery. Or a keyword may be, in the *OED*'s secondary definition, "a word or thing that is of great importance or significance," a term or symbol that organizes knowledge by allowing authors, book indexers, concordance makers, web designers, and database programmers to guide users to significant clusters of meaning. As these usages indicate, keywords are terms of great power and utility. Referred to in the field of information technology as "metadata" or "meta-tags," they sort through large quantities of print and digital information not only by providing quick access to specific content, but also by prioritizing and marketing some clusters of meaning and modes of contextualization over others.

When you look up a term in *Keywords for American Cultural Studies*, you will find that these technical definitions are both accurate and limited. Entries in this volume synthesize a great deal of information about the historical and contemporary meanings of many of the central terms that structure the fields of American studies and cultural studies; they provide contexts for the usage of those terms by discussing how their meanings have developed over time; and they may even unlock a few mysteries and break a few

codes. The volume serves, in this primary sense, as a snapshot of the dynamic, interdisciplinary, and cross-methodological research conversations that currently traverse the fields of American studies and cultural studies. But it would be a mistake to read *Keywords for American Cultural Studies* as a standard reference guide to an academic discipline. It is also designed to model a different kind of intellectual activity, and we intend it to provoke researchers, teachers, and students working across a wide range of intellectual formations to engage in problem-based forms of inquiry as they make claims about "America" and its various "cultures." Such inquiries differ from traditional academic research about "American culture" in two ways: they frame and pursue research questions that are explicitly responsive to shifts in contemporary political and social life; and they enable readers to think critically and creatively about how knowledge about "America" and its "cultures" has been, is, and should be made. *Keywords for American Cultural Studies* is, in this second sense, both a guide to some of the best existing research in and across the fields it maps and an argument for maintaining and enhancing a commitment to critical and interdisciplinary approaches to the future evolution of those fields.

Given these somewhat heterodox aims, it should come as no surprise that the immediate context for our usage of the term "keyword" is one that reference books like the *OED* tend not to mention: the writings of the British cultural studies scholar Raymond Williams. Upon his return from World War II, Williams became interested in how the meanings of certain words, which he later called "keywords," seemed to have shifted during his absence. The most notable of these keywords was "culture," a term Williams saw as taking on very different significances in the academic spheres of literary studies and anthropology, and as anchoring new clusters of meaning through its interactions in popular discourse with neighboring terms such as "art," "industry," "class," and "democracy." Two publications that would hold great importance for the emerging field of cultural studies resulted from this experiential insight. The first, *Culture and Society, 1780–1950* (1958), traced a genealogy of the complex and often contradictory mid-twentieth-century usages of the word "culture" back through nearly two centuries of writings by British intellectuals concerned with the antagonistic relations between political democracy and capitalist industrialization. The second, *Keywords: A Vocabulary of Culture and Society* (1976), collected 134 short entries (151 in the 1983 revised edition), all of which gloss the shifts over the same two centuries in the meanings of terms ranging from "behavior" and "charity" to "sensibility" and "work." As Williams explained in his introduction to the first edition of *Keywords*, he wrote these entries in his spare moments and originally conceived of them as an appendix to *Culture and Society*, but later developed them into a separate publication as their

sum grew in scope and complexity, and as he began to understand and articulate the methodological stakes of the project he had undertaken. *Keywords* is, Williams insisted, "not a dictionary or glossary of a particular academic subject. It is not a series of footnotes to dictionary histories or definitions of a number of words. It is, rather, the record of an inquiry into a *vocabulary*" (15).

The term "vocabulary" is in many ways the unacknowledged keyword of Williams's introduction, and his use of that term can help us to explain how our *Keywords* volume works as well. He deployed it in order to distinguish his project not only from those of dictionary editors and glossary makers, but also from the work of academic philologists and linguists who examine the formal and structural components of language systems and their evolution. In contrast, Williams focused his keyword entries on what he called "historical semantics" (23), a phrase that emphasizes the ways in which meanings are made and altered over time through contestations among the usages of diverse social groups and movements. "What can be done in dictionaries," Williams wrote, "is necessarily limited by their proper universality and by the long time-scale of revision which that, among other factors, imposes. The present inquiry, being more limited—not a dictionary, but a vocabulary—is more flexible" (26). This underlining of the flexibility of a "vocabulary"—as opposed to the universality of a "dictionary"—both points to Williams's general premise that language systems develop and change only in relation to local and practical usages, and explains his editorial decision to include blank pages at the end of his *Keywords* in order to signal that "the inquiry remains open, and that the author will welcome all amendments, corrections and revisions" (26). Like institutionally established academic methodologies and disciplines (philology and linguistics, in this case), dictionaries, glossaries, and other reference books reproduce a discourse of expertise by downplaying the creative, idiosyncratic, and unpredictable aspects of problem-based thinking and research. Like the forms of critical interdisciplinarity to which Williams's own work contributes, vocabularies provide a counterpoint to this discourse of expertise. They treat knowledge not as a product of research that can be validated only in established disciplines and by credentialing institutions, but as a process that is responsive to the diverse constituencies that use and revise the meanings of the keywords that govern our understandings of the present, the future, and the past.

Keywords for American Cultural Studies shares a number of these fundamental premises with Williams's volume, as well as its other successors (e.g., Bennett, Grossberg, and Morris 2005). It provides an accessible and readable introduction to some of the central terms and debates that shape the study of culture and society today. And it insists that those debates can be enhanced—rather than settled or shut down—by an increased understanding of the genealogies of their structuring terms and the conflicts and disagreements embedded in differing and even contradictory uses of those terms. To this end, we asked our contributors to address four basic questions as they wrote and revised

their entries: What kinds of critical projects does your keyword enable? What are the critical genealogies of the term and how do these genealogies affect its use today? Are there ways of thinking that are occluded or obstructed by the use of this term? What other keywords constellate around it? These questions were intended to spur our contributors to map the contemporary critical terrain as they see it developing in and around their keyword, and to ensure that a reader opening the book to any given entry could expect to encounter many of the same things: information about that term's genealogy; a specific thinker's take on the lines of inquiry that the term opens up or closes down; and links between the term and others in the volume or elsewhere. Attentive readers will note that individual authors responded in different ways to these prompts. Some entries are explicitly argumentative and polemical, while others are more descriptive and ecumenical. A few are willfully idiosyncratic, and several hint at implicit disagreements among the authors. Yet across all of the entries the reader will find scholarly writing that models critical and creative thinking, and authors who simultaneously analyze and evince the ways in which keywords are, as Williams put it, both "binding words in certain activities and their interpretation" and "indicative words in certain forms of thought" (15).

At the same time, there are several aspects of our *Keywords* that make it distinctive. Most obviously, it is a collaborative project involving more than sixty authors working across a range of disciplinary and interdisciplinary fields that overlap with, but seldom map neatly onto, either American studies or cultural studies. Most importantly, its exploration of culture and society is explicitly linked to a nation (the United States) or, at times, a geography (the Americas). The keyword "America" is thus central to the volume in two ways. First, the term in all of its mutations— "American," "Americas," "Americanization," "Americanist"—needs to be defined in relation to what Williams called "particular formations of meaning" (15). "America," in other words, is a category with particularizing effects that are as central to how we think about the possibilities and limitations of the field of American studies as the universalizing term "culture" is to our understanding of the shape of the field of cultural studies. Second, contemporary disagreements over the category's field-defining function point toward a wide range of debates related to what is now commonly called the postnational or transnational turn in American studies. Just as the universalizing referents of Williams's own project have been troubled by subsequent work in cultural studies that has rendered explicit his tendency to assume a narrowly "British" (largely white, working-class) readership and archive for that project (Gilroy 1987), the category "America" has been troubled within American studies in part through the field's interactions with cultural studies, though more pressingly by its engagements with new "formations of meaning" emerging from shifting patterns of migration and immigration, existing and evolving diasporic communities, and the cultural and economic effects of globalization. The fact that nine of the words in this last sentence—"culture,"

"white," "class," "America," "immigration," "diaspora," "community," "economy," and "globalization"—appear as keyword entries in this volume indicates how rich and complex this research has become.

In our editorial conversations with our contributors, we have attempted to draw out this richness and complexity by insisting—as Kirsten Silva Gruesz does in her entry on "America"—that authors specify when they are talking about "America" and when they are talking about the "United States." It is an editorial decision that has produced some interesting results. Nearly all of the entries reach across U.S. national borders to track usages of terms like "America," "South," and "West," and across disciplinary formations such as political philosophy and social theory where terms ranging from "liberalism" and "democracy" to "secularism" and "religion" may be inflected in particular ways in the United States, but cannot be subsumed under either an "American" or an "Americanist" rubric. Similarly, terms that might from one perspective be viewed as a subset of American studies (or cultural studies focused on the United States) are consistently shown to have transnational histories and future trajectories. Entries on "African," "Asian," "mestizo/a," "coolie," and "white"—not to mention "diaspora," "immigration," and "naturalization"—all map cultural formations and develop lines of inquiry that are neither exclusive to the United States nor exhausted by historically U.S.-based fields such as African American or Asian American studies. Transnational understandings of these keywords push us to re-imagine the political geographies of the United States, as well as the nation-based intellectual geographies of the institutions that study it. And they indicate the involvement of our contributors in a wide variety of critical interdisciplinarities, ranging from postcolonial studies to queer studies to community studies. One lesson taught by these relatively new intellectual formations is that attempts by traditionally nation-based fields such as American studies to contain "particularities" within a universalizing (U.S.) nationalism, no matter how "diverse" or "multicultural," always leave something—and often someone—out of the analytical frame.

Faced with this inevitability, it is tempting to apologize for specific terms and perspectives we have failed to include. Many keywords of American studies and cultural studies do not appear in this volume, some due to oversights that reflect our own intellectual and institutional orientations, but most because we wanted the book to be affordable and portable. This second factor required that we pare our original list of 145 entries to the current 64, a vexing process, but one that allowed several clusters of meaning to surface even as significant terms vanished. Take as an example the keyword "individual." A college student who in high school was exposed to the old saw that "American" (read: U.S.) culture is characterized by an ideology of "individualism" might at first be dismayed to find no entry for that term in this volume. But that student might then look for—or be guided to—terms closely related to the concept of individuality: most clearly "identity," but also "interiority" and "body."

From there, the student could move either to keywords that qualify and constitute individuality, such as "race," "ethnicity," "gender," "sex," and "disability," or to keywords that name places and concepts within which "individualism" is contested and constructed, such as "family," "religion," "corporation," "state," and "city." This line of inquiry could then bring the student to "public" and "community" for broader framings of the missing entry on "individual." And the student might even end up reading the entry on "society," remembering that a previous course had suggested that individualism is always in tension with social norms, though now reflecting more critically on that simplistic analytical framework. At this point, the student would have a much more nuanced understanding of what other keywords and concepts are necessary to map the relationship between "individual" and "society," and would be prepared to launch a research project around the problem of the "individual" that had been enriched by the simple fact that the term itself does *not* appear in this volume.

We imagine that this hypothetical example will strike some readers as persuasive, while others will remain skeptical of our editorial choices. To both groups, we want to extend an invitation to become collaborators in keywords projects that extend beyond the covers of this book. We ask you to revise, reject, and respond to the entries that do—and do not—appear in this volume, to create new clusters of meaning among them, and to develop deeper and richer discussions of what a given term does and can mean when used in specific local and global contexts. While we have not followed Williams's cue by providing blank pages for the reader's use at the back of our *Keywords*, we do want to offer the following, necessarily incomplete list of words about which we, as co-editors of this keywords project, would like to hear and read more: activism, age, agency, alien, anarchy, archive, art, black, book, bureaucracy, canon, celebrity, character, child, Christian, commodity, consent, conservative, country, creativity, creole, depression, desire, development, disciplinary, diversity, education, elite, equality, evolution, European, experience, expert, fascism, feminine, fiction, freedom, friendship, government, hegemony, heritage, heterosexual, history, homosexual, human, imagination, individual, intellectual, Islam, Jewish, justice, labor, Latino, liberty, literacy, local, masculine, management, manufacture, media, minority, mission, multicultural, Muslim, native, normal, opinion, oratory, patriotism, place, pluralism, policy, popular, poverty, pragmatism, psychology, radical, reality, representation, republicanism, reservation, resistance, revolution, rights, romance, security, segregation, settler, socialism, sodomy, sovereignty, space, subaltern, subjectivity, technology, terror, text, theory, tourism, tradition, transgender, translation, trauma, utopia, virtual, virtue, wealth, welfare, work.

This already too-long list could go on for pages, and even then it would be easy to conjure other possibilities. Whether keywords projects like this one take the form of classroom assignments, research and working groups, edited volumes, or public forums, they must remain open to further elaboration and amendment not simply due to dynamics of inclusion and exclusion or limitations of time and space. Rather, their incompletion is essential to any problem-based understanding of how research is conducted and how knowledge is made, both inside and outside of academic settings. Claiming the ability to map complex fields of knowledge while also maintaining a critical approach to how the problems that constitute those fields are—and should be—framed requires both intellectual modesty and an openness to further collaboration. One response to this modesty and openness is critique. We welcome this response, and we also want to encourage all of our readers to react by making something new, whether that thing is as minor as a new conversation or classroom assignment or as major as an edited volume, digital archive, or public initiative. The true measure of the success of *Keywords for American Cultural Studies* will be its ability to clear conceptual space for these future projects, as scholars, teachers, and students develop new and challenging research questions in dialogue with others who may not quite share a common vocabulary, but who do know something about where conflicts and debates over meaning come from, why they matter, and how they might matter differently in the future. We look forward to reading and hearing about the results of these inquiries.

1

Abolition

Robert Fanuzzi

"Children are taught that 'AB' stands for 'Abolition,'" fumed the mayor of Boston in 1835, who correctly grasped that abolition meant more than the end of slaveholding ("Mr. Otis's Speech" 1835). In the popular imagination of the early nineteenth century, abolition named a utopian program of mass reeducation that would indoctrinate its white listeners and readers into a new set of moral beliefs. The fact that even children were addressed by this pedagogy means that abolitionists considered it necessary to alienate future citizens from their allegiance to their government, and to remake the nation from the ground up. The concept of abolition that shaped the antislavery struggle of the nineteenth century thus challenged nothing less than the legitimacy of the entire U.S. political system.

The most radical arguments and implications of abolition had many precedents. One of the most influential was the early-nineteenth-century Christian evangelical movement, which pointedly refused to recognize secular institutions such as the nation-state as sources of moral norms and identities. From this movement, advocates of abolition adopted the psychic and ethical structure of the conversion experience, with its urgent demands for personal moral accountability and a direct encounter with truth. Abolition, thought of during the late eighteenth and early nineteenth centuries as a gradual process, was by the 1830s defined as something that could and should happen immediately.

And yet the concept of abolition that inspired antislavery activists also contained a set of possibilities that were designed to perpetuate and sustain U.S. citizens' faith in their political system: that the most corrupt government or social order might be repaired by a challenge from outside it; that the vehemence of this challenge bore witness to the original intent and principles of the political system; and that a single, decisive act therefore could restore continuity to a ruptured narrative of national history (Sundquist 1985; Fanuzzi 2003). The imperative of abolition, in other words, betrays a fundamental anxiety about the validity of the U.S. political system and promotes periodic tests of that system by forcing it to measure up to a specific policy priority: the abolition of slavery, the abolition of the death penalty, or the abolition of legalized abortion. The call made by a late-twentieth-century scholar for the "abolition of whiteness" suggests that the special status of abolition as final arbiter and ultimatum has given the field of American cultural studies not just one of its keywords, but also a moral vocation (Roediger 1994).

The concept of abolition has played an equally important role in the construction of a progressive national history. Several generations of American studies scholars have used the concept to chart a progressive history of the United States in which the end of chattel slavery serves as the climax and marker of an ongoing commitment to civil rights. In the early twentieth century, the civil rights leader W. E .B. Du Bois (1995) invoked the prospect of an "abolition democracy" in order to hold a still racially segregated United States accountable to this history. However, the wide range of conflicting initiatives that have been advanced under the rubric of abolition suggests that the concept cannot reveal a single historical trend or even denote a categorically progressive political actor. The unique feature of abolition is that it forces a disruption in the flow of political power in each of its iterations and deployments and helps to instigate a debate over the legitimacy of political means and ends in each of its historical contexts. By extending the title "abolitionist" to the advocates of abolition, we in fact imply that such a commitment is so all-consuming and incongruous that it cannot be reconciled with any other political affiliation or identity and that it easily supplants alternative designations such as "citizen."

The intensity and complexity of abolitionist resistance so frustrated its nineteenth-century opponents that they coined the term "ultraism" as a synonym for abolition. The scholarship of American cultural studies, on the other hand, has embraced the most transgressive examples of abolitionist politics—William Lloyd Garrison's campaign to disband the Union and neutralize the advantages of white citizenship (Castiglia 2002), the mobilization of white middle-class and African American women (Yellin 1989), the politicization of popular fiction (S. Samuels 1996)—and used them as creative sites for rethinking civic identity and political action.

The signature "abolitionist" in this sense of the word might well be John Brown, whose paramilitary assault on a munitions arsenal continues to compel scholars to wonder not just whether his violent methods were consistent with moral standards of political action but whether such an abolitionist commitment was rational (Reynolds 2005). His contemporary Henry David Thoreau (1973) helped to square the radicalism of abolition with a national tradition of civil disobedience when he eulogized Brown, executed as a traitor and terrorist, as a martyr to freedom. Of course, Thoreau had previously invented this tradition in order to rationalize his own idiosyncratic act of abolitionist defiance in the essay "Resistance to Civil Government."

Thoreau's efforts notwithstanding, Brown's abolitionism poses its most difficult questions when we widen our view to include his comrades in arms, the enslaved and free African Americans who opposed slavery. Can they be considered abolitionists too? Judgments about who and what is abolitionist inevitably reveal the racial construction that inheres within the concept. Indeed, abolition often identifies a special capacity or attribute of white people that compels them to discharge their moral responsibility (Wiegman 2002). Although fugitive slaves such as Frederick Douglass claimed leading roles as abolitionists and sought to align slave insurrections with the goals of the abolition movement, these exceptions continue to prove the rule of common usage. Abolition remained (and remains) understood as something that others do on behalf of inert, aggrieved parties; as such, it can seem opposed to the prospect of self-liberation.

However, historical research concerned with the enslaved and free black communities of the antebellum era promises to change this meaning of abolition. As Robert Levine (1997) and Paul Goodman (1998) have shown, the first abolitionists in the early-nineteenth-century antislavery struggle were the free black members of an anti-colonization movement, which sought to debunk the colonization policy championed by so-called liberal whites as the best answer to the slavery question. Colonizationists promoted the new African colony of Liberia as the best and, in fact, the only homeland for African Americans, while its opponents called it a racist scheme for the removal of free blacks from the United States. For African American civic leaders such as William Watkins and Samuel Cornish, abolition was an express alternative to colonization that entailed not just the liberation of the enslaved but also the coexistence of whites and blacks.

The egalitarian politics that black activists inscribed in this concept of abolition distinguish it so markedly from the original British meaning of the word that it is fair to say that they helped to Americanize the term. Abolition originated in the lexicon of eighteenth-century British anti-mercantilism as an argument for free trade, signifying the freedom of markets, not of enslaved people. Such arguments specifically stipulated the abolition of the infamous transatlantic slave trade, in large part because it profited from mercantilist policies of protectionism and monopoly (Smith 1776). Of course, this concept of abolition left Britain's capitalist middle class secure in its virtue, while the enslaved remained safely ensconced in West Indian plantations. The "humanitarian sensibility" ascribed by the historian Thomas Haskell (1985) to the supporters of abolition in fact stipulated that white people maintain a distant, hypothetical identification with the sufferings of black people that put off the prospect of social coexistence.

The American concept of abolition allows for no such distance, either in the United States or elsewhere. On the contrary, it makes geographical, social, and even personal proximity a condition for morally justified race relations. In the nineteenth-century antislavery struggle, the ever-present possibility of physical contact between the races so haunted the discussion of slavery and emancipation that many U.S. Americans believed abolition to be just another word for "amalgamism," or racial mixture. That same possibility, however, also helped abolition to become a powerful force for, and expression of, cross-racial solidarity, one that has continued to resonate within many fields of anti-racist scholarly inquiry. Even today, the prospect of what Karen Sánchez-Eppler (1992) refers to as a nineteenth-century "feminist-abolitionist politics" governed by "bodily bonds" remains a powerful language for describing both the intimacies of racial politics and the politics of racial intimacy.

2

Aesthetics

Russ Castronovo

At once universal and specific, transcendent as well as deeply historical, property of individual feeling but also affecting the mass subject, "aesthetics" have been notoriously difficult to define. This imprecision explains why aesthetics have often been invoked as a progressive force that opens new conceptual horizons and just as often derided as a tired elitist dodge that preserves the status quo. The divided and shifting ground upon which matters of beauty, perception, taste, and the sublime stand stems from elemental fissures between art and politics. Such fissures may be more fantasy than actuality, however; when aesthetics are historicized in terms of social practice, philosophy, and cultural criticism, they appear as profoundly material engagements with embodiment, collectivity, and social life.

In their narrowest sense, aesthetics are purely about the discernment of formal criteria such as unity, proportion, and balance within the domain of art. If we trace the term's origins back to the German Romantic tradition of Immanuel Kant and Friedrich von Schiller, aesthetics appear as a philosophical topic rather than a cultural conjuncture. Yet even this narrow sense resounds with expansive political and social possibility. Schiller (1954, 25) correlates aesthetic education with "true political freedom," and Kant (1952) orients aesthetic judgment around a shared sensibility that

would hold true for all individuals, engendering feelings of the universal. Historically, this utopian potential found practical application in the reformist energies of the "City Beautiful" movement of the late nineteenth and early twentieth centuries, which attempted to unify, uplift, and, perhaps most crucially, "Americanize" the heterogeneous populations of urban masses teeming with immigrants. Theoretically, this emphasis on universality and transformation found its expression in the work of John Dewey (1980), who construed aesthetic experience as a vital encounter that challenged the fixity of custom and precedent. These historical and theoretical currents merged in the efforts of pragmatists such as Jane Addams who, like Dewey, sought to make beauty and art a common feature of the modern social landscape. By linking magic lantern shows, art exhibitions, drama clubs, poetry readings, and film screenings to the cultivation of social ethics, reformers hoped that aesthetics could play a generative role in the democratization of culture. A central question for the political and cultural projects of both American studies and cultural studies is whether aesthetics can continue to play that role.

The narrow sense of aesthetics as a discourse on art thus leads almost inevitably to broader usages that understand the term to denote the entire "corporeal sensorium," including affect and emotion, pain and pleasure, feeling and sensibility (Buck-Morss 1992, 5). This emphasis on broad human reactions and responses suggests the potential force of commonality as a universal feeling that collides with and energizes political positions. One brief way of understanding this emergence of the political within the aesthetic is to say that Kant's idea of *sensus communis* (Kant 1952), a common standard of aesthetic judgment in which individual perception tallies with general taste, recalls Thomas Paine's notion of "common sense" (Paine 1953), which marshals public sentiment for the purposes of revolution. Structured by familiar responses and shared stimuli, aesthetics represent the possibility of mass mobilization. It is a possibility that echoes with political ambivalence; even as collective feeling resounds with democratic energy, the hum of a mass unified—and manipulated—by emotion also echoes with more ominous overtones of totalitarian control, as Walter Benjamin (1968) predicted in his famous essay on mechanical reproduction.

In the nineteenth-century United States, the potentially transformative effects of aesthetic feeling in galvanizing political opinion appeared in literary sentimentalism. Animating a host of reforms from temperance to women's rights, sentimentalism figured prominently in the antislavery crusade, culminating in Harriet Beecher Stowe's directive that individuals confronted with the awesome task of defeating the monster of slavery begin by making sure that "*they feel right*" (1852/1981, 624). Individual by individual, citizens could build a *sensus communis* that would change how the world acts and thinks. The problem, of course, was that individual feeling could remain individualized, forever private and never connected to shared action or thought. Indeed, Ralph Waldo Emerson, in the poem that introduces his essay "Art,"

seemed to imply that when art touches us, it reconciles and adjusts the individual to the social world as it is, instead of reshaping the world in accordance with a common regard for justice or fairness. The duty of art, according to Emerson's couplet, is "Man in Earth to acclimate, / And bend the exile to his fate" (1983, 429). Here, the politics that aesthetics produce come in the mode of resignation.

Identifying Emerson with this one-dimensional position ignores his belief that beauty could reinvent the ordinary forms of social life. Aesthetics for much of the twentieth century were prone to distortions and simplifications that cast beauty and art as the conservative guarantors of the social world as it is and not how it might be reimagined and reformed. Twentieth-century proponents of New Criticism often stressed aesthetics as a means of giving order and stability to sexual passion and political affect. "Aesthetic forms are a technique of restraint," announced John Crowe Ransom (1965, 31), advancing the position that the human rush to action, overflow of emotion, and unpredictable stir of social life could all be reined in by using art to formalize beauty and our responses to it.

These lingering effects of social governance and political containment are what motivate some American studies and cultural studies scholars to critique aesthetics as a conservative strategy of retrenchment that justifies art's putative evasion of political matters, mystifies class privilege as disinterestedness, and uses ideas of harmony and unity to excuse the status quo. As Sacvan Bercovitch and Myra Jehlen framed the issue in their landmark collection *Ideology and Classic*

American Literature (1986), the concentration on artistic qualities and literary effects among previous generations of critics diminished both the social impetus and the radical potential of literature. If we attend to the historicity of beauty and form, as this case against aesthetics goes, the scales of appreciation will drop from our eyes to reveal aesthetics as an evasion of culture. While this assessment is dead on, it finds its target only by aiming at notions of aesthetics that are themselves culturally thin, cut off from larger—and potentially alternative—histories of form, emotion, and representation. In short, the cultural critique of aesthetics risks overlooking varied strategies of interpretation, expression, and collaboration enabled by the aesthetic project itself. As a central term for American cultural studies, "aesthetics" can enable a questioning of the forms by which we organize domains of politics and art in the first place.

3

African

Kevin Gaines

The keyword "African" has been and remains a touchstone for African-descended peoples' struggle for identity and inclusion, encompassing extremes of racial denigration and vindication in a nation founded on the enslavement of Africans. Correspondingly, the African presence throughout the Americas and its significance for constructions of national culture in the United States have remained fraught with racialized and exclusionary power relations. In a nation that has traditionally imagined its culture and legislated its polity as "white," "African" has often provided for African Americans a default basis for identity in direct proportion to their exclusion from national citizenship.

As scholars ranging from Winthrop Jordan (1969) to Jennifer L. Morgan (2004) have noted, there was nothing natural or inevitable about the development of racial slavery in the Americas. Nor was the emergence of the racialized category of the African as permanent slave foreordained. European travelers who recorded their initial encounters with Africans did not perceive them as slaves. But their ethnocentric self-regard informed their descriptions of Africans as extremely different from themselves in appearance, religious beliefs, and behavior. European constructions of the bodily difference, heathenism, and beastliness of Africans mitigated occasional observations of their morality and humanity. As European nations experimented with systems of forced labor in the Americas, initially enlisting indigenous peoples and European indentured servants as well as Africans, ideologies of African inferiority facilitated the permanent enslavement of Africans as an expedient labor practice. With the legal codification of lifetime African slavery, European settlers completed the racial degradation of African men and women, a process anticipated in Enlightenment conceptions of difference and hierarchy. In keeping with the contingency of its origins, the idea of the African in America was subject to change and contestation. An awareness on the part of travelers and slave owners of ethnic and regional distinctions among peoples from Africa yielded to the homogenizing idea of *the* African. Throughout the eighteenth century, slave owners in the Caribbean and North America attributed rebellions to "wild and savage" Africans, leading, on occasion, to restrictions on the importation of African slaves.

During the nineteenth century free African Americans held an ambivalent attitude toward all things African. It could hardly have been otherwise, given the existential burdens of chattel slavery and the exclusion of Africa and its peoples from Enlightenment ideas of historical agency, modernity, and civilization. Such prominent African Americans as the shipping merchant Paul Cuffee championed emigration to West Africa. Despite his personal success, Cuffee despaired at the prospects for African-descended people to achieve equality in the United States. Inspired by the global antislavery movement, as well as the establishment of the British colony of Sierra Leone as an asylum for Africans rescued from the slave trade, Cuffee believed that emigration would allow Africans and African Americans to realize their full potential. But Cuffee led only one voyage of settlers to West Africa, leaving his entrepreneurial and evangelical objectives unfulfilled. African American enthusiasm for emigration was further dampened by the rise in the early nineteenth century of an explicitly racist colonization movement. The impetus for colonization, which sought the removal of free blacks and emancipated slaves to Africa, came from powerful whites, including slave owners and members of Congress.

Free blacks resented the proslavery motives of colonizationists and increasingly rejected an identification with Africa largely as a matter of self-defense. While the initial wave of schools, churches, mutual-aid societies, and other institutions established by northern free blacks in the late eighteenth century bore the name African, this nomenclature was largely abandoned by the mid-nineteenth century. The reasons for this shift were complex, including demands for U.S. citizenship, the dwindling population of African-born blacks, and an acknowledgment, at some level, of a black community "whitened" by the sexual oppression of enslaved women. Above all, "African" epitomized the stark conditions of exile faced by African Americans, excluded from U.S. society and deprived of an affirming connection to an ancestral homeland. Even for leaders of the African Methodist Episcopal (AME) Church, founded in Philadelphia in 1816 when white Methodists refused to worship alongside blacks, wariness toward Africa and a deep suspicion toward its indigenous cultures informed their evangelical efforts toward the continent (Campbell 1995).

While emigration and colonization movements resulted in the resettlement of relatively few African Americans, the violent exclusion of African Americans from southern politics after emancipation renewed the appeal of Africa as a foundation of African American identity. As Africa came under the sway of European missions and colonialism, the involvement of AME Church missions in Africa and the scholarship of Edward W. Blyden (1967) helped promote among some African Americans a general interest in the welfare of Africans and a greater tolerance for indigenous African cultures. Blyden's work was part of a longstanding African American intellectual tradition seeking to vindicate Africa by documenting its contributions to Western civilization (Moses 1998). Such scholarship, combined with the worldwide impact of Marcus Garvey's post–World War I movement, helped sow the seeds of African nationalism and anticolonialism. The Garvey movement, which flourished amid a national wave of urban race riots and antiblack violence, built on popular emigrationism and energized African-descended peoples all over the world with its secular gospel of economic cooperation toward African redemption, even as some African American intellectuals dismissed it as a "back to Africa" movement. Such controversy may well have informed subsequent debates among black studies scholars over whether it was valid to speak of African cultural retentions, or "survivals," among the descendants of enslaved Africans in the Americas. The sociologist E. Franklin Frazier and the social anthropologist Melville Herskovits represent the opposing positions in the debate (Raboteau 1978). Frazier believed that the traumas of enslavement and the rigors of urbanization had extinguished all cultural ties to Africa. Herskovits based his support for the idea of African cultural retentions on his research on Caribbean societies and cultural practices. If recent scholarship in history, anthropology, literary and cultural studies, historical archaeology, and population genetics is any indication, Herskovits's position appears to have prevailed.

As African national independence movements capitalized on the decline of European colonialism after World War II, the idea of the African underwent yet another profound revision in the minds of many African Americans, from intellectual and popular stereotypes of African savagery to images of black power and modernity. The emergence of newly independent African nations beginning in the late 1950s became a source of pride for many people of African descent. Even as blacks believed that the new African presence in world affairs signaled the continent's full participation in, if not redefinition of, the modern world, members of the U.S. and European political establishment opposed African demands for freedom and true self-determination, trafficking, more or less discreetly, in racist attitudes. In 1960, widely touted as "the year of Africa," more than thirty African states gained national independence; that year also witnessed the bloody repression of demands for freedom in apartheid South Africa and the Congo. For many northern urban African Americans not far removed from the violence of the Jim Crow South, and facing marginalization in such cities as New York, Chicago, and Detroit, new African states and their leaders, including Ghana's Kwame Nkrumah and the Congo's Patrice Lumumba, rivaled the southern civil rights movement in importance. When Lumumba was assassinated during the civil disorder fomented by Belgium, African Americans in Harlem and Chicago angrily demonstrated against the complicity of Western governments and the United Nations in the murder. In doing so, they joined members of the black left and working-class black nationalists in a nascent political formation that envisioned their U.S. citizenship in solidarity with African peoples, uniting their own demands for freedom and democracy in the United States with those of peoples of African descent the world over (Singh 2004; Gaines 2006).

Within this context of decolonization, the term "African" became a battleground. To the architects of U.S. foreign policy, such an affiliation exceeded the ideological boundaries of U.S. citizenship. African American criticism of U.S. foreign policy and advocacy on behalf of African peoples transgressed the limits imposed by a liberalism whose expressed support for civil rights and decolonization was qualified by Cold War national security concerns (and opposed outright by segregationist elements). As some African governments joined U.S. blacks in denouncing violent white resistance to demands for equality, U.S. officials' assertions of the American Negro's fundamental Americanness became a staple of liberal discourse. Their view was echoed in press accounts asserting that Africans and American Negroes were fundamentally estranged from one another. No doubt many African Americans still looked upon Africans with ambivalence. However, this normative notion of African American identity and citizenship provided a context for subsequent debates among African Americans throughout the 1960s over the terms of an authentic identity.

As a Janus-faced U.S. nationalism trumpeted its civil rights reforms—seemingly in exchange for consent to its political and military repression of African and, in the 1960s, Vietnamese nationalists—

mainstream civil rights leaders endeavored, without success, to formalize an African American position on U.S. foreign policy. It was Malcolm X, among African American spokespersons, who most effectively articulated a growing frustration with the federal government's domestic and foreign policies toward black and African peoples (Gaines 2006). Along with such post–World War II figures as Paul Robeson, St. Clair Drake, and Lorraine Hansberry, to name a few, Malcolm X reanimated W. E. B. Du Bois's decades-old assertion that African Americans sought no less than full U.S citizenship without sacrificing their "Negro" identity, helping African Americans to embrace rather than shun the designation "African" (Plummer 1996; Von Eschen 1997; Meriwether 2002).

During the 1980s, African American leadership, including many elected officials, waged an effective civil disobedience campaign against the apartheid regime in South Africa and the Reagan administration's support for it. The rapid acceptance of the term "African American," championed by Jesse Jackson and others and used in the context of the anti-apartheid struggle, represents a profound reversal of decades of shame and ambivalence. Yet it is unclear what relationship the prominent use of "African" as a marker of U.S. black identity bears to the black transnational consciousness that developed during the 1960s and that flourished during the Free South Africa movement. A major legacy of these social movements for black equality and African liberation has been the legitimation of scholarly investigations of the African foundations of African American history and culture, including studies of the African diaspora and what Paul Gilroy (1993) has termed the "Black Atlantic."

At the beginning of the twenty-first century, the term "African" remains highly contested in politics and popular culture. Crises of poverty, famine, disease (including the AIDS epidemic), and armed conflict reinforce an Afro-pessimism in the Western imagination not far removed from the colonial idea of the "Dark Continent," a place untouched by civility and modernity. While the human toll of such crises is undeniable, the U.S. media generally devote far less attention to democratically elected civilian governments, some of which have supplanted brutal and corrupt military dictatorships tolerated by the West during the Cold War. These representations continue to view Africans and African Americans through alternately romanticizing and demeaning prisms of race.

In one sense, the term "African" has come full circle within a society capable of sustaining contradictory views of race, and preoccupied with the manipulation of black identities. Recent news accounts have incorporated the African into the quintessential U.S. immigrant success narrative, as the latest immigrant whose mobility is depicted as an implicit reproach to underachieving native-born African American descendants of slaves. In such accounts, native-born African Americans are said to resent having been leapfrogged by African immigrants. That those foreign-born Africans and their children refer to themselves as "African Americans" adds insult to injury. Despite their ostensible objectivity, media narratives purporting tensions between African Americans and African immigrants

are the present-day equivalent of Tarzan movies, whose effect is to erase the history and modernity of transnational black subjectivities.

While recent scholarship in American cultural studies has called for a rethinking of the black-white color line in U.S. race relations, the tensions expressed by the question of who is an "African" and who is an "African American" are symptomatic of the nation's continued struggle over the significance of the African presence, past and present, real and symbolic. Of course, the contested meaning and legacy of the African presence is not peculiar to the United States, as many Latino immigrants to the United States bring with them histories and identities shaped by the vexed legacy of racial slavery in their countries of origin. The foundations of Latin American societies, with their diverse populations of Africans, indigenous peoples, Europeans, and Asians, suggests that the growth of the Hispanic population in the United States does not render the black-white color line obsolete, but rather makes it all the more salient as a benchmark for social affiliation.

4

America

Kirsten Silva Gruesz

"We hold these truths to be self-evident," begins the main body of the Declaration of Independence, and the definition of "America" may likewise seem utterly self-evident: the short form of the nation's official name. Yet the meaning of this well-worn term becomes more elusive the closer we scrutinize it. Since "America" names the entire hemisphere from the Yukon to Patagonia, its common use as a synonym for the United States of America is technically a misnomer, as Latin Americans and Canadians continually (if resignedly) point out. Given the nearly universal intelligibility of this usage, their objection may seem a small question of geographical semantics. But "America" carries multiple connotations that go far beyond its literal referent. In the statement "As Americans, we prize freedom," "American" may at first seem to refer simply to U.S. citizens, but the context of the sentence strongly implies a consensual understanding of shared *values*, not just shared passports; the literal and figurative meanings tend to collapse into each other. The self-evidence of "America" is thus troubled from the start by multiple ambiguities about the extent of the territory it delineates, as well as about its deeper connotations.

Seeking out the meaning of America might be said to be a national characteristic, if that proposition were not in itself tautological. The question prompts responses representing every conceivable point of view, from the documentary series packaged as *Ken Burns's America* (1996) to prizewinning essays by schoolchildren invited to tackle this hoary topic. Foodways, cultural practices, and even consumer products are readily made to symbolize the nation's essence ("baseball, hot dogs, apple pie, and Chevrolet," as a highly effective advertising campaign put it in the 1970s). Such metonyms gesture, in turn, at more abstract no-

tions: Freedom, Liberty, Democracy. Whether implicit or explicit, such responses to the enigma of Americanness tend to obscure the conditions under which they were formulated. Who gets to define what "America" means? What institutions support or undermine a particular definition? Under what historical conditions does one group's definition have more or less power than another's? How does the continued repetition of such ideological statements have real, material effects on the ways people are able to live their lives? Without looking critically at these questions of nomenclature, "American" cultural studies cannot claim self-awareness about its premises or its practices.

Because the meaning of "America" and its corollaries—American, Americanization, Americanism, and Americanness—seems so self-evident but is in fact so imprecise, using the term in conversation or debate tends to reinforce certain ways of thinking while repressing others. In his slyly comic *Devil's Dictionary* (1911), pundit Ambrose Bierce defines the term only through its opposite: "un-American, *adj.* Wicked, intolerable, heathenish." "American" and "un-American," Bierce implies, shut down genuine argument by impugning the values of one's opponent. A less cynical example may be found in Walt Whitman's preface to *Leaves of Grass*, which in several pages seeks to define the essence of America: "The genius of the United States is not best or most in its executives or legislatures, nor in its ambassadors or authors or colleges or churches or parlors . . . but always most in the common people." "America is the race of races," he writes. "The Americans of all nations at any time upon the earth have probably the fullest poetical nature. The United States themselves are essentially the greatest poem" (Whitman 1855/1999, 4–5). Whitman's claims about America work toward his larger project of celebrating "the common people," the heterogeneous mixing of immigrants into a "race of races," and everyday, vernacular speech as the stuff of poetry. Each variant of his definition bolsters this larger ideology. Although Whitman seems to use "United States" and "America" interchangeably, elsewhere in the document Mexico and the Caribbean are included as "American"—a slippage from the *political* meaning to the *geographical* one that reveals the expansionist beliefs Whitman held at the time.

If the substitution of the name of its most powerful nation for the hemisphere as a whole is a mistake sanctified by the passage of time, the same may be said of the origins of the term "America." Against Columbus's insistence that the landmass he had "discovered" was Asia, the Italian explorer Amerigo Vespucci first dubbed it a "New World" in his treatise by that name. It was not Vespucci himself but a contemporary mapmaker, Martin Waldseemuller, who then christened the region "America," though it originally referred only to the southern continent. Later cartographers broadened the designation to include the lesser-known north—a further irony of history. The sixteenth-century Dominican priest Bartolomé de las Casas initiated an argument that raged across both Americas over whether Vespucci had usurped an honor rightly due Columbus; he proposed rechristening it "Columba."

To this day alternative theories of the naming of the continent flourish, finding new devotees on the Internet. Solid evidence links a British merchant named Richard Ameryk to John Cabot's voyages along the North Atlantic coast, leading to speculation that Cabot named "America" for his patron a decade or so before Waldseemuller's map. Others have argued that the name comes from Vikings who called their Newfoundland settlement "Mark" or "Maruk"—"Land of Darkness." Still others have claimed, more circumstantially, that the root word derives from Phoenician, Hebrew, or Hindu terms, suggesting that one of these groups encountered America before Europeans did. Similar etymological evidence has been interpreted to show that the term ultimately stems from a word for Moors or Africans, so that "America" really means "land of the blacks." "America" is thus a product of the same misunderstanding that gave us the term "Indian." Given this similarity, one final theory about the term's origins is particularly provocative. An indigenous group in Nicaragua had referred to one gold-rich district in their territory as "Amerrique" since before the Conquest, and Mayan languages of tribes further north use a similar-sounding word. These discoveries have led to the radical proposition that the name "America" comes from *within* the New World rather than being imposed on it. The continuing life of this debate suggests that what's really at stake is not some ultimate etymological truth but a narrative of shared origins; each claim grants primacy and symbolic (if not literal) ancestry of the Americas to a different group.

The fact that only one of these foundational fables of America's origin involves an indigenous name is revealing. Throughout the colonies, settlers tended not to refer to themselves as Americans, since the term then conveyed an indigenous ancestry—or at least the associated taint of barbarism and backwardness—they were (with certain romanticizing exceptions) eager to avoid. Instead, they called their home-spaces "New-England," "Nieuw-Amsterdam," "Nueva España," reminders of the homeland reflecting a local, rather than continental, identification. Until well into the nineteenth century, as the example from Whitman indicates, "America" and its analogues in Spanish, French, and other European languages designated something called "the New World," not necessarily "the United States." And during the early modern period in particular, it was persistently represented as female, using an iconography that ranged from the savage devourer to the desirable exotic. Following the same pattern of feminization, a poem published during the Revolutionary War by the African American celebrity Phillis Wheatley first personified the nascent country as Columbia, an invented goddess who lent a tinge of classical refinement to the nation-building project. The image and name were quite popular during the century that followed. Referring specifically to the United States, "Columbia" distinguished the nation from the hemisphere, but it also came to carry its own ideological baggage and can thus be seen as a kind of predecessor to the contemporary usage of "America." It prompted patriotic musings on the true meaning of "the Columbian ideal," and inspired events like the 1893 World's Columbian Exposition in Chicago, calculated to draw international attention to a nation that increasingly celebrated modernity and progress. In addition, "Columbia" had an iconographic presence that "America" no longer does; the figure of the goddess appeared on coins into the early twentieth century.

At what point, then, did "America" become synonymous with the USA, within the nation itself if not worldwide? "Americanism" and "Americanization" had entered common usage by the beginning of the nineteenth century, referring at first to evolving linguistic differences from the "mother tongue." Such changes are gradual, of course, but the Civil War marks one watershed. The war brought about not only an upsurge in patriotic feeling but a marked increase in centralized governmental power. A more unified vision of national identity seemed necessary to counteract the effects of sectionalism, followed by the perceived threat of the great surges of immigration at the end of the century. "Americanization" came to signify the degree to which those immigrants altered their customs and values in accordance with the dominant view of Americanness at the time.

Of the many figurative meanings that "America" has acquired over time, many involve notions of novelty, new beginnings, and utopian promise. The Mexican historian Edmundo O'Gorman influentially wrote in 1958 that America was "invented" before it was "discovered," demonstrating that Europeans had long imagined a mythical land of marvels and riches they then projected onto the unfamiliar terrain. This projection was not always positive. The common representation of a "virgin land" waiting to be explored, dominated, and domesticated relegates the natural world to the passive, inferior position then associated with the feminine. The French naturalist George Louis Leclerc de Buffon even argued in 1789 that since the region was geologically newer, its very flora and fauna were less developed than Europe's—a claim Thomas Jefferson took pains to refute. Nonetheless, the notion of the novelty of the Americas persisted, extending to the supposedly immature culture of its inhabitants as well.

Early debates over literature and fine arts in English, Spanish, and French America focused on the question of whether the residents of a land without history could cultivate a genuine or original aesthetic. Some Romantic writers tried on "Indian" themes, while others spun this "historylessness" in America's favor. The philosopher G. W. F. Hegel delivered an influential address in 1830 that claimed, "America is therefore the land of the future, where, in all the ages that lie before us, the burden of the World's History shall reveal itself—perhaps in a contest between North and South America. It is a land of desire for all those who are weary of the historical lumber-room of old Europe" (Hegel 1837/1956, 86). Here Hegel uses "America," as Whitman would a few decades later, to indicate the whole region, not just the United States. Claims about the New World's salvational role in global history, then, gestated from without as well as from within. Given this longstanding tendency to define America in mythic terms, we must be skeptical of the common boast that the United States is the only

modern nation founded on an *idea*—democratic equality—rather than on a shared tribal or racial ancestry. Such a claim to exceptionalism is of course particularly appealing to intellectuals, who traffic in ideas. In the early years of American studies as an academic discipline, in the 1950s, the field's foundational texts located the essential meaning of America variously in its history of westward movement, in religious and philosophical individualism, or in the worship of progress and modernity. As the discipline has evolved, it now attempts to show how such mythic definitions arise in response to historically specific needs and conditions. When we go in search of what is most profoundly American, scholars now insist, we blinker our sights to the ways in which the actual history of U.S. actions and policies may have diverged from those expectations. Moreover, any single response to the prompt to define "America" tends to imply that this larger idea or ideal has remained essentially unchanged over time, transcending ethnic and racial differences. "America" has generally been used as a term of consolidation, homogenization, and unification, not a term that invites recognition of difference, dissonance, and plurality—all issues of crucial import in the post–civil rights movement era.

Such a recognition cuts to the heart of any Americanist pursuit, whether in historical, literary, or social studies, forcing scholars to confront fundamental questions of the field's scope and limits. Jan Radway's much-cited presidential address to the American Studies Association in 1998 repudiated the "imperial" arrogation by the United States of a name that originally belonged to an entire hemisphere, arguing that "American national identity is . . . constructed in and through relations of difference." She went so far as to suggest that the organization eliminate the term "American" from its name altogether in order to "reconceptualize the American as always relationally defined and therefore as intricately dependent on 'others' that are used both materially and conceptually to mark its boundaries" (Radway 2002, 54, 59).

Though her proposal to change the name of the organization was more a provocation than a promise, Radway's speech responded to challenges raised in preceding years by proponents of an "Americas" or "New World" cultural studies that would insist on a relational consideration of the United States within the larger context of the hemisphere. Inherently pluralistic, this transnational approach draws upon Latin American, Caribbean, and Canadian works and emphasizes their production within a history of U.S. imperial design. Rather than Alexis de Tocqueville and Michel Crèvecoeur, its canon of commentators on the meaning of America highlights lesser-known figures like the Cuban José Martí—who in an 1891 speech famously distinguished between "Nuestra" (Our) America, with its mestizo or mixed-race origins, and the racist, profit-driven culture he saw dominating the United States. Martí, like the later African American activist-writers W. E. B. Du Bois and C. L. R. James, was critical of the growing interventionist tendencies of the United States and sought to revive and provoke dissent and resistance. In addition to recovering such underappreciated figures, comparative Americanist work often locates its inquiry in spaces once relegated to the periphery of scholarly attention, such as the Spanish-speaking borderlands that were formerly part of Mexico. As contact zones between North and South, Anglo and Latino, such areas produce hybrid cultural formations that inflect mainstream U.S. culture with that of the "other" America.

"Americas" studies, capitalizing on the plurality of its name, seeks to relativize the status of the United States within the hemisphere and the world—and thus reaches well beyond matters involving Latin American and Latino cultures. Bell Gale Chevigny and Gari Laguardia, introducing their landmark essay collection *Reinventing the Americas* (1986, viii), write that "by dismantling the U.S. appropriation of the name 'America,' we will better see what the United States is and what it is not." The work of divorcing the name of the nation from the name of the continent has stumbled a bit on the lack of a ready adjectival form in English. A few scholars have recalled into service the neologism that Frank Lloyd Wright coined in the 1930s to describe his non-derivative, middle-class house designs: "Usonian." Others, like Chevigny and Laguardia, simply substitute "U.S." or "United Statesian" for "American," arguing that the very awkwardness of such terms has a certain heuristic value, recalling us to an historical moment before the pressure toward consensus and national unity became as pervasive as it is today.

Perhaps such consciousness-raising about the power of "self-evident" terms could begin the slow work of altering social relationships and structures of political power. On the other hand, pluralizing "America" to "Americas" does not in itself do away with imperial presumptions—indeed, some of its deployments may reiterate them. Proponents of the North American Free Trade Agreement (NAFTA), which took effect in 1994, argued that the treaty would open borders and promote cultural interchange—at the expense, many would contend, of subjecting Mexico's economy to tighter control by U.S.-based corporations than ever before. New proposals for a similarly structured "Free Trade Area of the Americas" could extend NAFTA to encompass thirty-four countries and some 800 million people. In this context, the plural term works opportunistically rather than critically, suggesting that in the future, the usage of "Americas" may require the same kind of critical scrutiny that we have just brought to "America."

5

Asian

John Kuo Wei Tchen

"Orientals are carpets!" is a common Asian American retort today, one that rejects the linkage between objects of desire—whether hand-woven carpets made in central and western Asia or porcelains made in China—and the people who make them. During the late-1960s phase of the civil rights movement, second- and third-generation, college-age, mainly Chinese and Japanese Americans from the United States and

Canada protested the term "Oriental," seeking to replace it with the seemingly less fraught term "Asian." But as in any debate about naming practices, the names rejected and defended reflect differing points of view, as groups trouble certain terms and adopt others in order to shape and reshape meanings for themselves. "Asia," "Asian," and "Asiatic" are still common, though the latter is far less preferred. Variations such as "Asianic," "Asiaticism," "Asiatise," "Asiatall," "Asiatican," and "Asiatically" are now archaic.

Each of these terms comes loaded with particular spatial orientations rooted in temporal relationships. "Asia" has Arabic, Aramaic, Ethiopian, and Greek origins signifying "was or became beautiful," "to rise" (said of the sun), "burst forth" or "went out," and "to go out." Demetrius J. Georgacas (1969, 33) speculates that "Asia" comes from the ancient Greeks, who adopted a cuneiform Hittite word *assuva* when traveling to the western shores of Anatolia (present-day Turkish Asia) around 1235 B.C.E. *Assuva*, in turn, may have originally been a pre-Persian name referring to a town in Crete with an ancient temple to Zeus or a "land or country with good soil" (73–75). Georgacas adds that Greek mariners first articulated a nautical boundary between the lands of the rising sun and those of the setting sun by traversing the saltwater straits of the Aegean through the Dardanelles, the Sea of Marmara, the Bosphorus, the Black Sea through the Straits of Kerch, and ending in the Sea of Azov where the landmass to the north did not have such a divide (711–12). Hence "Asia" as "east" began as a local definition.

"Asia" in these contexts appeared as separated by water from the Greek world, leading to the inaccurate idée fixe of a separable landmass and people. The categorization of continents that emerged from this idea reproduced early notions of racial superiority and inferiority. By the fifth century C.E. "Asiatic" was clearly associated with vulgarity, arbitrary authority, and luxurious splendor—qualities deemed antithetical to Greek values (Hay 1957, 3). An early-eleventh-century "T-O" map reveals a clear religious cosmos of the world. A "T" within a circle divides three continents: Asia, marked "oriens," is over Europe and Africa (or Libya), which are both marked "occidens." The "T" itself represented both a Christian cross and the Nile River, believed by some to be the divide between Africa, Asia, and the Mediterranean (ibid., Plate 1b, 54). Noah's sons, Japheth, Shem, and Ham, were said to have dispersed to Europe, Asia, and Africa, respectively, thereby fixing their characters to geographic spaces. For Western Christians, the Ottoman Empire to the east was formidable. As their city-states became more secular and colonized non-Christian lands westward, northward, and southward, Renaissance intellectuals redefined "civilization" and "progress" as moving westward like the arc of the sun. A double shift took place: the West became synonymous with Christianity, and Western ideologues claimed direct continuity with Greek civilization.

In this centuries-long process, the appropriation of the word "Europe" for this Western Christian political culture also projected the imagined heathenism affixed to peoples onto the continents of "Asia" and "Africa." Intercultural influences that produced overlapping renaissances in the Mediterranean world were appropriated as *the* (one and only) Renaissance, at once Eurocentric and colonizing. Taxonomist Carolus Linneaus (1708–1778) formulated "four races of mankind," from primitive Africans to civilized Europeans, with Asians or "Mongoloids" said to be the "semi-civilized" peoples of once-great material civilizations now stifled by despotic rulers. The formulation by Karl Marx (1867) of "the Asiatic mode of production" as despotic bore the assumptions of this worldview. The rising European and colonial middle classes desired Asian goods, with their cachet of luxury, opulence, and decadence—a practice emulating the European courts' consumption fashions. Yet this fascination was also laced by threat. Startled by Japan's swift defeat of China, Kaiser Wilhelm II first dreamed of an impending "yellow peril" in 1895. The *Fu Manchu* novels of Sax Rohmer (Arthur Sarsfield Ward) soon followed, selling millions throughout the twentieth century.

As Edward Said (1978) has pointed out, the formulation "Near East," as ascribed by self-named "Occidentists," represented "the Orient" as utterly opposite and alien to the European self. This alterity was both derisive and romantic, coding "Asian" difference as gendered and sexualized. French Orientalists, for example, were fascinated by the eroticism of Persian *odalisques*, such as those represented in Jean-León Gérôme's paintings. This alterity enabled the self-delusional Eurocentric myth of a singular Western modernity: "In adopting the name 'Europe' as a substitute for Western Christendom, the Modern Western World had replaced a misnomer that was merely an anachronism by a misnomer that was seriously misleading" (Georgacas 1969, 729).

This misnaming has a long history. In 1507 German mapmaker Martin Waldseemuller named "America" after the Italian explorer Amerigo Vespucci's charting of South America. At that moment, a fourth continent upset the tripartite "T-O" map, and the Americas became the place where populations—indigenous, Africans, Europeans, and Asians—would intermingle. Spanish colonials established the Manila-Acapulco trade from 1565 to 1815, bringing Filipinos/as, Chinese, and other "Asians" to the "New World." By 1635, Chinese barbers were reportedly monopolizing the trade in Mexico City. Chinese silk shawls and other desired goods traveled the Camino Real north to Santa Fe. Filipino sailors resettled in the French colonial lands of Louisiane. As the northeastern ports of the newly established United States began direct trade with China in 1784, people, goods, and influences crisscrossed with ports of the Pacific and Indian oceans. Yet with Euro-American colonization, transplanted Eurocentric ideas of "Asia," "the Orient," and "the East" were reproduced ever-further westward. The more the people of the Americas shared this Eurocentrism, the more their national identities proved to be a variation of white *herrenvolk* nationalism.

Despite this long genealogy, "Asian" bodies in the Americas have been viewed as phenotypically foreign—a demarcation of otherness as foundational as the "T-O" map. "Far Eastern" bodies, ideas,

and things were mapped onto existent binaries of "Near Eastern" Orientalism. Anglo-American phrases emerged, such as "the yellow peril," "Mongoloid idiot," and "Asiatic hordes," along with names for diseases such as "Asiatic cholera," and the omnipresent "Asian flu." "Asiatics" were portrayed as threatening and inferior to white Euro-American masculinity. The Asian American critique of stereotypes is useful here. Writer-critics Jeffrey Paul Chan and Frank Chin have delineated "racist hate" as what most U.S. Americans imagine anti-Asian racism to be, and "racist love" as the affections formed by the dominant culture toward those Asians who conform to stereotype (Chan and Chin 1972). The exotic-erotic lotus blossom geisha, for example, is the object of Orientalist desire—an extension of the *odalisque*. And detective Charlie Chan always solved the white man's mystery with good humble humor. At the same time, white straight male control has been repulsed (and titillated) by the dominatrix Dragon Lady type or "the devil incarnate" Fu Manchu role.

Contemporary U.S. notions of "terrorism" are undergirded by such stereotypical structures of thought. When media mogul Henry Luce celebrated the "American Century" as a mid-twentieth-century enlightenment project for the world, the primary area of U.S. economic and political expansion was westward into the Pacific. For 170 years U.S. military actions and wars in the Pacific Rim have been justified by national security and self-interest. The Asia Pacific War, usually understood as a response to Japan's expansionism and efforts to formulate an "Asian Co-Prosperity Sphere," might be better understood in this broader context of competition for Pacific and Asian resources and markets. Historian William Appleman Williams (1992) charted the linkages between U.S. western expansionism to U.S. "foreign" policy annexations into the Pacific. "Manifest Destiny" did not stop at the shores of California. A list of U.S. military, diplomatic, and trade initiatives clearly delineates deep, sustained U.S. involvements in the Asia Pacific region. Witness the U.S. involvement in the British-led opium trade and wars with China (1830s), Commodore Perry's "opening" of Japan (1853), the annexation of Hawai'i, Guam, and the Philippines (1898) and Samoa (1900), the countless military actions of the twentieth century establishing strategic military bases, and the current twenty-first-century battle with the "Axis of Evil."

Military actions, missionary work, and trade, along with labor recruitment and immigration policies, linked the fate of Asians and Pacific Islanders in the United States to national foreign policy in Asia and the Pacific. Liberation movements thus necessarily became critiques of U.S. expansionism and self-interest, while policies toward Asia and the Pacific were articulated to domestic civil rights. Harvard historian and advisor to the U.S. war against Japan, Edwin O. Reischauer, for example, urged improved treatment of interned Japanese Americans to counter Imperial Japan's criticism of Western racism and imperialism—the primary argument for developing a pan-Asian and pan-Pacific Japanese-controlled "prosperity" confederation. While pan-Asianism has mainly been identified with the reactionary expansionism of the Japanese empire, it is important to note that there have been many moments when pan-Asian ideas and actions emerged from revolutionary nationalists—often adapting U.S. ideals of freedom and liberty. Tokyo in the 1900s brought together many left-leaning Chinese and Koreans with Japanese socialists; anarchists and various radicals gathered in Paris before World War I; and the Bandung Conference in 1955 articulated an Asian and African "Third World" unity. These movements have argued for multiple modernities, not one singular "Western" path. The ongoing post–civil rights era "culture wars" have cast Asian American and other identity-based rights movements as a de facto "Balkanizing" of Euro-America (Schlesinger 1998; Huntington 2004b). More progressive scholars argue for the ongoing struggle to expand the meaning of "we, the people" and "the American experiment" at home, and democracy and human rights abroad.

Given this long and complex history, the challenges for American cultural studies scholarship and practice are numerous. A thorough critique of Eurocentric knowledge needs to continue and be extended into curricula. As Naoki Sakai (2000) insists, modernity needs to be pluralized to recognize multiple paths for a people's development. Those who have experienced disempowerment and marginalization help us understand and gain insight into the ways reality is constructed and policies are formulated. This insight, when cultivated with deeper historical, cultural, social, and political analysis, restructures what we understand and how we understand it. In addition, it enables the recognition and translation of diverse and dynamic economic, cultural, and political developments in various parts of "east," "southeast," "south," "central," and "western" Asia (all these directional terms are partial and misleading). This rethinking can begin with the available literature of those Asians, Pacific Islanders, and Asian Americans writing and being translated into English, but must be extended to help U.S. Americans understand the local struggles of grain farmers in Kazakhstan or female Nike factory workers in Bangladesh in terms truthful to those peoples' own worldviews. This requires dialogue and the insistence that disempowered peoples gain the capacity to "name" their own world.

How the United States and various Asian governments respond to the political-economic rivalries of the "New World Order" will frame the spaces in which this scholarship and activism can take place. Calls for pan-Asianism, used in various ways in different places and at different times, can contribute to a process that opens up participation and grassroots mobilizations, or they can serve to close down understanding by offering simplistic solutions to complex political economic questions. Uneven development and hierarchical knowledges challenge us to better imagine and work for a fair and equitable global vision. "Development" and "modernization" must be reformulated to produce sustainable local practices without romanticizing a pre-lapsarian past. Here, feminists, labor activists, and students who have access to both local and particular knowledges and transnational networks, via faxes and the Internet, have led the way, while ambitious corporate power-players from "developing nations" and peoples have become the new comprador managers of internationalizing North American, European, and Asian finance capital. The contestation of values and meanings is critical to our future collective well-being. Like other keywords of these globalized struggles, it is the fate of "Asian" to be contested locally and regionally—in contending, politicized practices of naming.

6

Body
Eva Cherniavsky

As a term that designates the physical or material frame of human and other living beings, "body" has a long career in the language and a relatively brief one as a focus of critical engagement in the study of culture. For Christian theology as for speculative philosophy in the West, the body figures as the devalued term in a structuring dualism of body/soul (in sacred thought) and body/mind (in secular traditions). These dualisms apprehend the body as a material substrate of human life that is fundamentally distinct from and subordinated to the privileged term in the dichotomy (mind, soul), which alone comprehends the human capacity for knowledge and self-knowledge, as well as the repertoire of human sensibilities, dispositions, and affects on which the salvation, expression, or advancement of humanity is understood to depend. In Christian theology as in humanist philosophy, the body turns up on the side of animality or merely mechanical existence and so dwells outside the bounded domain of what is proper or essential to human culture, a domain which the exclusion of the body guarantees.

At the same time, classic political economy and social contract theory grant the body a certain limited dignity as the organic container of human personhood. For social contract theory, the body constitutes the inalienable property of human subjects. To sell oneself bodily is tantamount to selling one's self, to an erasure of personhood that, paradoxically, would suspend the seller's ability to enter into such a contract in the first place. In this way, social contract theory affirms the rationality and justice of wage labor (the selling of one's capacity for physical or intellectual labor) by setting a specific limit on the attributes of personhood that may circulate in the marketplace. The claim to an inalienable property in the body animated moral opposition to chattel slavery in the New World, although as David Brion Davis (1975) has argued, abolitionism was at least as much an apology for the immiseration of wage labor under industrial capitalism as it was an indictment of slavery and plantation economics. For Marxist political economy (in contrast to the classic political economy of Locke), the very distinction between alienable labor and inalienable embodiment cannot hold, as the abstraction of labor from the embodied person of the laborer makes possible the theft of his energy and creativity in the production of value to which the laborer loses all claim. Marxism is certainly the major intellectual tradition before the twentieth century to understand human

creativity and the production of value as fully bound up in the materiality of embodied life. It refuses the dichotomization of body and soul, of matter and spirit, that otherwise dominates philosophical and theological inquiry in the West.

In the other main sense of the term relevant to contemporary cultural study, the body may be understood as a collective entity, "an artificial person created by legal authority for certain ends" (e.g., a corporation), or a political entity, a "body politic," which in its widest sense may signify "organized society" as such. This meaning of the term is of more modern provenance (the *Oxford English Dictionary* cites 1461 as the first recorded usage of "bodie corporate" and 1634 of "body politic"). As the product of legal discourse and political theory, the use of "body" to reference abstract collectivity is from its origins at once descriptive and analytic. In the twentieth century, the European tradition of the history of ideas began to give to this analytical concept an expressly culturalist turn, by framing the study of political bodies as a question about the iconography of power. This historiographical tradition considers how figuring institutionalized political power and identity as corporeal animates these abstractions; the power of the monarchical state is an abstraction remote from the lives of ordinary subjects that submit to its authority, but the sacred body of the king is an awesome iconic image that can be widely disseminated across the ranks of a stratified social order (Kantorowicz 1957; Starobinski 1988).

This type of critical reflection on the embodiment of political authority comes belatedly to American studies, perhaps because of the insistence in U.S. law and political theory on divorcing political bodies from most forms of sensational corporeality and so rendering them as pure abstractions. The reflections on the appropriate size of the representative bodies of government in the Federalist Papers, for example, underscore how such political bodies were *not* conceived as the practical means to reproduce the *agora* of the ancient Greek democracies in a modern state, where size and population make impossible the massing of all its citizens in any one physical space. Rather than an abridgement of this embodied totality of citizens thronging the *agora*, the representative bodies arrayed in the U.S. Constitution were envisioned as different sorts of "bodies" altogether, purged of the mass physicality of the crowd. In the early national period, to claim political authority in civic matters required that one speak in the guise of disinterested reason, rather than render one's particular viewpoint, so that print became the privileged medium of public debate, exactly because it detached the voice of the author from the evident partiality or particularity of his embodied person (Warner 1990). Citizenship on this model is an ideally *disembodied* identity, while citizens' bodies remain a private matter.

Critical attention to forms of material and abstract embodiment in American studies has been fostered through its interface with feminism, race and ethnic studies, and postcolonial studies. The latter critical projects enable a turn to those human subjects historically associated with the discredited life of the material body and so constituted as marginal to the arenas of cultural production and political representation: women, Africans and their New World descendants, indigenous peoples, mestizos, and Asians, among other categories of "overembodied" ethnic, sexual, and classed identity. As it emerges transformed from this intellectual contact zone, American studies has addressed how collective and impersonal forms of political agency are routinely embodied in propertied, white men, whose political privilege depends on the association of other genders, races, and classes with corporealized identities. The circulation of such "overembodied" identities as public icons and spectacle has been crucial to the protection of established political privilege. At the same time, the visibility of disqualified political subjects within public culture has also generated important opportunities for contesting their disqualification.

Minimally, these contestations require a denaturalized understanding of the physical body as a social text rather than a given form. While some critical accounts of embodiment continue to honor this very distinction by framing the human body as a quantity of physical matter imprinted with social meaning, theories of performative identity reject the idea of a natural body altogether. Judith Butler's account of performative gender is one example. It suggests that the sexed body does not precede its social realization as a gendered person, but rather the sexed body in its material configuration is itself an *effect* of gender norms that operate through imitation (Butler 1990). We "assume" a gender through the repeated bodily enactment of intelligible gendered identity, and it is this repetitious performance that constitutes the body in its very physicality (in its boundaries and receptivities; in the sensational geography of its surfaces). In this view, there are no bodies *without* culture, since the body as a kind of material composition requires a cultural *grammar* of embodiment. Although theories of performative identity have been most influential in the study of gender and sexuality, significant intellectual ground has also been broken in the study of race, ethnicity, and class as performative embodiments (Lott 1993; Muñoz 1999; Foster 1999).

The turn to cultural studies within American studies has also fostered critical attention on forms of public and political corporeality, particularly the orientation of cultural studies to mass culture. Because mass culture insistently links abstract identity to iconic embodiment, it proliferates the public bodies evacuated from early national political culture. The norms of commercial and political culture in the United States are thus historically at odds, yet today the life of the body politic is entirely transacted within the mass media, which may help to explain the contemporary salience of identity politics, as well as the tendency to stake claims for political recognition on the basis of embodied particularity. But mass culture also circulates bodies promiscuously; its technologies and commercial logic ensure the production of desirable body images made available to the widest market. Access to particular corporeal identities becomes paradoxically generalized; within mass culture, one can "have" (identify with or as) iconic forms of gendered, racial, ethnic, sexual, or classed embodiment that

have no necessary relation to the cultural consumer's assigned ("natural") body. (In virtual environments, for instance, a white, middle-class man might adopt the avatar of a working-class Asian woman.) Much of the contemporary scholarship on U.S. political culture, then, draws on notions of performative identity to parse the ways in which identity politics entail a *contest* over the grammar of embodiment (Spillers 1987; Harper 1994; Berlant 1997). The central question that arises from this new scholarship concerns which subjects will claim what forms of embodiment and with what effects.

7

Border

Mary Pat Brady

Were we to imagine an earlier iteration of this keywords project—one published around, say, 1989—"border" would most likely have been left off the list entirely, though "margin" or maybe "minor" might well have been included. In the intervening years, as violent border conflicts have erupted across the world and as the U.S. government has prepared to militarize its border with Mexico, the term has become prominent in academic work. Accounting for this shift—understanding the concept's fortunes, as it were—entails movement among academic concerns, theoretical conversations, and socio-political and economic developments over the last quarter of the twentieth century. To be sure, a loosely defined field of "border studies" has been around in some form or another since Frederick Jackson Turner (1893) argued for the significance of the frontier and Herbert Eugene Bolton (1921) published *The Spanish Borderlands: A Chronicle of Old Florida and the Southwest*, and certainly since the end of Word War II, when regional area studies began to receive sustained governmental support. During this period the most prominent borders were located between East and West Germany, North and South Vietnam, and the officially segregated U.S. South and the unofficially segregated U.S. North. By the mid-1980s, however, the United States had failed in its effort to maintain the border between North and South Vietnam, segregation had been rendered illegal if not eliminated in practice, and efforts to dismantle the border between East and West Germany were gaining momentum. At the same time, philosophers, artists, novelists, and scholars who had been meditating on the less prominent international border between Mexico and the United States began to gain broad attention and to publish significant new work.

That new work emerged along with the effort to create a North American Free Trade Zone, the subsequent Zapatista revolutionary response, the acceleration of other globalizing forces, and the attendant anxieties these forces generated among citizenry of various nations—many of which were manifested in political and grassroots efforts to further militarize national borders, narrow access to citizenship, and withdraw humane support for workers without papers. Borders were very much in the news because of the ongoing violence of national borders around the world, particularly in regions immediately affected by the break up of the Soviet Union, the Palestinian-Israeli conflict, the continuing impact of anticolonial struggles, and regional economic recessions. Furthermore, during this period capital accelerated its transition from its base in the nation-state to a new global scale that entailed more flexible modes of accumulation and citizenship. Under a series of new trade agreements, national borders no longer contained national economies as they had in prior decades. This economic shift accelerated a broad new series of global flows not only of capital and resources but also of jobs and people across national and regional borders. Alongside these developments, researchers in African American and postcolonial studies, feminist theory, post-structuralism, and the cultural studies of the Birmingham school, attuned to the experiences of exile and diaspora, drew attention to the manner in which the making and unmaking of various kinds of borders affects everyone (C. Fox 1999). Thus scholars were particularly interested in the theoretical analyses of Chicano and Chicana intellectuals who connected the study of ethnicity, racialization, and immigration to empire building, imperialism, and international relations (Paredes 1958; Gutiérrez-Jones 1995; Saldívar 1997).

Perhaps most significant among these new border theorists was the late philosopher Gloria Anzaldúa. Already well-known among feminists of color as coeditor of the groundbreaking anthology *This Bridge Called My Back* (Moraga and Anzaldúa 1981), Anzaldúa, in *Borderlands/La Frontera: The New Mestiza* (1987), mapped the violence of U.S. colonialism, patriarchy, and capitalism by exploring some historical aspects of the Texas-Mexico border. In doing so, Anzaldúa drew attention to the violent history of anti-Mexican racism, noting the borderland rapes, murders, land grabs, and police detentions largely ignored in standard U.S. histories. At the same time, she roundly critiqued what she saw as misogynist and homophobic practices prevalent in both Anglo and Mexican cultures. In a brilliant act of reappropriation, she mined the term "border," unveiling its metaphoricity in an effort to envision the impact of the border in less degrading and more sustainable ways. In keeping with the critical theoretical work of other feminists of color, Anzaldúa questioned the production and maintenance of binaries, their exclusionary force, and the maxims that suggest that living with contradiction necessarily entails psychosis. Instead, she mobilized a second spatial metaphor—that of the *frontera* or borderlands—to insist that one can embrace multiple contradictions and refuse the impossible effort to synthesize them fully, thus turning apparent contradictions into a source of insight and personal strength.

Rapidly disseminated in the United States and elsewhere, this concept of the *frontera* or borderlands enabled other writers to consider culture not through a dominant narrative of synthesis but from a more subaltern perspective of heterogeneity and messiness. "The borderlands are physically present," Anzaldúa (1987, 19) writes, "wherever two or more cultures edge each other, where people of different races occupy the same territory, where under, lower, middle and upper classes touch, where the space between two individuals shrinks with intimacy." This deliberately universalizing turn provided a language for discussing difference while invoking an imaginary geography. It allowed other scholars and performance artists to build on Anzaldúa's insights, focusing particularly on the conceptual possibilities contained in metaphors of borders, border-crossings, and borderlands. Some, such as Guillermo Gómez-Peña (1990), Néstor García Canclini (1995), and Homi K. Bhabha (1994), found much to celebrate in the hybridizing effects of borders. They too argued for the latent power and innovative possibilities of conflictive regions and binaries and suggested that working with contradictions, drawing humor and insight from them rather than repressing or resolving them, would challenge an epistemological structure that enabled economic oppression, racism, misogyny, and homophobia.

"Border" subsequently became a common analytical tool and reference point for scholars working across the fields of American studies and cultural studies (Aparicio 2003). It particularly appealed to researchers intent on analyzing the violence of racism and the naturalizing effects of various structures, from gender to nation. It also appealed to a much wider range of academics and nonacademics interested in exploring various forms of structural conflict. Scholars of romantic literature and medieval history held conferences in which "border" served as an organizing thematic. Prominent journals of critical theory and philosophy organized special issues around the theme of "borders." And a number of scholarly texts were published featuring "border" in their title—many of which were not particularly interested in geopolitical borders. At the same time, business and advertising copywriters celebrated the arrival of a world in which national borders no longer prohibited the movement of people and material. Since these celebrations of a borderless world often appeared in the very same magazines that reported economic blockades and efforts to restrict informal movements across national borders, the contradictory function of borders could not be ignored. Indeed, these contradictions highlighted the extent to which borders are crucial to capital management—they serve as revenue-producers for states, as wage-depressers for corporations, and as instantiations of national identity for citizens.

Within academic research in particular, the term began to do some very peculiar work. Because of its simultaneous material and metaphoric resonances, "border" could be used to locate an argument by apparently materializing it, while often dislocating it from any historically specific geopolitical referents. Such a function might not have been so available had borders not been so regularly the subject of news reports. Because of the unending violence of many geopolitical borders, including the thousands of people who have died attempting to cross the Mexico–U.S. border, scholars could use the term and implicitly invoke its violence without documenting or narrating that violence with any real precision (Berestein 2005). In a manner that worried some scholars, the seem-

ingly nonproductive status of a border (as object, wall, fence, riverbed) and its visual familiarity as a national-spatial icon disguised geopolitical and metaphoric borders' nefarious productivity (Brady 2000; Villa 2003).

José Saldívar (1997, xii) argues that the border as it has evolved in the hands of Chicano and Chicana intellectuals must be understood at least in part as a "paradigm," one that leads to an "ontological question: what kinds of world or worlds are we in?" Taking such a question seriously provides the opportunity for "border thinking," that is, moves beyond the constraining effects of Western epistemology's categories of knowledge and the explanatory macronarratives that have structured both the emergence of state power and the resistance to it (Mignolo 2000). Border thinking entails a shift in perspective to coloniality, to thinking, as Norma Alarcón (1996) would put it, "on the hyphen." Beginning with a geopolitical term, the best border theorists have developed an epistemological approach equally cognizant of "real" borders and of their fantastic, fantastically violent effects.

8

Capitalism

David F. Ruccio

While the capitalist system is generally celebrated within mainstream economic research, American cultural studies scholars will search in vain through those writings for actual discussions of the term "capitalism." Instead, neoclassical and Keynesian economists take as their object a system that is variously referred to as the "market economy" (in which individuals and private firms make decisions about consumption and production in decentralized markets), a "mixed economy" (in which marketplace activities are mixed with government "commands"), or just "the economy" (defined by scarce means and unlimited desires, the correct balancing of which is said to characterize all societies) (Stiglitz and Walsh 2002; Bhagwati 2003; Krugman and Wells 2004; Samuelson and Nordhaus 2004).

In contrast, the term "capitalism" has long occupied a central position in the vocabulary of Marxian economic theory. References to capitalism in American studies and cultural studies thus draw, implicitly or explicitly, on a two-fold critique of political economy: on one hand, a critique of capitalism as an economic and social system; on the other hand, a critique of mainstream economic theory. Karl Marx and latter-day Marxists criticize capitalism because it is based on exploitation, in the sense that capitalists appropriate and decide how to distribute the surplus labor performed by wage-laborers. They also criticize the work of mainstream economists for celebrating the existence of capitalism and for treating capitalist institutions and behaviors as corresponding to human nature (Mandel 1976; Resnick and Wolff 1987; Harvey 1989).

Much of this scholarship draws on Karl Marx and Frederick Engels's critique of political economy in the *Manifesto of the Communist Party* (1848) and the three volumes of *Capital* (1867, 1884, 1894). In the *Manifesto*, Marx and Engels compare capitalism to other forms of economic and social organization such as feudalism and slavery. What feudalism, slavery, and capitalism have in common is that all are based on class exploitation, defined as one group (feudal lords, slaveowners, and capitalists) appropriating the surplus labor of another (serfs, slaves, and wage-laborers). At the same time, capitalism exhibits a distinct dynamic. For the first time in history, it "established the world market," making it possible for the capitalist class to "nestle everywhere, settle everywhere, establish connexions everywhere" and giving "a cosmopolitan character to production and consumption in every country" (1848, 486, 487). It leads to radical and continuous changes throughout the economy and society, since, as Marx famously put it, "all that is solid melts into air" (487). And it is based on the development of a class of wage-laborers that is capable of ending class antagonisms and creating a new form of society, in which "the free development of each is the condition for the free development of all" (506).

If the goal of the *Manifesto* was to challenge the prevailing belief that capitalism had eliminated classes and class struggles, the point of *Capital* was to analyze the specific conditions and consequences of the class dimensions of a society in which the capitalist mode of production prevails. Capitalism presumes that the products of labor have become commodities, which means that the goods and services human beings produce have both a use-value (they satisfy some social need) and an exchange-value (they can be exchanged for other commodities or money). The existence of commodity exchange, in turn, presupposes a culture congruent with the "fetishism of commodities": a culture whereby individuals come to believe and act such that they have the freedom to buy and sell commodities; that the commodities they exchange are equal in value and that the commodity owners meet one another as equals in the marketplace; that individuals have well-defined property rights in the commodities they sell and purchase; and that they are able to calculate the ability of external objects to satisfy their needs and desires. The existence of commodity exchange is thus not based on the essential and universal human rationality assumed within mainstream economics from Adam Smith to the present. Nor can the cultures and identities of commodity-exchanging individuals be derived solely from economic activities and institutions. Rather, commodity exchange both presumes and constitutes particular forms of individual economic rationality (Amariglio and Callari 1993).

In both the *Manifesto* and *Capital*, "capitalism" refers to a system in which capitalists are able to produce commodities that will, at least in principle, yield them a profit. The source of the profit is the value created by the laborers who have been forced (historically, through a process Marx referred to as "primitive accumulation," and, socially, through capitalist institutions and cultures [1867, 871–940]) to exercise the specifically capitalist "freedom" to sell their ability to labor as a commodity. Capitalists profit within this system by extracting value above and beyond the cost of labor power (the necessary labor of the direct producers). Under the assumption that all commodities (including labor power) are exchanged at their values, a surplus-value arises based on the ability of capitalists to appropriate the surplus labor performed by the wage-laborers and to realize that extra labor by selling the commodities that are produced. Struggles consequently arise over the "rate of exploitation" (the ratio of surplus labor to necessary labor) and over the subsequent distributions of surplus-value (to managers, state officials, and other capitalists, who receive portions of the surplus). The culture of societies in which capitalism exists is stamped by the effects of such class struggles. The keyword "capitalism" thus designates not just an economic structure, but also the conflicts and contradictions inherent in that structure. Both the initial emergence and the continued reproduction of capitalism, if and when they occur, can and often do lead to tremendous social dislocations and acute crises; they are also conditioned by the most varied cultures and social identities.

In the case of the United States, the last two centuries might well be referred to as the era of the widening and deepening of capitalism, both domestically and internationally. Initially a market for foreign (especially British) capitalist commodities, the original thirteen colonies oversaw the establishment and growth of domestic capitalist enterprises, which sought both raw materials and markets for final goods within expanding geographical boundaries and across a heterogeneous class landscape. One result was that noncapitalist—communal, independent, slave, and feudal—producers located outside the urban centers of the Northeast were eventually undermined or displaced, thereby causing waves of rural peoples—men, women, and children of diverse racial and ethnic origins—to migrate to existing and newly established cities and to sell their labor power to industrial capitalists. The opening up of new domestic markets (through the determined efforts of retail merchants and advertisers), capitalist competition (which drove down the unit costs of production), and government programs (to establish a national currency and regulate trusts and working conditions) spurred further capitalist growth. The continued development of capitalist manufacturing required vast international migrations of laborers: initially, from Africa and Western Europe; later, and continuing to this day, from Latin America, Asia, Eastern Europe, and Africa (Dowd 1977; Duboff 1989; Amott and Matthaei 1996).

The movement of capital that accompanied the expansion of markets and the search for cheaper raw materials transformed previously noncapitalist regions outside the Northeast, including the relocation of textile mills to the South, the creation of foundries and automobile factories in the Midwest, the development of the oil industry in the Southwest, and the flourishing of capitalist agriculture and the movie industry on the West Coast. Capital was also exported to other countries to take advantage of lower wage levels and other cost advantages, introducing economic and social dislocations similar to those that had occurred inside the United States. In both cases, governments, business groups, and social movements (such as trade unions, civil rights organizations, and political parties) struggled over the economic and social conditions and consequences of the new industrial capitalist investments—the boom and bust cycles of domestic economic growth; large-scale movements of populations; the formation of new social identities; and military adventures and imperial interventions. The uneven development of capitalism has left its mark on the culture of the United States, now as in the past (Kaplan and Pease 1993; Jacobson 2000).

In the analysis of this nexus of capitalism and U.S. culture, we face three major challenges that in turn open up new paths of investigation for American cultural studies. The first concerns globalization. It is often assumed that the internationalization of the U.S. economy and society is a radically new phenomenon, something that burst on the scene in the 1980s. However, when measured in terms of movements of people (migration), goods and services (imports and exports), and money (capital inflows and outflows), the globalization of capitalism with respect to the United States achieved, beginning in the 1980s, levels that are quite similar to those experienced almost a century earlier (Ruccio 2003). Because of these similarities and others (particularly the rise in the rate of exploitation and, with it, the increasingly unequal distribution of income and wealth), it is a mistake to describe contemporary developments as unprecedented (Phillips 2002). This is not to say that the forms of capitalist development during the two periods are the same. One of the challenges for students of American culture is to register these differences—such as the outsourcing of jobs, the growth of Wal-Mart, the spread of financial markets, the conduct of wars to protect petroleum supplies, the emergence of new media and communication technologies—without losing sight of the past.

The second challenge is to avoid treating capitalism as a purely economic system, separate from culture. The influence of capitalism on the culture industry—including the rise of a capitalist film industry and the export of U.S. culture (Miller et al. 2001; Wayne 2003)—has been widely studied and debated. What is less clear is that the capitalist economy is "saturated" by and cannot exist apart from cultural meanings and identities. From this perspective, each moment of capitalism, from the existence of commodity exchange to the export of capital, is simultaneously economic and cultural. The point is not to substitute cultural studies for political economy, but to recognize—and analyze, concretely and historically—the cultural conditions of capitalism. Money, labor, labor power, surplus labor, profits, capital, capitalists, enterprises: all of these economic forms require the performance of specific, historically and socially constructed meanings and identities. It is also important to understand the role of economic thought (mainstream, Marxian, Keynesian, and others) in influencing the development of U.S. capitalism and U.S. culture generally. These topics remain open, though a fruitful place to begin is by understanding the commodity phase in the social life of things (Appadurai 1986), the role that "languages of class" play in creating new class identities (Gibson-Graham et al. 2001), and the complex interplay of capitalist and noncapitalist economic imaginaries (Watkins 1998).

The third potential stumbling block is the treatment of capitalism as an all-encompassing, unitary system that has colonized every social arena and region of the globe. While capitalism certainly represents a powerful project for making and remaking the world, deploying the concept of capitalism as a complete mapping of the economic and social landscape has the effect of obscuring noncapitalist forms of economic organization and cultural sense-making. "Capitalocentrism" (akin to the role played by "phallocentrism" and "logocentrism" with respect to gender and language) hides from view the diverse ways in which people in the United States and elsewhere engage with individual and collective noncapitalist economies—including barter, communal production, gift-making, and solidarity—that fall outside the practices and presumed logic of capitalism (Gibson-Graham 1996; Ruccio and Gibson-Graham 2001). On this view, U.S. culture is heterogeneous and contradictory with respect to different class structures. It contains elements that foster and reproduce capitalism and, at the same time, its noncapitalist others.

9

Citizenship "politically intimate"

Lauren Berlant

Although we tend to think of citizenship as something national, originally the *citizen* was simply a certain kind of someone who lived in a Greek *city*: a member of an elite class who was said to be capable of self-governance and therefore of the legal and military governance of the city. But the ancient history of the term tells us little about the constellation of rights, laws, obligations, interests, fantasies, and expectations that shape the modern scene of citizenship, which is generally said to have been initiated by the democratic revolutions of the eighteenth century (B. Anderson 1991; B. Turner 1993; Mouffe 1995). Most simply, citizenship refers to a standing within the law (this is often called *formal* citizenship); *jus soli* citizenship allots citizenship to people born within the geographical territory, and *jus sanguinis* awards citizenship by way of a parental inheritance.

At the same time, citizenship is a relation among strangers who learn to feel it as a common identity based on shared historical, legal, or familial connection to a geopolitical space. Many institutional and social practices are aimed at inducing a visceral identification of personal identity with nationality. In the United States, this has often involved the orchestration of fantasies about the promise of the state and the nation to cultivate and protect a consensually recognized ideal of the "good life"; in return for cultural, legal, and military security, people are asked to love their country, and to recognize certain stories, events, experiences, practices, and ways of life as related to the core of who they are, their public status, and their resemblance to other people. This training in politicized intimacy has also served as a way of turning political boundaries into visceral, emotional, and seemingly hardwired responses of "insiders" to "outsiders." Thus we can say that citizenship's legal architecture manifests itself and is continually reshaped in the space of transactions between intimates and strangers. The term *civil society* is often applied to these scenes of *substantive* citizenship, though discussions of civil society tend to focus only on the rational aspects of communication and interaction that contribute to the state's reproduction of mainstream society, and not to the ordinary affective or interactive aspects of social exchange (Habermas 1999).

The concept of *sovereignty* is a crucial bridge between the legal and the substantive domains of U.S. citizenship. This term presupposes a relation between the nation's legal control over what happens in its territory and the presumption that citizens should have control over their lives and bodies, a condition of limited personal autonomy that the state has a responsibility to protect. But the promise of U.S. citizenship to deliver sovereignty to all of its citizens has always been practiced unevenly, in contradiction with most understandings of democratic ideals (Rancière 1998). The historical conditions of legal and social belonging have been manipulated to serve the concentration of economic, racial, and sexual power in the society's ruling blocs.

This shaping of the political experience of citizens and noncitizens has been a focus of much recent scholarship and political struggle. These discussions contest the term *citizenship* in various ways: *cultural citizenship* describes the histories of subordinated groups within the nation-state that might not be covered by official legal or political narratives (T. Miller 1993, 2001; Ong 1996; R. Rosaldo 1999); *consumer citizenship* designates contemporary practices of social belonging and political pacification in the United States (Shanley 1997; Cronin 2000; L. Cohen 2003); *sexual citizenship* references the ongoing struggle to gain full legal rights for gendered and sexual minorities (Berlant and Warner 2000; Cott 2000; M. Kaplan 1997); and *global citizenship* describes a project of deriving a concept of justice from linkages among people on a transnational or global scale (Falk 1994; Bosniak 1998; Hardt and Negri 2000). This list could be vastly expanded. Patriotic citizenship, economic citizenship, and legal citizenship have all been shaped not just within a political public sphere, not just within the logic of mass culture and consumer capitalism, but also within a discussion among various collective interest groups struggling over the core norms, practices, and mentalities of a putatively general U.S. population.

The histories of racial and sexual standing in the United States provide the clearest examples of the uneven access to the full benefits of citizenship. But historically citizenship has also shaped less recognized kinds of distinction. Central among these is that U.S.

citizenship has always involved tensions between federal and state systems. Indeed, for most of U.S. history, state citizenship had priority, and the history of civil and suffrage rights centrally involved arguments over the relative priority of state versus federal law. For example, the 1967 Supreme Court case *Loving v. Virginia*, which deemed it unconstitutional to forbid marriage among heterosexuals identified as being of different races, nullified "anti-miscegenation" laws not only in Virginia but in thirty-seven other states as well. In so doing, the Supreme Court argued that it is a general rule of *U.S.* citizenship that marriage cannot be governed by racial restrictions. Prior to that, states were more important than the nation in determining the racial component of legal marriage among heterosexuals, as well as in many other sexual, familial, and commercial matters, including the legal standing of Mormon, lesbian, gay, and women's marital practices, age of consent, marital rape, reproduction (e.g., abortion, surrogacy, and adoption), and child protection.

Given these complex legal and social histories, U.S. citizenship may be best thought of as an intricate scene where competing forces, definitions, and geographies of freedom and liberty are lived concretely. Citizenship is the practical site of a theoretical existence, in that it allows for the reproduction of a variety of kinds of law in everyday life. It is an abstract idea on behalf of which people engage in personal and political acts, from cheating on taxes to pledging allegiance to fomenting revolutions. It is also, importantly, an ordinary space of activity that many people occupy without thinking much about it, as the administration of citizenship is usually delegated to the political sphere and only periodically worried over during exceptional crises or the election season.

Recent scholarship has pursued this insight into the everyday life of citizenship by exploring some of the most contested scenes in which citizenship has been battled over in U.S. history: immigration, voting rights, sexuality, and labor. Immigration and suffrage have been closely linked at least since the U.S. Naturalization Act of 1790 allowed only "free white persons" to be naturalized as full U.S. citizens. Implicitly this act began the shift from a definition of citizenship through the *ownership of property* to citizenship as the *ownership of labor*, since the word "free" in this act defined freedom as not being economically enslaved—that is, free to sell one's labor in a market for wages (Glenn 2004). The history of U.S. immigrant rights (and exclusions) is thus tied up with desires to control the conditions under which certain populations would be "free" to perform labor in the United States without access to many of the privileges of "free white persons," such as the vote and the legal standing to enforce contracts (Haney-Lopez 1996; Lipsitz 1998; Roediger 1999).

So, for example, between 1882 and 1952 virtually all Asian immigrants except for a small number of Filipino laborers were excluded from full U.S. citizenship. During this period the United States was also opening and closing the gates to Latin American peoples, especially Mexicans, hundreds of thousands of whom were forcibly repatriated to Mexico a number of times, following fluctuations in capitalists' needs and white racial anxieties about disease and moral degeneracy, along with the usual and always false fear that "alien" poor people take more from the economy than they contribute to it. The courts adjudicating these shifts veered between using racial science and "common knowledge," especially in the visual register, as justification for discrimination (Honig 1998; Jacobson 1998, 2000; Roberts 1998). Similarly, arguments for *and* against suffrage for women appealed to common sense, racist science, and biblical authority to protect patriarchal privilege. Suffrage was achieved only when President Woodrow Wilson found it politically expedient to use an image of emancipated femininity to establish U.S. modernity and moral superiority on a global scale (Berlant 2002). Federal and state manipulation of voting rights continues to threaten the representation of many citizens, especially the poor and the incarcerated.

The same pseudo-scientific rationales that maintained white supremacy in the performance of U.S. citizenship were also crucial in shaping reproductive law. It may not seem a question of citizenship when a court determines, as it did in the early twentieth century, that it is proper to sterilize women deemed mentally ill, intellectually limited, or epileptic. But the presumption was that these women would be incompetent as mothers and would pass their incompetence on to their children, and that the nation would be burdened by the social and economic costs of reproduction by the poor. Poor women and women of color, especially African American and Native American women, were isolated by this juridical-medical ideology: in California, until the late nineteenth century Native American children could be taken from their families without due process; until 1972, the State of Virginia routinely sterilized poor women without their consent if their offspring were deemed vulnerable to taking on a "degenerate" form (Ginsburg 1998; Stern 1999b). These examples demonstrate that certain perquisites of citizenship, such as the material experience of sovereignty and sexual "privacy" (a modern development within sovereignty), have often been unavailable to the poor, thereby privileging the wealthier classes and the sexually "normal."

What connects these cases to the keyword "citizenship" is not that they are denials of state-protected *rights* (there has never been a "right" to medical care in the United States). Rather, the contradiction between the sovereignty of abstract citizens and the everyday lives of embodied subjects has been structured by the administration of class hierarchies alongside formal democracy. So it is no surprise that citizenship norms and laws have been highly contested in the workplace as well. Should places of business be allowed to function by different standards than the public domain? Should the protections of citizenship punch out when the worker punches in? Should there be different rules for free speech and political speech on private property and public property? These and other legal questions of citizen sovereignty are put to the test in labor relations. It was not until the last decades of the nineteenth century that workers won the right to an eight-hour day; and during the post–World War II era many

employers made "concessions" to their workers such as the family wage, health insurance, pensions, and protecting workers from undue physical harm on the job. None of these concessions would have happened without the organizing energy of the labor movement, as we can see when, in tight economic times, corporations renege on contracts with workers and states cut back on oversight of corporations' economic, environmental, and worker health practices. Most histories of U.S. citizenship would not place worker rights at the center of a consideration of the practice of equality in the law and social spaces. But insofar as citizens and workers live citizenship as an experience of sovereignty in their everyday lives, the conditions of labor and the formal and informal rules about organizing worker demands for employer accountability have to be at the center of the story.

Many other vectors of normative and legal adjudication that have structured citizenship could be isolated and enumerated, such as human rights, family law, public education, military conscription, real estate zoning, tax structure, religion, and various state entitlement programs. Such seemingly separate domains are actually mutually defining. What, for example, has Christianity had to do with U.S. citizenship, given the constitutionally mandated prohibition of an official state religion? While some theorists have correlated the development of modern public spheres with the secularization of the shared social world, this evolutionary liberal model has recently been shattered by a cluster of different arguments: that the founding fathers were installing political modernity within the strictures of a Protestant morality of conscience; that the history of legislation around marriage, the family, and children has inevitably been influenced by religious movements advocating for and against traditional patriarchal control; that religious organizations have shaped powerfully the historical relation of the public and the private in terms of rights and proprieties; that the development of the welfare state and the civil rights understanding of the economic basis of rights was crucially shaped by religious thinkers (Harding 2001; Morone 2003; Bruce and Voas 2004). At the same time, local communities often engender notions of proper citizenship through churches, schools, and other institutions that involve face-to-face social participation (Ong 1996). The religious question has also been central to the story of the citizenship of Mormons, Native Americans, and many immigrant groups, involving taxation, reproductive rights, free speech, public education, and diverse discussions of the material relation of morality to political and economic concerns.

Many of the progressive developments in U.S. citizenship would not have been achieved without the internationally based struggles of socialism, feminism, and the labor movement. Today the United States feels pressure from other international movements dedicated to transforming its practices of citizenship: religious movements (Christian fundamentalism and evangelicalism, Islam, Catholicism); anti-neoliberalism (anti-globalization movements dedicated to a sustaining rather than exploitative and depleting version of global integration); international legal and policy institutions (the United Nations and the Hague; Doctors without Borders). While international institutions tend to be oriented toward a one-world model of justice, resource distribution, and peace, there is no singular direction or vision of the good life projected by these movements. Anti-neoliberalism is a *motive* rather than a program, coordinating liberal reformist models of ameliorative activity (environmentalism, welfare statism) with more radical anarchist, queer, anti-racist models of refusal and demand. Global religious movements link anti-capitalist (anti-poverty) messages with a variety of assertions of local sovereignty against the abstract imperialism and general liberality of the modernist state.

Innovations in communication and transportation technology, most notably the Internet, have revitalized and even enabled new inter- and transnational movements, and have often produced new understandings of citizenship (Dahlberg 2001; Graeber 2002; Poster 1999/2005). Local determination is not a major stress-point among Internet utopians: personal attachments across the globe are made possible by the speed of information transmission. The seemingly infinitely expanding possibilities of niche political developments and micro-movements have reanimated citizenship as an aspirational concept in discussions of diverse communities, real and imagined. Thus the nation-state as such has become only one player in struggles over political and social justice, so much so that many states feel threatened by the transnational flow of information and have responded with censorship. Still, the delocalization of citizenship has not made the world simply postnational. Corporations are like empires; both work transnationally to reshape national standards of conduct. So too the activity of ordinary people to force accountability and to imagine new possibilities for democratic collective life and the sovereignty of people—whether or not they are citizens—continues to revitalize the political sphere everywhere.

10

City

Micaela di Leonardo

Raymond Williams (1973) demonstrated the overarching significance of the keywords "city" and "country," establishing the simultaneously positive and negative inflections of urbanity. On the positive side were the values of learning, light, progress, civilization, cosmopolitanism, tolerance and civil liberties, excitement and sophistication; on the negative lay the countervalues of sin, darkness and noise, corruption and devolution, danger and violence, irreligion, mob rule, and anomie. In short, urban modernity and its discontents.

As Williams noted, these city/country oppositions are always invoked in the service of political interests. Diverse social actors described European and, later, U.S. urban life in ways that shifted and evolved with cities themselves. Troubadours, priests, ministers, and Romantic poets gave way to flaneurs and other urban

observers, who then gave way to social statisticians, settlement-house workers, novelists, playwrights, and painters. The new social scientists and artists took cities and urban dwellers as their research objects, as problems to be solved, and as material to be dramatized. In this thrifty recycling of tropes, a set of symbolic associations arose linking the European and American urban poor to colonized others through their mutual need for instruction from their betters (di Leonardo 1998). The voluminous writings of missionaries, journalists, and reformers in Victorian Britain provided a template for later U.S. constructions of "urban jungles" filled with the "near-savage" poor. Socialist novelist Jack London (1903, 288), in an account of life among East London's homeless at the time of Edward's coronation, declared passionately that it was "far better to be a people of the wilderness and desert, of the cave and the squatting-place, than to be a people of the machine and the Abyss."

The long history of American and U.S. urban imaginaries include the Puritan vision of the blessed gathering of the elect as a "city on a hill"; the revolutionary republican associations attached to Boston and Philadelphia; the new nation's classically planned capital of Washington, D.C.; and diverse nineteenth-century texts that American studies pioneer Leo Marx (1964) catalogued under the heading of the "machine in the garden." The nineteenth century brought the westward expansion of the new republic and the rapid growth of New York and Boston; the legal end of slavery and the "great migration" of freedmen and women to northern cities; the rapid rise of capitalist industrialization and its associated second major wave of labor migration from Europe and Asia; the first wave of the women's movement and of home-grown radicalisms hatched in urban environments; and U.S. imperial actions in the Caribbean, Latin America, and the Pacific, all of which created bridges for future migration to U.S. cities. These historical developments, along with many others, were connected to vast urban growth fueled by external and internal migration.

Dominant urban imaginaries reflected and interpreted these sea-changes. The "Chicago school" social scientists, from the 1910s forward, tended to envision inevitable progress as repeated waves of migrants of every nationality settled first in center cities and then moved to outer and suburban rings as they experienced upward social mobility. This narrative credited even the poorest of urban dwellers with civility and the capacity for self-organization. Other scholars, journalists, and artists focused instead on the dirt, pollution, noise, and overcrowding of rapidly expanding U.S. cities, though from contrasting political perspectives. Progressives such as Upton Sinclair (1906) described the capitalist exploitation of downtrodden urban dwellers and the corrupt urban machines (such as New York's infamous "Tammany Hall") that failed to ameliorate their lot. Their opponents, such as Madison Grant (1916), envisioned cities as cesspools harboring the genetically unfit and overly procreative, particularly Italians, Irish, Jews, and Slavs and other southeastern European immigrants. The associations of these new immigrants with poverty, crime, disease,

and hyperfertility have been recycled across the decades to apply to populations now construed as "racial," particularly blacks and Latinos. Related associations of urban worlds and their racialized populations with sexual danger and "perversion" have obscured the role cities have played in women's emancipation and interracial and queer community-building since at least the nineteenth century (Chauncey 1994; Mumford 1997; Delany 2001).

At the same time, mainstream social scientists continue to frame sexual and racial forms of capitalist exploitation as expressions of cultural difference and pathology. Counterempirical descriptions of a "culture of poverty" in the 1960s shifted in the 1980s into a contrast between the "urban underclass" and new "model minorities" (largely new Asian and select Latino migrants), even as urban renewal projects destroyed low-cost housing. "Asphalt jungles" gave way to "welfare queens" and journalistic hysteria over inner-city crime, drugs, and gangs. Replicating the oppositional structure of earlier figurations, the late twentieth century saw the rise of rap, hip-hop, and break-dancing, and the marketing of the virtues of urban "diversity," even as gentrification was raising real estate values in minority neighborhood after neighborhood, thus pricing out "diverse" populations.

The global neoliberal shift of the 1990s forward—the wholesale privatization of public goods and cutbacks in all social programs combined with an identity-based reading of human rights—and U.S. imperial responses to global terrorism have further complicated urban representations and realities. Among the factors reconfiguring U.S. urban life are the representation of cities as targets of terrorist attacks; the uncertainty occasioned by simultaneous economic growth, unstable markets, rising public deficits, and wholesale layoffs; the outsourcing of white- and blue-collar jobs to non-U.S. urban workers; the explosion of "urban contemporary" (black and Latino) music, dance, and fashion; the hyper-gentrification of urban housing markets; and the development of urban cores as tourist destinations. Simultaneously, the development of a network of "global cities"—New York, London, and Tokyo, among others—has centralized the administration and growth of finance capital (Sassen 1991). At the dawn of the twenty-first century, cities continue to serve as metonyms of both nations and their discontents.

11
Civilization
David S. Shields

"Civilization" refers to an ideal perpetually contested, a condition perpetually threatened, and a practice perpetually prescribed. It is a term employed by academics and cultural theorists, policy pundits, and government officials in the United States and around the world. In the view of G. R. Collingwood (1971) and a host of lesser defenders of "Western heritage," it is the political order and cultural treasure of the West threatened by totalitarian, proletarian, and jihadist barbarities. It is the globally exportable condition of social development promoted by the United Nations Civil Society Organizations and Participation Programme. It is the seductive discipline of decorum prescribed by colonizing powers upon subaltern populations critiqued in Homi K. Bhabha's essay "Sly Civility" (1985/1994). It is an abstract set of conditions, found in any number of world cultures throughout history, described by sociologists such as Benjamin Nelson (1973) and Stanford M. Lyman (1990).

These various usages have long jostled in print and public media. Yet they share a common history that was initially concerned with distinguishing the different social conditions discovered by Europe's early modern exploration of the world and by the development of the empirical investigation of the past. The word was born of the Enlightenment, and not all of its subsequent usages have escaped the Enlightenment tendency to conceive matters in the form of binary oppositions. Yet its first usage in English resulted from the desire to go beyond the conventional opposition between civil and uncivil.

"Civilization" came into English sometime in the 1760s or 1770s, adapted from the French word *civilisation* to supplant the phrase "civil life." Since the time of the 1579 treatise *Of Cyuil and Uncyuil Life*, English authors had debated whether rural simplicity or urbanity made a subject better able to serve the crown. Civil life referred here to the harmonious incorporation of the subject into the public world of a nation and presupposed an effective traditional culture. The final decades of the eighteenth century made the question of civility broader than the formation of serviceable political subjects in a given nation. The revolutionary social and political agitations in British America and France framed the condition of the citizenry (as distinguished from a realm of subjects) in the generalities of abstract rights, universal laws, and utopian institutions. Civilization came into prominence in the discourse of the French Revolution, where it named an enduring cultural and communal organization more fundamental than the political constitution of the state and more reasonable than the cultus of religion.

"Civilization" thus began to operate in tension with "culture," "nation," "barbarity," and "rural primitivism." It now owed less to "civil life" than to "civility," a term that spoke of an orderliness and integrity of society that enabled the conversation and commerce of various classes and orders within a community. Civility had a more inclusive and normative character than the older courtly value of courtesy. It also had a range of application extending beyond one's own community. Externally, "civility" stood in contrast with the disorders and social simplicity of "savagery"; it enabled conversation, diplomacy, and trade between peoples. Internally, civility spoke of the condition of a people at one moment in time. "Civilization," in distinction, invoked a narrative of development or progress that depended upon a stage-based theory of civil refinement.

This narrative became popular in the wake of early modern explorations of the world. Contacts with illiterate, pastoral peoples who had mastered the smelting and casting of iron set Europeans pondering the characteristics of civility. The capacity of "savage peoples" to learn technology and understand European concepts, coupled with the Europeans' wish to incorporate these peoples as laborers and suppliers in Western imperial commerce, suggested that such persons were in a more primitive state of development. For these savage peoples to attain civilization meant that they must be educated into the arts of peace and commerce. The example of China, which Enlightenment philosophers recognized as an integral civilization, further indicated that the history of development might have more than one trajectory.

Sociologist Norbert Elias (1939/1969) described the mechanism that underlay these cultural and societal developments in the early modern West as the "civilizing process." Elias saw this process as occurring in two cultural registers. In the nation-states of the West, a regime of masculine power centered in monarchy and a martial aristocracy, operating under an ethic of honor and valor, was transformed into a "civil society" centered in social institutions outside the royal court, where conflict was sublimated in contests of aesthetic display, gentility, and heterosocial conversation. Outside of these nation-states, particularly in places seen as lacking literacy, centralized government, social order, and law, civilization involved a process of acculturation, enabled by commerce and the exchange of knowledge, in which civil society was created and developed.

In contrast to many of the writers he surveyed, Elias was careful to speak of process, not progress. He described a development, not a scheme of evolution or perfection. Elias thus argued for the second of two models of civil improvement that have long contended: the utopian and the processive. In the former, a civil community is perfected in accord with an ideal; in the latter, civilization is a process with an implicit but unprogrammatic tendency. The French Revolution brought the conflict between these two views into the open. The Enlightenment philosopher the Marquis de Condorcet, in *Esquisse d'un tableau historique des progrès de l'esprit humain* (1793), viewed civilization as culminating in a perfection of human knowledge, spirit, and will. The problem with this model of civilization—of utopia as a program of social change—was announced in the ironic title of the masterwork of revolutionary wit composed by one of its partisans and victims, the collection of aphorisms entitled "Produits de la civilization perfectionée" by Nicolas Chamfort (1984). Perfected civilization for Chamfort was vanity institutionalized and enforced by the coercive power of the state.

In the wake of the French Revolution, literary Romanticism, disillusioned by the political fallout of the Enlightenment, complicated the resulting dialectics of civilization and savagery, civility and barbarity. Romantic suspicion of civilization can be traced to Jean-Jacques Rousseau's celebration of the primitive in "Discourse on Inequality" (1754). Civilization's attributes—urbanity, politeness, commerce—became associated with corruptions of man. In Romantic ideology, nature and individual human genius became the counterforces to civilization. In Europe, this Romantic

ideology spawned a politics of anarchism. In the United States, a less overtly political version of Romantic individualism found expression in canonical writings ranging from Ralph Waldo Emerson's "The American Scholar" (1837) to Mark Twain's *Adventures of Huckleberry Finn* (1885/1985).

Still, the utopian impulses unleashed by the Enlightenment were not halted by the Romantic cult of nature. A faith in the capacity of humans to intervene in history drove various experiments in utopian community and nation-building. Civilization became a set of programs applied to myriad peoples and nations, from social communes in the U.S. hinterlands to blueprints for European and Latin American revolutions. Civilization became one of the keywords in debates over the character of the new nations created by the independence movements in South America. Domingo F. Sarmiento (1845/2004), in his classic *Civilization and Barbarism*, praised the liberalism, urbanity, and creativity of his native Argentina's cities against the political and cultural legacy of the *pampa*, where ignorance, authoritarianism, and rigid custom ruled. Sarmiento anticipated many nineteenth- and twentieth-century thinkers in his use of "civilization" as an ideal from which to criticize the "nation." Conversely, José Martí in "Our America" (1891) identified "civilization" as the counterforce of liberty, a trace of colonial ideology, and a synonym for luxury. The debate between Sarmiento and Martí typifies Romantic agony over civilization in its linkage of civilization with the question of national destiny. Post-Romantic politics posed civilization as the other by which the limits of nationhood were revealed.

As the manifestations and expressions of nationalism became increasingly extreme in the twentieth century, thinkers embraced the nonprogrammatic sense of civilization to counter the rhetoric of state self-glorification. G. R. Collingwood and other critics described the nationalist self-celebration of Germany under National Socialism and Fascist Spain as "anti-civilizational." Collingwood memorably redefined the term "barbarity," retiring its traditional sense of alien crudity and supplying in its stead the willful selfishness and philistinism of a modern nation-state.

At the same time, the nonprogrammatic view of civilization developed descriptive and critical uses. Emile Durkheim and Marcel Mauss argued in their "Note on the Notion of Civilization" (1913) that certain phenomena have long existed that are "supranational" in their operation, such as tools, languages, styles of aesthetic expression, and rituals of exchange. Their interdependence and systemic reciprocity are not located within a politically determined boundary. In its descriptive and historical manifestations, "civilization" thus names a rough set of conditions, influenced by human action, recognized in many times and places, yet lacking an immutable essence. Civilization not only has a material face, but a social one as well. This human, institutional character of civilization—embodied in the phrase "civil society"— during the late twentieth century increasingly eclipsed "civilization" in the lexicon of governmental agencies and international bodies.

World officialdom, in the form of the United Nations and other international organizations, thus avoids the question of whether a "nation" will be a "civilization." Instead, these organizations ask whether a nation possesses a "civil society." This shift in terminology avoids the programmatic implications of civilization and its history of colonial violence, yet it alludes to a condition of political stability, urbanity, commerce, and social enrichment. The U.N. Civil Society Organizations and Participation Programme has viewed the formation of civil society as the goal of political development for states characterized by strongly centralized, authoritarian polities where independent institutions have not been permitted, and for unconsolidated societies lacking an institutional sphere. Since 2000, the Civil Society Programme has expanded its purview considerably to include initiatives related to democratic governance, poverty reduction, crisis prevention and recovery, HIV/AIDS, energy, and the environment. In effect, a global pragmatics of civility—marked by a citizenry's enjoyment of civil order, a right of association, and venues for expressing public opinion, projecting communal interest, and envisioning the good life—now encompasses the whole realm of social welfare, with the exceptions of civil rights and commerce.

Witnessing the growing semantic amorphousness of the term "civil society," we can understand why it is difficult to conceive of a clash of civil societies, but not difficult to envision clashes between civilizations. Civilization retains its denotative character, pointing to communities that possess certain qualities of development and pursuing distinctly formed purposes. These purposes sometimes stand opposed to others. History abounds in such conflicts: Egypt and Babylonia, Greece and Rome, Catholic Spain and Protestant North Europe. Samuel Huntington attempted to theorize these recurring conflicts in his *The Clash of Civilizations* (1996), but failed to grasp the differences between cultures and civilizations. For a neoconservative, he is unusual in believing that an incommensurability of values exists among cultures. He fails to recognize the pragmatics of global exchange in values and goods now operating even among enemy states.

Contrary to Huntington's thesis, civilization's critical function in global political discourse has not been to explain the deep grammar of international conflicts, but to propose a quality of social existence that rebukes barbarity and supplies an extralegal standard for the comportment of nations. Civilization is therefore not utopia, but an enriched condition of social existence acknowledged both by those who enjoy it and those who wish to enjoy it. "Civilization" thus brings to light inequality. Efforts to understand the origins of inequality among individuals and social groups can be traced to nineteenth-century thinkers who turned away from the definition of civilization as essence to definitions that took into account practices of social interaction that permitted an enriched quality of communal life: the stability of law, a disinclination to violence, an inclination to cooperation, and an ethic of sociability based on tolerance of strangers. Arthur de Gobineau, in "An Essay on the Inequality of the Races" (1853–55/1967), gave this analysis a racial

cast. Certain biological races were fated to savagery due in part to their intolerance of the other. Gobineau's linkage of an interactional sociology of civilization with essentialized racism fathered a hybrid picture of civilization of great and pernicious influence that has not been fully exorcised by the new "civilization analysis" developed by Nelson (1973) and Lyman (1990), an interactionalist sociology that frees social descriptions from essentialist explanations in order to develop a global inquiry that ranges from micro to macro scenes of social action.

Of greater power in countering Gobineau's legacy has been postcolonial studies, whose leading practitioners take care to expose how the descriptive and prescriptive features of the Western discourse of civilization are characteristically intermingled. Civilization always appears in the service of some presumptive project, whether territorial conquest, commercial hegemony, evangelical mission, cultural imperialism, or the enslavement of non-Western populations (Bernal 1995; Paranjape 1998). Most, but not all, postcolonial critics are concerned with strategies for resisting the enchantment of Western civilization. These range from outright rejection to more complex engagements with the legacies of colonial power. Interestingly, some recent postcolonial thinkers embrace a pragmatics of civility and the form of civilization, seeing it as a remedy to tribalism and sectarianism. Leon de Kock (2001), for instance, offers a model of postcoloniality that disavows simple oppositionality by exploring a moment in the history of nascent African nationalism in South Africa when African subject formation was framed in apparent complicity with prescribed forms of Western civility. Similar work on the conceptual homologies between transnationalism, a favored conceptual orientation for American studies, and civilization as now understood by interactionalist sociology, would do much to enhance the conversation in the field. Transnationalism and the interactionalist sociology of civilization both explore the pragmatics of cultural permeability on a global scale, pursuing knowledge of those values, practices, institutions, and objects shared among states and peoples that contribute to responsible action among nations and persons.

12

Class

Eric Lott

As an analytical tool and historiographical category, class has an important place in American cultural studies, if only because so many have thought it irrelevant to the study of the United States. Unlike Europe's old countries, with their feudal pasts and monarchical legacies, the United States, it has often been said, is a land of unlimited economic and geographical mobility. Abraham Lincoln was only one of the most notable believers in "American exceptionalism," the idea that the United States, uniquely among the globe's nations, assigned its citizens no fixed class definition and afforded boundless opportunity to those who would only work hard and look beyond the next horizon. The reality is much more complicated, as scholars and critics have to some extent always known, and over the last forty years have demonstrated in studies of U.S. class formation, cultural allegiance, and artistic expression.

Some form of class consciousness has existed in North America at least since white settlers arrived; John Winthrop's well-known sermon aboard the *Arbella* in 1630, "A Model of Christian Charity," in part justifies the existence of class differences by making them crucial to God's plan of binding through charity the socially stratified community of Puritan believers. The descendants of those believers would become an ever-rising post-Puritan middle class, as German sociologist Max Weber (1905) famously suggested when he linked the "Protestant ethic" with capitalist economic energies. Simultaneously, the development of a specifically working-class or "plebeian" consciousness would come out of the early U.S. situation of class stratification, and the scholarly dilemma ever since has been how to account for such stratification historically, socially, and culturally.

Closely related to such categories as "station," "status," "group," and "kind," class resonates with implications of value, quality, respectability, and religious virtue. Goodness is gilded in much U.S. cultural thought, and it has been difficult to pry capital loose from rectitude. A related difficulty is that class can seem a natural and fixed category; certainly one strain of social and historical analysis in American studies has been marked by a static account of class and class belonging, with discrete strata exhibiting characteristic habits and allegiances and existing in hierarchical formation. In one of the best theoretical accounts, Erik Olin Wright (1985) makes useful distinctions among class *structure*, class *formation*, and class *consciousness*. Class structure is that ensemble of social relations into which individuals enter and which shapes their class consciousness; class formations are those organized collectivities that come about as a result of the interests shaped by the class structure or system. As Wright sums it up, classes "have a structural existence which is irreducible to the kinds of collective organizations which develop historically (class formations), the class ideologies held by individuals and organizations (class consciousness) or the forms of conflict engaged in by individuals as class members or by class organizations (class struggle), and . . . such class structures impose basic constraints on these other elements in the concept of class" (28).

These distinctions help keep in view the fact that class and classification are dynamic processes, more the result than the cause of historical events. Class, as British historian and cultural studies scholar E. P. Thompson (1963) insisted, is a *relational* category, always defined against and in tension with its dialectical others. In response to British cultural theorist Raymond Williams's (1958) claim that culture should be defined as a "whole way of life," Thompson (1961a, 1961b) redefined culture as a "whole way of conflict," structured in dominance and constantly contested by its various social actors. Work on class in American studies has done much to substantiate Thompson's

thesis, and the connections between Thompson's historical reconstruction of British working-class formation, Williams's influential model of cultural studies, and American cultural studies scholarship focused on class have been often intimate.

This emphasis has battered time-honored and influential ideas about U.S. culture and society, such as Frederick Jackson Turner's "frontier thesis" (1893), in which westward-roving U.S. Americans continually reestablish the conditions for social mobility and rising wages, or Louis Hartz's lament that a hegemonic "liberal tradition" rendered U.S. Americans incapable of thinking outside the contours of social consensus (1955). American studies scholars have shown, for example, how self-conscious, articulate, and combative early working-class or "artisan republican" ideologies were in waging rhetorical—and sometimes actual— war on what they termed the "non-producing classes" or "the upper ten." Sean Wilentz's *Chants Democratic: New York City and the Rise of the American Working Class, 1788–1850* (1984) is one of the finest studies of the former, while Stuart Blumin's *The Emergence of the Middle Class: Social Experience in the American City, 1760–1900* (1989) is one of the best on the latter. Both capture how extensively the cultural and affective life of social class shaped democracy in the United States.

Each of these studies exemplifies a body of historiography that first emerged in the 1960s to explain the shape and nature of various class formations. Wilentz is the beneficiary of the "new social history," of which Herbert Gutman (1976) was perhaps the chief U.S. representative. Subsequent studies of the labor process, shop-floor cultures, workers' leisure activities, and other matters have decisively demonstrated the tenacious, conflictual character of working-class belonging—even, or most particularly, when that belonging is overdetermined by being African American or female (Peiss 1986; Kelley 1994). Meanwhile, extensive studies of bourgeois or middle-class cultural formations in major books by Warren Susman (1984), Jackson Lears (1981), and many others have shown how ruling-class desires and cultural investments have influenced everything from modern art to modern therapy, as well as the degree to which such canonical ideas as the "American character," "American progress," and the "American Dream" are inflected by class. Perhaps most illuminating have been studies by such scholars as Christine Stansell (1986), Richard Slotkin (1985), Hazel Carby (1987), Alan Trachtenberg (1982), and Lizabeth Cohen (2003) that examine the complex interrelations among various class fractions and formations.

One of the common findings of the latter sort of study is how often cross-class interaction works not to dissolve class boundaries but to buttress them—in, for instance, middle-class philanthropic enterprises that wind up solidifying bourgeois formations and alienating their would-be working-class wards, or African American strategies of racial uplift that too often demonize the black working class. For this reason and others, the category of class has been immensely useful in American cultural studies as an analytical tool capable of unpacking the sometimes surprising dynamics of cultural and textual processes and products,

from social clubs and theatrical performances to dime novels and Disney films. The class segregation of mid-nineteenth-century U.S. theaters, for example, has earned a whole tradition of scholarship, with its attention to class-bound characters, plots, settings, and themes; much the same has been done for the history of U.S. fiction, which has, scholars argue, differing trajectories based not only on plot, character, and outcome but also on mode of production and distribution. Cultural forms hardly recognized at all under erstwhile rubrics of U.S. cultural expression—balladry, mob action, table manners, amusement parks—have found a place in scholarly debates precisely as classed forms of cultural life. The saloon is now recognized no less than the literary salon as a space of cultural and social self-organization.

Just as importantly, quintessential public artifacts of U.S. culture such as New York City's Central Park need to be understood as complex mediations of conflicting class, party, and historical factors. Witness too studies of U.S. newspapers, in which various class accents have been seen to vie for control of a given editorial tendency, newsworthy event, or style of audience address. The key, and often exhilarating, emphasis in such studies is that U.S. cultural forms do not so much belong to a given class or class fraction as they become sites in which class struggles are fought out. In recent years, studies of American "hemispheric" and even global class struggles have moved to the fore, whether focused on the emergence of internationalist social movements (Reed 2005), the character and function of manufacturing sweatshops (Ross

1997), or the place of U.S. cultural formations in the world system (Denning 2004).

At their best, class-sensitive versions of American cultural studies are animated by the attempt to grasp the complex dialectic of work and leisure—the structuring of U.S. society by the unequal and uneven social relations of labor and the ways in which those relations give rise to a vast array of cultural forms. The social location of the artist, the assembly-line production of films and cheap fiction: whatever the case, class analysis has immeasurably benefited our understanding of the cultural scene. The United States may be an exceptional place—what country isn't?—but it has seen its fair share of class conflict in the sphere of culture, conflict that is intense, productive, and ongoing.

13

Colonial

David Kazanjian

"Colonial" has very old roots. The Latin word *colonia* was used during the Roman empire to mean a settlement of Roman citizens in a newly conquered territory. Often these citizens were retired soldiers who received land as a reward for their service and as a display of Roman authority to the conquered inhabitants. For Roman writers, *colonia* translated the Greek word *apoikia*, which meant a settlement away from one's home state, as opposed to the *polis*, meaning one's own city or country as well as a community of

citizens, or the *metropolis*, literally one's mother-city or mother-country.

Though it has these etymological ties to the violence and power of conquest, the English word "colony" was until the eighteenth century as likely to mean simply a farm, a rural settlement, or a country estate as a settlement in conquered land subject to a parent state. The cognate "colonial" was not coined until the late eighteenth century (it is not in Samuel Johnson's 1755 dictionary), when it was used as an adjective to mean "of a colony" and as a noun to mean "a person from a colony," most often referring to Europeans who conquered and settled in North America and the West Indies.

This eighteenth-century usage acquired an important and odd wrinkle in the United States, one that is particularly relevant to American cultural studies: "colonial" and "colonist" have often been used as if they were simple descriptors for early Americans, and unrelated to conquest. For instance, while the recent popular dictionary *Colonial American English* does not include a definition for the word "colonial," it does define "colony" as "A government in which the governor is elected by the inhabitants under a charter of incorporation by the king, in contrast to one in which the governor is appointed" (Lederer 1985, 54). Here, we can see how far this usage strays from the word's roots in conquest by suggesting that "colonial" signifies a kind of democracy. Indeed, "colonials," "American colonists," "the colonial period," and "colonial literature" in the U.S. context have often invoked images of plucky settlers fleeing persecution in

Europe, overthrowing their oppressive European rulers, establishing rich new states and cultures against all odds through hard work, and founding a free, democratic, and unified nation. The word "colonial" thus oddly comes to figure resistance *to* the violence and power of conquest.

In 1847, the influential political economist Henry Charles Carey (1967, 345) extended this usage in a way that links it to a history of American exceptionalism: "The colonization of the United States differs from that of the two countries we have considered [Britain and France], in the great fact that they [the United States] desire no subjects. The colonists are equal with the people of the States from which they sprang, and hence the quiet and beautiful action of the system." While Britain and France send their citizens to the far corners of the world to conquer territory and subjugate native inhabitants, Carey tautologically claims, the United States was founded by colonists who colonized themselves. As he goes on to argue, the resulting nation is both exceptional, or unique in the history of the world, and exemplary, or destined to be emulated by the rest of the world.

This U.S. understanding of colonization expresses a deeply nationalist mythology that continues to thrive today: The United States was founded exclusively upon the just and noble principles of freedom, equality, and democracy, and it continues to spread those principles around the world. This mythology has been challenged from a number of directions. Scholars and activists in African American and Native American studies have shown how the "quiet and beautiful ac-

tion" Carey describes actually involved some of the most brutal "systems" of dispossession the modern world has known: the conquest of Native American lands, the enslavement and genocide of native peoples and Africans, and the establishment of a vast transatlantic and transcontinental system of race-based chattel slavery. Much of this scholarship has argued that these systems were not simply aberrations from or exceptions to the history and culture of the United States, but rather constitutive of all that it would become.

We can also see how the myth of the American colonial as a "quiet and beautiful," even heroic actor finesses histories of slavery and white-settler colonialism by examining a text that has long embodied this myth: the Declaration of Independence. The Declaration represents American colonials as innocent victims of British tyranny ("Such has been the patient sufferance of these Colonies"), as well as harmless witnesses to violence against Native Americans, by blaming both the Crown and Native Americans themselves for Indian resistance to colonization ("the present king of Great Britain . . . has endeavored to bring on the inhabitants of our frontiers the merciless Indian savages) (Jefferson 1984, 19, 21). Even as they were doing battle with Indians, however, white settlers paradoxically drew on their fantasies about Indians to fashion their own identities as American colonials distinct from their British brethren. Sometimes they "played Indian," as Philip J. Deloria (1998) has carefully recounted, in private societies and at protests like the Boston Tea Party. At other times they combed through

Indian graves to show that America had its own ancient history to rival that of Europe (Jefferson 1984b, 223–28). And increasingly after the Revolution, white U.S. American writers depicted Indians in order to distinguish "American" from "English" literature. Performed alongside violence against Native Americans, this fashioning of an American identity helped to generate the mythology of the innocent American colonial who became a heroic rebel and eventually an exceptional U.S. citizen.

While the Declaration of Independence does not mention slavery directly, in an early draft it did include a passage that both criticized slavery and perpetuated the mythology of American colonials as innocent victims of conquest. The passage personified the entire transatlantic slave trade in the king ("He has waged cruel war against human nature itself"), and equated enslaved Africans with free white settlers as fellow victims ("he is now exciting those very people [slaves] to rise in arms among us, and to purchase the liberty of which he has deprived them, by murdering the people on whom he also obtruded them"). By suppressing the alliance between Europeans and American colonials in the system of chattel slavery, this passage transforms American colonials from conquerors to conquered. Unabashedly proslavery colonials found even this argument too threatening to their interests and fought successfully for its deletion (Jefferson 1984a, 22).

By recovering and reinterpreting early colonial and national texts that were crucial in their day but had long been excluded from disciplinary canons, twenti-eth-century scholars have also shown us how early Americans themselves all along challenged this mythological conception of the American colonial. New social historians have reminded us that the list of men who signed the Declaration of Independence is not simply a list of heroic rebels; it is a list of elites. Their Declaration would have had no force behind it had poor people throughout the colonies not been struggling for decades against exploitation at the hands of wealthy and powerful colonials as well as British authorities. The American colonial looks neither innocent nor uniform from the perspectives of an early dissident like Stephen Hopkins, who helped to organize a rebellion and then a furtive utopian community after a Virginia Company vessel shipwrecked on Bermuda in 1609 (Strackey 1964); or Richard Frethhorn, an indentured servant who was transported to Virginia in 1623 and wrote back to his parents of the brutal conditions he faced (Jehlen and Warner 1997, 123); or Anne Bonny and Mary Read, two cross-dressing women pirates who worked with the predominately male pirate population of the early eighteenth century to disrupt the social and cultural norms, and the emerging imperial state, of the British empire (Hogeland and Klages et al. 2004, 98–106); or rural colonial rebels who challenged the British colonial elite for control over land and political decision-making before the American Revolution, and then took on the early social and political elite in the Shays rebellion of 1786 (A. Young 1976, 1993; Zinn 1980; G. Nash 1986; New Social History Project 1989, 1992; Raphael 2001).

In the eighteenth and nineteenth centuries, African Americans and Native Americans took the lead in challenging the mythology of the American colonial. In 1829, a free black tailor and activist from Boston named David Walker published a pamphlet that excoriated whites for their systematic racism and called upon blacks to claim the land that slavery had forcibly made their own, effectively recalling the etymological roots of "colonial" in the violence and power of conquest and disrupting analogies between white settler colonials and slaves (Walker 1995, 74–76). William Apess, a Pequot born in 1798, published an 1833 essay in which he charged that U.S. Christians failed to live up to the revolutionary ideals of freedom and equality as well as the spirit of Christianity: "By what you read, you may learn how deep your principles are. I should say they were skin-deep" (1992, 160). Even in the title of his essay ("An Indian's Looking-Glass for the White Man"), Apess reverses the dynamic of "playing Indian"; he claims a European technology, the looking-glass, and turns it on white men so that they may see themselves not as innocent colonials but as violent colonizers.

This minority tradition of challenging the mythology of the American colonial was renewed after the U.S.-Mexico War of 1846–48 by Mexicanos, Tejanos, and, in the twentieth century, Chicanos who insisted that it was U.S. imperialism—not innocent, plucky settlers—that made them as well as the entire geography of the Southwest and California part of the United States. Chicanos in the second half of the twentieth century collaborated with African Americans, Asian Americans, and Native Americans to appropriate the word "colonial" by situating their own histories in the context of Third World liberation movements ("Alcatraz Reclaimed" 1971; "El Plan" 1972; Ho 2000). Black activists Stokely Carmichael and Charles Hamilton (1967, 5–6) exemplify this mode of analysis in their book *Black Power: The Politics of Liberation in America*: "Black people are legal citizens of the United States with, for the most part, the same *legal* rights as other citizens. Yet they stand as colonial subjects in relation to the white society. Thus institutional racism has another name: colonialism. Obviously, the analogy is not perfect." By acknowledging the imperfections of this "internal colonization" argument at the very moment of formulating it, Carmichael and Hamilton foreground both the difficulty and the importance of thinking the keyword "colonial" in an international context.

Such international thinking took place in the early United States as well: Walker's *Appeal*, for instance, is addressed to "the coloured citizens of the world." And it continues today: In an echo of the Declaration of Independence's claim that white American colonials are victims of imperialism along with slaves and Indians, some contemporary scholars have suggested that the United States be considered a postcolonial nation (Ashcroft, Griffiths, and Tiffin 1989; Buell 1995). By contrast, others have picked up on the implications of the internal colonization thesis and insisted on the differential relations among variously racialized minorities and whites (Spivak 1993; Sharpe 1995; Saldaña-Portillo 2001). The latter scholarship relies on richly historical understandings of the differences among modes of imperialism, particularly white settler colonialism, comprador capitalism, and neo-colonialism.

Contemporary scholars have also shown how an historical understanding of these differences requires a close attention to gender and sexuality. Indeed, we can hear an echo of gender and sexuality in the very word "colonial." As noted above, the Latin *colonia* was a translation of the Greek word *apoikia* (literally, away from the domestic sphere), which itself was opposed in Greek to the *polis* and the *metropolis*, the city and the mother-country. This distinction survives in English in the opposition between "metropole" and "colony." If the home or domestic sphere is figured as maternal, then the colonial sphere is readily figured as public, political, and masculine, which makes the word "colonial" subject to the vast feminist scholarship on the separation—or inseparability—of public and private spheres (Kerber 1980; Isenberg 1998; Davidson and Hatcher 2002). One aspect of this scholarship is exemplified by studies of American colonial women like Anne Hutchinson, who challenged the male dominance of mainstream Puritanism in seventeenth-century New England (Kerber and De Hart 2004, 25–120). Other studies suggest that the very concept of the domestic invokes the process of domestication, the incorporation and subjection of that which is not yet fully domesticated (A. Kaplan 2002).

It is thus not surprising to see early champions of women's work in the domestic sphere, such as Catharine Beecher (1841), imagine in imperial terms the ordering and unifying of the home as an ever-expanding, American process destined to encompass the entire world. In addition, black women who were enslaved in the Americas, as well as contemporary black feminist critics, have shown how the gendering of the colonial had deep racial implications (A. Davis 1983; H. Wilson 1983; Hartman 1997; Prince 2000; Spillers 2003). Eighteenth-century laws that based a black person's status as free or enslaved on that of the mother effectively encouraged the sexual exploitation of black women by white men. Consequently, the black domestic sphere became, to white men, a breeding ground for slavery. To further complicate matters, feminist postcolonial scholars have shown how the colony as such is often figured as feminine in order to make it subject to the power and authority of the metropole, while others have complicated this general model by tracking the uneven deployments of gender across the postcolonial world (Mohanty 1991; McClintock 1995; Yuval-Davis 1997; Spivak 1999). Queer studies has also opened up the study of sexuality in the colonial context, examining closely the ways heterosexuality was made culturally and legally normative among early American colonists, and in turn revealed the challenges sexually dissident cultures presented to this normativity (Goldberg 1992; Burgett 1998).

The complex history of the word "colonial" indexes the equally complex politics that have characterized U.S. imperialism. At the dawn of the twenty-first century, when struggles over the future of the U.S. empire are proliferating, it is all the more urgent for American cultural studies to take stock of the history of such a contested keyword.

14

Community

Miranda Joseph

In the contemporary United States, the term "community" is used so pervasively it would appear to be nearly meaningless. And in fact the term is often deployed more for its performative effect of being "warmly persuasive" than for any descriptive work it accomplishes (R. Williams 1983, 76). Carrying only positive connotations—a sense of belonging, understanding, caring, cooperation, equality—"community" is deployed to mobilize support not only for a huge variety of causes but also for the speaker using the term. It functions in this way for Starbucks and McDonald's, both of which display pamphlets in their stores proclaiming their commitment to community, as well as for the feminist scholar who seeks to legitimize her research by saying she works "in the community." It is deployed across the political spectrum to promote everything from identity-based movements (on behalf of women, gays and lesbians, African Americans, and others), to liberal and neoliberal visions of "civil society," to movements seeking to restore or reaffirm so-called "traditional" social values and hierarchies.

The relentless invocation of "community" is all the more remarkable given the persistent critique to which it has been subjected. Beginning in the late twentieth century, scholars have examined its use in the contexts of identity politics, liberalism, and na-

tionalism, in each case pointing to its disciplining, exclusionary, racist, sexist, and often violent implications (Joseph 2002). Feminist activists and scholars have argued that the desire for communion, unity, and identity among women tended in practice to make the women's movement white, bourgeois, and U.S.-centric (Martin and Mohanty 1986). Feminist critics of liberalism have pointed out that the supposedly abstract political community constituted through the liberal state actually universalized exclusionary gendered and racial norms (W. Brown 1995). Critics of European and postcolonial nationalisms have historicized the communal origin stories used to legitimate those nationalisms and emphasized the hierarchies and exclusions likewise legitimated by those narratives. Post-structuralist theories have underwritten many of these critiques, enabling scholars to argue that the presence, identity, purity, and communion connoted by "community" are impossible and even dystopic fantasies (I. Young 1990). In light of these critiques, many scholars have tried to reinvent community, to reconceptualize it as a space of difference and exposure to alterity (Mouffe 1992; Agamben 1993). Such stubborn efforts to build a better theory and practice of community only emphasize that the crucial question to pose about "community" as a keyword is this: Why is it so persistent and pervasive?

One answer to this question lies in the realization that particular deployments of the term can be understood as instances of a larger discourse that positions "community" as the defining other of capitalist "modernity." As Raymond Williams (1983) notes, "community" has been used since the nineteenth century to contrast immediate, direct, local relationships among those with something in common to the more abstract relations connoted by "society." While community is often presumed to involve face-to-face relations, capital is taken to be global and faceless. Community concerns boundaries between us and them that are naturalized through reference to place or race or culture or identity; capital, on the other hand, would seem to denature, crossing all borders, and making everything and everyone equivalent. The discourse of community includes a Romantic narrative that places it prior to "society," locating community in a long lost past for which we yearn nostalgically from our current fallen state of alienation, bureaucratization, and rationalization. This discourse also contrasts community with modern capitalist society structurally; the foundation of community is supposed to be social values, while capitalist society is based only on economic value. At the same time, community is often understood to be a problematic remnant of the past, standing in the way of modernization and progress.

The narrative of community as destroyed by capitalism and modernity, as supplanted by society, can be found across a wide range of popular and academic texts; one might say that it is one of the structuring narratives of the field of sociology (Bender 1978). And it has taken on a fresh life in the works of contemporary communitarians such as Robert Bellah (1985), Robert Putnam (1993), Amitai Etzioni (1993), E. J. Dionne (1998), and others, all of which are aimed at least in part at nonacademic audiences. These works inevitably misread Alexis de Tocqueville's *Democracy in America* (1835) as describing a now lost form of local community that they believe would, if revived, promote democracy and economic prosperity and solve many contemporary problems, including drug use, crime, and poverty. In the post-Soviet era, "community," in the guise of nongovernmental organizations, has featured prominently in the promotion of "civil society" in both former communist countries and "developing" countries of the "Third World."

The discursive opposition of community and society provides a crucial clue to the former's pervasiveness in contemporary discourse; community is a creature of modernity and capitalism. Williams optimistically suggests that modernity positively constitutes communities of collective action. In *The Country and the City* (1973, 102, 104), he argues against the nostalgic idealization of pre-enclosure communities that he finds in late-eighteenth- and early-nineteenth-century British literature, pointing out that pre-enclosure villages supported "inequalities of condition" and that "community only became a reality when economic and political rights were fought for and partially gained." More pessimistically, Nikolas Rose (1999, 172, 174) reads the invocation of community as a central technology of power, arguing that in its contemporary deployments "community" is used to invoke "emotional relationships" that can then be instrumentalized. He suggests that the communities so invoked are required to take on responsibilities for "order, security, health and productivity" formerly carried by the state. And certainly there is substantial evidence for his argument in the proliferation of public-private partnerships, neighborhood watch programs, restorative justice initiatives, and the like, all of which mobilize familial and communal relations to promote subjection to law and order rather than to fight for economic or political rights (Lacey and Zedner 1995; Lacey 1996; Joseph 2006).

Community thus can be understood as a supplement to the circulation of state power and capital; it not only enables capital and power to flow, it also has the potential to displace those flows. Because the circulation of abstract capital depends on the embodiment of capital in particular subjects, the expansion and accumulation of capital requires that capitalists engage in an ongoing process of disrupting, transforming, galvanizing, and constituting new social formations, including communities. Community is performatively constituted in capitalism, in the processes of production and consumption, through discourses of pluralism, multiculturalism, and diversity, through niche marketing, niche production, and divisions of labor by race, gender, and nation.

This complex relation of community to capitalism is particularly evident in the promotion of nonprofit and nongovernmental organizations (NPOs and NGOs)—"civil society"—in the context of "development" in the United States and internationally. In the United States, nonprofit organizations are said to express community and often stand in for community metonymically. They are the institutional sites where people contribute labor or money to "the community." And they are posited as the form through which community might be reinvigorated as a complement to capitalism, providing those goods and services that capitalism does not. In the context of "development," NGOs have been explicitly promoted as a means for developing human and social capital and involving the poor in development projects—as, in other words, sites for constituting liberal capitalist subjects and subjectivities. At the same time, the necessity for such organizations suggests that subjects are not always already capitalist subjects. And in fact, the promotion of NPOs and NGOs has often been explicitly intended to stave off socialism or communism (Joseph 2002). The incorporation of subjects as community members at the site of the NGO can be understood as hegemonizing, wedding potentially resistant subjects (potentially or actually communist subjects) to capitalism.

The centrality of community to capitalism has been made even more explicit in the context of globalization. Politically diverse iterations of globalization discourse, both popular and academic, argue that capitalism now depends on communities, localities, cultures, and kinship to provide the social norms and trust that enable businesses to function, and that contemporary globalized capitalism is and should be more attuned to particular communities, localities, and cultures (Piore and Sabel 1984; Fukuyama 1995). While a number of scholars have portrayed the localization and culturalization of capitalism as a positive development, creating opportunities for local or communal resistance, others have emphasized the weakness, dependence, and vulnerability of the local. The claim that capitalism has just now discovered community is, however, problematic. It suggests that communities, and the economic inequalities between them, have not themselves been constituted by capitalism. To the contrary, the explicit deployment of community within globalization discourse tends to legitimate economic inequalities and exploitation as the expression of authentic cultural difference even as it articulates all communities and cultures as analogous sites for production and consumption (M. Wright 1999).

The project of examining "the seductions of community" remains a crucial one (Creed 2006). Exploring the ways in which community is constituted by or complicit with capital and power can reshape our understandings of the dimensions of our communities and the connections among them. Such exploration might enable us to recuperate and rearticulate the needs and desires for social change that are so often coopted by the uncritical deployment of the term.

15

Contract

Amy Dru Stanley

Contract is at least as old as the Old Testament and as new as the market transactions of the moment—local, national, and global. It encompasses the provinces of religion and commodities, state and civil society, public and private exchange, the rights of persons and the rights to property. Puritan theology speaks of

covenants, Enlightenment liberalism of social contracts, political economy of commercial contracts, the law of liberty of contract. Informed by those traditions, U.S. culture has long been infused by contract. Just after the Civil War, a primer handed out by Yankee liberators to former slaves testified to contract's vast province: "You have all heard a great deal about contracts, have you not since you have been free? . . . Contracts are very numerous; numerous as the leaves on the trees almost; and, in fact, the world could not get on at all without them" (Fisk 1866, 47). The lesson of freedom was not simply that contract was essential, but that it was virtually a fact of nature. In other words, "contract" stood as a keyword of U.S. culture. Never was this more so than in the nineteenth century, when "contract" prevailed as a metaphor for social relations in free society.

Implicit in the vocabulary of contract is a set of fundamental terms denoting human subjectivity, agency, and social intercourse. As opposed to prescriptive duties or formally coercive bonds of personal dominion and dependence, a contract is, in principle, a purely voluntary obligation undertaken in the expectation of gaining a reciprocal benefit—an equivalent of some sort, a quid pro quo, or, in the language of the law, "consideration." Thus contract implies both individual volition and mutual exchange, reconciling freedom and obligation, creating rights and duties, and imposing social order through myriad transactions among ostensibly free persons. Above all, contract implies conditions of self-ownership. In order to cede a portion of liberty by choosing to incur duties, contract makers must, in theory, be sovereigns of themselves—possessive individuals, entitled to their own persons, labor, and faculties. A lasting axiom of Enlightenment thought is that contract derives from and governs individual will and that free will is tethered to rights of proprietorship. Early in the nineteenth century, Hegel (1979, 58) philosophized that under a contract a person "ceases to be an owner and yet is and remains one. It is the mediation of the will to give up a property . . . and the will to take up another, i.e. another belonging to someone else." Or as an American professor of political science explained a half-century later: "I cannot make that the property of another *by contract* which is not *mine* already" (Woolsey 1878, 74). Equally enduring in this intellectual tradition is the notion that contract's fundamental properties — self-ownership, consent, and exchange—belonged fundamentally to men. That notion, though, like the very meaning of consent, exchange, and self-ownership, has provoked a longstanding dispute over the cultural significance of contract.

Notably, contract is not simply a language, a metaphor, a set of principles, or a worldview. A contract is also a palpable transaction. It is a social relation—an exchange relation—involving what the eighteenth-century British legal theorist Sir William Blackstone (1765–69/1979, 118) called the "rights of things" and the "rights of persons." Abstract principles of entitlement and volition find concrete embodiment in contracts of state, of church, of sale, of debt, of labor, and of marriage. In the realm of U.S. law, the nineteenth century has long been considered the age of contract—with contract figuring as the legal apparatus of classical political economy and laissez-faire liberalism. Yet the authority of contract reached well beyond the law, and contract law itself was heir to older religious and political traditions. In the Middle Ages, contracts of rulership reflected Christian doctrine as well as Roman codes, and ancient, informal customs of covenant shaped the advent of early contract law (Gordley 1991). In the modern era, the roots of contract extend back to understandings of the origins of the state, the Puritan church, and market society in the seventeenth and eighteenth centuries, and, following the paths of the common law, became embedded in debates over the meaning of slavery and emancipation (Hopfyl and Thompson 1979).

Since the British settlement of the New World, the tenets of self-ownership, consent, and exchange remained central to contract theory and practice; yet the meaning of those tenets subtly altered as they were understood to validate changing institutions and social relations. The doctrine of covenant, or contract, lay at the heart of dissenting Protestantism, reconciling divine supremacy and human agency, explaining the relationship between God and humanity as a bargain, and establishing consent as the basis for human obedience to biblical edicts. The Enlightenment theory of the social contract gave secular political formulation to this notion of voluntary submission to the rule of law, thereby legitimating the obedience of citizens to the authority of the state in return for protection of their lives and property. Here, contract entailed volition and reciprocity, while also justifying a degree of subordination. But, as a paradigm of commercial society, contract came to embody exchange between individuals who were formally equal as well as formally free. It defined the relations of the free market rather than the rules of sovereignty. For Adam Smith (1776/1937, 31) and his disciples, contract presupposed "rough equality" among persons involved in commodity exchange. And the antislavery claim of the nineteenth century was that contract represented the absolute antithesis of chattel bondage, with the abstract rights of freedom concretely lodged in the contracts of wage labor and marriage, which entitled ex-slaves to own and sell their labor and to marry and maintain a home.

Most famously, contract has been associated in U.S. culture with the career of classical liberalism, an association that past and present critics have deemed the source of contract's most infamous illusions and contradictions. The criticisms have become canonical, and are virtually synonymous with those directed at other core liberal institutions and intellectual traditions—laissez-faire political economy, the negative state, the market calculus of supply and demand, commodity relations, possessive individualism, the abstractions of rights theory. In contract, so the argument goes, the core liberal tenets of formal equality and freedom cloak actual differences of power, thereby obscuring the underlying social inequalities, dependencies, and informal compulsions that nullify the vaunted rights of individual contract freedom. Since the early-nineteenth century this argument has been advanced by a multitude of U.S. citizens—by

wage workers seeking to form unions and fashion collective work contracts; by ex-slaves resisting free labor's coercions; by churchmen, reformers, and intellectuals critical of the moral callousness and inequities of the free market; by statesmen and jurists who, like Justice Oliver Wendell Holmes in his landmark dissent in the 1905 *Lochner* case, insisted that the Fourteenth Amendment had been wrongly construed to enshrine liberty of contract as an absolute constitutional right. As one freedman vividly decried the falsity of the contract regime: "I would not sign anything. I said, 'I might sign to be killed. I believe the white people is trying to fool us'" (Sterling 1976, 6).

Another strain of critique has brought to light the contradictions of contract in affirming individual rights while also validating sexual inequality on the basis of putatively immutable physical difference. Thus the "sexual contract" stands alongside the social contract, anointing men with property in women, who accordingly are dispossessed of rights to their own persons, labor, sexuality, and property (Pateman 1988). That was the outcry of generations of feminists against the marriage contract, which gave the husband dominion over his wife, binding her to serve and obey him in return for his protection and support. "If the contract be equal, whence come the terms 'marital power,' 'marital rights,' 'obedience and restraint,' 'dominion and control?'" Elizabeth Cady Stanton protested in 1868. "According to man's idea, as set forth in his creeds and codes, marriage is a condition of slavery" (quoted in Stanley 1998, 5). Subject to the will of a master, the wife had no rights of contract, a fact that led Stanton and others to bitter comparisons between marriage and chattel slavery. Prostitution also figured as an analogy for marriage; reformers argued that both were contracts centered on the sale of sex as a commodity in which women were not fully free or equal to men. The point was that only in the context of an ideal marriage, contracted freely between husband and wife who were utter equals, could sex be a legitimate token of exchange; otherwise, sex counted as a uniquely inalienable aspect of self (Stanley 1998).

Yet to highlight only the critical tradition is to lose sight of the emancipatory prospects of contract. Absent such insight, the cultural power of contract ideals becomes inexplicable, even mysterious. For the generation who witnessed the transition from slavery to freedom and argued over the meaning of that transformation, contract offered a way of making sense of the changes in their world and of distinguishing between the relations of freedom and slavery. Contract opened up ways of thinking about the perplexities of a culture that condemned the traffic in slaves while otherwise celebrating the boundlessness of the free market. It did not offer a common vantage point to differently situated persons, but instead some common principles for expressing differing visions of the genuine meaning of self-ownership, consent, and reciprocal exchange. It was a language of aspiration as well as of criticism.

Thus, objections to existing contract relations often translated into demands for universalizing and authenticating the ideals of contract—for more perfectly realizing contract's promise, as opposed to rejecting it outright. However much ex-slaves disavowed the equation of freedom and the wage contract, they tended to choose willingly to marry, and many expressly invoked their "rights under . . . contract" in challenging the control of ex-masters (Berlin et al. 1990, 614). Notably, however much freedwomen joined with freedmen in affirming the collective dimensions of emancipation, they simultaneously asserted individual rights of property and person and protested the inequalities of marriage. At least some black women, both those born as slaves and those born free, explicitly strove to be self-owning. That was also the vision of generations of white feminists who proclaimed equal rights of contract as a central goal. And however much some critics condemned the entire wage system, many more, through methods ranging from unions and labor legislation to partnerships, cooperatives, and Christian brotherhood, sought to bring greater equality to the wage contract.

Precisely because contract held such emancipatory meaning, its ideals also could mask existing inequalities. That ideological paradox endures along with more palpable contract practices. Today, however, public debate dwells less on the legitimacy of contract than it did a century ago, when the age of contract waned with the advent of the welfare state and the new creeds of liberalism advanced by reformers in the Progressive Era. Then, intellectuals and reformers disputed whether industrial capitalism subverted or sustained individual liberty of contract; indeed, many concluded that contract freedom had become illusory. And that conclusion still finds credence among some scholars today, who agree with the famous interpretation put forth by law professor Grant Gilmore in *The Death of Contract* (1974, 95–96): "The decline and fall of the general theory of contract and, in most quarters, of laissez-faire economics, may be taken as remote reflections of the transition from nineteenth-century individualism to the welfare state and beyond." But, again, the association of contract simply with the ideal world of Adam Smith is too narrow. "Contract" remains a keyword of both U.S. culture and American cultural studies, signifying not only free-market capitalism, consensual government, and the rule of law but also the sovereignty of self that underlies the right of free individuals to choose what to do with their bodies and property. It is not hard to imagine emissaries of the global dispersion of U.S. culture distributing primers just like those put in the hands of freed people after the Civil War.

16

Coolie

Moon-Ho Jung

The word "coolie" is first and foremost a product of European expansion into Asia and the Americas. Of Tamil, Chinese, or other origin, it was popularized by Portuguese sailors and merchants across Asia beginning in the sixteenth century and later adopted by fellow European traders on the high seas and in port cities. By the eighteenth century, "coolie" referred to a laborer of India or China, hired locally or shipped

abroad. The word took on a new significance in the nineteenth century, as the beginnings of abolition remade "coolies" into indentured laborers in high demand across the world, particularly in the tropical colonies of the Caribbean. Emerging out of struggles over British emancipation and Cuban slavery in particular, "coolies" and "coolieism"—defined by the late nineteenth century as "the importation of coolies as labourers into foreign countries" (*Oxford English Dictionary*, 1989 edition)—came to denote the systematic shipment and employment of Asian laborers on sugar plantations formerly worked by enslaved Africans (Tinker 1974; Irick 1982; Prashad 2001).

The word entered mainstream U.S. culture as a result of these intensifying global debates over slavery, making its first appearance in Noah Webster's American dictionary in 1842. Reports on the Caribbean, including the status of "coolies," circulated widely in the antebellum United States, with antislavery newspapers hailing Asian workers as a "free" alternative to enslaved labor early on. By the outbreak of the Civil War, however, widespread news of violent abuses and rebellions aboard "coolie" ships and on Caribbean plantations generated a powerfully enduring image that would haunt generations of Asian migrants. Represented as a coerced and submissive labor force by anti- and proslavery forces alike, "coolies" came to embody slavery in the age of emancipation. From Hawai'i to California to Massachusetts, employers of all sorts demanded "coolies" while white workers and politicians clamored for their exclusion from a "free" America. Well into the twentieth century, U.S. labor leaders such as Samuel Gompers attacked Asian workers as nothing but hordes of "coolies" undermining "American" manhood and wages.

In response, Asian migrants, their liberal allies, and, more recently, Asian Americanist scholars have tried to refute such racist charges by claiming that Asians in the United States were not "coolies." "Coolies," they have insisted, were shipped to the Caribbean, while Asians in the United States were immigrants who came voluntarily (Takaki 1989). Given the ubiquity of the word in virtually every discussion on Chinese migrants (and, subsequently, other Asians), these denials have proven neither historically effective nor critically revelatory. It is far more instructive to argue that no one in the United States or the Caribbean was really a "coolie," a racialized and racializing figure that denied Asian migrants the liberal subjectivity that "immigrants" presumably possessed (Jung 2006).

If we approach the term as a conglomeration of racial imaginings that materialized worldwide in the era of slave emancipation—as a product of the imaginers rather than the imagined—we can begin to see how pivotal "coolies" were in defining racial and national boundaries and hierarchies in the nineteenth century. Racialized as an enslaved labor force in the emergent age of free labor and free trade, "coolies" ultimately reflected the hopes, fears, and contradictions of emancipation. The ambiguous qualities ascribed to "coolies" served to confuse and collapse seemingly indissoluble divides at the heart of race (black and white), class (enslaved and free), and nation (alien and citizen, domestic and foreign) in U.S. culture. Locating, defining, and outlawing "coolies," at home and abroad, in turn evolved into an endless and indispensable exercise that resolved and reproduced the contradictory aims—racial exclusion and legal inclusion, enslavement and emancipation, parochial nationalism and unbridled imperialism—of a nation deeply rooted in race, slavery, and empire.

Racial fantasies of "coolies" as docile and apolitical made the reality of the Reconstruction amendments (the abolition of slavery, the enfranchisement of black men) and black labor struggles bearable and seemingly surmountable, particularly to white planters in the U.S. South. The mobilization of white workers against dependent "coolies" symbolically restored the racial meanings of whiteness—namely, political and economic independence—when industrial capital's expansion threatened to kill the Jeffersonian agrarian ideal for good. The impulse to drive out "coolies" (and prostitutes) from the United States, in large part a cultural legacy of the antislavery movement, justified the earliest legal restrictions on immigration (the Page Law of 1875 and the Chinese Exclusion Act of 1882). The historical process of excluding "coolies" simultaneously racialized "immigrants"—those worthy of entering the "nation of immigrants"—as white and European in U.S. culture; Asians would remain "aliens ineligible to citizenship" until the World War II era. And, whether in China, Cuba, or, later, the Philippines, the existence of "coolies"—and the moral imperative to prohibit slavery—fueled and rationalized U.S. imperialism, even as U.S. Americans imported and consumed "un-American" products made by "coolies," like sugar from Cuba and Hawai'i.

"Coolie," then, is a term crucial to understanding the formations of the U.S. nation, state, and empire at a historical moment of great turmoil and promise. Racial imaginings of "coolies" helped to remake the United States into a "free," "white," and "modern" nation, revealing both its intricate ties to a wider world and its dogged pursuit of an exceptionalist self-image. The violent and mythical legacies of those imaginings would go a long way toward shaping the United States and the world in the twentieth century and beyond.

17

Corporation

Christopher Newfield

In current usage, the keyword "corporation" is synonymous with "business corporation," generally referring to a for-profit organization that can operate at the discretion of its owners and managers free of social and legislative control. The term is derived from the Latin *corporatus*, the present participle of *corporare*, which means "form into a body," and appeared in English by 1530. A business corporation can own property; buy, sell, and control assets, including other corporations; pay or avoid taxes; write or break contracts; make and market products; and engage in every kind of economic activity. At the same time, the persons involved in a corporation have under most cir-

cumstance no liability for its debts. Since 1900, the corporation has been the dominant form for organizing capital, production, and financial transactions. By 2000, the corporation had become a dominant force in the global economy, the only alternative to the state as an organizer of large-scale production, a rival to national governments, and a powerful presence in the world's cultures. Of the world's hundred largest economies in 2000, forty-seven were nation-states and fifty-three were corporations.

American cultural studies generally has not focused on the corporation or the corporate form but rather on features of culture and society that the corporation has affected (Trachtenberg 1982; Horwitz 1987; Michaels 1987). This research has produced major reconsiderations of civil rights, community formation, consumerism, culture industries, discrimination, environmental justice, imperialism and colonialism, labor, political agency, and underdevelopment, domains where business has played a major and sometimes controlling role. But the corporate world as such has only rarely been an object of study in itself; even the cultural effects of the corporation have been the province of historians, legal scholars, and sociologists. The prominent critic Fredric Jameson (1993, 50) noted the reluctance of cultural studies to "look out upon the true Other, the bureaucrat or corporate figure." The situation has changed little since that time; for instance, the word "corporation" does not make a single appearance in a comprehensive bibliographical essay on the 2005 American Studies Association website (Reed, "Theory and Method").

Before the mid-nineteenth century, the corporation was a public franchise—a ferry or turnpike company, for example—that received a profit in exchange for reliable service to the common or public good. After the Civil War, corporations increasingly came to reflect private economic interests. Though the Supreme Court, in the early case *Trustees of Dartmouth College v. Woodward* (1819), had held that a public charter possessed the legal status of a private contract, most of the legal foundations for this change were laid in the 1870s and 1880s. In the Slaughter-House Cases (1873), the Supreme Court denied that labor had a property interest in a job that required compensation upon dismissal, which left the firm itself as the sole legitimate property interest. In *Santa Clara County v. Southern Pacific Railway* (1886), the Court asserted, with little supporting argumentation, that the corporation was a legal person and could not have its property regulated in a way not in conformity with the due process provisions of the Fourteenth Amendment. Through a series of small but unswerving steps, the courts freed the corporation from both public purpose and direct legislative will.

This movement toward corporate independence consolidated several important features of the corporate form. One was limited liability, in which the shareholder was personally insulated from claims for damages or the repayment of debts. Limited liability made it easier to attract a large amount of capital from many investors while retaining concentrated control, since the investor was less likely to insist on control in the absence of liability. Through two further changes,

corporations gained the right to own stock in other companies, which had been denied to ordinary proprietorships, and stabilized the managerial authority of boards of directors (Roy 1997). A firm could grow through cross-ownership or, even without ownership, control other firms through interlocking board memberships. This legal framework gave the firm's executives significant independence from the firm's owners, influentially defined as the separation of ownership and control (Berle and Means 1932). This phenomenon allowed the corporation even greater distance from the surrounding society, for it was relatively sheltered not only from immediate legislative influence and community pressure but also from the collective will of its own investors. The simultaneous development of concentration of control and immunity from interference transformed the corporation from a public trust into a potential monopoly power with most of the capacities of a parallel government.

Twentieth-century corporate law took the existence of the corporation for granted and sought not to regulate the form so much as to regulate particular industry sectors and management practices. The landmark Sherman Anti-Trust Act (1890) was so vague that its powers were in effect created through enforcement or through later legislation such as the Hepburn Act (1906) and the Mann-Elkins Act (1910), which focused on the power to regulate monopoly pricing or constrain concentrated ownership, and was extended through later New Deal legislation such as the Glass-Steagall Act (1933) and, still later, the Bank Holding Company Act (1956). The courts generally rejected the idea that big is bad; rather, plaintiffs had to show that big had a materially bad effect. To the contrary, by the late twentieth century, enormous size was seen by regulators as a competitive necessity; in the 1980s, "ten thousand merger notifications were filed with the antitrust division. . . . The antitrust division challenged exactly twenty-eight." One legal historian summarized the situation by saying that "corporation law had evolved into a flexible, open system of nonrules" that "allowed corporations to do whatever they wished" (L. Friedman 2002, 392, 389).

Support for the corporation came more frequently from courts and legislators than from public opinion. The labor movement consistently challenged three of the corporation's most important impacts on working conditions: the accelerated absorption of skilled, relatively independent workers into the factory system; Taylorization, in which mass production was transformed into a routinized assembly-line process strictly regulated for maximum time-efficiency; and managerialism, whose meaning for labor was unilateral control of pay and working conditions by layers of management separated from and generally set against labor. More than a century of major strikes—such as those at Carnegie's steel works at Homestead, Pennsylvania (1892), and the Loray Mill in Gastonia, North Carolina (1929), down through the United Parcel Service strike (1997) and the Los Angeles janitor strike (2000)—were among the most visible expressions of popular opposition to the corporation's independence of, or sovereignty over, the wider society in which it operated.

Corporate power prompted a decades-long movement for "industrial democracy" that sought to put corporate governance on a constitutionalist and democratic footing. Some saw collective bargaining, finally legalized by the Wagner Act (1935), as an industrial civil rights movement that transformed management into a government of laws (Lichtenstein 2002, 32–38). But labor never did achieve meaningful joint sovereignty with management in the context of the large corporation. The Taft-Hartley Act (1947) required all trade-union officials to sign an affidavit that they were not Communists, impugning the collective loyalty of labor leaders (managers were not required to sign), and also forbade cross-firm and cross-industry labor coordination (ibid., 114–18). Union membership and influence declined precipitously from the 1970s onward, and the idea of industrial democracy had by the end of the century virtually disappeared from public view. Even as it continued to rely on the state for favorable environmental legislation, tax law, educated workers, and the like, the corporation consolidated its relative autonomy from employees and the public.

As this brief history reveals, from the mid-nineteenth century on, the corporation has had an enormous influence on society. The corporation became part of the culture of the United States and other countries, and the resulting corporate culture had four dominant features. First, consumption became central. When the corporation collectivized labor and coordinated the production process on a large scale, it enabled the mass production of consumer goods for the first time. This led to increases in the general standard of living and to the rise of a consumer society in which consumption came to be a virtually universal activity and a primary means of expressing personal identity and desire. Second, democracy was equated with capitalism. Mass production and consumption, freedom, self-expression, and personal satisfaction came to be seen as interchangeable and as enabled by corporate capitalism; consumption came to eclipse, if not exactly replace, political sovereignty. Conversely, democracy's best outcome seemed to be affluence rather than public control of the economy and other social forces. Third, efficient organization became synonymous with hierarchical bureaucracy. As the twentieth century wore on, it became increasingly difficult to imagine truth, power, or innovation arising from personal effort, insight, and inspiration unharnessed by economic roles, or effective cooperation without command from above. Compared to corporate command-and-control, self-organizing political agency seemed obsolete. Fourth, philosophical, spiritual, cultural, and social definitions of progress were eclipsed by technological ones. The rapid commercialization of technical inventions—radio, radiology, transistors—became the measure of the health of a society, and thus society came to require healthy corporations. Building on a long tradition of presenting themselves as public benefactors (Marchand 1998), corporations by the 1980s and 1990s were regarded by most political leaders and opinion makers as the leading progressive force in society.

Across these changes, the economy began to appear as a natural system, accessible only to highly trained experts in production, management, and finance, and resisting all attempts to soften its effects through public services and social programs. In this new common sense, society had to adapt to the economy, and the corporation was the privileged agent of that adaptation. By 2000, the majority of U.S. leaders appeared to accept the priority of economic laws to social needs, and the corporate system as the authentic voice of those laws. Concurrently, U.S. society lost its feel for the traditional labor theory of value. Real value now seemed to be created by a combination of technological invention and corporate activity. At the end of the twentieth century, cheap manual labor and advanced mental labor had become more important than ever to steadily increasing corporate revenues, and yet the individual's labor contribution was less valued and more difficult to picture.

The tremendous cultural power of the corporate form has not spared it turbulence and even decline. Annual economic growth in the United States and Europe slowed markedly in the 1970s, as did rates of increase in profitability and productivity. Business efforts to maintain profit margins led to continuous price increases that in turn increased wage demands and overall inflation. The United States lost its unchallenged economic preeminence as countries like France, Germany, Italy, and Japan fully recovered from the devastation of World War II, and as the newly industrializing countries of Asia became important competitors. Oil price shocks and the end of the Bretton Woods currency system were only the most visible sign of this changing economic order (Rosenberg

2003). Internal pressures added to external ones. Job satisfaction was low enough to prompt an important study from the Nixon Administration's Department of Labor, and "human relations" management theory increased its attacks on Taylorist regimentation (Newfield 1998). These trends contributed to a sense among some observers that the large corporation was part of the problem, that it had become too inflexible, hierarchical, and expensive to lead the way in a new era of "post-Fordist" globalization (Harvey 1989).

In response to these threats, corporations began a rehabilitation campaign, recasting themselves as the world's only true modernizers, capable of moving the economy and society relentlessly forward, often against their will (T. Friedman 2000, 2005). Executives, journalists, politicians, and scholars generally overstated the novelty of these arguments for a new corporate system underwriting a new economy in a new era of globalization. Nearly all of these claims were tried-and-true standards of the economic liberalism of previous periods: that the markets are inherently efficient and self-regulating in the absence of government interference; that attempts to stabilize employment and incomes place unnatural burdens on these efficient markets, as do consumer protections, banking restrictions, environmental legislation, regional planning, and the like; that the tireless search for ever-cheaper labor, now fully internationalized, is legitimate because it benefits consumers; that corporate giants can "learn to dance" by "reengineering" their companies to simplify their cumbersome bureaucratic layers and routines (Kanter 1990; Hammer and Champy 1993);

and that corporations have rejected monopoly in favor of entrepreneurship. Though the terminology and images had changed, so that chief executive officers could by the late 1990s wear leather astride Harley-Davidson motorcycles on the cover of *Business Week*, the intellectual content was derived from models developed during the corporation's infancy and adolescence. By the turn of the twenty-first century, no single corporation or corporate group could be called an empire, but as a group they had unchallenged sovereignty over the economy.

Or almost unchallenged. Economic problems continued: overall growth remained historically weak while economic inequality mounted steadily, work became less secure, and the public was treated to a long series of trials for corporate fraud. Opposition to corporate influence grew at the end of the twentieth century, though the strongest movements appeared outside the United States. Examples included Argentina, which had modified the regime imposed on it in the 1990s by the U.S.-dominated International Monetary Fund; India, where protests against development projects and intellectual property regimes sponsored by multinational corporations became routine; Malaysia, whose conservative regime rejected U.S. recipes for recovery from the economic crisis of 1997–98; Mexico, where nongovernmental organizations began to build social infrastructure; Venezuela, where strong popular support for social development proved capable of prevailing in elections; and Bolivia, where native peoples toppled two presidents in their attempt to nationalize natural gas reserves. In the United

States, protests against the World Trade Organization and the "Washington Consensus" broke out in Seattle in 1999, though they did not become as widespread or sustained as they have been elsewhere.

Evidence continues to grow that the hierarchical, multidivisional corporation of the twentieth century—with its enormous managerial and executive costs, its monopoly market goals, its mixtures of empowerment and authoritarianism, its definitions of value that exclude social benefits—is less functional and affordable than most leaders had assumed (D. Gordon 1996; Ross 1997; Bamberger and Davidson 1999). And yet, any process of inventing postcorporate economic forms would require deeper public knowledge of corporate operations than prevails in the wealthy countries of the early twenty-first century, as well as clearer, more imaginative definitions of democratic economics.

18

Culture

George Yúdice

The concept of "culture" has had widespread use since the late eighteenth century, when it was synonymous with civilization and still indicated a sense of cultivation and growth derived from its Latin root *colere*, which also included in its original meanings "inhabit" (as in colonize), "protect," and "honor with worship" (as in cult). According to Raymond Williams (1976),

the noun form took, by extension, three inflections that encompass most of its modern uses: intellectual, spiritual, and aesthetic development; the way of life of a people, group, or humanity in general; and the works and practices of intellectual and artistic activity (music, literature, painting, theater, and film, among many others). Although Williams considers the last to be the most prevalent usage, the extension of anthropology to urban life and the rise of identity politics in the 1980s (two changes that have left a mark on both cultural studies and American studies) have given greater force to the communal definition, particularly since this notion of culture serves as a warrant for legitimizing identity-based group claims and for differentiating among groups, societies, and nations. More recently, the centrality of culture as the spawning ground of creativity, which in turn is the major resource in the so-called new economy, has opened up a relatively unprecedented understanding of culture in which all three usages are harnessed to utility.

The meaning of culture varies within and across disciplines, thus making it difficult to narrate a neat linear history. Nevertheless, one can discern a major dichotomy between a universalist notion of development and progress, and a pluralistic or relativistic understanding of diverse and incommensurate cultures that resist change from outside and cannot be ranked according to one set of criteria. Beginning in the late eighteenth century, universalist formulations understood culture as a disinterested end in itself (Kant 1790/1952), and aesthetic judgment as the foundation for all freedom (Schiller 1794/1982). Anglo-American versions of this universalism later linked it to specific cultural canons: Matthew Arnold (1869/1971, 6) referred to culture as "the best which has been thought and said in the world" and posed it as an antidote to "anarchy"; T. S. Eliot (1949, 106) legitimated Europe's claim to be "the highest culture that the world has ever known." Such assertions, which justified U.S. and European imperialism, are currently disputed in postcolonial studies (Said 1993), but they were already rejected early on by defenders of cultural pluralism and relativism such as Johann Gottfried von Herder (1766/2002), who argued that each particular culture has its own value that cannot be measured according to criteria derived from another culture. This critique of the culture-civilization equation had its ideological correlate, first formulated by Karl Marx and Frederick Engels (1845-46/1972), in the premise that culture is the superstructure that emanates from the social relations involved in economic production; hence, it is simply a translation of the ruling class's domination into the realm of ideas.

The view of culture—and the civilizing process—as a form of control is consistent with the recent turn in cultural studies and cultural policy toward a focus on the ways in which institutions discipline populations. In the post-Enlightenment, when sovereignty is posited in the people, the institutions of civil society deploy "culture" as a means of internalizing control, not in an obviously coercive manner but by constituting citizens as well-tempered, manageable subjects who collaborate in the collective exercise of power (T. Miller 1993; Bennett 1995). The universal address of cultural institutions, ranging from museums to literary canons, tends either to obliterate difference or to stereotype it through racist and imperialist appropriation and scientism, sexist exclusion and mystification, and class-based narratives of progress. Populations that "fail" to meet standards of taste or conduct, or that "reject culture" because it is defined against their own values, are subject to constitutive exclusion within these canons and institutions (Bourdieu 1987). Challenges to these exclusions generate a politics of representational proportionality such that culture becomes the space of incremental incorporation whereby diverse social groups struggle to establish their intellectual, cultural, and moral influence over each other. Rather than privilege the role of the economic in determining social relations, this process of hegemony, first described by Antonio Gramsci (1971, 247), pays attention to the "multiplicity of fronts" on which struggle must take place. The Gramscian turn in cultural studies (American and otherwise) is evident in Williams's (1977/97, 108–9) incorporation of hegemony into his focus on the "whole way of life": "[Hegemony] is in the strongest sense a 'culture,' but a culture which has also to be seen as the lived dominance and subordination of particular classes."

But hegemony is not synonymous with domination. It also names the realm in which subcultures and subaltern groups wield their politics in the registers of style and culture (Hebdige 1979). Indeed, in societies like the United States, where needs are often interpreted in relation to identity factors and cultural difference, culture becomes a significant ground for extending a right to groups that have otherwise been excluded on those terms. The very notion of cultural citizenship implies recognition of cultural difference as a basis for making claims. This view has even been incorporated in epistemology to capture the premise that groups with different cultural horizons have different and hence legitimate bases for construing knowledge; they develop different "standpoint epistemologies" (Haraway 1991; Delgado Bernal 1998). The problem is that bureaucracies often establish the terms by which cultural difference is recognized and rewarded. In response, some subcultures (and their spokespersons) reject bureaucratic forms of recognition and identification, not permitting their identities and practices to become functional in the process of "governmentality," the term Michel Foucault (1982, 21) uses to capture "the way in which the conduct of individuals or groups might be directed." On this view, strategies and policies for inclusion are an exercise of power through which, in the U.S. post–civil rights era, institutional administrators recognize women, "people of color," and gays and lesbians as "others" according to a multiculturalist paradigm, a form of recognition that often empowers those administrators to act as "brokers" of otherness (Cruikshank 1994).

These contemporary struggles over cultural citizenship and recognition can be traced to earlier battles over the attributes according to which anthropologists and sociologists in the 1950s and 1960s catalogued certain non-European and minority populations as "cultures of poverty." This diagnostic label, first formulated by Oscar Lewis in 1959, references the presumed characterological traits—passivity, apathy, and impulsivity—that in underdeveloped societies impede social and economic mobility. We see at work here the narrative of progress and civilization that had been the frame within which anthropology emerged more than a hundred years earlier. Most anthropologists' method had been comparative in a non-relativistic sense, as they assumed that all societies passed through a single evolutionary process from the most primitive to the most advanced. Culture, which has been variously defined as the structured set or pattern of behaviors, beliefs, traditions, symbols, and practices (Tylor 1871; Boas 1911; Benedict 1934; Mead 1937; Kroeber and Kluckhohn 1952) by means of which humans "communicate, perpetuate and develop their knowledge about and attitudes toward life" (Geertz 1965, 86), was the ground on which anthropologists, even into the 1920s, sought to track the origins of all societies as well as their progress toward (European and/or Anglo-American) modernity.

In partial contrast, the relativist or pluralist cultural anthropology (often associated with Franz Boas) that arose during the 1920s began to critique the scientific racism that underwrote many of these accounts, to question the premise that any such accounting could be objective, and to argue that there were neither superior nor inferior cultures (Boas 1928). Nevertheless, Boas and his U.S. and Latin American followers (Kroeber 1917; Freyre 1933; Benedict 1934; Mead 1937; Ortiz 1946) believed that culture could be studied objectively, as a science, so long as description and analysis were not hamstrung by the anthropologist's cultural horizon. Many of the U.S. studies were explicitly designed, in Margaret Mead's words, to "giv[e] Americans a sense of their particular strengths as a people and of the part they may play in the world" (1942/1965, xlii).

By the end of the 1950s (coincident with the rise of cultural studies in Britain and American studies in the United States), the Boasian legacy as well as other salient anthropological tendencies such as British structural-functionalism and U.S. evolutionism waned and other trends rose in influence: symbolic anthropology (culture as social communication and action by means of symbols [Geertz 1965]), cultural ecology (culture as a means of adaptation to environment and maintenance of social systems [M. Harris 1977]), and structuralism (culture as a universal grammar arranged in binary oppositions that rendered intelligible the form of a society [Lévi-Strauss 1963]). These largely systemic analyses then gave way in the 1980s to a focus on practice, action, and agency as the main categories of anthropological explanation, and also to a self-reflexivity that put the very enterprise of cultural analysis in question. Self-reflexive or postmodern anthropology criticized the writing practices of ethnographers for obscuring the power relations that subtend the ethnographic encounter, the status of the knowledge that is derived from that encounter, the relationship of ethnography to other genres (Marcus and Fisher 1986; Clifford and Marcus 1986), and even the analytical and political usefulness of the concept of culture itself (Abu-Lughod 1991; Gupta and Ferguson 1992; R. Fox 1995). Related developments in postcolonial studies focused on transnational hybridity in contradistinction to national cultural homogeneity. With the introduction of television and other electronic media, mass migrations from former colonies to metropolitan centers, and modern transportation and communications technologies, cultures could no longer be imagined as circumscribed by national boundaries. Metaphors like montage and pastiche replaced the melting pot in accounts of Brazilian culture (Schwarz 1970/1992; Santiago 1971/1973), echoing Néstor García Canclini's description of popular culture as the product of "'complex hybrid processes' in which signs from diverse classes and nations' are combined" (Dunn 2001, 97; García Canclini 1995; Appadurai 1996). More recently, García Canclini (2004) has added *access* to new information and communication technologies as another dimension to consider when weighing the effects that globalization has on culture-based understandings of difference and equality.

For many U.S. scholars, this troubling of culture as a category of analysis opened up a critique of the ways in which culture expanded in the late twentieth century to serve as an almost knee-jerk descriptor of nearly any identity group. While this expansion responds to the political desire to incorporate "cultures of difference" within (or against) the mainstream, it often ends up weakening culture's critical value. Especially frustrating for critics working in these fields is the cooptation of local culture and difference by a relativism that becomes indifferent to difference, and by a cultural capitalism that feeds off and makes a profit from difference (Eagleton 2000). If a key premise of modernity is that tradition is eroded by the constant changes introduced by industrialization, new divisions of labor, and concomitant effects such as migration and consumer capitalism, recent theories of disorganized capitalism entertain the possibility that the "system" itself gains by the erosion of such traditions, for it can capitalize on them through commodity consumption, cultural tourism, and increasing attention to heritage. In this case, both the changes and the attempts to recuperate tradition feed the political-economic and cultural system; nonnormative behavior, rather than threatening the system in a counter- or subcultural mode, actually enhances it. Such a "flexible system" can make action and agency oriented toward political opposition seem beside the point.

While these critical responses to corporate and bureaucratic modes of multicultural recognition are useful, they often lack a grounded account of how the expedient use of culture as resource emerged. Today, culture is increasingly wielded as a resource for enhancing participation in this era of waning political involvement, conflicts over citizenship (I. Young 2000), and the rise of what Jeremy Rifkin (2000, 251) has called "cultural capitalism." The immaterialization characteristic of many new sources of economic growth (intellectual property rights as defined by the General Agreement on Tariffs and Trade and the World Trade Organization) and the increasing share of world trade captured by symbolic goods (movies, TV pro-

grams, music, tourism) have given the cultural sphere greater importance than at any other moment in the history of modernity. Culture may have simply become a pretext for sociopolitical amelioration and economic growth. But even if that were the case, the proliferation of such arguments, in forums provided by local culture-and-development projects as well as by the United Nations Educational Scientific and Cultural Organization (UNESCO), the World Bank, and the so-called globalized civil society of international foundations and nongovernmental organizations (NGOs), has produced a transformation in what we understand by the notion of culture and what we do in its name (Yúdice 2003). Applying the logic that a creative environment begets innovation, urban culture has been touted as the foundation for the so-called new economy based on "content provision," which is supposed to be the engine of accumulation (Castells 2000b). This premise is quite widespread, with the U.S. and British hype about the "creative economy" echoing in similar initiatives throughout the world (Caves 2000; Landry 2000; Venturelli 2001; Florida 2002).

As should be clear, current understandings and practices of culture are complex, located at the intersection of economic and social justice agendas. Considered as a keyword, "culture" is undergoing a transformation that "already is challenging many of our most basic assumptions about what constitutes human society" (Rifkin 2000, 10–11). In the first half of the twentieth century, Theodor Adorno (1984, 25) could define art as the process through which the individual gains freedom by externalizing himself, in contrast to the philistine "who craves art for what he can get out of it." Today, it is nearly impossible to find public statements that do not recruit art and culture either to better social conditions through the creation of multicultural tolerance and civic participation or to spur economic growth through urban cultural development projects and the concomitant proliferation of museums for cultural tourism, epitomized by the increasing number of Guggenheim franchises. At the same time, this blurring of distinctions between cultural, economic, and social programs has created a conservative backlash. Political scientists such as Samuel Huntington have argued (once again) that cultural factors account for the prosperity or backwardness, transparency or corruption, entrepreneurship or bureaucratic inertia of "world cultures" such as Asia, Latin America, and Africa (Huntington 1996; Harrison and Huntington 2000), while the Rand Corporation's policy paper *Gifts of the Muse: Reframing the Debate about the Benefits of the Arts* has resurrected the understanding of culture as referring to the "intrinsic benefits" of pleasure and captivation, which are "central in . . . generating all benefits deriving from the arts" (McCarthy et al. 2005, 12). The challenge today for both cultural studies and American studies is to think through this double-bind. Beyond either the economic and social expediency of culture or its depoliticized "intrinsic" benefits lies its critical potential. This potential is not realizable on its own, but must be fought for in and across educational and cultural institutions.

19
Democracy
Fred Moten

"Democracy" is the name that has been assigned to a dream as well as to certain already existing realities that are lived, by many, as a nightmare. The dream is of government by the people; government in which the common people hold sway; in which the dispensation of the commons—"the universality of individual needs, capacities, pleasures, productive forces, etc., created through universal exchange" that Karl Marx called wealth—is collectively determined; in which the trace of any enclosure of the commons whatever is an object of the severest vigilance since such dispensation will have been understood as ending not in tragedy but in romance (Marx 1858/1993; Hardin 1968). This is the fantasy of democracy *as* fantasy, as the contrapuntal arrangement of the many voices of the whole. The materialization of this dream will have been real democracy.

Authority in democracy can be exercised directly, in the immediate participation of each member of a given polity, or it can be ceded to representatives of the people, mediated not only by an individual person but also by whatever persons, codes, forms, and structures comprise the mode in which a representative is chosen. Every element that intervenes between the commons and authority constitutes a danger for the democracy to come; every idea and procedure that limits or circumscribes common participation is, similarly, a danger. And of the myriad ways in which the democratic dream is deferred and direct participation eclipsed, the most important are those in which the consent of the governed is manufactured by governors and boards of governors in the name of saving already existing democracy. When considering "democracy" as a keyword in culture and cultural studies in the United States, one must come to grips with the severity of the difference between what exists and what is yet to come under the name of "democracy" while inhabiting a state that constantly announces itself—in musical, poetic, and architectural languages—to be democracy's very incarnation.

It is partly by way of the shrill ubiquity of such celebratory announcements that we become aware that democracy in the United States has always been in crisis. This fact is further indexed by constant contradictory assertions that the United States is democracy's unique and solitary home and that the nation has the right and duty violently to export what it calls democracy. What it has meant to be a part of the intellectual cohort of the U.S. ruling class, at least in part, is to have participated in the ongoing identification and amelioration of that crisis. The constant crisis of democracy in the United States—something recognized with clarity in the normative national intellectual formation from James Madison to Samuel Huntington, something whose proper management is celebrated as I write today, January 20, 2005, the date of George W. Bush's second inauguration, in what journalist Cokie Roberts beamingly describes as a ritual of continuity, a series of spectacles in which the

abortive nature of repetitive beginning is everywhere present, though almost nowhere remarked, *as exclusion*—is precisely that democracy constantly threatens to overflow its limits, to emerge from the shadows in the outlaw form of an excluded, but also degraded, middle. It is not that which is given but that which invades, as it were, from an alienated inside, from the interior that it has been the business of already existing democracy, throughout the long history of its devolution, to expunge and criminalize (whether in the form of a duplicitous speaking for that middle by the ones who call themselves conservatives [e.g., Rush Limbaugh], or in the forms of abandonment and dismissal, of condescension and mischaracterization, of that middle by the ones who call themselves progressives [e.g., Al Franken]). Thus U.S. democracy is, on the one hand, what exists now as crisis management and, on the other hand, the set of acts, dispositions, improvisations, collectivities, and gestures that constitute and will have constituted the crisis.

Noam Chomsky, who has had much to say about what Huntington calls "the crisis of democracy," is fond of invoking John Dewey as a kind of conceptual antidote to Huntington (Crozier and Huntington et. al. 1975). Early in the last century, Dewey already recognized that "politics is the shadow cast by big business over society" (Chomsky 2005). We could expand upon this now by saying that U.S. democratic politics is a mode of crisis management whose most conspicuous and extravagant rituals—elections and the inaugural celebrations and protests that each in their way confirm them—operate at the level of the demonstration. All too often, the shadow demonstrates the irrelevance of public opinion, moving to obscure it in the convergent discourses of public relations and punditry, both of which are steeped in the rhetoric of positivist demonstration even as they eschew actual empirical investigation and the dangers of participation that such investigation always carries. In the refusal of self-styled public opinion makers, public intellectuals, and public servants actually to talk—and, deeper still, listen—to the common voice or voices a more genuine publicness lies submerged.

This entry is being written during the interval between elections in the United States and in Iraq that are meant, above all, to demonstrate a democratic actuality that falls short, often brutally and tragically, of the democracy of which many dream. The elections are meant to demonstrate, finally, that an election took place—a central consideration for structures of authority that depend upon the eclipse of democratic content by the ritual reanimation of supposedly democratic forms. We might examine, along with Chomsky and Edward Herman, the history of the U.S.-mandated demonstration election that is a central element of U. S. foreign policy in the American Century, while emphasizing the fact that such demonstrations were first enacted domestically (Chomsky and Herman 1979). We operate within a long history of the self-nomination of the elect and their restriction of elections, and, more importantly because more generally, of antinomian political voicing that, as poet and critic Susan Howe (1993) points out, goes at least as far back as Anne Hutchinson.

Straining against pseudodemocratic formality is a question whose utterance defines membership in the underground: Where will democracy, which is to say the democracy that is to come, have been found? The answer remains on the outskirts and in anticipation of the American *polis*.

It remains possible and necessary, then, for anyone who aspires to do cultural studies in the United States, to consider and to participate in what Chomsky (2005) calls the "public attitudes that are kept in the shadows." When one dreams, along with C. L. R. James (1956), of the government of cooks, of government that cooks or swings in ways that belie facile identifications of the music that cooks and swings with what is called, or what already exists under the name of, American Democracy; when one imagines the common and fantastic counterpoint and countertime that moves in perpetual disturbance of the American exception and the imperial acquisitiveness and domestic predation, the ongoing endangering of internal and external aliens, that exception is supposed to justify; then one could be said to move in as well as toward the outskirts and shadows—which are, in fact, the essence—of the *polis* and of the political. Intimations of this city, which is not on a hill but underground, are given in those occult forms where participation and mediation, participation and representation, interact by way of linkage and articulation rather than eclipse: for instance, in the paramusical, intervallic space where Ray Charles's voicing and phrasing submits itself to the force of an exteriority that comes, paradoxically, from his own, alien interiority; or in speculative fiction writer Samuel R. Delany's paraliterary excursions into the diffuse origins of the city and of writing, where he extends his continuing invocation of what one of Delany's critics, fellow novelist Joanna Russ, calls "the subjunctivity of science fiction" in order both to illuminate and inhabit that excess of the mundane that characterizes (the politics of) everyday life in the shadows (Russ 1995; L. Harris 2005).

Such illumination, such *theoria*, such fantasy, links Delany and Charles because in both it is enabled by their placement in the tradition of black radicalism, a tradition of alternative vision predicated on the enabling inability to see (which is to say the capacity and curse of seeing through) the glaring light of already existing democracy and its demonstrations. What the Reverend Al Sharpton said of Charles—that his blindness is the condition of possibility of a rendition of "America the Beautiful" that is at every moment infused with phonographic insight and foresight—helps us to understand how Delany's documentary writing on Times Square is given only through the lens of submerged cities and fragmentary texts of lands that have never, or have not yet, been (Charles 1972; Delany 1994, 2001). Charles and Delany see shades of red and blue that are wholly outside the spectrum of intellectual and pseudo-intellectual democratic management. Moreover, Sharpton's formulations make clear once again what must be understood, at least in part, as the Afro-diasporic constitution—and invasion (the incursion of what Cedric Robinson calls the eternal internal alien, the *metoikos*)—of a problematic Greek revival, the violently suppressed and nevertheless ongoing work that W. E. B. Du Bois (1935) called the "black reconstruction of American democracy."

Reading and re-reading work like that of Du Bois sharpens our awareness that the United States is the land of formal democratic enclosure and, moreover, the land in which critical analysis of such oxymoronic forms is relegated to the shadows. Such analysis occurs in nonstandard languages and styles; at the same time, whatever democratic energy that remains in the practically empty interior of our democratic forms makes itself manifest as dissatisfaction with those forms. Of course, the irregularity of common cries and common dreams is manifest as both mourning and hope at the very outset and from the very outskirts of the *polis*. Recent analyses of the constitutive irruption of the outside (and the outsider) in Athenian democracy bear this out while providing transcendental clues regarding the constant irruptions into the democracy that now exists of the democracy that is to come (Loraux 1998; Butler 2000). At the same time, democrats of the outside, the partyless democrats who like to party, who rock the party, recognize that the gap between what is and what is to come is filled by a constant and total mobilization against, that moves as if in regulation of, such irruption (Hanchard 2006). Democracy is the rupture of any exclusion, however common that exclusion might appear to be; the recalibration of the *polis*, of the city, by and according to the most irregular measures. In the United States and in every place subject to U.S. authority, there are multitudes who work to discover it.

20

Dialect

Shelley Fisher Fishkin

It is probably both fortuitous and overdetermined that the critic most responsible for the view of dialect writing that American cultural studies critics are challenging today was a man by the name of Krapp. Writing in the 1920s, George Philip Krapp (1925, 1926) insisted that dialect writing was a highbrow literary convention that always involved a patronizing class-based condescension. Krapp's view came to dominate scholarship on the topic through much of the twentieth century. Indeed, it is echoed in the ten-volume *Encyclopedia of Language and Linguistics* published in 1994, which avers that dialect speakers in literature are usually presented as inferior, primitive, and backward (Asher and Simpson 1994). To be sure, the hierarchy that Krapp and others invoke was, historically, a component of much dialect writing. But recent scholarship emphasizes that the story is more complex and more interesting: dialect writing can be subversive as well as repressive, radical as well as conservative, as capable of interrogating status quo distributions of power as of reaffirming them. For these reasons, scholars of American cultural studies are now considering dialect writing in more nuanced ways, increasingly recognizing that a practice previously sidelined as ephemeral and retrograde can be seen, in many cases, as the forerunner to many of the important vernacular voices that have enriched twentieth- and twenty-first-century U.S. and American culture.

Long dismissed by scholars as unworthy of serious attention, dialect writing carries a lot of baggage, conjuring up visions of elitist disdain, class bias, cheap humor, ethnocentrism, and racism. But contemporary scholars increasingly argue that dialect writing can also be a site of subversion, resistance, empathy, respect, and social critique. Gavin Jones (1999, 11), for example, questions the idea that the principal function of dialect in the Gilded Age (1865-1901) was to reinforce an elitist ideology, and he urges scholars to attend to "the political dynamic of subordination *and* resistance that defined linguistic conflict at the end of the nineteenth century." Holger Kersten (1996, 2000) similarly rejects critical evaluations of dialect writing as "inferior," and instead argues that departures from "correct" traditions of usage often represent consciously innovative literary experiments, including those that use the perspective and speech of ethnic immigrant characters to present a critique of U.S. culture from the outside. The humor may have mitigated the satire to some extent, allowing a mainstream audience to both recognize certain weaknesses of their own culture and distance themselves from the criticism; but the form was a vehicle for getting the criticism out. Eric Lott (1993) and Michael North (1994) argue that an analogous critique informs the centrality of black dialect in both popular and elite white cultural forms ranging from nineteenth-century minstrelsy to twentieth-century modernist poetry.

Because of the longstanding assumption (articulated by Krapp) that the use of dialect in literature implied the subordinate status of the dialect speaker, for over a century readers have often misinterpreted the work of writers such as Mark Twain and Paul Laurence Dunbar (D. Smith 1991; Braxton 1993; Fishkin and Bradley 2005). Neither Twain nor Dunbar considered dialect speakers inferior or undeserving of respect; on the contrary, both authors were sometimes apt to assign *superior* qualities to dialect speakers, thereby inverting the presumptive hierarchies of value embodied in the linguistic choices that they made. Far from being presented as objects of ridicule, black vernacular speakers in work by Twain and Dunbar often underscore, through the compelling power of their voice and their message, the superficiality and thinness of the dominant white culture. Aunt Rachel in Twain's "A True Story" (1874) and Jim in *Huckleberry Finn* (1885)—both speakers of "black dialect," as traditional literary terminology would have it—are the figures we admire most in their respective texts. Through them Twain undermines the ideology of black inferiority that pervaded both popular belief and "scientific" opinion of his time. The signifying slave preacher in Dunbar's poem "An Ante-Bellum Sermon" similarly embodies the richness and depth of black vernacular speech and makes all other speech look one-dimensional and pallid by comparison. We need to attend more closely to the subversion behind the stereotype in Dunbar's work if we are to grasp the complexity of his project as a poet.

"Dialect," as it turns out, in the hands of sly and talented artists and astute and sensitive critics, may do cultural work that is a good deal more complicated than we may have thought. Rather than reifying a hi-erarchy that postulates something called "Standard English" on top and "dialect" of various sorts at the bottom, scholars today increasingly recognize the ways in which U.S. English is a dynamic amalgam of a range of varieties of speech and writing in which vernacular forms have always played, and continue to play, critical roles. Late-twentieth-century literary experiments such as Alice Walker's vernacular, epistolary novel *The Color Purple* (1982) and Gloria Anzaldúa's code-switching blend of poetry and nonfiction, *Border-lands/La Frontera* (1987), remind us of the distinctive and radical energy and vitality of some of dialect writing's contemporary heirs.

21

Diaspora

Brent Hayes Edwards

Until only a few decades ago, "diaspora" was a relatively esoteric word restricted in meaning to the historical dispersion of particular communities around the Mediterranean basin. Since then, it has become a privileged term of reference in scholarship, journalism, and popular discourse, used broadly and at times indiscriminately to denote a number of different kinds of movement and situations of mobility among human populations. *Diaspora* is a Greek word, a combination of the prefix *dia-* (meaning "through") and the verb *sperein* (meaning "to sow" or "to scatter"). It was used in the Septuagint, the translation of the Hebrew

Torah prepared for the ruler of Alexandria in Egypt around 250 B.C.E. by a specially appointed group of Jewish scholars. Subsequently, the word came to be employed as a self-designation among the Jewish populations that spread throughout the Mediterranean during the Hellenic period.

In recent deployments of the term, it is sometimes assumed that *diaspora* was used to translate a relatively wide number of Hebrew words in the Septuagint, including words relating both to scattering and to exile. However, as scholars of the Hellenic period have long pointed out, the Greek word never translates the important Hebrew words for exile (such as *galut* and *golah*) (Davies 1982). Instead, *diaspora* is limited to the translation of terms describing literal or figurative processes of scattering, separation, branching off, departure, banishment, and winnowing. Most of these terms, such as *tephutzot* (or "dispersal"), are derived from the Hebrew root *pvtz* ("scatter"). In the Septuagint, many such terms are found in passages dealing with the divine expulsion of the Jewish people, particularly in the books of Leviticus and Deuteronomy, as in Leviticus 26:33, which reads, "And I will scatter you among the heathen, and will draw out a sword after you: and your land shall be desolate, and your cities waste."

In fact, there is a deeply significant distinction in the Jewish intellectual tradition between diaspora and exile. Often "diaspora" is used to indicate a state of dispersal resulting from voluntary migration, as with the far-flung Jewish communities of the Hellenic period. In this context, the term is not necessarily laced with a sense of violence, suffering, and punishment,

in part because Jewish populations maintained a rich sense of an original "homeland," physically symbolized by the Temple in Jerusalem. (Strikingly, Jewish settlements around the Mediterranean were commonly called *apoikiai*, or "colonies.") Very differently, the term exile (*galut*) connotes "anguish, forced homelessness, and the sense of things being not as they should be" (Wettstein 2002, 2), and is often considered to be the result of the loss of that "homeland" with the destruction of the Second Temple in 70 C.E. As Haim Hillel Ben-Sasson (n.d., 275) explains, "The residence of a great number of members of a nation, even the majority, outside their homeland is not definable as *galut* so long as the homeland remains in that nation's possession. . . . Only the loss of a political-ethnic center and the feeling of uprootedness turns Diaspora (Dispersion) into *galut* (Exile)."

This nuanced history is almost always overlooked in the current appropriations of the term "diaspora" that render it as a loose equivalent for a range of other words, conflating it with exile, migration, immigration, expatriation, transnationalism, minority or refugee status, and racial or ethnic difference. Scholars have also debated the "primacy" of the Jewish model in any definition of diaspora (Tölölyan 1996; Boyarin and Boyarin 2002). Yet the genealogy of the term in the Jewish intellectual tradition itself might be taken as an indication that the Jewish diaspora should not be considered to be an "ideal type," as some scholars of comparative diasporas would have it (Safran 1991). "Diaspora" is first of all a translation, a foreign word adopted in the Jewish intellectual discourse of community. As such, it should serve as a reminder that there is never a "first," single dispersion of a single people, but instead a complex historical overlay of a variety of kinds of population movement, narrated and imbued with value in different ways and to different ends. As the historian Erich Gruen (2002, 19) has explained with regard to Jewish populations in the Hellenic period, "a Greek diaspora, in short, brought the Jewish one in its wake." With regard to the study of the movement of peoples under globalization in the contemporary period, this history of usage should make us skeptical of an overarching concern with the movement of groups considered as discrete or self-contained, and compel us to focus on the ways in which those movements always intersect, leading to exchange, assimilation, expropriation, coalition, or dissension. This is to say that any study of diaspora is also a study of "overlapping diasporas" (E. Lewis 1995, 786–87; Edwards 2003b).

In the United States, the term "diaspora" has been invoked in interdisciplinary academic initiatives, first and foremost in attempts to institutionalize Africana and black studies programs, as well as in popular culture at least as early as the late 1960s. Yet it became especially prevalent in scholarly discourse as a result of the international influence in the late 1980s and early 1990s of a group of intellectuals associated with the Centre for Contemporary Cultural Studies at the University of Birmingham (Edwards 2001). In the writings of Stuart Hall and Paul Gilroy, diaspora is invoked expressly in a critique of previous scholarship in cultural studies and labor history (by Raymond Williams, Richard Hoggart, and E. P. Thompson, among others),

which was limited above all by its implicit assumptions about the racial character of Englishness. It is reductive to discuss such forms of national belonging, Hall (1993) and Gilroy (1993) argued, without taking into account the ways in which English identity itself has been defined through the exclusion of a range of "others," particularly populations of the former British colonies who have been forcibly denied the rights and privileges of citizenship. This critique opened an entire arena of study, as the younger generation of Birmingham scholars began to consider culture "within the framework of a diaspora as an alternative to the different varieties of absolutism which would confine culture in 'racial,' ethnic or national essences" (Gilroy 1987, 155).

Despite the anti-essentialism of the Birmingham model, clearly diaspora has been theorized in relation to the scattering of populations from sub-Saharan Africa in particular, as a result of the slave trade and European colonialism. As some scholars have cautioned, given the historical peculiarities of the African diaspora, this model should not be taken as a template for any inquiry into the dynamics of diasporic forms of community (Tölölyan 1996; Edwards 2001). Moreover, diaspora structured in terms of race may be qualitatively different from diaspora structured in terms of religion (as evident, for instance, in recent scholarship on the "Sikh diaspora"), nation (as in the "Indian diaspora," the "Cuban diaspora," or the "Palestinian diaspora"), ethnicity (as in the "Berber diaspora" or some definitions of the "Chinese diaspora"), region (as in the "Caribbean diaspora"), or sexuality (as in the "queer diaspora").

Especially in historical and sociological work on diaspora, much scholarship continues to take what Kim Butler (2001, 193) has termed the "checklist" approach, testing a given history of dispersal against a set of typological characteristics: to be "authentic," a diaspora must involve, for instance, the forced migration of a people to two or more locations; a collective memory or narrative of the homeland; the maintenance of autonomous group identity against the backdrop of the host environment; and, in some versions, a persistent network of ties to the homeland, or ongoing agitation for its redemption. In contrast, "diaspora" tends to be used in American studies and cultural studies scholarship as a term that runs against the grain of any fixed notion of belonging; cultural identity is thereby understood as necessarily "unstable points of identification or suture," as Stuart Hall (1990, 226) puts it: "not an essence but a *positioning*." This emphasis on diaspora as a politics of process or practice, especially in anthropology and literary studies, has resulted in scholarship investigating the uneven and dialogic interplay of material, ideological, and discursive phenomena in transnational cultural circuits (Nandy 1990; Warren 1993; E. Gordon 1998; Matory 1999; Yelvington 2001). Some of this scholarship insists on language difference as a key structural feature of transnational culture, and thus theorizes diaspora through the intricacies of translation (Rafael 1988; Gruesz 2002; Edwards 2003a; Hofmeyr 2004).

Given that "diaspora offers an alternative 'ground' to that of the territorial state for the intricate and al-ways contentious linkage between cultural identity and political organization," the term inherently represents a challenge to any mode of knowledge production framed around the nation-state as an organizing principle (Boyarin and Boyarin 2002, 10). In this sense, the term must unavoidably reframe and transform the discussion of a wide variety of issues in an area-based field such as American studies. Seen through the lens of diaspora, some of the traditional, even paradigmatic concerns of American studies (for example, immigration and assimilation) are thrown into question or rendered peripheral (Mishra 1996). With regard to community affiliation and self-description in the contemporary conjuncture, it is crucial to consider the reasons that groups that not long ago might have called themselves "minorities" are increasingly calling themselves "diasporas" (Clifford 1997). An emphasis on diaspora also necessitates a new approach to the study of foreign policy, as evinced in the growing scholarship that has begun to consider the impact of "mobilized" diasporic pressure groups on U.S. foreign affairs (Mathias 1981; Edmondson 1986; Shain 1994/95; Von Eschen 2004). The term likewise opens up new avenues of inquiry into the history of U.S. imperialism, not just in relation to its attendant dispersal of military, labor, diplomatic, and administrative populations, but also because of the ways in which transnational population movements in the Americas, especially those involving groups of those considered "others" in the U.S. nation-state, necessarily take shape in the shadow of U.S. globe-straddling ambitions.

22

Disability

Kanta Kochhar-Lindgren

As a keyword in American studies and cultural studies, the site of a political movement, and the name of an emergent interdisciplinary field, "disability" articulates vital connections among public histories, the many communities formed by people with disabilities, and various modes of cultural theory. The term by necessity foregrounds the social construction of disability and the way the disabled are all too often rendered invisible and powerless due to the mainstream tendency to valorize the normal body. Legal changes, as well as concomitant activist work at the grassroots level, shifted the emphasis on disability as a set of medical conditions toward the notion of disability as a political category. By the 1980s, disability activists had begun to move into the academy and to formulate a wide range of disability scholarship. In the first phase, this work centered on the analysis and reform of public policy. By the early 1990s, a second phase had emerged in the humanities that analyzed the implications of representation for how people think about disability.

Disability studies, and work in American studies and cultural studies influenced by it, seeks to revise the place disability holds in various cultural imaginaries, challenging the tendency of the social mainstream to consider disability a personal problem, a source of pity, or as something that can be overcome with the help of medical intervention. Activists and scholars alike note that disability is often a significant but hidden marker of inferiority, linked to other identity categories such as race, gender, sex, and class. This emerging framing of disability as a cultural problematic rather than a fixed category extends important work already being done on the body, eugenics, biopolitics, immigration, nation-building, and the practice of everyday life.

Among the factors that contributed to the rise of disability studies, the most prominent are the civil rights movement of the 1960s, disability activism in the 1960s and 1970s, and the implementation of the Americans with Disabilities Act (ADA) in the 1990s. Spearheaded by Ed Roberts's advocacy for independent living, disability activism in the United States began in the 1960s at two university campuses: the University of Illinois and the University of California–Berkeley, where demands for alternatives to the previously dominant rehabilitation model led to the creation of the Center for Independent Living. Important shifts in U.S. law resulted from this activism, such as Section 504 of the Rehabilitation Act of 1973, which granted the right of equal access to federal programs to people with disabilities. In 1975, the Education of All Handicapped Children Act (renamed IDEA in 1990) was passed, leading to the mainstreaming of children with disabilities. Equal access to public transportation also became more common as a result of grassroots activism and subsequent legal interventions. The ADA accords people with disabilities the right to protection against employment discrimination. Nevertheless, law and practice are often not in accord, and a large percentage of the cases brought before the Supreme Court have not been decided in favor of the disabled person.

Partly as a result of this gap between legal reform and social practice, recent work on disability has turned to questions of cultural representation. The disabled body—whether diseased, deaf, blind, physically handicapped, or cognitively different—marks the other of the able body, an unmarked norm that gained its force as an implicit corollary to Enlightenment notions of citizenship and work. Since at least the eighteenth century, the disabled body has been relegated to the provenance of medicine in order to codify, classify, control, and where possible (and of interest) fix it. This pattern has led to extensive institutionalization of the mentally insane, the "feebleminded," and the physically disabled. At the turn of the twentieth century, eugenics programs, fostered in part at the Carnegie Institution's Cold Spring Harbor complex in Long Island, New York, furthered this approach by implementing state-sanctioned sterilization as a means of limiting the proliferation of the disabled and other populations deemed undesirable (Carlson 2001; Black 2003). This pattern of removing the disabled from everyday life reinforced the valorization of the able-bodied paradigm, the authority of the medical model of treatment, and the common understanding of the disabled body as a site of abjection—based on an "out-of-sight, out-of-mind" logic. Nevertheless, the instantiation of "able-bodied" carries within it a discomfort with disability and the frailty of the human body, since, as disability activists often point out, anyone

can become a member of the disabled population at any time.

These various attempts to control the disabled were congruent with nationalism's increasing tendency to classify and regulate diverse populations. The institutionalization of the deaf, for example, began in the 1800s in Europe and spread to the United States. While this form of regulation served to remove deaf people from the cultural mainstream, it also acted as a site where the deaf could begin to form a unique subculture. The first school for the deaf, the American Asylum for the Education and Instruction of Deaf and Dumb Persons, was founded by Thomas Hopkins Gallaudet in Hartford, Connecticut, in 1817; by 1863 there were thirty-two such schools in the United States. This movement led to the education of a large deaf community as well as the development of a community identity enabled by a shared language—American Sign Language (ASL). However, as the rise of nationalism precipitated interest in monolingual societies, the use of sign language was suppressed and oralism was promoted. Even in deaf schools, new technologies and elocution methods were developed to train the deaf to behave as if hearing. Often operating in league with this monolingual nationalism, educators influenced by Social Darwinism argued that the use of sign language indicated intellectual inferiority and lack of social and cultural progress. It was not until the 1960s (at approximately the same time that disability activism was beginning to gain force) that Gallaudet University professor and linguist William Stokoe validated ASL as a full language in its own right through his extensive research into its linguistic structures. As a result, deaf schools, particularly Gallaudet University, began to incorporate ASL in their instructional methods, and the deaf community became more fully identified as a linguistic and ethnic minority rather than one with impairments. This led the deaf students at Gallaudet to protest successfully for the hiring of the first deaf university president in 1988 (Christiansen and Barartt 2002; Burch 2004).

This sort of critical analysis of the history of a single disability demonstrates how social practices maintain and reinforce disability as a category of the marginalized other, what the consequences of that othering are, and how these techniques of othering are exacted on the body. These practices have serious implications not only for how we treat the disabled, but also for how we understand the limits of the human body. Scholars have, for instance, remarked on the characteristic first response of the able-bodied to the disabled as being one of unease (L. Davis 1995). Subjected to strong cultural mores about the normal body as a site of orderliness, even progressive and radical able-bodied responses tend to repress anxiety about dealing with sensory, physical, or cognitive differences (E. Samuels 2002). Yet there is much to be gained from a critique of knowledge produced about and through theories of the body, difference, and disability. Donna Haraway's (1991) work on cyborgs, for instance, is helpful for its articulation of a disability identity and its theorization of the use of prosthetics as a mixture of human and machine. Similarly, Rosemarie Garland Thomson has applied Eve Kosofsky

Sedgwick's (1990) distinction between "minoritizing" and "universalizing" theories of sexual difference to disability. While the former links the politics of disability to a specific population, the latter opens onto a broader understanding of disability as "structuring a wide range of thought, language, and perception" (Thomson 1997, 22; Porter 1997).

As this brief survey indicates, there is now a discrete interdisciplinary field of disability studies—a field that has emerged through the pioneering work of Paul Longmore (2001, Longmore and Umansky 2003), Simi Linton (1998), Rosemarie Garland Thomson (1997), David Mitchell and Sharon Snyder (2001), and Lennard Davis (1995). At the same time, a number of scholars are working at and across the edges of that field to create new connections regarding the significance of disability, including linkages to genetic engineering (Asch and Fine 1988; Asch and Parens 2000), immigration and labor studies (Longmore 2001; Baynton 1998), literary studies (Mitchell and Snyder 1997, 2001), everyday life (Thomson 1997; R. Adams 2001), performance studies (Kuppers 2003; V. Lewis 2005; Sandahl and Auslander 2005; Kochhar-Lindgren 2006), philosophy (Silvers 1998), and medical humanities (S. Gilman 1995). Across all of this work, disability, as a socially constructed category, is understood as deeply embedded in our biopolitical technologies and cultural imaginaries.

While this innovative scholarship has advanced a more nuanced understanding of the underlying assumptions that make disability the other of normalcy, one of the problems in using disability as an organizing trope is that it often artificially consolidates a wide array of physical and mental differences under a single term. Like other keywords that organize identity-based legal and cultural fields, the current use of the term helps to politicize our understanding of disability, but it also tends to create an abstract concept in which the particularities of peoples' histories are erased. In order to recuperate a more embodied reference point for disability and claim a more visible social space in the public sphere, a number of disability scholars have begun to address the importance of reclaiming individual bodily experience through art, performance, and literature (Corker 2001; Mitchell 2001; Snyder and Mitchell 2001; Siebers 2004; Kochhar-Lindgren 2006). With regard to the fields of American studies and cultural studies, the ongoing challenge will be to identify disability as a discrete category, while also pluralizing our understanding of its manifestations. Considered as a keyword that indexes this challenge, "disability" has newly problematized and invigorated work on the body by naming an identity category that enables us to understand the diverse lived experiences of bodies and their many sensorial differences.

23

Domestic

Rosemary Marangoly George

The keyword "domestic" conjures up several different yet linked meanings. It evokes the private home and all its accoutrements and, in a secondary fashion, hired household help. It also refers to the "national" as opposed to the "foreign," and to the "tame" as opposed to the "natural" or "wild." American cultural studies scholarship has only recently begun to think through the connections among these usages of the term, and to make visible the racial and class bias of much of the scholarship on domesticity in relation to the United States.

Theorizing the domestic has been integral to many academic disciplines: architecture and design, anthropology, sociology, history, economics, philosophy, psychoanalysis, and literary and cultural criticism. Expressed in binary terms such as male/female, public/private, and production/reproduction, a relatively stable home/work dichotomy has formed the basis of scholarly writing on domesticity across these disciplines. Newer studies of domesticity are more attentive to its complex political entrenchment in the so-called public and private: to the entanglement of the domestic with nationalist discourses and, in feminist economic analyses, to the home as a workplace where industrial "homework" is done. Researchers such as Jeanne Boydston (1990) and Alice Kessler-Harris (1990) see the impact of domesticity on the determination of wages and on labor issues that were hitherto understood to be purely market driven. In her studies of women's labor history in the West and the reliance on domestic ideologies to buttress capitalist expansion, Eileen Boris (1993) notes that while a home/work split was an essential component for industrialization, the two arenas were also fundamentally constitutive of each other. Thus domesticity, in these discussions, has ideological functions that do not stop at constructions of the private life of individual persons, of homes and families.

Much work on domesticity has focused on the white middle classes. This work tends to trace what is essentially an Anglo history of the "American" home from its utilitarian use in the seventeenth century as an unadorned place for storage and shelter, to the emergence of the cult of domesticity or true womanhood in the mid-nineteenth century, to the mid-twentieth-century articulation of the home as a prison where countless white middle-class women suffered unnamable sorrows (Matthews 1987). The prevalence and familiarity of this story indexes both the success and the limitations of liberal feminism as a social movement. Even as it sought to reformulate domesticity in relatively gender-equitable ways, liberal feminism failed to address other factors that shape the domestic arena, most notably the economic and racial connections that hold different domestic sites adjacent and yet unequal within a national or global framework.

A very differently oriented genealogy of domesticity in the United States can be traced through the history of the domestic (as household servant) over the same three centuries. This history moves from the seventeenth century use of indentured servants and "hired help" who worked alongside family members in the household, to the use of servants and slaves in the eighteenth and nineteenth centuries, to the centrality of domestic laborers in establishing U.S. notions of ideal domesticity in the mid-twentieth century. It is worth speculating that what Betty Friedan referred to in *The Feminine Mystique* (1963) as the "problem with no name," the anxieties that beset countless white women in the late 1950s, arose in part because the era of ample cheap domestic labor came to an end as women of color found other employment avenues open to them. In recent years, career women in the United States may be reversing this trend, as they increasingly turn to non-familial domestic labor provided mainly by a service economy made up of documented and undocumented immigrants and other women of color, in order to juggle the tasks of maintaining both a career and high standards of child-care and home maintenance. A complex network of economic, racial, and gendered arrangements needs to be in place on a national and international footing before respectable middle- and upper-middle-class homemaking is successfully achieved in the United States (M. Romero 1992; Parreñas 2001).

Scholarship on European and U.S. imperialism has also begun to examine "the spatial and political interdependence of home and empire," what Amy Kaplan (1998) has called "Manifest Domesticity." Such scholarship demonstrates that the domestic sentimentalization of the white middle-class home from the nineteenth century onward was intimately intertwined with the ongoing and violent expansion of U.S. interests across the North American continent and beyond. One example of this work is Laura Wexler's (2000, 8) notable study of late-nineteenth- and early-twentieth-century women photographers and the multiple ways in which "nineteenth century domestic photographs shaped the look and power of white supremacy at the century's end." Wexler argues that Frances Johnston's photographs of Admiral George Dewey and his crew, taken in 1899 aboard the battleship *Olympia* after they had routed the Spanish forces in the Philippines, celebrate and consolidate the "American" heroism that Dewey and his band of sailors embodied even as these photos bear witness to the "American" domestic world that was re-created on the ship. Such "domestic images" function both to deny and to showcase the violence with which the differences between home and alien spaces or alien peoples are constructed, managed, and policed.

Research of this type demonstrates that the "domestic" is a dynamic and changing concept, one that serves as a regulative norm that continually refigures families, homes, and belonging. In its early forms, the domestic was a primary site where modernity was made manifest; the concept of "family" changed from a largely temporal organization of kinship into a spatially organized sphere of activity. In narratives and practices of domesticity, the trauma of such transformation is absorbed (imperfectly at times) and the do-

mestic is reissued as usable or, in rare cases, abandoned altogether. The wholesomeness associated with the domestic, as in Witold Rybczynski's (1988, 217) assessment of "domestic well-being [as] a fundamental human need that is deeply rooted in us, and that must be satisfied," is rarely discarded even when specific domestic arrangements are. Even liberal-radical accounts that seek to contest the mainstream-conservative reduction of domesticity to the nuclear family often remain firmly committed to family values. These values may be alternative, but they nonetheless retain the pleasures of the normative: private comfort, safety, exclusivity. And at the national level, the demand for the comfort and safety of the enfranchised citizenry has put into place a rigorous screening process that excludes from the "homeland" those who threaten "the American way of life," even as it lets slip in an underclass whose labor is necessary for maintaining the domestic comforts of everyday life.

Much of the literary and cultural studies scholarship on the rise of these normative forms of domesticity focuses on the mid-nineteenth century, when a new ideology of the home and of women's role in its maintenance took hold of the U.S. imagination. Catharine E. Beecher's *A Treatise on Domestic Economy for the Use of Young Ladies at Home and at School* (1841) was a significant inaugurator of this ideology, since it newly venerated the white, middle-class home and placed central responsibility for it in the hands of the housewife. This widespread rhetoric sentimentalized both the home and the housewife as the sources and locations of national virtue and was manifest in a variety of cultural texts, including women's magazines like *Godey's Lady's Book* (published 1830-98), religious tracts, newspapers, home design innovations, home management guides, and the "domestic fiction" written in this period. In the late twentieth century, a whole generation of U.S. feminists investigated the cultural impact of the latter phenomenon, produced by what Nathaniel Hawthorne famously called the "d——d mob of scribbling women." Influential studies such as Ann Douglas's *Feminization of American Culture* (1977) and Jane Tompkins's *Sensational Designs* (1985) revised the U.S. literary canon by insisting on the importance of mass culture in the nineteenth century and of women as powerful consumers and producers in this arena. More recently David Reynolds (1989), Lora Romero (1997, 14), and others have argued that "the reign of women [should be understood as] a cultural artifact produced by the antebellum period," rather than as an accurate assessment of the power of middle-class white women in the antebellum years.

Regardless of the degree to which the nineteenth-century cult of domesticity authorized white women in the context of U.S. cultural production, the "domestic fiction" formula reigned supreme. When African American women writers in the late nineteenth century utilized this genre, it was indicative of the different political charge of domesticity for a people struggling with the burden of slavery that had placed heavy prohibitions on both the means and contents of such pleasures. Denied access to reading, writing, state-recognized marriage, and homeownership, de-

nied the luxury or right to play the pure lady of the house or even to be a child learning at her mother's knee, these writers produced domestic fiction that revealed very little dissonance between attending to the claims and duties of domestic life (especially motherhood) and attending to those of activism on behalf of the race. The establishment and celebration of happy marriages within domestic havens in these black women's writings did powerful political and cultural work in a period when the attainment of a private sphere, whether through homeownership or by other means, was something fought for daily even as it was recorded and celebrated in cultural texts (Tate 1992; DuCille 1993). More than a century later, welfare reform programs and policies, the recruitment of disproportionate numbers of people of color into the armed forces and police, and racially biased criminal sentencing and incarceration patterns all indicate that, in Aida Hurtado's (1989, 849) words, "there is no such thing as a private sphere for people of Color except that which they manage to create and protect in an otherwise hostile environment." Whether we look at housing-loan records, zoning laws, civic amenities in specific neighborhoods, the location of toxic industries, the differential funding to schools, or levels of prenatal care, we see that state intervention into domestic life continues to be systematically beneficial to white middle- and upper-class citizens and detrimental to the everyday lives of lower-class whites and people of color.

Partly due to this complex history, "domestication" has often been deployed for metaphorical purposes in academic discourse, including feminist discourse, to signify the opposite of radical thought, a usage that draws on the opposition of the domestic to the wild. Literary and cultural critic Rachel Bowlby (1995, 73), for instance, notes that domestication "refers generally to processes of simplification, assimilation and distortion—any or all of these—to which the theory in question falls victim or which it is powerless to resist." Yet if we consider the name chosen by the founders of Kitchen Table / Women of Color Press, we encounter a radical feminism that harnesses the wisdom and labor of this homely location to a far-reaching feminist politics. As in the nineteenth century, "marriage," "family," and "homemaking" continue to be differently inflected terms and spaces for different groups of people and are fabricated with local variations across national borders and social classes. What is truly remarkable are the ways in which dominant domestic ideologies and practices have become globally hegemonic as a result of colonial and capitalist expansion and modernization, even as they have entered into contestation with other local forms of domesticity. Class, race, and geographic location place heavy inflections on domesticity, and yet, like love, childhood, and death, the domestic is most often portrayed as transcending all specifics, or rather as blurring all distinctions in the warm glow of its splendor. Ultimately, the enormous attention that domesticity has received, and the enshrinement of heterosexuality therein, has severely stymied the representation and even recognition of other forms of establishing intimacy and affiliation.

24
Economy
Timothy Mitchell

The term "economy" in its contemporary sense came into use only quite recently. It is often assumed that the idea of the economy, defined as the relations of material production and exchange in a given territory and understood as an object of expert knowledge and government administration, was introduced by political economists such as William Petty, François Quesnay, and Adam Smith in the seventeenth and eighteenth centuries, or even by Aristotle. In fact, however, this use of the term developed only in the 1930s and 1940s and was well established only by the 1950s (Mitchell 2005).

In earlier periods, "economy" (usually with no definite article) referred to a way of acting and to the forms of knowledge required for effective action. It was the term for the proper husbanding of material resources or the proper management of a lord's estate or a sovereign's realm. Political economy came to mean the knowledge and practice required for governing the state and managing its population and resources (Tribe 1978; Poovey 1998). Michel Foucault (1991) connects the development of this expertise to the wider range of practices known as "government," in an older sense of that term referring not to the official institutions of rule but to a variety of forms of knowledge and technique concerned with governing personal conduct, managing the health and livelihoods of a population, and controlling the circulation of material and political resources.

What is the difference between the older meaning of economy, understood as a *way* of exercising power and accumulating knowledge, and the contemporary idea of the economy, understood as an *object* of power and knowledge? Foucault (1991, 92) does not address this question, but simply relates the two meanings by suggesting that "the very essence of government—that is the art of exercising power in the form of economy—is to have as its main object that which we are today accustomed to call 'the economy.'" This conflation has led several scholars to argue that the economy emerged as a distinct object in the late eighteenth or early nineteenth century. Others read Karl Polanyi's (1944/2001) argument that in the same period market relations were "disembedded" from society as another version of this idea. Polanyi, however, is describing the emergence not of the economy but of society, formed as an object of political discourse in response to the increasingly unrestrained relations of what he calls "market economy."

The emergence of the economy in the mid-twentieth century differs from the era of nineteenth-century governmentality in at least three important senses. First, economists and government agencies defined the economy in a way that enabled them to claim new powers to measure it, manage it, and make it grow. They defined it not in terms of human labor, or the management of resources, or the accumulation of national wealth, but as the circulation of money. The economy is the sum of all those transactions in which money changes hands, and its size and growth are calculated by estimating this sum. Second, the idea of the economy belongs to the postimperial era of nation-states, in which human sociality is understood as a series of equivalent national units. Each of these units claims the right to its own national state, replacing the earlier system of European colonial empires, and each is thought to be composed of a series of distinct socio-technical spaces: a society, an economy, and a culture (Mitchell 2002). Third, the emergence of the idea that state, society, economy, and culture exist as separate spheres, which collectively fill the space of the nation-state, coincided with the twentieth-century development of the social and cultural sciences as distinct professional and academic fields. Political science, sociology, economics, and anthropology (and the study of national literatures and histories in the case of Western societies) each contributed to the making of its respective object, providing it with concepts, calculations, agents, and methods of evaluation. Portrayed as merely an *object* of knowledge, the economy, along with these other spheres, was in fact enmeshed in the new forms of academic expertise and professional knowledge.

Acknowledging the role of economics and other professional expertise in making the economy does not mean that the economy is just a "representation" or merely a "social construction." Making the economy involved a wide range of socio-technical projects that embedded people and things in new machineries of calculation, new techniques of accounting, and new impulsions of discipline and desire. The development of marketing and brand identity, the management of the flow of money by corporate and national banks, New Deal programs such as electrification and the building of dams, colonial development schemes and the postwar projects of development agencies and the World Bank: all contributed to the organization of worlds that could now be described and measured as the economy.

Firmly established by the 1950s, the modern idea of the economy was soon subject to criticism. Researchers pointed out that its measurement does not take proper account of unpaid labor, especially the work of maintaining and reproducing households performed largely by women. It cannot measure illegal, unreported, or unregistered economic activity, such as the global arms trade or the informal, small-scale farming, manufacturing, and commerce that play a large role in many countries. It treats the natural world only as resources to be consumed and cannot express the cost of the exhaustion of nonrenewable resources, the destruction of species, or irreversible changes in the global climate.

These criticisms were made by writers mostly operating outside the academic discipline of economics. But even economists began to acknowledge the increasing difficulty of accurately measuring or describing the economy. The growth in the production of film and music, tourism and information, telecommunications and the Internet, legal and consulting services, health care, and other forms of expertise and culture created economies whose products seem increasingly ethereal. Even in the case of consumer goods such as food, clothing, cars, and electronics, the creation of value through brand identity and through the shaping of fashion and taste has made the economic world seem less material and more difficult to measure or predict.

These changes in the economy have sometimes been described in American cultural studies, as in cultural studies more broadly, as marking the transition to a postmodern stage of capitalism (Jameson 1991; Lowe and Lloyd 1997). Such accounts homogenize the changes and attribute them to the force of an underlying logic of the development of capital. They also invoke an earlier era, modernity, in which representations were more firmly anchored to material realities. The genealogy of the concept of the economy cautions against this view. There was never an era in which a simple, material reality could be captured and represented as the economy. The possibility of representing the economy as the object of economic knowledge rested upon the proliferation of socio-technical processes of representation. It was the spread of new forms of representational practice that made it possible to attempt the social-scientific representation of that world. The economy, the new object of economics, was constructed out of not only numerical quantifications but an entire process of branding, product development, information production, and image-making that formed both the possibility of the modern economy and the increasing impossibility of its representation.

The contemporary idea of the economy has also been affected by the rise of neoliberal economics, which has turned attention away from the economy and back toward the seemingly simpler idea of "the market." Like economies, however, markets must be made. They are produced not by the natural working of self-interest but by the complex organization of desire, agency, price, ownership, and dispossession. Economics (especially in a wider sense of the term, encompassing fields such as accounting and management) helps to produce these arrangements, by providing instruments of calculation and other necessary equipment (Callon 1998), just as it helped to produce the economy. However, while the idea of the economy refers to a specific territory, usually the nation-state, the market has no particular spatial connotation. It can refer to the trading floor of a futures exchange or a transnational network. Unlike the economy, therefore, it does not invoke the role of the state, as the power that governs economic space and defines its task as the management and growth of the economy and the nurturing and regulation of economic actors. The regulation of markets and the forming and governing of market agencies is dispersed at numerous levels.

The idea of the economy survives today as much as a political concept as an object of economic theory. A sign taped to the wall in the Democratic Party campaign headquarters for the 1992 U.S. presidential election proclaimed, "It's the economy, stupid!" Placed there, it is said, as a reminder of where the campaign should keep its focus, it reminds us today of the work that is done to make the existence of the economy appear obvious and its truths uncontestable. It also should remind us that the goal of fixing what the

economy refers to has remained surprisingly resilient. While the field of cultural studies (American and otherwise) has paid much attention to other organizing concepts, such as nation, class, gender, society, and of course culture itself, it has often left the idea of the economy untouched. There have been a number of interesting studies of different "representations" of the economy. These usually assume, however, that the economy itself remains as a kind of underlying material reality, somehow independent of the intellectual equipment and machinery of representation with which it is set up and managed. In the same way, academic economics is often criticized for misrepresenting the "true nature" of the economy. The task now is to account for the great success of economics and related forms of expertise in helping to make the economy in the first place.

25

Empire

Shelley Streeby

In the aftermath of the 2003 U.S. invasion of Iraq, it was often observed that the word "empire" was becoming increasingly popular as a way to describe the current form of U.S. power in the world. Many commentators noted that while the meanings of the word had previously been overwhelmingly negative, a host of best-selling books, policy statements, newspaper editorials, and other sources promoted the idea of an

American empire. One example among many was Vice President Dick Cheney's 2003 Christmas card, which contained the following quotation, attributed to Benjamin Franklin: "And if a sparrow cannot fall to the ground without His notice, is it probable that an empire can rise without His aid?"

As Cheney's citation of Franklin suggests, this embrace of the word "empire" was not really a new phenomenon. Even though the United States established its political independence from the British empire by winning the Revolutionary War, understandings of empire as necessarily tyrannical and as an Old World vice competed with arguments about the possible virtues of U.S. empire. As historian Richard Van Alstyne pointed out in his 1960 study *The Rising American Empire* (a title which, as he noted, "comes straight from George Washington"), many of the founders were invested in the idea of an American "imperium— a dominion, state, or sovereignty that would expand in population and territory, and increase in strength and power" (1). Such ideas were strengthened by the notion that civilization was moving westward, and that the United States would be the next (and perhaps last) great incarnation of civilization. The idea of a U.S. empire was also partly driven by fears of the other empires—British, French, and Spanish—that claimed vast territorial possessions in North America. In competition with these powerful imperial states, U.S. policymakers often claimed, in spite of the much longer presence of indigenous peoples, a natural right to the continent based on geographical factors as well as the migrations of U.S. settlers.

Thomas Jefferson's Louisiana Purchase of 1803, which massively increased the size of the United States, went a long way toward realizing those continental ambitions. And Jefferson's statement that U.S. territorial expansion enlarged the space of freedom and enabled an "empire for liberty" has been echoed by many subsequent empire-builders. But the founders' readings in republican political theory also provoked debates about whether a great extent of territory might endanger a republic and ultimately lead to its downfall. Some versions of republicanism (notably those influenced by Montesquieu) warned that the pursuit of empire threatened a republic with corruption and decline through overextension and by engendering luxury, incorporating alien peoples, and promoting the maintenance of standing armies. Such fears are displayed in Thomas Cole's famous set of paintings called *The Course of Empire* (1833–66), which represent what he and many others imagined as the five stages of empire: the Savage State, the Arcadian or Pastoral State, Consummation, Destruction, and Desolation (A. Miller 1993). While Jefferson and the U.S. empire-builders who followed him hoped that exceptional American conditions would prevent the United States from sharing the fate of other empires, the darker strains of republican theory continued to provide resources for those who wanted to argue against the nation's imperial ambitions.

Comparisons to other empires and questions about the annexation of new lands also provoked both pro- and antiwar arguments during the U.S.-Mexico War (1846–48). Along with the more familiar allusions to the Roman empire, Spain and England increasingly became important reference points for such comparisons. On the one hand, U.S. Americans sometimes imagined themselves as the heirs to the Spanish empire in the New World. The popularity of W. H. Prescott's *History of the Conquest of Mexico* during the 1840s inspired many soldiers and commentators to imagine that U.S. armed forces were retracing the steps of the Spanish invaders as they marched on Mexico City during the war. On the other hand, such a comparison was potentially disturbing because of the Black Legend: the idea that the Spanish conquest of the New World was uniquely bloody and vicious. And although the Black Legend positioned the British colonists as more enlightened and humane than the Spanish, mid-nineteenth-century events in India and Ireland also made the British empire a potentially unsettling point of comparison. In a powerful antiwar speech delivered in 1847, for instance, Boston Unitarian clergyman Theodore Parker (1863/1973, 26) compared the U.S. invasion of Mexico to England's "butchering" of Sikhs in India and seizure of lands in Ireland. Debates over the imperial annexation of new territories also raised divisive questions about the incorporation of heterogeneous elements—notably Catholics and nonwhite people—into the nation, as well as about the extension of slavery. During these years the issues of empire and slavery became fatally conjoined; soon after the United States increased its size at the expense of Mexico after the signing of the Treaty of Guadalupe Hidalgo, this conjunction would culminate in the U.S. Civil War.

While commentators such as Parker opposed the U.S.-Mexico War by calling the nation an empire and invoking pessimistic comparisons to other empires both classical and contemporaneous, many who supported the war tried to sidestep such comparisons by using other words to describe U.S. expansion. One especially influential formulation was coined in 1845 by *Democratic Review* editor John O'Sullivan, who argued that it was "our manifest destiny to overspread the continent allotted by Providence for the free development of our yearly multiplying millions" (quoted in Horsman 1981, 219). The concept of Manifest Destiny derived in part from earlier ideas about the Puritan settlers as God's chosen people, who were working out their destiny in the Promised Land. It also built on eighteenth-century Lockean arguments that possession of land was justified by use, as well as the Jeffersonian notion that the extension of agrarian democracy was coterminous with the extension of freedom. The use of the concept of Manifest Destiny instead of "empire" gave divine sanction to U.S. expansion and implied that it was a natural and nonviolent process. This concept even influenced subsequent scholarship by twentieth-century researchers, who tended to distinguish continental expansion from imperialism, thereby disconnecting earlier moments of U.S. empire-building from later imperial conflicts, such as those of the 1890s.

In much of that scholarship, U.S. wars in the Caribbean and the Pacific during and after the 1890s were regarded as part of an aberrant period in which the nation uncharacteristically acted as an empire.

This disavowal was coincident with the coinage, around 1860 according to the *Oxford English Dictionary* (*OED*), of the word "imperialism," which has very different connotations than the much older word "empire." In its earliest and subsequent usages, imperialism was often associated with "arbitrary" or "despotic" rule, as well as the "advocacy of imperial interests," including "trading interests and investments." The *OED* even states: "In the United States, imperialism is similarly applied to the new policy of extending the rule of the American people over foreign countries, and of acquiring and holding distant dependencies, in the way in which colonies and dependencies are held by European states." That the *OED* writers, who compiled their definitions in the early twentieth century, would see U.S. imperialism as a "new policy" shows the pervasiveness of the idea that U.S. empire-building before the 1890s did not count as imperialism.

The definition of a "new" U.S. imperialism included three key elements. First, it depended upon the identification of similarities between U.S. imperialism and the various European imperialisms that were in their heyday during the late nineteenth and twentieth centuries. Although many advocates of the Spanish-American War (1898) argued, especially early on, that U.S. forces were liberators rather than conquerors, comparisons to European-style imperialisms became more difficult to dismiss as the United States turned from warring with Spain to warring with Filipinos, Cubans, and others who sought independence. Second, the concept of a new U.S. empire (LaFeber 1963)

was based on an understanding of imperialism as necessarily involving the extension of rule over "distant places," particularly places located overseas. Third, this new definition emphasized the pursuit of commercial "interests and investments," as well as the establishment of military bases, in addition to or instead of the formal annexation of new lands.

Of course, none of these elements was particularly new. During the U.S.-Mexico War, antiwar activists pressed the comparison to the British and Spanish empires; the United States had long had an interest in trying to take over or control "distant places," such as the islands in the Caribbean; and the notion of a commercial empire extends back to the early days of the United States and was strongly articulated by Abraham Lincoln's secretary of state, William Steward, among others. While it is true that after the 1890s the nation tended to back away from the previous pattern of annexing new territories and making them into states, this development was more of an innovation in the administration of empire than an absolute break with the past. But by viewing late-nineteenth-century U.S. imperialism as a new development, and by distinguishing continental expansionism from overseas imperialism, U.S. commentators promoted the notion that the pursuit of empire was an exceptional episode in U.S. history, rather than the norm.

This view of the 1890s as an aberration is especially ironic given the extent of the U.S. military presence and the reach of U.S. commercial imperialism in the decades that followed the 1890s. In his 1904 corollary to the Monroe Doctrine, for instance, Theodore Roosevelt stated that "chronic wrongdoing, or an impotence which results in a general loosening of the ties of civilization, may in America, as elsewhere, ultimately require intervention by some civilized nation, and in the Western Hemisphere . . . may force the U.S., however reluctantly . . . to the exercise of an international police power" (quoted in Stephanson 1995, 107). This understanding of the United States as a police force devoted to the defense of civilization would be used to justify multiple interventions in Latin America and elsewhere, from the early twentieth century to the present. Indeed, although Theodore Roosevelt has often been contrasted with Woodrow Wilson, largely because of Roosevelt's frank endorsement of empire-building and Wilson's emphasis on creating international institutions, the two shared a vision of the United States as a sort of "world cop" (Hardt and Negri 2000, 177). Although Wilson was ostensibly devoted to preserving peace and Roosevelt was committed to the war of civilization against savagery, Wilson was also determined to establish governments he approved of in strategically important locations, and so sent U.S. troops to Russia, Mexico, Haiti, Central America, and the Dominican Republic. Perhaps Wilson's most important contribution to the empire question was his idealistic, Jeffersonian recasting of U.S. imperialism as the protection and extension of universal values; his declaration, in 1917, that the nation was devoted to "making the world safe for democracy" has often been echoed by more recent empire-builders.

After World War II, U.S. military involvement in other parts of the world, especially Asia, was often said to be motivated by the need to contain communism and to counter Soviet expansion. According to many Cold War thinkers, it was the Soviet Union, and not the United States, that was imperialist; this logic suggested that an aggressive U.S. military policy was a defensive response to the threat that communist expansion posed to capitalist democracies. Within such binary schemas, the United States was cast in the role of the defender of freedom and liberty, and therefore its interventions around the world were not viewed by U.S. policymakers as imperialist. This helps to explain why, during the Cold War years, so many historians, literary critics, and other American studies scholars maintained that the United States was not and had never been an empire, except perhaps for that brief period during and after the Spanish-American War. Scholars such as diplomatic historian William Appleman Williams, who argued that empire had been a "way of life" from the beginning of the nation, were definitely in the minority during the Cold War years.

The question of empire was posed anew during the Vietnam War and particularly in educational activists' battles for ethnic studies during the 1960s and 1970s. Social movements pressing for justice, including the antiwar movement and the movements of people of color working both outside and inside the academy, helped to make U.S. empire an issue in revisionist scholarly work of the Vietnam War era and after. We could go back even further, of course, and find critical work on U.S. imperialism, often linked to the collective endeavors of social movements and to interdisciplinary concerns, in the writings of W. E. B. Du Bois,

Americo Paredes, C. L. R. James, Ricardo Flores Magón, Lucy Parsons, and many others. In the late 1970s and 1980s, the literatures and theories of decolonization, work on internal colonialism in U.S. ethnic studies (especially Native American studies and Chicano studies), as well as the impact of postcolonial studies, all helped to make U.S. empire visible as a problem. When we define American studies in terms of programs and institutions, we need to recognize how it emerged as a post–World War II form of area studies that had ties on some campuses to the CIA, the Cold War national security state, and the imperatives of U.S. empire. But we should also attend to what George Lipsitz (2001, 27) has called "the other American studies, the organic grassroots theorizing about culture and power that has informed cultural practice, social movements, and academic work for many years."

From that perspective, the influential 1993 anthology *Cultures of U.S. Imperialism*, edited by Amy Kaplan and Donald Pease, is best understood as an important contribution to ongoing debates within American studies and cultural studies, not as an origin point for work on U.S. empire. The book grew out of a 1991 conference that was organized, according to Pease (1993, 22), "in the shadow of three macropolitical events—the end of the cold war, the Persian Gulf War, and the Columbus quincentennial." Each of these events, which involved multiple imperial histories, generated public debates that helped to shape the conversation about empire in American studies. Many of the essays in the volume linked recent episodes of U.S. empire-building to longer histories of imperialism, and several extended insights from contemporary cultural studies research (Ashcroft et al. 1989; Gilroy 1987, 1993). Michael Rogin, for instance, explored how political spectacles of covert operations in popular culture contributed to an amnesia about U.S. empire. And in her introductory essay, Kaplan (1993, 5) similarly focused on imperial amnesia as she argued that "imperialism has been simultaneously formative and disavowed in the foundational discourses of American Studies." She thereby helped to inspire a large body of new work on forgotten histories of U.S. imperialism.

While many American studies scholars responded to this call by focusing on imperial amnesia and hoping that the naming of the empire would help to challenge it, public policymakers and popular pundits were busy remembering and championing that history, although often in highly selective and misleading ways (Kaplan 2002). This does not mean that the idea of an empire was universally acknowledged and endorsed. Even within the administration of George W. Bush, there is still some discomfort with the word "empire": when reporters asked Dick Cheney about his Christmas card, he denied that the United States was really an empire and jokingly blamed his wife Lynne for choosing Franklin's quotation. It is certainly true, however, that naming and exposing the empire does not automatically undermine its power, especially at a moment when U.S. empire is being identified, once again, with "universal" values such as democracy and freedom. As Kaplan (2004, 6) suggests, an American studies critique of U.S. empire must involve not only "disinterring the buried history of imperialism," but also "debating its meanings and lessons for the present" and showing "how U.S. interventions have worked from the perspective of comparative imperialisms, in relation to other historical changes and movements across the globe."

26

Environment

Vermonja R. Alston

In its broadest sense, the term "environment" indexes contested terrains located at the intersections of political, social, cultural, and ecological economies. In its narrowest sense, it refers to the place of nature in human history. In each of these usages, representations of the natural world are understood as having decisive force in shaping environmental policy and the environmental imagination. Conservation politics were inspired by interpretations of particular places as untouched by the industrial revolutions of the nineteenth century, while much contemporary ecocriticism has continued the mainstream preoccupation with wilderness traditions, pastoralism, and the Romantic impulse of nature writing. Environmental justice activists and some ecofeminists have questioned these preoccupations, as have indigenous and postcolonial writers and scholars across the Americas who point out that imaginative writing about "nature" has a long tradition among colonial settlers attempting to mythologize and indigenize their relationships to place. This polyphony of competing voices and genealogies may be best understood as an interplay among many environmentalisms.

In his *Keywords*, Raymond Williams (1983, 219, 223) notes that "[n]ature is perhaps the most complex word in the language . . . Nature has meant the 'countryside', the 'unspoiled places', plants and creatures other than man . . . nature is what man has not made." At the heart of this conception of nature lies the sense that there exists inherent, universal, and primary law beyond the corrupt societies of "man." While "environment" is not one of Williams's keywords, "ecology" does make an appearance, even though the term was not common in the English language until the middle of the twentieth century. Ecology, defined as the "study of the relations of plants and animals with each other and their habitat," replaced environment, a word in use since the early nineteenth century but derived from the mid-fourteenth-century borrowing from Old French, *environ*, meaning to surround or enclose (111). In American cultural studies, "environment" has undergone a renewal among scholars and activists, owing in part to resistance to the bracketing of "nature" and "wilderness" as privileged sites of national identity, and its acceptance as a shorthand for research on ecosystems and diverse environmental movements. Curiously, even as the term "ecology" is used less often, it has been condensed to a prefix in the names of social and intellectual movements, notably ecocriticism and ecofeminism.

In the late eighteenth century, a transatlantic Romantic movement coincided with U.S. independence to produce a nationalism whereby nature, understood as "wilderness," came to underwrite a new national identity. A harmonious relationship with sublime, wild nature became a way of articulating civilized U.S. American purity against the perceived decadence of Europe. With Henry David Thoreau's version of Transcendentalism, "wildness" came to symbolize absolute freedom: "in wildness is the preservation of the World" (R. Nash 1982, 84). For Thoreau, preservation of wilderness was important for the preservation of civilization, though his own notion of wilderness was the pastoral, a liminal space between the technologically driven pursuit of progress and the savagery of wilderness. Lawrence Buell (1995) locates the "American environmental imagination" in the canonization of Thoreau as a naturalist by late-nineteenth-century ecologists such as John Muir. Muir developed an environmental ethos that was later central to the philosophy of deep ecology: first, abuse of nature is wrong; second, "nature has intrinsic value and consequently possesses at least the right to exist" (Payne 1996, 5). During this period characterized by increasing fear of Eastern urbanization, environmental protection became synonymous with wilderness preservation. Thus urban environments, along with the diverse human populations who inhabit them, mediated (and continue to mediate) perceptions of nonhuman, "natural" environments.

The narrow sense of "environment" as a discourse on wilderness protection has fueled criticism by ecofeminists, urban ecologists, and environmental justice activists. Ecofeminists suggest that human relationships with the natural world have been engendered by a masculinist impulse to imagine and experience the land as feminine. For Annette Kolodny (1975, 58), the pastoral impulse is at once a desire for exclusive possession, leading to exploitation, and an urge to protect the primal forest, so as "to return in order to begin anew." In response, ecofeminism attempts to deconstruct the nature/culture dualism that situates nature, women, and ethnic minorities as passive "others" against which the Anglo-American male constructs himself. By linking the salvation of the planet Earth to issues of social equality, ecofeminism contributes to our understanding of the place of human structures of domination and power in environmental change. Yet the process of deconstructing the nature/culture dualism also risks enshrining a gender dualism. The problem is that neither "women" nor "ethnic minorities" are unitary categories of analysis. Rather they are diverse groups differentially situated with respect to their environments, communities, and identities (Di Chiro 1996).

In response to this problem, Marxist streams of ecofeminism have focused on issues of social class and environmental degradation, while grassroots environmental justice movements have successfully mobilized urban poor communities in the United States. In different ways, each has pointed out that the anti-urban bias of preservation politics has often resulted in the creation of toxic ghettoes in cities while cordoning off scenic wonderlands. William Cronon (1995) argues that wilderness preservation may encourage the migration of dirty industries to poor communities whose members lack access to networks of power; Robert D. Bullard (2002) adds that the term "environmental racism" more accurately describes the environmental policies and industry practices that provide benefits to whites while shifting costs to people of color. Environmental justice movements, including the "environmentalism of the poor" in developing countries, place the survival of poor and marginalized people at the center of environmental activism. These movements seek freedom from state-centered and international development projects that excrete the toxins of affluent nations and local communities into poor communities.

Environmental justice activists charge deep ecologists with ignoring the problems of social and economic inequality on a global scale. Deep ecologists counter with the charge that the environmental justice position is reformist and anthropocentric, too firmly rooted in human communities. In contrast, deep ecology establishes itself as biocentric or ecocentric. The advantage of the latter position lies in its emphasis on the notion that "everything is connected"; its disadvantage is that it can be accused of ventriloquizing a natural world that cannot speak for itself. Herein lies the central paradox: Speaking for a natural world is a representational practice requiring the intervention of an authorized human agent. Biocentrism's radical displacement of human agency means that a powerful speaking human subject vanishes into nature, setting up an ideological fantasy of a world of total equality

among humans, and between humans and nonhuman "nature" (van Wyck 1997). As Jim Tarter (2002, 213) puts this critique of biocentrism, "some live more downstream than others," and those people tend to be poorer and darker, and to have little or no access to environmental policymakers. In short, biocentrism risks masking the relationship between environmental exploitation and human exploitation. By contrast, the broader sense of the term "environment" can enable a questioning of relations of power, agency, and responsibility to human and nonhuman environments.

27

Ethnicity

Henry Yu

The term "ethnicity" gained widespread currency in the mid- to late twentieth century, naming a process by which individuals or groups came to be understood, or to understand themselves, as separate or different from others. This meaning of ethnicity commonly referred to the consciousness of exclusion or subordination, though it also indexed social practices—language, religion, rituals, and other patterns of behavior—that define the content of a group's culture. The spread of this theory of ethnic culture created two mutually exclusive, analytically separate categories: "ethnicity," defined as cultural traits, was utterly divorced from the workings of the physical body, defined as "race." When anthropologists such as Franz

Boas (1940) of Columbia University and sociologists and anthropologists from the University of Chicago began to teach students in the early twentieth century that cultural characteristics were the most interesting social phenomena for study, they spread at the same time the idea that any attention to physical characteristics was intellectually inappropriate. Attacking justifications for racial hierarchy grounded in biology, social scientists used the concept of ethnicity as a weapon against racial thinking.

"Ethnicity" thus became the term that named an alternative to the earlier biological emphases of racial hierarchy. In *Man's Most Dangerous Myth: The Fallacy of Race* (1942), one of the most significant anti-racist books published in the twentieth century, anthropologist Ashley Montagu argued that race as a category of analysis should be dropped as a dangerous invention, and that "ethnic group" was a more neutral term. Ethnicity became synonymous with cultural difference, and any theory dependent upon physical characteristics was dismissed as racist. Similarly, the attempt by anthropologists such as Ruth Benedict (1934) to array societies in a spectrum of cultures aided this flattening of all human distinction into a matter of cultural or ethnic difference. Possibilities for the elimination of racial prejudice (defined specifically as the expression of conscious attitudes about a group of people considered racially different) depended upon a very specific definition of race as a form of consciousness. Race was a myth because it had no basis in biology, yet race as a consciousness about the importance of a set of physical attributes could still exist. Because consciousness of race was claimed to be merely one form of ethnic consciousness, race and ethnicity were concepts simultaneously distinct and indistinct from each other.

The subsuming of race under the broader category of ethnicity was both a significant attempt at offering a solution to racial conflict and a sign of the persistent difficulties with distinguishing between the two. As a matter of consciousness, the racial culture of "Negro Americans" was no different in kind than the ethnic culture of "Polish Americans," and purely cultural processes of assimilation could eliminate all differences between them. However, there were chronic difficulties with the distinction between race and ethnicity. W. Lloyd Warner and Leo Srole's widely read *Social Systems of American Ethnic Groups* (1945) exemplified the paradox inherent in this distinction. According to them, the host society accepted some groups more easily than others. Class differences tended to fragment ethnic groups, and the class mobility of some members of ethnic groups was the major determinant of acceptance within the host society. Most difficult to accept, however, were those groups seen to be racially different. Although Warner and Srole argued that group conflict was a matter of ethnic identification (in the sense that the host society viewed a group as different, and the group viewed themselves as different), they also assumed that there was some characteristic that set apart ethnic groups that were racially defined. The "future of American ethnic groups seems to be limited," Warner and Srole concluded; "it is likely that they will be quickly absorbed. When this happens one of the great epochs of

American history will have ended and another, that of race, will begin" (295).

This sense that a great epoch of ethnicity was about to end at mid-century was a product of a crucial social transformation in the decades following the explicitly racialized immigration exclusion policies of the late nineteenth and early twentieth centuries. By the 1920s, U.S. social scientists (some of whom were themselves either migrants or children of migrants) had created a body of theories of race and culture that had grown out of studying mass migration (Yu 2001). The most significant of these studies were associated with sociologists such as William I. Thomas (1918–20) and Robert E. Park (1950) at the University of Chicago. Park and Thomas were at the forefront of an attempt to advance a new theory about social interaction based upon the concept of culture. In opposition to earlier theories about the importance of inherited characteristics and physical bodies in determining human behavior, cultural theories emphasized the centrality of consciousness, of the mental attitudes and forms of self-understanding that people communicated through writing, speech, and other media. One of the most important of these theories concerned what Park and Thomas labeled "cultural assimilation," the process by which two groups communicated with each other and came to share common experiences, memories, and histories. Applied specifically to U.S. immigrants, the theory of assimilation promised that any migrant, no matter how different in language, religion, or other social practices at the moment of arrival, could learn to assimilate national cultural norms. This historically progressive vision of the United States became the foundation for later arguments about ethnic consciousness, self-identity, and group identity.

At the same time, the twentieth-century "alchemy of race" (Jacobson 1998) had its origins in the mechanisms by which European immigrants who were defined at the beginning of the century as racially different came to be seen as "white" ethnics by the end of the century (Brodkin 1998). Along with the intellectual transformation wrought by cultural theory, popular writers such as Louis Adamic, who was himself of recent immigrant ancestry, pushed for an overcoming of the nativist divide between old and new U.S. Americans. In books such as *From Many Lands* (1940) and *Nation of Nations* (1944), Adamic reconceived the United States as a land of immigrants, subsuming what had earlier been major dividing lines such as religion and language into mere differences of ethnic culture. At the same time (and with Adamic's assistance), organizations such as the National Council of Christians and Jews, founded in 1928, were striving to unify Protestants, Catholics, Orthodox Christians, and Jews into a so-called Judeo-Christian tradition. This period also saw widespread mass-cultural arguments for the end of religious discrimination, perhaps most visibly in 1950s Hollywood motion pictures such as *The Ten Commandments* (1956) and *Ben-Hur* (1959). The focus upon the assimilation of religious differences, powerfully propelled by wartime propaganda against the genocidal science of Nazism, helped label anti-Semitism and anti-Catholicism as un-American.

By the end of the 1950s, class mobility fueled by the postwar Montgomery G.I. Bill and federal subsidies of suburban housing had made Adamic's dream of an amalgamation of new and old seem viable.

The truth is that such programs of social engineering were predominantly focused on men able to pass as white. Immigrants who had been treated in the period between 1890 and 1920 as racially different (Slavs, Jews, Southern Europeans such as Italians, Greeks, and Armenians) were now transformed into white ethnics, mere varieties of white people. Just as dividing lines over religion, which had seemed intractable a generation before, were now reduced to mere denominational differences, all such culturally defined elements of difference had disappeared into a generic whiteness marked only superficially by vestiges of ethnic culture. Ironically, the civil rights movement of the 1950s helped reinforce this process of ethnic transformation. Jewish American intellectuals of the 1930s and 1940s had been at the forefront of political coalitions with African Americans seeking civil rights. Similarities in discrimination and exclusion at work, and in the legal segregation of housing and public facilities, had drawn Jewish and African Americans together to fight for civil rights. However, paralleling the larger transformation of white ethnics, Jewish Americans by the end of the civil rights era had become solidly white, even if anti-Semitism remained in vestigial and virulent forms. The civil rights movement for blacks ended up helping immigrant groups that previously had been the targets of racial nativism to amalgamate into a new ethnic "whiteness."

Despite these formidable intellectual and political problems, "ethnicity" has continued to be used widely as a description of and prescription for social life. Indeed, the acceptance and eventual celebration of ethnic difference was one of the most significant transitions of the twentieth century. Coincident with the increasing awareness of migration at the beginning of the century, a cosmopolitan appreciation of exotic difference arose. Writing in the days before World War I, a number of New York intellectuals embraced the rich diversity of the city, forecasting that the eclectic mix of global migrants was the future of U.S. society. Randolph Bourne's vision of a "transnational America" (1916) and Horace Kallen's description of "cultural pluralism" (1915) argued against the xenophobia that fueled the immigration exclusion acts of the same period, replacing it with an embrace of the different. The consumption by elite whites of the music and art of the Harlem Renaissance in the 1920s, along with periodic fads for Oriental art and so-called primitive tribal objects, reflected an embrace of the exotic as valuable. The celebration of exoticism in theories about the cosmopolitan self laid the groundwork for two major developments concerning ethnicity. The first was the theoretical foundation for the commercialization of ethnic difference; the second was the creation of a new definition of elite, enlightened whiteness.

Beginning with the fascination with exotic art forms in modernism, but also embodied in the hunger for ethnic food and objects, a tasteful appreciation of the exotic became part of an educational program to combat racism and ignorance in the 1960s. At the same time that education was touted as the answer to race relations, ethnic music and other forms of exotic art and entertainment were offered at first as alternatives to the mass productions of popular culture, and by the 1990s as important commodities distributed and consumed in the marketplace. Interestingly, the rise and spread of a cosmopolitan embrace of exotic difference helped expand the boundaries of whiteness. One of the ways in which those individuals formerly excluded as racially or ethnically suspect could "whiten" themselves was by embracing cosmopolitan ideas. Those who continued to express racist opinions were subsumed under the newly enlarged rubric of white racists (a category that "whitened" former ethnics at the same time that it tarred them as ignorant bigots of the lower classes). The embrace of cosmopolitan ideals offered a way of becoming an elite, enlightened white. Whether it was black music or Chinese food, an appreciation of exotic difference signaled one's aspiration to a higher class status. These ideas were spread through advertising and by an education system that began in the 1940s to promote this outlook on ethnicity and class.

By the end of the twentieth century, objects associated with ethnicity enjoyed a popular boom as commercial goods. Ethnic objects that had assumed the status of collectible art (such as African tribal masks and Native American totem poles); items of everyday use (such as Chinese woks and chopsticks or Scottish tartan kilts); performances of identity that could be consumed (ethnic music and dance): all were packaged as desirable objects of consumption. Ethnicity was something to be collected by a tasteful consumer able to appreciate an array of objects. This commercialization of ethnicity also allowed those identified as different to turn that identification into an object with value. Musical styles such as rhythm and blues, rock and roll, soul, rap, and hip-hop were marketed through an association with their black origins. By the 1970s, the commercialization of ethnicity extended to those ethnics who had been targets of xenophobia but were now comfortably white. White ethnics could continue to express cosmopolitan appreciation for the exoticism of nonwhites, but they could also embrace signs of their own ethnicity without fear of exclusion from the privileges of whiteness. White ethnicity was thus securely different from nonwhite racial ethnicity, and white ethnics drew upon a history as victims of discrimination in ways that attenuated their own enjoyment of the privileges of being white, even as it evoked parallels to the historical suffering of nonwhites.

There are many long-term legacies of this history of ethnicity, including the rise of "whiteness studies" and the current use of the term "ethnicity" in the U.S. media to describe a wide array of subnational and transnational conflicts. The ethnic cultural theory that underwrites these legacies derived its popular appeal from the combination of two elements. One was the description of how European immigrants were transformed into white ethnics during the mid-twentieth century; the other was the hope that this social process would also work for U.S. Americans subordinated as nonwhite. However, the extension of what Nathan Glazer (1983) called the "ethnic analogy" to the problems of racial hierarchy has often foundered because of a widespread belief that ethnicity is a matter of choice. This mistake is a direct result of the way the concept was modeled upon the extension of the privileges of white supremacy to those who could voluntarily erase signs of their foreign origins, and the withholding of those privileges from those who could not. The process of forgetting the historical origins of ethnicity in white supremacy continues today in arguments about its definition.

28

Exceptionalism

Donald E. Pease

Given the significance of the keyword "exceptionalism" within the field of American studies, it is ironic that the word is not originally an "American" coinage. Joseph Stalin devised the phrase "the heresy of American Exceptionalism" in 1929 to justify his excommunication of the Lovestoneites from the ranks of the Communist International (J. Alexander 1981; Tyrell 1991). The Lovestoneites were a faction whose leader, Jay Lovestone, had already broken with the American Communist Party over what was then referred to as the national question, specifically the question of whether and how to work with established U.S. trade unions. The Lovestoneites provoked Stalin's condemnation when they proposed that the United States was "unique" because it lacked the social and historical conditions that had led to Europe's economic collapse. In sharp contrast, the founders of American studies as an academic discipline (or interdiscipline) reappropriated the term in the 1930s in an effort to portray the United States as destined to perform a special role in the world of nations. By installing a uniquely "American" exceptionalism as the foundational tenet of American studies, the field's founders elevated the United States into a model that offered European societies an image of a future liberated from the incursions of both Marxism and socialism.

In having emerged at the site of the geopolitical face-off between the United States and the Soviet Union, "exceptionalism" delineated the irreducible incommensurability of the two global powers. The fundamental recasting that the term underwent in this context transposed it into a multilayered academic discourse: as an explanatory framework, exceptionalism supplied scholars of U.S. culture and society with the horizon of intelligibility that shaped their research practice; as an interpretive paradigm, it regulated how they went about identifying, selecting, formulating, and resolving scholarly problems; as the keystone for interdisciplinary pedagogy, the term supplied fields of inquiry across the humanities and the social sciences with an overarching orientation; as an ethos, it codified the attitudes and beliefs through which "Americanists" (in and out of the academy) practiced their mode of national belonging. Throughout the Cold War era, American studies research, teaching, and publication proved themselves indispensable to the state by constructing a nationalist and, ultimately, an imperialist discourse out of the exceptionalist norms that they propagated throughout Europe and the so-called Third World.

The discourse of exceptionalism may be best characterized by its account of the United States's unique place in world history—the "redeemer nation," "conqueror of the world's markets," and, more recently, the "global security state" (Commager 1947; Hartz 1955; P. Miller 1960; Lipset 1963; Bush 2001). But this discourse drew its structure out of its difference from the historical trajectories that it attributed to Europe, to the Soviet Union, and to the Third World. The exceptionalist paradigm described U.S. uniqueness in terms of what the nation lacked—a landed aristocracy, a feudal monarchy, a territorial empire, a society hierarchized by class, a deeply anchored socialist tradition. Exceptionalist historians noted these "lacks" in order to portray the U.S. nation-state not merely as different from, but also as qualitatively better than, the European nation-states whose social orders were described as having been devastated by Marxism (Commager 1947; Hartz 1955; Bell 1960; Lipset 1963). The discourse of American exceptionalism imagined a Soviet empire that threatened to overthrow the world order through the spread of revolutionary socialism, and it represented Europe as especially susceptible to this threat.

American exceptionalism was thus an academic discourse, a political doctrine, and a regulatory ideal assigned responsibility for defining, supporting, and developing the U.S. national identity. But the power of the doctrine to solicit the belief that the United States was unencumbered by Europe's historical traditions depended upon the recognition of European observers for its validation. In the transition from World War II to the Cold War, widely read U.S. consensus historians such as Arthur Schlesinger, Jr. (1945) and Henry Steele Commager (1947) cited Alexis de Tocqueville's nineteenth-century account of his travels through the United States in *Democracy in America* (1835/2004) as definitive verification of the doctrine of exceptionalism. Daniel Bell (1960), observing that Tocqueville had found U.S. political society lacking in the feudal traditions that had precipitated the violent confrontations in France's moment of revolutionary transition, grounded his "end of ideology" thesis upon this absence. Louis Hartz advanced a similar claim in *The Liberal Tradition in America* (1955) that the absence of class conflict from a liberal capitalist order had rendered impossible the emergence of socialism within U.S. territorial borders. In arriving at this thesis, Hartz depicted Frederick Jackson Turner's "frontier thesis" as the articulation of a complementary representation of American exceptionalism. Turner famously described the frontier as the space on the map where lingering European influences were perfected into an absence through the inexhaustible wilderness promised to all of the "Americans" who answered the call of the wild frontier (F. Turner 1893; Slotkin 1973). By describing the nation's past as lacking the history of class antagonism that they posited as the precondition for world communism, American studies scholars cooperated with policymakers and the press in constructing a culture of national uniqueness whose narrative themes informed U.S. citizens' imaginary relations to the Cold War state. In doing so, they disseminated a specifically cultural supplement to the political nationalism promoted by the state.

Practitioners of the "Myth and Symbol" school of American studies endowed the cultural forms and historical events under their analysis with traits that further corroborated exceptionalist assumptions. Scholars ranging from Henry Nash Smith (1950) to Richard Slotkin (1973) produced a thematically coherent tradition that they described as the repository of the collective representations, communally held images, and core narratives (myths and symbols) that underpinned a historically continuous "American civilization." These scholars articulated trans-historical themes (assimilation, political liberation, cultural rebirth, and social mobility) to the national myths through which they were idealized (the melting pot, the endless frontier, American Adam, Virgin Land) (H. Smith 1950; R. Lewis 1955; L. Marx 1964; Slotkin 1973). These mythic aspects of self-representation became the deeply engrained tropes through which U.S. citizens conceptualized and legitimated the uniqueness of their national identity. Events on a world scale were thereafter assimilated to this cultural typology that was made to translate them.

U.S. policymakers depended upon this academic discourse to authorize their practices of governance, while for historians and literary scholars it became the principle by which they decided what events to give representation in the historical record and what literary and cultural works to include in the U.S. canon. Historians and political theorists approached the past in search of historical confirmations of the nation's unique mission and destiny. Examining the past became for scholars who were steeped in exceptionalist convictions a personal quest whereby they would understand the meaning of their "American" identity by uncovering the special significance of the nation's institutions (Chase 1949; P. Miller 1960).

The U.S. state presupposed the centrality of these convictions to its citizenry's identity whenever it found it necessary to justify "exceptions" to exceptionalist norms. In recasting Japanese internment camps, Operation Wetback, and the Vietnam War as deviations within the historical record, scholars aligned themselves with state policymakers by removing these troubling events from the orderly temporal succession organizing the nation's official history. But if the doctrine of exceptionalism has produced beliefs to which the state has regularly taken exception, the state has nevertheless needed the doctrine to solicit its citizenry's assent to its monopoly over actual and symbolic violence. In light of these contradictions, the relations between U.S. citizens' belief in exceptionalism and the state's production of exceptions to it might be best described in psychological terms as structures of denial. By enabling U.S. citizens to disavow the state's exceptions that threatened their beliefs, the discourse of exceptionalism regulated U.S. citizens' responses to historical events.

Throughout the Cold War, U.S. dominance was sustained through its self-representation as an exception to the rules through which it regulated the rest of the global order. But with the dismantling of the Soviet

Union and the formation of the European Union, the United States lost its threatening socialist-totalitarian-Russian antagonist as well as its destabilized, dependent European ally. This historical dismantling of the exceptionalist paradigm resulted in a fundamental reshaping of academic accounts of U.S. culture and society and its place in world history. American exceptionalism had legitimated U.S. global sovereignty by basing it upon representations of a dichotomized world order over which the United States exercised the legal power to rule. After the conditions that lent the exceptionalist frame its plausibility passed away, the disavowed underside of American exceptionalism suddenly reappeared. With the disappearance of the Cold War's macropolitical dichotomies, heterogeneous developments emerged that were irreducible to such stabilized oppositions. In the wake of American exceptionalism, the demands of a newly globalized world order required an understanding of the United States' embeddedness within transnational and transcultural forces rather than a reaffirmation of its splendid isolation from them.

During the Cold War, American exceptionalism had produced an image of U.S. national unity in which the significance of gender, class, race, and ethnic differences was massively downgraded. The discourse of exceptionalism erected the image of a hardworking, unified national monoculture to ward off the dangers posed by the globalizing of economic exchanges. It also represented internal differences between classes, genders, and ethnic groups as threatening to national unity. But racial, ethnic, and gender

minorities who refused to be aggregated within these marginalized spaces have effected fundamental recastings of the exceptionalist paradigm. New American studies scholarship has begun to document these anti-exceptionalist movements. This scholarship is characterized by its understanding of globalization (rather than exceptionalism) as its horizon of intelligibility, and its practitioners have supplanted the "frontier" and the "melting pot" with the "borderlands" and the "contact zone" as the cultural tropes that inform their scholarship (Anzaldúa 1987; Rowe 2000).

In the aftermath of this paradigm shift, American studies scholars have been compelled to confront the contradictory relationship between an increasingly postcolonial world and a U.S. monoculture that remains tethered to exceptionalist assumptions. Globalization does not merely require an increased understanding of "American" minority cultures and subcultures; it also demands an understanding of the relationships of these subnational formations to migrant and diasporic communities across the globe. In response to these demands, American studies scholars have redescribed the United States as one node in an interlocking network of commercial, political, and cultural forces, and have developed archives variously organized through the geographies of Aztlán, the Pacific Rim, the Afro-Caribbean, and the Transatlantic (Saldívar 1997; R. Wilson 2000; Giles 2001; Bogues 2003). Rather than construing American exceptionalism as the instrument for representing and evaluating these exchanges, these transnational and transregional models conceptualize social movements and modes of

cultural transmission as passing back and forth between disparate local and global systems of power.
These emergent forms of comparativist analysis describe cultural production in ways that facilitate an
understanding of the intricate and global relationships
that pertain among literary texts, historical explanations, and lived cultural experience.

Despite the rise of these nonexceptionalist and
post-exceptionalist forms of scholarship, the credo of
American exceptionalism has not lost its power to justify new policy. When President George W. Bush
(2001) described "9/11" as a fundamental transformation *of* history that took place *in* history ("Everything
changed after 9/11"), he added a new mytheme to the
mythology of exceptionalism. Bush associated the U.S.
monopoly on the legal use of global violence with the
intervention in human time of a higher law (what he
called his "higher father"). In doing so, he endowed
the doctrine of American exceptionalism with a metaphysical and arguably theological supplement, claiming that the preemptive violence through which the
United States would defend the globe against the
threat of Islamic terrorism was metaphysically superior to that of other nation-states. The apocalyptic and
Christian millennialist register of Bush's invocation of
this higher law has not merely reestablished the nation's claim to historical uniqueness; it has positioned
the United States outside the world of nations as *the*
divinely ordained exception. The future organization
of the field of American studies will depend on how
scholars respond to this latest turn in the discourse of
American exceptionalism.

29

Family

Carla L. Peterson

"Family" is one of the most widely invoked words today. Friends and colleagues talk about family. It is a
central topic in biography, autobiography, and fiction.
TV sitcoms, theater, and film regularly portray families
in their many variegated forms. In addition, family is
a significant point of reference in public policy,
whether in debates over welfare, AFDC (Aid to Families with Dependent Children), immigration laws, or,
most recently, "family values." The word has of course
a long history in U.S. culture. In 1869, for example,
Catharine Beecher and Harriet Beecher Stowe began
their book *The American Woman's Home* by posing the
question, "What, then, is the end designed by the
family state?" For them, the makeup of the family
state was self-evident: it consists of a "stronger and
wiser" father who "undergoes toil and self-denial to
provide a home," a mother who becomes a "self-
sacrificing laborer to train its inmates," and the inmates themselves, children (18). This family, the
Beechers insisted, is resolutely Christian.

The Beechers' definition of family suggests additional keywords. One set is "kinship," "blood," and
"lineage." Persons making up a family or bound
through kinship are biologically related by blood.
Linking descendants to progenitors across generations, blood creates lineage. Furthermore, the title of
the Beechers' book explicitly invokes the term

"home," which in turn brings to mind its frequent qualifier "domestic." The text itself pointedly distinguishes between "out-door," where the father labors, and the "domestic home"—a physical and emotionally charged space—realized by his labor. Finally, "family" invites inclusion of words like "patriarchy," "property," "woman," and "reproduction." The man of the family acquires and controls property, while the woman ensures its orderly transmission—in the form of both estate and blood—by producing legitimate heirs.

In his own musings on family, Raymond Williams (1976) argued that both the actuality and the image of the nuclear, bourgeois family were nineteenth-century "inventions" and that the term has in fact a richly diverse prehistory. "Family" derives from the Latin *famulus*, meaning servant, and *familia*, meaning household. Hence, the early English meaning of "family" was that of the "*household*, either in the sense of a group of servants or a group of blood-relations and servants living together in one house" (108) By extension, "familiar" came to connote feelings of friendship and intimacy born of "the experience of people living together in a household, in close relations with each other and well used to each other's ways" (109).

As inventions, definitions of family serve ideological purposes and often contradict historical reality. They are necessarily partial and incomplete. Contrary to the Beechers' contention, family is not a "state" but a malleable process; its connotations range from a delimited social practice involving specific persons and spaces, to broader notions of feeling and experience, and finally to metaphor. Yet each of these usages—even when extended and metaphoric—commonly works to limit the family's parameters; the family is seen as a system of inclusion that reserves the right to exclude strangers not related by blood, not descended from the same ancestor, not living under the same roof, not belonging to the same class or race.

Categories of inclusion and exclusion have all too often been rearticulated as "norm" and "deviance." These terms still dominate today's public debates about family. They reverberate, for example, in discussions of family values that define the social, religious (Christian), and sexual (heterosexual) *norms* that give birth to and maintain the family, or of gay marriage deemed *deviant* because its sexual practices disallow the production of children and therefore of legitimate families. Family, it turns out, is not a private, but very much a public, affair.

In the 1970s and 1980s, feminist historians, anthropologists, and literary critics such as Stephanie Coontz (1988), Michelle Rosaldo (1984), Alice Rossi (1973), Mary Ryan (1975), Gayle Rubin (1984), and Jane Tompkins (1985) embarked on the critical process of exposing the bourgeois family as a nineteenth-century invention. Working on topics as diverse as gender, slavery, sentimentality, and nationhood, they mined the archives and drew on earlier theoretical texts—notably John Locke's *Second Treatise of Civil Government* (1690/1988), John Stuart Mill's *The Subjection of Women* (1869/1976), and Frederick Engels's *Origin of the Family, Private Property and the State* (1884/1972)—to trace the evolution of the family from the American colonial period onward. In the earlier periods, domestic home and workplace formed a single economic unit located in the household; whether working on farms or in trades, all of a family's members—father, mother, and children—contributed to its sustenance. By the early nineteenth century, work became increasingly separated from household as fathers engaged in "out-door" labor, and the domestic work of mothers became privatized. This division of labor gave rise to the ideology of separate spheres.

Whereas writers like the Beechers naturalized this separate-spheres dichotomy, feminist thinkers—then and now—critiqued it as a patriarchal system of sexual and property relations supporting state interests; the father alone is entitled to property, which includes his wife and children, while the wife, as *feme covert*, is herself property and denied power of ownership. As remedy, nineteenth-century feminists such as Elizabeth Cady Stanton sought legal redress by demanding the right to contract. Later feminist theorists, however, have astutely pointed out how legal intervention frequently results in state intrusion that infringes on rights to privacy, particularly women's reproductive rights.

If the nineteenth-century bourgeois family was constructed as the norm, what can be said of other familial forms? *Who*, other than the bourgeoisie, creates families, and *how* might these be structured? Family, as noted earlier, often functions as a code word intended to stigmatize the deviant, those placed beyond the norm by virtue of their race, sexuality, class, or other social identities. Yet analysis of alternative family structures complicates this opposition between norm and deviance by forcing a shift from an either/or to a both/and paradigm, and, in so doing, challenges conventional systems of classification and evaluation.

The history of the African American family provides a wealth of examples. Defining slaves as property, U.S. law denied them the right to create families, rejecting both the legality of slave marriage and the legitimacy of its children. Bent on economic profit, slaveholders refused to acknowledge that slaves could experience familiarity, or feelings of intimacy for one another, thereby justifying the separation of slave families. To the extent that U.S. blacks in and out of slavery were able to form families, these were, as anthropologists such as Niara Sudarkasa (1988) have argued, extended kin families, adapted from African culture. In *Incidents in the Life of a Slave Girl* (1861), Harriet Jacobs described her childhood family as composed of a brother, an uncle, and a grandmother. They both follow and counter the bourgeois family's prescribed gender roles. Harriet's uncle is a nurturer. Her grandmother is the family's economic provider who strictly upholds the cult of true womanhood. If her adherence to true womanhood is normative, her application of it to slave women is deviant. Conversely, if her "male" role as primary provider appears deviant, her goal of capital accumulation (to purchase enslaved family members) is normative.

The postbellum era established the legality of African American marriage and family. A radical social event, it affirmed U.S. blacks' capacity to establish affective bonds just as it granted them the ability to acquire and transmit property. Many African American writers of the period took as their subject the untangling of what Jacobs called the "tangled skeins" of slave genealogies by reconstructing family lineages. Here too, the writers followed a normative impulse in reconstituting the family as bourgeois and patriarchal and emphasizing lineage and inheritance. Yet, once again this family structure may be seen as deviant in its application to African Americans. It diminished differences between whites and blacks and proved a powerful threat to the norms of white supremacy.

Even progressive public policymakers have not been able to discard binaristic notions in their evaluations of the black family. In *Family Limitation* (1914), social reformer Margaret Sanger promoted birth control as a means of relieving poor women burdened with children. But she came to envision it as a tool of eugenics meant to ensure that the "unfit"—poor immigrants and African Americans—would not reproduce. Fifty years later, ignoring both past and present social history, Daniel Patrick Moynihan (1965) issued a report that reduced the African American family to one single structure—the female-headed household—and classified it, in an uncanny echo of Jacobs's language, as a "tangle of pathology."

The concept of the household returns us to Williams's *familia*, in which physical and emotional familiarity brings non-kin persons together under one roof, albeit in forms far more complex than Williams intimates. Here too, U.S. history is rich in examples that defy binaristic thinking. In the antebellum period, defenders of the slave system in the South imagined the plantation as a family in which the slave master, as God's steward on earth, figured as the benevolent patriarch of those he oppressed. In the North, managers of the Lowell Mills cast their workplace as a family designed to protect working girls. Yet, this family pointedly excluded those who were racially different, and its patriarchal structure left its daughters without protection. In cities, boarding houses assembled individuals not related by blood who bonded to form households resistant to the pressures of urban life. The late nineteenth century gave rise to settlement houses such as Jane Addams's Hull House in Chicago. Seeking alternatives to marriage and traditional family life, middle-class women entered city slums to provide a gathering place and social services to the urban poor, all the while creating alternative family structures for themselves.

In its broadest extension, family becomes a metaphor for nation and even humankind. It functions as a site of contestation over who is familiar and who is a stranger, what is normal and what is deviant. Amy Kaplan (1998) has noted how nineteenth-century writers often cast the nation in familial terms as an expansion of the bourgeois, domestic home; its members are kin, belong to the same lineage, share the same blood. From a highly idealized perspective, postbellum writers imagined national Reconstruction as a romantic reunion between a masculine North and a feminine South, producing a new nation that nevertheless continued to exclude African Americans and other minority groups. Turning this convention on its head, African American writer Anna Julia Cooper (1892) cunningly represented the nation as a family squabble between a big brother (the North) and a spoiled, headstrong younger sister (the South), thus foreclosing the possibility of marriage and progeny (unless incestuous). In its most expansive metaphoric manifestation, that of the family of man, nineteenth-century pseudo-scientific theories of polygenesis argued for the separate creation of races in opposition to the Christian concept of humanity's shared blood: "He hath made of one blood all nations of men for to dwell on all the face of the earth" (Acts 17:26).

In the wake of world wars and social and economic upheavals, the United States is currently experiencing the proliferation of families indifferent to traditional concepts of blood, nuclear structures, and lineage. These include communal households; blended families formed through divorce; and families created by means of adoption, artificial insemination, or surrogate mothering for heterosexual or gay couples and single parents. To social conservatives, such families signal the breakdown of traditional norms and underscore their failure to exclude deviants from the national family. They have protested in various ways, encouraging school boards to pull books like *Heather Has Two Mommies* from libraries and family courts to favor adoptive parents over single surrogate mothers, as in the case of "Baby M." To sociologists like Judith Stacey (1990), however, these "brave new families" are the result of resourceful and creative action. In fact, these postmodern families hark back to Williams's premodern *familia*. We are progressing, it seems, back to the future in a movement that demands analysis by American cultural theorists and public policymakers alike.

30
Gender
Judith Halberstam

In American studies and cultural studies, as in the humanities more broadly, scholars use the term "gender" when they wish to expose a seemingly neutral analysis as male oriented and when they wish to turn critical attention from men to women. In this way, a gender analysis exposes the false universalization of male subjectivity and remarks upon the differences produced by the social marking we call "sex" or "sexual difference." Post-structuralist feminist theory queries this common usage by suggesting that the critique of male bias or gender neutrality comes with its own set of problems: namely, a premature and problematic stabilization of the meaning of "woman" and "female." In 1990, Judith Butler famously named and theorized the "trouble" that "gender" both performs and covers up. In doing so, she consolidated a new form of gender theory focused upon what is now widely (and variably) referred to as "performativity." In recent years, this focus on gender as something that is performed has enabled new modes of thinking about how the transgendered body is (and can be) inhabited, about the emergence of queer subcultures, and about practices that promise to radically destabilize the meaning of all social genders.

As a term, "gender" comes to cultural studies from American (U.S.) sexology, most explicitly from the work of psychologist John Money (Money and

Ehrhardt 1972). Money is credited with (and readily claimed) the invention of the term in 1955 to describe the social enactment of sex roles; he used the term to formalize the distinction between bodily sex (male and female) and social roles (masculinity and femininity), and to note the frequent discontinuities between sex and role. Since sex neither predicts nor guarantees gender role, there is some flexibility built into the sex-gender system. This reasoning led Money to recommend sex reassignment in a now infamous case where a young boy lost his penis during circumcision. Given the boy's young age, Money proposed to the parents that they raise him as a girl and predicted that there would be no ill effects. Money's prediction proved disastrously wrong, as the young girl grew up troubled and eventually committed suicide after being told about the decisions that had been made on his/her behalf as a baby.

This case has reanimated claims that gender is a biological fact rather than a cultural invention and has led some medical practitioners to reinvest in the essential relationship between sex and gender. It has also been used by some gender theorists to argue that the gendering of the sexed body begins immediately, as soon as the child is born, and that this socio-biological process is every bit as rigid and immutable as a genetic code. The latter claim (concerning the immutability of socialization) has been critiqued by post-structuralist thinkers who suggest that our understanding of the relation between sex and gender ought to be reversed: gender ideology produces the epistemological framework within which sex takes on meaning rather than

the other way around (Laqueur 1990; Fausto-Sterling 1993).

All of these arguments about how we ought to talk and think about sex and gender today assume a related question about how the modern sex-gender system came into being in the first place. Different disciplines answer this question differently. In anthropology, Gayle Rubin's work on "The Traffic in Women" (1975) builds on Claude Levi-Strauss's structuralist analysis of kinship (1971) to locate the roots of the hierarchical organization of a binary gender system in precapitalist societies where kinship relied upon incest taboos and the exchange of women between men. Esther Newton's (1972) ethnographic research on drag queens in Chicago in the 1960s and 1970s finds gender to be an interlocking system of performances and forms of self-knowing that only become visible as such when we see them theatricalized in the drag queen's cabaret act. In sociology, Suzanne Kessler and Wendy McKenna (1990) have produced a brilliant handbook on the production of gendered bodies, providing readers with a vocabulary and a set of definitions for the study of gender as a system of norms.

Working across these disciplinary formations, American studies and cultural studies scholarship on gender continues under numerous headings and rubrics. Researchers studying the effects of globalization have paid particular attention to transformations in the labor of women under new phases of capitalism (Enloe 1989; Kempadoo and Doezema 1998). Scholars working on race have traced very specific histories of gender formation in relation to racial projects that attribute gender and sexual pathology to oppressed groups. In African American contexts, for example, black femininity has often been represented as vexed by the idealization of white femininity on the one hand and the cultural stereotyping of black women as strong, physical, and tough on the other (Hammonds 1997). Other scholars seeking to denaturalize cultural conceptions of manhood have examined masculinity in terms of new forms of work, new roles for men in the home, the function of racialized masculinities, new styles of classed masculinity, the impact of immigrant masculinities upon national manhood, and the influence of minority and nonmale masculinities upon gender norms (Bederman 1995; Sinha 1995; Harper 1996). Queer theorists have detached gender from the sexed body, often documenting the productive nature of gender variance and its impact upon the way gender is understood and lived.

In all of these research contexts, gender is understood as a marker of social difference, a bodily performance of normativity and the challenges made to it. It names a social relation that subjects often experience as organic, ingrained, "real," invisible, and immutable; it also names a primary mode of oppression that sorts human bodies into binary categories in order to assign labor, responsibilities, moral attributes, and emotional styles. In recent years, cultural work dedicated to shifting and rearticulating the signifying field of gender has been ongoing in queer and transgender subcultures. Drag-king shows, for example, have developed along very different lines than their drag-queen counterparts (including those docu-

mented by Newton). While drag queens tend to embody and enact an explicitly ironic relation to gender that has come to be called "camp," drag kings often apply pressure to the notion of natural genders by imitating, inhabiting, and performing masculinity in intensely sincere modes. Where camp formulations of gender by gay men have relied heavily upon the idea that the viewer knows and can see the intense disidentifications between the drag queen and femininity, drag-king acts more often depend upon the sedimented and earnest investments made by the dyke and trans-performers in their masculinities. Drag-king acts disorient the spectator and make her unsure of the proper markings of sex, gender, desire, and attraction. In the process, they produce potent new constellations of sex and theater (Halberstam 1998).

Understood as queer interventions into gender deconstruction, drag-king performances emerge quite specifically from feminist critiques of dominant masculinities. In this sense, they can be viewed as growing out of earlier practices of feminist theory and activism. Consider Valerie Solanas's infamous and outrageous 1968 *SCUM Manifesto* (SCUM stood for "Society for Cutting up Men"), in which she argued that we should do away with men and attach all the positive attributes that are currently assigned to males to females. As long as we have sperm banks and the means for artificial reproduction, she argued, men have become irrelevant. While Solanas's manifesto is hard to read as anything more than a Swiftian modest proposal, her hilarious conclusions about the redundancy of the male sex ("he is a half-dead, unresponsive lump, incapable of giving or receiving pleasure or happiness; consequently he is an utter bore, an inoffensive blob . . . etc") take a refreshingly extreme approach to the gender question (1970/2004). The performative work of the manifesto (its theatricalization of refusal, failure, and female anger and resentment; its combination of seriousness and humor) links it to contemporary queer and transgender theaters of gender. Like Solanas's manifesto, drag-king cultures offer a vision of the ways in which subcultural groups and theorists busily reinvent the meaning of gender even as the culture at large confirms its stability.

It is revealing, then, that Solanas is at once the most utopian and dystopian of gender theorists. While Butler, in her commitment to deconstructive undecidability, cannot possibly foretell any of gender's possible futures (even as she describes how gender is "done" and "undone"), Solanas is quite happy to make grand predictions about endings. Many academic and nonacademic gender theorists after Solanas have also called for the end of gender, noted the redundancy of the category, and argued for new and alternative systems of making sense of bodily difference (Bornstein 1994; Kessler 1998). But socially sedimented categories are hard to erase, and efforts to do so often have more toxic effects than the decision to inhabit them. Other theorists, therefore, have responded by calling for more categories, a wider range of possible identifications, and a more eclectic and open-ended understanding of the meanings of those categories (Fausto-Sterling 2000). It seems, then, that

we are probably not quite ready do away with gender, or with one gender in particular, but we can at least begin to imagine other genders.

Whether by manifesto or reasoned argumentation, scholars in the fields of American studies and cultural studies have made gender into a primary lens of intellectual inquiry, and the evolution of gender studies marks one of the more successful versions of interdisciplinarity in the academy. Indeed, as U.S. universities continue to experience the dissolution of disciplinarity, a critical gender studies paradigm could well surge to the forefront of new arrangements of knowledge production. At a time when both students and administrators are questioning the usefulness and relevance of fields like English and comparative literature, gender studies may provide a better way of framing, asking, and even answering hard questions about ideology, social formations, political movements, and shifts in perceptions of embodiment and community. Gender studies programs and departments, many of which emerged out of women's studies initiatives in the 1970s, are poised to make the transition into the next era of knowledge production in ways that less interdisciplinary areas are not. The quarrels and struggles that have made gender studies such a difficult place to be are also the building blocks of change. While the traditional disciplines often lack the institutional and intellectual flexibility to transform quickly, gender studies is and has always been an evolving project, one that can provide a particularly generative site for new work that, at its best, responds creatively and dynamically to emerging research questions and cultural forms, while also entering into dialogue with other (more or less established) interdisciplinary projects, including cultural studies, American studies, film studies, science studies, ethnic studies, postcolonial studies, and queer studies.

31
Globalization
Lisa Lowe

"Globalization" is a contemporary term used in academic and non-academic contexts to describe a late-twentieth-century condition of economic, social, and political interdependence across cultures, societies, nations, and regions precipitated by an unprecedented expansion of capitalism on a global scale. One problem with this usage is that it obscures a much longer history of global contacts and connections. In the ancient world, there were empires, conquests, slavery, and diasporas; in medieval and early modern times, Asian, Arab, and European civilizations mingled through trade, travel, and settlement. Only with European colonial expansion, beginning in the sixteenth century and reaching its height in the nineteenth, did global contacts involve Western European and North American dominance; the rise of Western industrialized modernity made possible by labor and resources in the "new world" of the Americas was, in this sense, a relatively recent global interconnection. Yet today the term "globalization" is used to name a specific set

of late-twentieth-century transformations: changes in world political structure after World War II that included the ascendancy of the United States and the decolonization of the formerly colonized world; a shift from the concept of the modern nation-state as bounded and independent toward a range of economic, social, and political links that articulate interdependencies across nations; and an acceleration in the scale, mode, and volume of exchange and interdependency in nearly all spheres of human activity.

Even with this caveat, "globalization" is not a self-evident phenomenon, and the debates to which it gives rise in American studies, cultural studies, and elsewhere mark it as a problem of knowledge. For economists, political scientists, sociologists, historians, and cultural critics, globalization is a phenomenon that exceeds existing means of explanation and representation. It involves processes and transformations that bring pressure upon the paradigms formerly used to study their privileged objects—whether society, the sovereign nation-state, national economy, history, or culture—the meanings of which have shifted and changed. Globalization is both celebrated by free-market advocates as fulfilling the promises of neoliberalism and free trade, and criticized by scholars, policymakers, and activists as a world economic program aggressively commanded by the United States, enacted directly through U.S. foreign policies and indirectly through institutions such as the World Bank, the International Monetary Fund, and the World Trade Organization, exacerbating economic divides with devastating effects for the poor in "developing" countries and in systematically "underdeveloped" ones (Amin 1997; Stiglitz 2002; Pollin 2003).

Political scientists argued in the 1980s that the global expansion of the economy had created asymmetries among nations and regions that provided sources of "complex interdependence" (Keohane and Nye 1989). Adherents of their "neoliberal" school of political science, dominant for nearly two decades, agreed that international laws and institutions, global commerce, and diplomatic networks of cooperation had lessened the need for war and militarism. Yet since 2001 and the unilateral U.S. invasions of Afghanistan and Iraq, the U.S. government has embraced "neoconservative" political thinking, reviving "neorealist" arguments from the Cold War period to contend that despite economic or social links between nations, "national security" has never ceased to be the most important issue, and that war constitutes a viable, "rational," and effective instrument of policy and of wielding power (Kagan and Kagan 2000). Such lethal contentions about the nature of global conditions have demonstrated that the epistemological problem of what can be known about "globalization" is never distant from ethical or political issues of life and death.

Sociologists adopted Max Weber's (1968) original observations about the contradictions of rationalizing modernity within a single society to study globalization as an acceleration and expansion of capitalist bureaucracy through transnational corporations (Sklair 1991). In this view, globalization both deepens the interconnection *and* widens the dissymmetries represented as "core" and "periphery" in an earlier "world-system" (Wallerstein 1976). At the same time, cultural critics observed that flexible capital accumulation and mixed production fragmented subjectivities and collectivities according to a "cultural logic of postmodernism" (Jameson 1991), an apparent shrinking or elimination of distances and a general reduction of time spent (Harvey 1989). The rise of a new "global" culture comprised of cross-border communities, multilingual immigrants, and syncretic religions revised earlier presumptions that place, culture, language, and identity could be mapped onto one another (Gupta and Ferguson 1992; Sassen 1998; Fregoso 2003). The coexistence of migrant diasporas and indigenous peoples creates material imaginaries dictated less by citizenship and traditional national sovereignty than by new social identities and overlapping affinities (Appadurai 1996; Clifford 1997). At the same time, some social identities are policed, and criminalized, by the refortified articulations of "national security" states.

One position in debates about the globalization of culture argues that globalization is a form of cultural imperialism that has eroded nation-states and flattened national cultural differences through the vast spread of consumerism (Miyoshi 1993). Another emphasizes that global encounter, migration, and contact have produced more hybrid forms of "cultural complexity" (Hannerz 1992). The best critical cultural studies of globalization move beyond the polarized theses of cultural imperialism or hybridization, or the simplified idea that culture flows from center to margin, overcoming or corrupting the periphery. To study "culture" within globalization is to understand it neither as merely commodified, nor as simply the inert effects or ideological correlative of transnational capitalism. Rather, contemporary culture, as the "structure of feeling" (R. Williams 1977) of globalization, mediates the uneven spaces linked through geohistorical, political, economic, and social logics (P. Taylor 1999). Whether it is the medium through which groups are persuaded to live and die as patriotic subjects or the inspiration for their transgression or protest, "culture" expresses dynamic contradictions precisely at those intersections, borders, and zones where normative regimes contact, enlist, restrict, or coerce. Critical studies of the United States within global processes may demonstrate, through the study of culture, that normative modes differentiate as they regulate, and discipline as they include and assimilate.

American cultural studies follows this line of inquiry by situating U.S. culture (its traditional object) in an international context, from its origins up through contemporary globalization. It identifies in cultural products (literature, music, art, mass and popular cultures) and in cultural practices (the organization of cities and public spaces, schooling, religion) both the longer world history within which the United States emerged and the contemporary U.S. understanding of itself within a global entirety, increasingly, yet unevenly mediated through electronic information technologies. Manuel Castells (2000b) has suggested that state, military, and economic processes are now entirely coordinated, in real time across distances, through the vast reach of global information networks. As "information" becomes a pervasive new medium of global production, "cultures" of globalization will include information technologies, like the Internet, as sites of both production and critique.

The restructuring of the U.S. economy by globalization has entailed a shift from vertically integrated national industries to transnational finance capitalism, a conversion of traditionally male jobs in manufacturing to more feminized forms of service operations, and an unsettling of historical neighborhoods by the influx of new transnational migrants. Communities of color in deindustrializing U.S. cities of the 1980s were hit hard by loss of jobs as manufacturing moved to export-processing zones in Asia and Latin America, even as the urban poor suffered from the simultaneous reduction of social welfare and build-up of the U.S. prison system (R. Gilmore 1998). Transnational immigration that appeared to bring more racial and ethnic diversity often rendered these worsening inequalities more complex, and certainly more difficult to decipher. New critical and comparative work on race considers U.S. cities as locations for understanding the history of racial inequalities and its rearticulation within neoliberal political and economic policies from the 1980s onward (Lee 2004).

For some in American cultural studies, globalization signifies the "end" of modern U.S. myths of purity: of "man" as the white race, redeemed by the authenticity of rural life, as leader of the "free world" and "the American century." For others, it is a "crisis," a "chaos of governance," and the "end" of the Enlightenment, liberal humanism, or civil society. Noting the weakening of states and the waning social power of subordinated groups, some suggest that globalization changes the balance of power between "civilizations." Projected apocalyptically, it appears as a "clash of civilizations" between Western modernity and the Confucian-Islamic East (Huntington 1996). Others interpret Chinese modernization as a probable sign of emerging Asian economic supremacy (Krugman 1997). Still others herald the impact of anti-globalization movements, transnational feminism, global environmentalism, and international human rights activism and express cautious hope about the possibilities for countering poverty and creating sustainable growth (Lowe and Lloyd 1997; Mohanty and Alexander 1997; Sen 1999). Some observe that transnational capitalism not only effects a "denationalization" of corporate power, but also draws new workforces that express themselves in movements articulated in terms other than the "national," for example in transnational feminist work by U.S. and U.K. women of color and immigrant women from the formerly colonized world (Sudbury 1998; Mohanty 2003; Hong 2006). Globalization not only "unbundles" the territorial organization of sovereignty, defying earlier maps of "core" and "periphery," it also changes the means, agents, and strategies employed in contesting the "new world order." Global cities such as New York, London, Tokyo, or São Paolo gather both the infrastructure to coordinate global finance and the transnational migrant workers who perform the service labors for these operations (Sassen 1991; Eade 1997).

Women, immigrants, political prisoners, refugees, "squatters," and other non–state subjects are among the important new social actors who are transforming how we ought to conceive of ethics, justice, and change in globalization.

32

Identity

Carla Kaplan

One of our most common terms, "identity" is rarely defined. In everyday language, its most common usages—"personal identity" and "social identity"—designate meanings not only distinct from one another but also hierarchically related. Personal identity is often assumed to mediate between social identities and make sense of them. Whereas our social identities shift throughout the day, what allows us to move coherently from one to another is often imagined to be our personal identity, or "who we are"—our constant.

Hence, personal identity conventionally arbitrates taste and lifestyle. "It's just not me," a potential homebuyer says to her realtor. "That's so you," a helpful friend appraises as the shopper steps out of the dressing room. An "identity crisis" is a *crisis* rather than an "identity opportunity" because personal identity demands proper and unimpeded expression. It is a value, something we prize. This sense of identity as ours implies an immutable essence unchanged by physical development or external circumstances. The *Oxford English*

Dictionary dates the origins of this usage to the late sixteenth century, but this meaning has recently been challenged by social theory and postmodern conceptions of subjectivity, and feminist theory has generated especially rich rethinkings of our notions of identity.

In reference to social categories, identity has long carried the meaning of relational and mutable identifications, actuated either by the individual's chosen identifications or by others who label individuals or groups based on characteristics and behaviors that seem shared. Whereas we commonly talk of having *a* unitary personal identity (our "personality"), social identity is regarded as a constellation of different and often competing identifications or "cultural negotiations" (Alcoff 2000, 315). Adrienne Rich's volume of poetry, *Your Native Land, Your Life* (1986), is one example of such a negotiation, drawing on feminism, Jewish history, and progressive social struggles to ask what in identity is chosen and what is given:

> *With whom do you believe your lot is cast?*
> *From where does your strength come?*
>
> . . . There is a *whom*, a *where*
> that is not chosen that is given and sometimes
> falsely given
>
> In the beginning we grasp whatever we can
> to survive

W. E. B. Du Bois's famous formulation of "double consciousness"—"one ever feels his two-ness,—an American, a Negro" (1903/1986, 364)—also speaks to this sense of not merely negotiated but "warring" social identities. If personal and social identity are seen as "warring"—if I must keep "who I am" intact and unrestrained by "who I am supposed to be"—then the stakes of such negotiation are inevitably raised. Recognition of our multiplicity may not seem as important as resolution of it.

Identity politics, as it emerged in the United States from the women's movement, the civil rights movement, gay rights struggles, and the New Left in the 1960s, offered new conceptualizations of the importance of recognizing—and valuing—previously denigrated or devalued identities. This "politics of recognition" expanded the kinds of rights claims earlier associated with progressive demands for the redistribution of social goods. As Charles Taylor (1992, 25) influentially put it, "a person or group of people can suffer real damage, real distortion, if the people or society around them mirror back to them a conflicting or demeaning or contemptible picture of themselves." At the same time, identity politics articulated coalitional strategies for linking those social identities to one another and to a range of social struggles for justice, equity, and rights.

Since its inception, however, identity politics has also aroused suspicion and criticism from the very avenues where it originated. Because group identities—religious, tribal, and national loyalties especially—can be obstacles to building broader political coalitions and often have been the excuse for systemic social violence, the limits of group identity sometimes seem to outweigh any political benefit or affective comfort to be had by such belonging. Hence, the struggle *for* recognition becomes a questioning *of* recognition. Rather than taking personal or political recognition for granted as a social good, some argue that recognition is a red herring that hooks us to concepts of belonging and being that can only prove exclusionary. As Ernesto Laclau (1994, 5) argues, how to legitimize and affirm "the proliferation of political identities in the contemporary world" (by whom and under what social practices) has now become "the question that sets the agenda for democratic politics."

On the one hand, then, identity politics has been understood as grounding new democratic possibilities through its reinvigoration of ideals of representation, voice, and self-determination. On the other hand, it has also been seen as limiting new democratic possibilities by encouraging narrow solidarities rather than broader identifications. In a complex defense of a more nuanced identity politics, James Clifford (2000, 106) writes: "Given the constitutive tension of positive and negative impulses in claims to peoplehood, all assertive identity movements, including those that empower the dispossessed, can seem to be symptoms of a general disease." The negative view, Clifford notes, associates identity claims with the violence and scapegoating that make "people kill their neighbors." A fluid sense of identity categories may provide a more positive resolution to the contradiction, since it sees the categories we want recognized as positions we move through in complex, challenging, and changing ways, not as boxes we're stuck in for all time (Carla Kaplan 1996). And while it may seem that we are caught

between two views of social identity—one of which demands that overlooked and denigrated identities be recognized and affirmed, and another that sees the immutable self as a socially constructed fiction from which we need to free our selves—the tension between these two strains in contemporary theorizations of identity can be productive. In practice, it can inform a progressive identity politics capable of embracing this tension as its own.

Within the academy, acknowledging that social identities matter, that they make a difference, and that we may need to both contest and celebrate them has led to some of the most sweeping changes in the history of postsecondary education; disciplines have been reconfigured and vital new models of knowledge production created. These new fields are often focused on the recognition and exploration of different social identities, most prominently in ethnic studies, women's studies, and lesbian and gay studies programs. While these *institutional* formations tend to be premised on recognition of diverse social identities in their intersectional relations to one another, the *intellectual* work these formations generate and support has been able to challenge the very idea of identity.

Rejecting the notion of the self as a centered, transparent, or realized presence, a deconstructive notion of the subject argues that identification, the chief mechanism of identity formation, reveals identity's lack or absence. On this account, identity is neither something we possess nor something that defines us, but is instead an *unending* linguistic process of becoming. Where identity politics, the politics of recognition, and multiculturalism insist that a lack of affirmation for some identities is a social insult needing rectification, a post-structuralist or deconstructive perspective names identity itself as the problem. When ascriptions are placed onto individuals and groups by others, and when those ascriptions limit or constrain the myriad personal and social identities one might wish to claim, recognition of our identities no longer seems a mechanism of social justice, but rather to *be* the social insult. In the global marketplace, moreover, multiculturalism and a diverse politics of identity always risk reinscription as just another commodity, offering us a "superficial shopping mall of identities" to keep capital flowing (Clifford 2000, 101).

Some theorists suggest that what we need is the subversion of identity, not its recognition. But *how* do we subvert "what we are"? One answer has been that we use identity categories only strategically, refusing to treat them as if they referenced an independent or transcendent reality. This is what is meant by the often-repeated injunction to be "strategically essentialist" in one's thinking about and practice of identity (Spivak 1990). Another answer has been that in place of *seeking* recognition, we *play* with it, and that we do so in such a way as to make clear that recognition is a circuit of power, not a naming of reality. If identity is, in Judith Butler's words, a "*regulatory* fiction" and if political appeals based on available social categories reinforce "limitation, prohibition, regulation, control" by addressing "ready-made subjects," we can subvert identity by revealing *how* it is "ready-made" (1990, 2, 149). This subversion is what is meant by "performa-

tivity," a concept with enormous impact on American studies, cultural studies, and related interdisciplines. Performativity is understood to unfix regulatory identity by exposing the reiterations by which "a phenomenon is named into being," a process called "citationality" (Butler 1993, 13). A performative understanding of gender's citationality, for example, can reveal how gender does not name "what we are," but rather *constitutes* the identities it purports to name through chains of repetitive citational signs. Performativity can be a subversive practice because it reveals that identities are not really "our own" and that we are not really "what we are"; rather, we are how we identify—a process that is mutable and changeable. As a citational practice, performativity can refigure available norms as contingent and open to change.

The subversiveness of performativity cannot be determined in the absolute, outside of specific practices, acts, and situations. This may account, in part, for why the appeal of performativity as a theory of resistance has proved limited outside of the academy. Accepting that there is no "there there" and that identity is a "regulatory fiction" does not, moreover, necessarily lead people away from a *desire* for identity. From popular culture to the reinvigoration of identity politics to the rise of new nationalisms, we see a persistent desire *for* identity, however much identity may be constructed, illusory, and unstable. One of the tasks of a new American cultural studies will be to explain that persistence, to trace its workings, and to offer suggestions for how to make contradictions enabling and liberatory. The recent call for "a realistic identity politics" is one such attempt to recognize "the dynamic, variable, and negotiated character of identity" (Alcoff 2000, 340, 341) in ways that reposition us toward a more just and equitable world.

33

Immigration

Eithne Luibhéid

Immigration is one of the most frequently discussed and multivalent concepts in scholarship on the U.S. experience. A subcategory within studies of "migration," "immigration" refers in the *American Heritage Dictionary* (4th ed.) to the activity of "enter[ing] and settl[ing] in a region or country to which one is not native." The "Usage Note" at "migrate" adds, "*Migrate*, which is used of people or animals, sometimes implies a lack of permanent settlement, especially as a result of seasonal or periodic movement. *Emigrate* and *immigrate* are used only of people and imply a permanent move, generally across a political boundary." As this wide-ranging definition indicates, many kinds of relocation may be described in everyday vernacular as "immigration." In partial contrast, academic studies of immigration generally focus on geographic relocations across political boundaries, usually of nation-states. These relocations are often imagined as permanent, thus differentiating immigrants from groups such as temporary migrant laborers, tourists, business visitors, and international students. The "Note" confirms this usage: "*Emigrate* describes the move relative to the point of departure. . . . By contrast, *immigrate* describes the move relative to the destination: *The promise of prosperity in the United States encouraged many people to immigrate.*"

Definitions like this one tend to make nation-states seem natural, to overstate the extent to which both emigration and immigration involve individual choice, and to make mobile people seem like problems. In contrast, the treatment of immigration in much recent work in American cultural studies focuses on the historical construction of nation-states and the peoples who populate them. Early nation-states did not try to control human movement across national borders, nor did they conceive of immigration control as a matter of national sovereignty. During the second half of the nineteenth century, however, as waves of immigrants arrived from Europe, Asia, and the Americas, the United States nationalized its immigration policies and procedures and implemented them in an increasingly exclusionary way. Claims that immigration control involved national sovereignty were reinforced in the 1880s and 1890s through efforts to exclude Chinese immigrants on racial grounds. A national sovereignty framework meant that Congress's powers over immigration were not constrained by the Constitution, and it legitimized reduced due-process protections and explicitly discriminatory practices, including race-based exclusion. Also in the 1890s, the United States acquired significant overseas territories, including the Philippines, Puerto Rico, and Guam. In this expanding imperial context, immigration control gained significance as an expression of and tool for actively constituting racialized national sovereignty.

The link between immigration control and national sovereignty both reinforced and was aided by the rise of a centralized state bureaucracy. Given the filtering demands of immigration policy, officials needed ways to establish clearly who belonged to the nation-state. This need, in turn, required the development of identity documents and systems of verification such as the passport, which became widely used after World War I. These documentation practices tied individuals to bureaucratic identities in ways that allowed for their monitoring and surveillance. Such practices did not map identities that people already had; rather, they were tools to divide up and classify populations in relation to state-making projects at local, national, and imperial levels. They depended on, deployed, and refined forms of racial, colonial, and sexual knowledge about bodies, and they relied on technologies such as photography and fingerprinting that developed in the context of empire, the transformation of policing, and the rise of human sciences (Wiegman 1997). Contemporary uses of biometric technologies have extended this history, which Gérard Noiriel (1991) calls "the identification revolution," in new ways.

Through these processes, "the immigrant" became defined as a person who crosses a nation-state boundary and takes on the legal status of "alien," with associated regimes of identification, surveillance, rights, and constraints. The figure of the "illegal immigrant" is produced through similar processes. Popularly treated as a sociological category, "the illegal" actually refers not to any particular "type" of person, but to the shifting ways in which the nation-state produces registers of legitimate and illegitimate entrants. While "illegals" are denied many fundamental rights, their labor is often welcomed, even demanded. Furthermore, the production of "illegals" connects to histories of systemic inequality between the United States and other nation-states within an imperial global order. For example, many suggest that Mexicans have become the paradigmatic "illegals" through historical, legal, political, and economic processes that derive from enduring neocolonial relationships between the United States and Mexico (Nevins 2002; Ngai 2004). Moreover, efforts to police Mexican and other "illegals" are thoroughly implicated in the production of the nation-state in a manner that emphasizes its territorial borders. Since "illegals" live inside the national territory, borders within the nation-state have also proliferated in a manner that often racializes Latin Americans and Asians as "foreigners" (while equating citizenship with whiteness).

Understanding that immigration control "illegalizes" particular migrants in an act of state power requires revising the common conception of immigration as simply a matter of individuals deciding to relocate permanently to another nation-state. This conception has been elaborated through theories of immigration as a consequence of push/pull forces or cost/benefit economic decision-making. These theories suggest, in line with the *American Heritage Dictionary*, that immigration is primarily driven by people making rational decisions to migrate due to poor conditions at home (poverty, repression, violence) and the promise of a better life elsewhere (wealth, freedom, peace). Other theories, however, resituate the dynamics of immigration by exploring how histories of imperialism, invasion, investment, trade, and political influence create what Saskia Sassen (1992) calls "bridges for migration" between and among regions within nation-states. While individuals certainly make choices, their choices are inevitably conditioned by the larger contexts that Sassen describes. And they are influenced by social networks including family, friends, and community members, and by intermediaries including labor recruiters, attorneys, and smugglers.

Immigration bridges may also be created through more symbolic means, including narratives and images of immigration and immigrants. Common representations characterize the United States as a "nation of immigrants," a "melting pot," or a "multicultural mosaic." Such images frequently gloss histories of genocide, slavery, racialized patriarchy, and economic exploitation as necessary moments of national consolidation, thus contributing to a culture that normalizes and privileges white, male, middle-class, and heterosexual statuses. Nonetheless, representational systems remain inherently ambiguous, thereby opening up possibilities for resistant identifications, counter-cultural practices, and contestation.

Popular representations produce these effects in part by drawing on forms of expertise created and inhabited by sociologists, demographers, economists, policymakers, and health professionals. Such expertise never involves simply collecting and analyzing "facts" that already exist; rather, there is an ongoing and reciprocal relationship between governance and knowledge production. These types of expert knowledge function in a complex relationship to more critical modes of scholarship. For instance, in the early twentieth century, Robert Park and the "Chicago school" social scientists effectively established the sociological study of immigration. Many of Park's concepts—such as the four-stage assimilation cycle of competition, conflict, accommodation, and assimilation—remain with us today. Park's scholarship contested the racist orthodoxy of his day, but it also served nationalist agendas and governance structures by positing assimilation to existing national norms as the endpoint of migration.

With the contemporary turn toward models of transnationalism, globalization, diaspora, and border studies that map more varied trajectories of migration, scholars have begun to rethink many of the foundational concepts of immigration scholarship, including static or place-bound ideas of culture, community, nation, race, gender, identity, and settlement. Much of this rethinking challenges concepts that are framed by trajectories of evolutionary development within the boundaries of the nation-state. Instead, newer work attends to contradiction, relationality, and back-and-forth dynamics and strives to undo conceptual binaries, theorize liminal positions, and resituate the border as a contact zone. These studies rethink immigrant agency and resistance by connecting material conditions to subject-formation processes, while also emphasizing multiple, interlocking inequalities at various scales.

Recent scholarship focused on sexuality can usefully illustrate these multidisciplinary efforts to reconceptualize the study of immigration. Though often overlooked or naturalized in immigration scholarship, sexuality is directly implicated in racial, gender, class, cultural, and imperial inequalities. It also thoroughly structures and is restructured by immigration, not merely at the level of metaphor and symbol, but also in material ways. For example, when the United States established military bases and sent troops to Asia for "rest and recreation" in the latter half of the twentieth century, it also generated bridges for immigration movements shaped by interlocking sexual, racial, gender, and economic inequalities within a (neo)colonial framework (Yuh 2002). More generally, links between capitalism and sexual identities, ideologies, imaginaries, and practices have continued to restructure and transform sexuality in ways that directly shape immigration movements (Brennan 2004). Contemporary neoliberalism, which both relies on and naturalizes racialized, patriarchal heterosexuality as a tool for governance (particularly through "family values" discourses and projects), simultaneously extends this complex history and contributes to the theoretical erasure of sexuality within mainstream thinking about immigration.

While histories of (neo)colonialism, economic inequality, racism, and (hetero)sexism on a global scale materially shape immigration, U.S. laws and policies remain largely unresponsive to these complexities, and instead react within a dominant nationalist framework that privileges heterosexuality channeled into marriage and family. The heterosexual family has long served as a model for nation-making that inscribes and naturalizes important hierarchies, including a patriarchal order that constructs women's sexualities as the property of males, and a racial and cultural order that valorizes whiteness (McClintock 1993). The heterosexual family and its associated hierarchies provide the abstract model, concrete mechanism, and means for measuring a wide range of social processes affecting immigrants. Take the example of racial and ethnic "mixing," which has been a central concern in the governance and study of immigration. "Mixing" has generated two of the major discourses that have structured popular and academic thinking about immigration—the color line and the melting pot—and the heterosexual family has been central to each.

In regard to the color line, anti-miscegenation laws, which were grounded in the history of slavery, were in many cases revived or extended to prevent single immigrant men from Asia, Africa, and Latin America from becoming sexually involved with native-born white women. Single immigrant women were also figured as potentially threatening—most vividly in nineteenth-century claims that Chinese women engaged in sex work were corrupting white men and boys, stripping them of their money, and infecting them with deadly diseases. Patriarchal marriage within the boundaries of one's "race" and "ethnic group" was deemed a good solution to all manner of potential social disorders associated with immigrant sexuality—including challenges to the color line. Yet when sexuality was channeled into intraracial marriage within racialized immigrant groups, the resulting childbearing often became constructed as a threat to the color line in a different way. Immigrants have regularly been accused of deliberately attempting to "(re)colonize" parts of the United States through birthing children who were legal citizens, but considered racially and culturally "unassimilable," prompting new cycles of exclusionary and eugenic measures.

At the same time, the heterosexual family has been viewed as a mechanism to assimilate immigrants into "American" culture and citizenship; in this respect, it has also been the focus of "melting pot" discourses, desires, strategies, systems of governance, and modes of representation, including versions of assimilation, pluralism, Americanization, and multiculturalism. For example, inter-racial and inter-ethnic marriage has regularly been characterized as the most effective mechanism to erase the color line and studied accordingly (Yu 2001). Similarly, the promotion of companionate marriage in both popular discourse and social science research has provided a technology for immigrant assimilation and driven more than a century of public policies and programs.

This history of "mixing" points to a larger issue. Normative heterosexuality has served as the unexamined ground for elaborating many foundational concepts in the study and governance of immigration. The core concept of "assimilation," for example, came to serve as a model for immigrant life that draws on and recapitulates the norm of heterosexuality as the desired outcome of a developmental process on which racial and national hierarchies depended (Somerville 2000). Generational conflict within heterosexual immigrant families became the model for conceiving and narrating cultural change. "Settlement"—another key concept in mainstream immigration scholarship—similarly hinged on whether immigrants entered into patriarchal marriages. Models of family, culture, community, economic advancement, race, and nation presumed heterosexuality as their actual mechanism and as the normative standard for evaluation. Recent scholarship that centers on sexuality in a manner that recognizes its direct imbrication in racial, gendered, colonial, and class regimes has contributed to rethinking these and other foundational concepts—not only in nation-centered accounts of immigration but also in global, diasporic, and transnational models of migration that implicitly rely on heterosexual logics (Manalansan 2006). This research is useful for all scholars of immigration, whatever their discipline or approach, since it provides a basis for rethinking the epistemologies, methodologies, and representational forms that govern our collective understanding of the histories and futures of migration in, across, and beyond national borders.

34

Indian

Robert Warrior

"Indian" is a word that has deep and conflicting roots in the history of the Western hemisphere and in the contemporary imaginations and attitudes of those who live in the Americas. The issue of the proper usage of this term and others related to it ("Native American," "American Indian," "Amerindian," "Native," "Indigenous," and "First Nations," among others) can be frustrating since the question is so basic; that is, it does little to open up the depths of historical or contemporary indigenous experiences. But it is also a way of beginning a discussion of what students and practitioners of American cultural studies ought to be learning and researching about the aboriginal history of the Americas.

Broad agreement exists that the term "Indian," referring to people in the Americas, originated in Christopher Columbus's mistaken idea that he had discovered a new route to India when he arrived in this hemisphere. Since Columbus's errors of navigation and nomenclature, variations on this term have often been used derisively, as in its bastardized form "Injun" or in its contemporary use in Mexico and other places south of the United States to describe people thought of as poor, backwards, and racially disadvantaged. In light of this, most scholars in Native American studies and many Native people themselves advise against the use of the word "Indian" alone as a

noun (singular or plural) in favor of "American Indian," though the adjectival form (as in Indian culture) is widely acceptable in the United States. This preference seems to derive from the fact that "American Indian" is a unique term, but also roughly equivalent in form to other terms that delineate ethnic and racial difference and identity in the United States, such as Italian American, Asian American, and African American.

"Native American" has gained currency more recently in the United States and Europe, though some American Indian people bristle at its use, in part because "Native American" would seem to refer to anyone who is born on the continent, and perhaps also because the term gained momentum among sympathetic non-Indian people in the 1970s—as if these sympathizers assumed that American Indian people, like African Americans, must surely have wanted to be referred to differently, and so came up with what they imagined Indians wanted to be called. Still, one clear advantage of the term "Native American" is that it includes all indigenous people of the countries in the Americas. In the United States, that means it references Alaskan Eskimos, Inuits, Aleuts, and Native Hawai'ians, none of whom consider themselves American Indians. Native, a shortened form, has become a preferred term among many academics, students, and others.

The issue of proper nomenclature is nowhere near settled, and specific usages usually reflect regional and national histories and realities. In Mexico and other South and Meso-American countries in which "Indian" (or Indio) is highly insulting, "indigenous" (or *indigena*) has come into usage. Many within these same indigenous communities also reject the term "Latin America" to describe those countries, since, as indigenous people (many of whom do not speak Spanish), they do not consider themselves Latin. In Canada, the main political term for indigenous groups is "First Nations," and the people who belong to those nations are Aboriginal, Native, or First Nations people.

Although nothing close to a consensus exists among Native people as to a preferred term for themselves in general, wide agreement has developed over the past several decades that it is most appropriate to use the names specific tribal groups have for themselves (Diné, Dakota, Yupik, Ojibwe, or Yakama), or at least the names by which they have come to be known since the European colonization of the Americas (Navajo, Sioux, Eskimo, Chippewa, or Yakima, respectively). This specificity generally affords respect for the vast differences among the indigenous peoples of the Americas, standing in marked contrast to references to *the* Indian, *the* Native American, or *the* original American, which are monolithic and help bolster the misimpression that all indigenous people are the same. This preference has grown up alongside social and political movements focused on the needs and prospects of individual tribal nations and local communities, rather than the more broadly defined politics of the 1970s. While that earlier era of activism and protest witnessed calls for wholesale changes in Indian affairs, the period since has seen a concern for economic de-

velopment, cultural preservation, governmental reform, and community control at the local level.

In spite of these areas of wide agreement, many individual Native people in the United States feel completely comfortable calling themselves and other people Indians. A shortened form, usually represented in writing as "Ind'n" (or now, in the sort of shorthand people use in the digital world, "ndn"), speaks to the persistence and acceptability of the term in urban, rural, and reservation settings. Thus, while the movement toward understanding oneself as a member of a specific tribal group is one contemporary dynamic, a significant sense of generational cohesiveness is also common among indigenous youth.

The fact that most college students do not even have this basic knowledge about how to refer to indigenous people of the Americas speaks to how little the average student who grows up in the United States learns about Natives in elementary and secondary school. Much of this results from the persistence of poor school curriculums in regard to the history and contemporary realities of Native life, but it also reflects the fact that the vast majority of U.S. schoolchildren have had little or no exposure to living, breathing Indian people, except perhaps on a family vacation through the Southwest or someplace else where large concentrations of Natives live. Nor do they encounter Native recording artists, television or film actors, authors, or politicians, though there are some exceptions, both historical (including Will Rogers, Jim Thorpe, the ballerina Maria Tallchief, and Vice President Charles Curtis) and contemporary (including activist/actor

Russell Means, singer Rita Coolidge, and professional golfer Tiger Woods, who is Native along with being Thai, white, and African American). Even in the major cities with the highest concentrations of Natives (Minneapolis and Oakland, for instance), no single neighborhood has much more than 10 percent Natives living in it.

Indian people, then, for the most part live either in enclaves in which they are a major focus of social life (reservations or towns bordering them) or in places where they are mostly invisible to the people with whom they share the world. Outside of occasional news stories on exceptionally severe social problems (poverty, substance abuse, unemployment, poor health) or feature stories on cultural events (powwows, art exhibits), neither local nor national media pay much attention to Native issues. While this might be said for any number of other groups in the Americas, none share the history or contemporary situation of Native Americans. To use just the most obvious example, no other group in the United States or Canada has an entire federal bureaucracy dedicated to it as Natives do with, respectively, the Bureau of Indian Affairs (BIA) and the Department of Indian Affairs (DIA). Taxpayers in these countries support their governments' day-to-day managing of the lives of Native people in spite of the fact that few of those taxpayers can say much about what their money funds.

Being inclusive of Native American experiences in American studies, then, requires something more than creating a new branch of the field that accounts for yet another group clamoring for the attention of scholars and students. Craig Womack makes this point forcefully in his work on Native American literature. "Tribal literatures," he writes, "are not some branch waiting to be grafted onto the main trunk. Tribal literatures are the *tree*, the oldest literatures in the Americas, the most American of American literatures. We *are* the canon. Without Native American literature, *there is no American canon*. . . . Let Americanists struggle for *their* place in the canon" (1999, 6–7). Native American studies is an invitation for American studies to rethink its understanding of the continent and the people who have made it their home. It requires attention to the ways in which historians have often skewed their work at the expense of an accurate portrait of how Native people have developed their own sophisticated ways of life, including responses to the circumstances that the European colonization of the Americas brought to them. But confronting ignorance also entails recognition of the contemporary realities that Native people inhabit.

Though American studies, when it has paid attention to Native Americans at all, has mostly focused on historical topics, other recent approaches in the field could create deeper scholarly understandings of features of contemporary Native life. Native American literature and visual art, for example, are now established as serious areas of artistic achievement and scholarly study, but numerous forms of contemporary Native expression have yet to capture much of the attention of the scholarly world, and interdisciplinary work could reveal important levels of meaning. Sporadic attempts have been made over the past two decades to establish Native versions of speculative fiction, graphic novels, and comic books (Justice 2005; Mindt 2005). These attempts, many of them interesting in and of themselves, could lead to rich discussions about what it means for indigenous youth to grow up without representations of themselves in most of the popular culture they experience. Similar work could be done in contemporary Native music, including jazz, rock, and hip-hop, or in the blending of traditional and contemporary crafts. Studies have barely begun of the development of professionalism or entrepreneurialism among Natives or of women's involvement in traditionally male roles. Along with striking a balance between the historical and contemporary, American studies students and scholars would do well to balance topics that are trendy (Native American "Barbie" or cruise packages marketed to Native professionals) with those that are not (the structure of the BIA and the history of federal Indian policymaking).

Impressive gains have been made in American studies and other academic fields over the past three decades in developing stronger scholarship regarding Native people, their histories, and their contemporary lives. Given that virtually every square foot of the Americas has an aboriginal past and much of the hemisphere has an aboriginal present, a fair question would seem to be why there has not been more. Students and scholars alike would do well to ask themselves whether American cultural studies can consider itself "American" without American Indians being much more central to how the field defines itself.

35

Interiority

Christopher Castiglia

An amorphous space located somewhere "inside" the human body, generating conviction ("that's just how I feel inside"), satisfaction ("I felt all warm inside"), and even identity ("I have to be who I am inside"), "interiority" has preoccupied recent work in American cultural studies. This preoccupation arguably stems from the influence of Michel Foucault's (1975) analysis of the institutional discourses shaping, implementing, and managing subjectivity and will. "Interiority," in these contexts, is the precondition and outcome of power as new knowledge regimes (pedagogical, medical, and penal) have shifted social control from forces exerted *on* the body (punishment) to institutional incentives to increase the productive forces of the body in managed systems of normalcy (discipline).

Attention to interiority emerged in the late eighteenth and early nineteenth centuries out of new institutional discourses that sought to maintain social order without impinging on Enlightenment principles of self-governance and rational liberty. Institutional knowledge permitted discipline to appear as objective benevolence, manifest in penal and educational reform and in new forms of science, psychology, and sexology. Nineteenth-century phrenology, for instance, read bumps and recesses on the skull to determine a person's "nature," locating *within* the body traits that formerly characterized social organization (the capacity for love or friendship), labor (the abilities to calculate or reason), and interaction (combativeness, acquisitiveness, or veneration).

This version of interiority required self-cultivation, making possible the individualism for which the United States became (in)famous. As citizens felt less control over public cultures made increasingly inaccessible by print, urbanization, and migration, the human interior became something they *could* control, allowing them to feel civically active without needing to engage in public affairs. To compensate citizens for the increased privatization of agency, interiority yoked obedience and pleasure. As phrenologist O. S. Fowler (1844, 21) promised, "all enjoyment flows in the direct *line* of the obedience, and all suffering bears a close analogy to that sin which causes it. The pleasure is *like* the obedience, and the suffering partakes of the same *cast and character* with the transgression."

Obedience and pleasure become especially conflated in the form of interiority called "identity." Arguing that apparently autonomous subjectivity arises from reiterative performances of cultural discourses, philosopher Judith Butler (1990, 279) conceives gender not as "a *role* which either expresses or disguises an interior 'self,' whether that 'self' is conceived as sexed or not," but as "an 'act,' broadly construed, which constructs the social fiction of its own psychological interiority." Again, phrenology provides a valuable example and precedent, since it popularized the idea that identities are the spontaneous manifestations of inner "natures" that correspond to gender

and race ("I have always found Eventuality very large in Jews," Fowler reports. "The same is true of the North American Indians, who perpetuate their history in the memories of the rising race" [135]), regions (Yankees possess strong organs of acquisitiveness, as opposed to New Yorkers [133]), and nations (the English and Germans have powers of concentration, but not Americans, "which corresponds with their national habits" [132]). The nationalization of bodily "natures" supports Paul Giles's (2003) contention that allegories of interiority have maintained fictions of American exceptionalism, impeding a fuller understanding of the culture of the United States in its global context.

Other cultural critics have bridled at the tendency to isolate the study of interiority from that of material social relationships. Terry Eagleton (1990), for instance, analyzes judgments of taste as presuming (and constructing) an interiorized realm of affective integration that insufficiently compensates people living in a postmodern age of alienating self-fragmentation and among the ephemeral pleasures of consumption, aesthetic sensation, and fashion. Gilles Deleuze and Félix Guattari (1983, 270) share Eagleton's desire to move out from the interior, faulting Freud for making the family the domain of libidinous subjectivity, establishing "interiority in place of a new relationship with the outside." Similar challenges to inflexible and predictable formulations of interiority surfaced in the nineteenth century. In the "Cetology" chapter of *Moby-Dick* (1851/1971), Herman Melville ridicules the "systemized exhibition" (116) of interior traits that will produce a clear taxonomy of whales. Instead of aligning interiority with law, whales' "internal parts" (122) reveal "peculiarities . . . indiscriminately dispersed among all sorts of whales, without any regard to what may be the nature of their structure" (122). If "a rabble of uncertain, fugitive, half-fabulous whales" (127) can defy "right classification" (122), surely the laws of human interiority ineffectively contain the social possibilities of an "almost frantic democracy" (135).

Melville's faith in the "half-fabulous" reminds us that "interiority" is not just a realm of containment and isolation, but also of imagination, fantasy, affect, aesthetics, and sensation, all of which have become sites, in recent cultural criticism, for the reinvigoration of a less-than-frantic American democracy. Despite Hayden White's (1982, 115) claim that the persistent belief in human interiority has made it "not only impossible but also undesirable even to aspire to the creation of full-blown sciences of man, culture, and society," the world-making powers of desire and pleasure, the political deployments of aesthetic sensation, the unprecedented social possibilities of fantasy, and the cultural demands made audible through melancholy and suffering have all been analyzed by cultural critics eager to trace the transformative possibilities, as well as the disciplinary dangers, of the human interior. At a moment in U.S. cultural history when politicians feel our pain, when "reality television" provides the giddy sensations absent in the mass-mediated "everyday," when elections are decided over issues of affective union, and when "terror" animates the cultural

landscape of an unevenly global security state, "interiority" is likely to remain a keyword for cultural critics well into the twenty-first century.

36

Internment

Caroline Chung Simpson

For many American studies scholars, "internment" identifies the specific process of relocation and resettlement of Japanese Americans during the early years of World War II. Indeed, the *Oxford English Dictionary*'s definition of "intern," the verb form on which "internment" is based, as "to confine as a prisoner" is an obvious and essential starting point for the discussion of internment. Yet a further investigation of the significance of internment as a keyword in American studies also requires an understanding of internment not simply as an unusual act of confining or imprisoning citizens in a racial democracy, but as typical of U.S. racial-disciplinary projects in the twentieth century. In the wake of the Cold War, political and legal comparisons tended to liken the internment to an earlier phase of Native American removal and dispersal, or, perhaps more ominously, to the system of concentration camps in wartime Europe. As the case of the Guantanamo Bay Naval Base makes clear today, these ongoing debates about the distinctive significance of internment as a system of racialization will continue to shape discussions of

Americanism and racial nationalism well into the twenty-first century.

The processes and representations of the Japanese American internment—which officially began in January of 1942 with the identification and removal of some 120,000 individuals of Japanese ancestry from their West Coast homes and into one of ten inland "relocation centers," and which lasted through 1944—have been duly recorded and widely discussed. Overwhelmingly, historical and autobiographical accounts have approached the internment of Japanese Americans as a shocking historical event, one that stands against the Enlightenment ideals of individual freedom and rights that founded the nation's mission. The most visible of these accounts is characterized by a familiar teleology of crisis and resolution that depends on a faith in neoliberal appeals to the "legal rights" and "justice" discourse shaped by modern democratic capitalism. A string of popular narratives, ranging from Monica Sone's autobiographical story *Nisei Daughter* (1953/1979) to David Guterson's novel *Snow Falling on Cedars* (1995), have explicitly promoted such resolutions.

In recent years, however, the Japanese American internment has also been cast within a broader political discussion about the mutual genealogies of racial liberalism and citizenship. Scholars interested in the development of racial liberalism have found it useful to explore the work of government social scientists stationed in the camps as a case in point. While the initial task of the camp analysts was to distinguish loyal from disloyal Japanese subjects and to suggest ways to maintain order and morale in the camps, their surveillance of Japanese Americans quickly evolved into an influential policy of racial reform that advocated the geographical and political dispersal and displacement of former Japanese communities as the answer to fears of Japanese alienage and disloyalty. The predominantly liberal and progressive anthropologists and sociologists working in the internment camps had previously studied the adaptability and assimilation of Native groups, and most of the camps were located on reservation lands that enabled a visible system of surveillance, often emblematized in memoirs of the internment as the disturbing specter of the guard tower and the barbed-wire fence.

This structural and material relationship between Native relocation and assimilation policies at the turn of the century and Japanese American internment policies during the middle of the twentieth century reverses the assumption that the agendas of liberal racial reform and militaristic suspension of rights are disconnected or contradictory gestures. What is more, the unblinking acceptance of a myth of racial progressivism and American exceptionalism may help to rationalize contemporary cases of government invasion, occupation, and violence at home and abroad. Liberal racial reform efforts proceeding from domestic crises or the imminence of war often work to reproduce racial nationalism and the stratified socio-economic relations on which it depends. Some critics have called internment "the most remembered 'forgotten' event of World War II," pointing out how the remembering of internment in many mainstream accounts presents it as a mistake whose long-neglected resolution actually reaffirms the rightness of democratic capitalism and citizenship (Fujitani 2001). More recently, critics have depicted the Japanese American internment as part of an ongoing early-twentieth-century policy of labor management through land reform and the dispossession of racialized populations (Lye 2004). This emerging critique has established internment less as an isolated historical event or ideological crisis than as part of the very logic of U.S. democratic capitalism, which reproduces its inevitability in the regulation of categories of citizenship and alienage.

Thus, internment—which we may define more precisely as the involuntary incarceration of any citizen, alien, or enemy alien, in a time of war or peace, for an indefinite period of interrogation without the filing of valid criminal charges—clearly has relevance for the twenty-first century. When an early poll conducted in the months after the September 11, 2001, attacks found that over a third of U.S. Americans approved of incarcerating all Arab Americans, Japanese American groups and progressive legal scholars were quick to react, warning of the danger of violations of civil and human rights (Kim 2001). Soon after these warnings, the Justice Department moved to abridge the civil rights of foreign nationals from predominantly Muslim nations, a decision that includes requiring the annual registration, fingerprinting, and interviewing of all male foreign nationals, as well as the monitoring of their movements within the United States and the restriction of their right to travel. The government's reliance on the unrestricted detainment

and interrogation of foreign nationals as "enemy combatants," suspected of, but not charged with, crimes at detention camps like Guantanamo Bay Naval Base, and the added revelations of abuse in violation of the Geneva Convention at Abu Ghraib prison in Iraq, have made the early warnings of former Japanese American internees seem, at the very least, more compelling. For the foreseeable future, the question of the political relevance of internment to detainment will be critically important for anyone who wants to comprehend the unfolding simultaneity of the U.S. projects of domestic racial reform and neoliberal global democracy.

37

Liberalism

Nikhil Pal Singh

"Liberalism" is one of the most important terms in Anglo-American and, more broadly, Euro-American political and philosophical discourse. It derives from the English term "liberal," which initially referred to a class of "free men" as opposed to the unfree—that is, people embedded within or bound by one or another form of socially restrictive hierarchy (Williams 1976). Liberalism has never shed the class meanings and elitist connotations at its root and origin, in large part because it indexes tensions and ambiguities at the heart of what are now referred to as liberal-democratic nation-states. At the same time, the term "liberal" has also retained longstanding associations with universality, open-mindedness, and tolerance linked to an advocacy of individual freedom and an antipathy to socially determined, collectively defined forms of ascription. As such, it has special purchase for scholars of U.S. politics and culture from Louis Hartz's seminal critique in the 1950s to the contemporary affirmations of Michael Ignatieff, as intellectual assertions about a consistent and thoroughgoing liberalism generally underpin a discourse of American exceptionalism (Singh 2004).

Colloquial uses of the term "liberal" complicate efforts to understand liberalism as one of the foundational intellectual discourses of political modernity. The conventional discussion in the United States illustrates this clearly, as "liberals" have been under sustained attack by "conservatives" for the past thirty years for what is alleged to be a reckless disregard for traditional values and moral virtue, and for a sentimental adherence to overly inclusive notions of human rights, political participation, economic distribution, and international norms. While these arguments reflect broad antinomies internal to the political history of liberalism, they also manifest a particular historical conjuncture in a much longer struggle over the prior meanings and future directions of a liberalism that is broadly shared across a spectrum of particular political positions.

Liberalism, in this larger sense, has been characterized by deep continuities as well as periodic revisions to the political, economic, and normative dimensions underlying its defining orientations. The latter can be summed up rather easily with reference to the *Oxford English Dictionary*, which defines liberalism as "respectful of individual rights and freedoms, favoring free trade and gradual political and social reform that tends toward individual freedom and democracy." This definition, replete with its characteristic repetition ("freedoms," "free," "freedom") and allusion to vague temporalities of progress ("gradual," "tends toward"), encapsulates some of the key attributes and ambiguities of liberalism. Central to every version of liberalism is an insistent, quasi-naturalistic link between human and market "freedom." What remains ambiguous is the specific historical character of liberalism's supposedly inherent "tendency" toward "democracy" and social "reform."

The modern conflation "liberal-democracy" quietly resolves this central and enduring problematic for liberalism and its adherents: how to combine an expansive, even utopian, defense of individual freedom with a stable and cohesive structure of social organization. Theorists of liberalism have looked toward two institutional mechanisms to manage this fundamental task: the self-regulating market, and one or another form of political democracy or representative government, incarnated in the nation-state. At least provisionally, therefore, we might distinguish between two strains within liberalism: *market liberalism* as exemplified by the work of Adam Smith, in which the individual is imagined as *homo œconomicus*, a person whose conduct is naturally coordinated and regulated through competition and trade with others with minimal state interference; and *political liberalism*, exemplified by the work of John Stuart Mill, in which individuals are posited as *citizen-subjects*, formally equal within a civic order whose political institutions are designed to balance and preserve individual liberty and equality (Smith 1776/1937; Mill 1976; W. Brown 2003).

One of the strongest critics of both variants of liberalism, Karl Marx (1867/1976) argued that capitalist market relations could only emerge in societies where human equality had attained the status of a popular prejudice. Yet, despite the fact that they both share a conception of the abstract and interchangeable human individual as the basis of all social organization, the coordination between the economic and political aspects of liberalism—freedom as the freedom of unregulated market activity, and freedom as a "tendency" toward political equality—has been highly uneven and has required a range of innovative thought experiments and institutional arrangements to give a "common-sense" cast to what is in fact a contradictory and unstable cohabitation. A work that illuminates this (and an important touchstone for liberalism as an intellectual project) is John Locke's *Second Treatise on Civil Government* (1690/1988), which envisions individuals in the state of "natural liberty," defined by an unlimited impulse to accumulate status and possessions, who consensually enter into a "social contract" with one another, arrogating their theoretically unlimited natural rights within civil society, and in turn establishing a government whose legitimacy rests upon its ability to secure the life, liberty, and property of its members.

Locke's theory implants property rights and class inequality at the heart of the liberal order by restricting political participation and decision-making to men of property and status, namely those whose pre-existent social credentials and private accumulation (that is, what they have supposedly "earned" in the "state of nature," *before* they voluntarily entered into civil society) is most in need of protection and legitimation (Macpherson 1962). Amplifying this critique, several thinkers suggest that Locke's theory of natural rights rests upon a broad range of social norms and conventions that the "individual, equipped with universal capacities, must negotiate before these capacities assume the form necessary for political inclusion" (Mehta 1999, 63). Those without an adequate stake in the social order, including the propertyless, those temporarily or permanently unable to exercise reason (i.e., children and the insane), and those whose presumed conjugal or domestic status supersedes their claim to public individuality (i.e., women) can in this view be governed without their consent (Pateman 1988).

The problems of political domination, exclusion, and inequality within liberalism are deepened dramatically when we consider the historical record of liberal-democratic nation-states founded in racial slavery and colonial expansion. Lockean liberalism in this context encodes a split view of the "state of nature," one that is idealized and viewed retrospectively from the standpoint of established civil society, and another that is historical, comprised of people who purportedly lack reason and who thus exist (in Locke's words) like "wild Savage Beasts, with whom Men can have no Society or

Security" (quoted in Mills 1997, 87). This liberalism contrasts an already "moralized" state of nature, defined by private property, with a wild, uncultivated nature. Indeed, this is the basis for Locke's famous advancement of historically extant justifications for the dispossession of Native lands in British settler colonies—North America in particular: Indians did not possess any property rights due to their failure to create value through commercial cultivation, or the steady, patient admixture of their labor with the land. Although he opposed hereditary slavery, Locke himself was heavily invested in the transatlantic slave trade, revealing what was at best an inconsistency, and at worst the divided normative vision that would gradually codify "racial" difference as a principle technology naturalizing exclusion within liberal-democratic societies.

How an unlimited—indeed a universal and universalizing—concept of human freedom could be so consistently combined with and underpinned by differentialist logics of exclusion and exploitation—of the propertyless, of women, of slaves and aboriginal peoples—would become the most vexing theoretical and political problem of twentieth-century liberalism. One of the crucial, unresolved debates among critics and defenders of liberalism is whether political exclusion is inherent within liberalism, or whether it is an artifact of historically contingent divergences between the theoretical universalism of liberalism and exclusionary social practices of liberal societies founded on race, class, and gender inequality. The latter view opens up the possibility of a politically productive dynamic in which demands for political and civic equality among excluded groups and categories of persons (women, racial and sexual minorities, colonized subjects, disabled people) have steadily advanced the convergence of the theoretical universalism of liberalism and the social and political boundaries of liberal-democratic nation-states across the world-system (Myrdal 1944).

Even if one resists the strong teleological presumption behind this last claim, it is possible to suggest that the idealized schematics of liberal universalism yielded distinctive patterns of political struggle and transformation. As Karl Polanyi (1944/2001 155) argued, nineteenth-century liberal doctrines of laissez-faire capitalism actually promoted "an enormous increase in the administrative functions of the state"—to enclose common lands, create pools of wage-labor, police vagrants, provide relief for the poor, open colonial markets, manipulate money and credit, and so on. At the same time, these powerfully destabilizing processes and events engendered counter-movements for the reasonable "self-protection of society," in the form of trade unions, voluntary associations, public health initiatives, and rural and environmental conservation, as well as anti-colonial movements for national sovereignty. What Polanyi called the "double movement" developed over time into a strong critique of the ideology of the self-regulating market, culminating in the social institutions and economic redistributions of the modern welfare-state.

Against the backdrop of the crisis of the Great Depression, the U.S. philosopher John Dewey (1927) denominated "renascent liberalism" as those efforts of "organized society" to develop and use political administration to produce the "actual" and not merely the theoretical liberty of the national citizenry. This meant first and foremost the emergence of state-directed policies toward equalizing the distribution of the national income. The key innovations here were in the economic domain and are generally ascribed to the British economist John Maynard Keynes, who argued for a more extensive regime of market regulation, economic planning, and public spending against the old "orthodoxies" of laissez-faire capitalism. Although Keynes was undoubtedly concerned to stave off revolutionary challenges from below, it is reasonable to ask whether the kind of social liberalism developed under the auspices of Keynesian economic policy is a fundamental deviation from what we still want to call liberalism. Polanyi (1944/2001, 242), for example, described "socialism" as "the tendency inherent in an industrial civilization to transcend the self-regulating market by consciously subordinating it to a democratic society," and he viewed the U.S. New Deal as a decisive step in that direction.

Other writers have been less sanguine about the inner tendencies of liberalism, particularly against the backdrop of mass democracy. In the face of the political crisis of post–World War I Germany, for example, political philosopher (and later Nazi jurist) Carl Schmitt (1985) presciently warned that "states of emergency" would force liberal-democracy to "decide between its elements." Schmitt identified democratic unanimity with sovereign capacity to decide on excep-

tions to the law, and he argued that this conjunction revealed the political anemia of liberal proceduralism (that is, parliamentary deliberation, separation of powers, and protection of individual rights). Advancing a sharp critique of the universalizing claims of liberalism, Schmitt defined democracy as "the equality of equals" and the production of a homogeneous "form of life." In doing so, he once again envisioned a doubled space where the rule of law and right enjoyed by "civilized" peoples was predicated on the violent suppression and control of contiguous or adjacent "wild" spaces, as exemplified by European (and U.S.) colonial history.

Writing at the height of the McCarthy period in the U.S. (but with a different political agenda and sympathies), Louis Hartz (1955) decried what he called the "dogmatic liberalism of a liberal American way of life." According to Hartz, this "liberal tradition," despite its expansive individualism, was inherently conservative and "conformitarian," possessing a "deep and unwritten tyrannical compulsion" at its core that led to periodic outbursts of nationalist hysteria, moral panics, "deportation deliriums," and "red scares" (12). Hartz's critique marks a seminal moment in the development of a critical American studies discourse as it emerged from wider streams of reflection on the meaning and import of culture in the moment of U.S. global ascendancy. For despite his generally cynical and ironic standpoint, Hartz proposed an "unconscious" or "mass Lockeanism" as the key to the national character, and as an answer to the old American exceptionalist saw: Why is there no socialism in the United

States? The puzzle for Hartz was that "Americanism" so consistently "combined McCarthy with [Woodrow] Wilson" (13). Thus, U.S. liberalism was marked both by a cosmopolitan, expansionist drive to "transform things alien," and by insular, parochial withdrawals into home and nation (286).

Hartz's critique lent itself to a certain political quiescence; it also underplayed the ongoing racial and imperial crisis of modern liberalism. In this sense, thinkers from the political left and those associated with new social movements of the 1960s and 1970s developed more powerful critiques of post–World War II liberalism (particularly as it had been leavened with anti-communism) as a regime of political compromise and coordination within the North Atlantic world that forestalled more radical potentials for working-class self-organization at home and decolonization abroad. Thus, anti-colonial theorist Frantz Fanon (1963) denounced the "universal violence" of a Pax Americana that preserved what he called "luxury socialism" for Europe, while subjecting the rest of the world to a violent and capricious decolonization, under the shadow of global nuclear annihilation. From within modern welfare states, feminist and antiracist activists excoriated the racial and gender hierarchies and differential inclusions that continued to skew material distribution and symbolic recognition for those long subordinated within the liberal order. A further line of criticism, associated with Michel Foucault (1975), cast the long historical development of the administrative or governmental state as a deepening of disciplinary techniques and normalizing logics that enmeshed individual subjects in an extensive network of power relations and intensive systems of social control.

Even as it was attacked from the left, however, liberalism was, to paraphrase British cultural studies scholar Stuart Hall (1978), moving to the right. As Irving Kristol famously quipped in the late 1960s, a neoconservative was merely a liberal who had been "mugged by reality." The image of a mugging invoked the specter of black street crime, the alleged soft tolerance of "liberal" inclusion, and rage at the perception that the U.S. had lost its moral claim to be the world's exemplary liberal-democracy in the wake of the Vietnam War. It is clear that since the 1970s another renovation of liberalism—often arrayed under the moniker "neoliberalism"—has been underway and gaining momentum. A hybrid (like all forms of liberalism), neoliberalism resurrects "pre-Keynesian" assumptions that free markets automatically generate civic order and economic prosperity, even while it gradually eviscerates democratic norms of political participation by an informed citizenry, re-imagining both individuals and groups as primarily "entrepreneurial actors" (W. Brown 2003, 5).

A significant challenge for critical intellectual work in the coming years will be to track the political contours and consequences of neoliberalism in a moment of resurgent U.S. imperialism. As Locke famously wrote, "In the beginning, all the world was America." Today it appears at times that we have come full circle, with the United States attempting to turn the world into itself. "A deep continuity connects U.S. global ambition from the eighteenth to the twenty-first century," something that may have a lot to do with Hartz's Lockean political unconscious (N. Smith 2004, 11). A danger is that the U.S. face of neoliberal globalization, with its consumptive excesses, blunt force, casual racism, and crude market calculus, augurs the exhaustion of the politically productive, incipiently democratic "double-movement" of liberal universalism and liberal exclusion and a turn to something far more ominous. As long as liberalism continues to dominate the political horizon, however, the ongoing and wholly consequential struggle to determine the character of its distinctive precipitates of economic liberty and political equality, individual freedom and normative exclusion, reformist perfectionism and counterrevolutionary animus, cosmopolitan vision and provincial blindness, are likely to continue.

38

Literature

Sandra M. Gustafson

Derived from the Latin *littera*, or letter, "literature" for many centuries referred to a personal quality ("having literature") that meant possessing polite learning through reading. To call someone "illiterate" in the seventeenth century did not mean that the person could not read; it meant that the individual was not possessed of learning, notably knowledge of the clas-

sics. Any formal written work—for instance, a scientific treatise, a sermon text, a work of philosophy, or an ethnographic narrative—counted as "literature." Then around 1750 the historic associations of literature with literacy and polite learning began to change. Literacy rates rose, printing presses became more common, and the products of the presses became increasingly varied. Reading styles slowly shifted from intensive reading of a few works to wide reading of many works, authorship emerged as a distinct profession, and printed works were increasingly treated as intellectual property. All these factors undermined the association of literacy with polite learning and affected the definition of literature, until eventually it was restricted primarily to works of imaginative literature, notably poetry, drama, and fiction (Kernan 1990; Amory and Hall 2000; McGill 2003).

This account of the emerging conception of literature summarizes developments in Europe and in creole communities in the Americas. Some distinctions are worth stressing. The colonies of British North America were among the most literate communities of their day. The Protestant tradition, which stresses the authority of scripture and the priesthood of all believers, justified the extension of literacy as a tool of spiritual enlightenment and of redemption from bondage to sin. Literacy contributed as well to religious community, uniting like-minded people around the reading of the Bible (Amory and Hall 2000). A parallel but secular narrative that links literacy, enlightenment, political freedom, and civic community emerged somewhat later, gaining prominence in the age of revolution (D. Hall 1996). Often entwined, these two liberationist narratives explained and promoted the high rates of literacy, particularly in New England, where the Common School movement joined other efforts to expand access to education during the antebellum period.

Even as literacy came to be understood as the basis for an informed citizenry and an essential component of democratic civic responsibility, the expanding array of reading materials available to the literate was a matter of concern to guardians of social order. From the beginning of the nineteenth century, when ministers and cultural elites fretted over the potential of the novel to distract women and the lower classes from their prescribed tasks and roles, to Anthony Comstock's campaign against "dangerous books" at the end of the century, to current debates about "banned books" and the Internet, the increasing availability of cheap and often sensational or politically charged texts produced a backlash from those who believed that literature should function as a tool of social discipline (Davidson 1986/2004).

Works of literature could be used to nurture critique as well as conformity. Among those who identified critique as a central function of literature were the writers now associated with the project of creating a U.S. national literature, notably Ralph Waldo Emerson, Henry David Thoreau, Margaret Fuller, Walt Whitman, and Herman Melville. Writing at the moment when European national identities coalesced around distinct literatures constituted by a shared language and allegedly bearing the marks of the genius of the "race" that produced them, writers associated with the Transcendentalist and Young America movements began in the 1830s to create what they considered to be a distinctively "American literature" (Matthiessen 1941; Widmer 1999). Literature came to be defined less in relation to categories of fiction and nonfiction than by its efforts to manifest a uniquely "American spirit" through its subject matter and form. Some writers and reformers identified the uniqueness of "American literature" in its use of critique to nurture social progress (M. Gilmore 1985).

Such overtly nationalistic literary efforts were more the exception than the rule on the literary scene of the United States, however. Until 1891, when an international copyright law was passed giving foreign authors intellectual property in their works, the U.S. book and periodical markets were dominated by reprints, many of them works by English writers. Moreover, in contrast to the more centralized publishing institutions of Europe, the U.S. book market was regional and heterogeneous until after the Civil War. In many instances the market was multilingual, with regional presses publishing works in a wide range of languages, particularly German, Spanish, and French. The multilingual nature of the U.S. market grew with the acquisition of formerly French and Mexican territories and with the enormous influx of immigrants after the Civil War (Sollors 1998; Shell 2002; McGill 2003).

The consolidation of a mass book market in the twentieth century tempered but did not eliminate the heterogeneity of the literary marketplace in the United States. For many decades, literature was defined by its representative and inclusive nature. The consolidation of a more exclusive, more narrowly "literary" canon during the Cold War was soon challenged, first by the democratization of universities that began in the 1950s and later through the canon-busting movements of the 1960s through the 1980s. The rise of ethnic literatures and the emergence of performance art contributed to these broadening trends as well. Other factors influencing the expanded notion of the "literary" in American cultural studies include the development of interdisciplinary methodologies and programs; the rise of theory within English departments; and the impact of British cultural studies, with its emphasis on social forms, media, and "communication." Debates about "cultural literacy" led to the conceptualization of multiple literacies (Graff 1987; Kernan 1990).

The challenges that these social, cultural, and intellectual movements pose to a narrow conception of literature are not novel features of a debased modern mass culture, as is sometimes argued. Manuscript, performance, and electronic forms of verbal expression have always complicated and resisted the consolidation of a restrictive, print-based sense of the literary. For instance, the circulation of poetry in manuscript form had an important vogue in the middle of the nineteenth century, at the height of what is often called "print culture," a trend most famously instantiated in the fascicles of Emily Dickinson (Cameron 1992; Howe 1993; M. Smith 1998). Beginning in the late nineteenth century, and with growing vigor during the following century, artists' books reflect a vital interest in visual elements and non-print modes of literary production (Drucker 1995).

For much of the nineteenth century, political and religious oratory were central to the world of letters. Even as U.S. writers suffered the contempt of the English reviewers and the competition of foreign reprints, the nation's orators were celebrated (not always without irony) as peers of Demosthenes and Cicero. Oratory was perceived as the ideal verbal art, a consummate republican form. Compilations of "great American speeches" were produced in substantial numbers. Critics wrote books analyzing the qualities and strengths of various orators. Elocution was a popular subject of study, and students rehearsed Patrick Henry's famous words in schools. In 1851, Daniel Webster's collected speeches were published, perhaps the first such collection to appear during an orator's lifetime. Thirty years later his speeches were still being analyzed for their contributions to U.S. American letters. The influence of oratory runs through the essays, fiction, and poetry of the antebellum period and constitutes an important element in the era's literary culture. Performance art, poetry readings, standup comedy, and other verbal arts are all heirs of the spoken word from this earlier era (Gustafson 2000).

The continued influence of oral genres has been particularly important for ethnic writers. Alphabetic literacy not only was in some instances prohibited to African Americans and Native Americans, as in the slave codes outlawing literacy training. It also came with the added burden of being identified as a skill derived from and properly belonging to whites and often used to advance their interests through false treaties and unjust laws. For some ethnic-minority verbal artists, literacy was a tool of oppression and, at times, of self-division, separating an individual from a community distinguished by oral forms of verbal art. In the twentieth century, writers and other artists associated with the Black Arts movement, as well as many Native American writers, reflected on the paradoxes of oppression and liberation intrinsic to the alphabetic literacy central to their artistic projects. U.S. literary history cannot be fully understood without reference to the oral forms that it excludes in its very name, the forms that modern critics call "orature" (Lauter 1990; Gustafson 2000).

Today the rise of electronic media poses important challenges to print culture. Beginning in 1990, a series of books and studies has tracked the impending "death of literature," linking its demise to social trends such as the democratization of the university and, increasingly, to technological developments, notably the rise of the World Wide Web. These critics characteristically employ the most restrictive definition of "literature," limiting it to poetry, drama (in a book, not on the stage), and, above all, the novel. The novel has special status for these writers, who often take it to be the paradigmatic literary form because of its length, the "linear" reading that it encourages, and the solitude and consequent richness of subjectivity that novel-reading is supposed to produce. They trace certain forms of social order and cultural organization to widespread engagement with "the literary," in this narrow definition (Birkerts 1994; Edmundson 2004).

These claims for and about "literature" have not gone unchallenged. One of the most striking recent developments in American cultural studies is the emergence of a critical discourse focused on recognizing and understanding the range of textual media and their varied modalities of creative verbal and visual expression. Studies of electronic media demand that scholars rethink the heterogeneous nature of textuality and the varied forms of reading that these textualities produce (McGann 2001). This approach opens new avenues for interpreting older textual forms, such as "Aboriginal oral, glyphic, artefactual modes, and conceptualizations of communication" (Battiste 2004). This new work foregrounds the specific historical and contemporary institutions and practices that are organized by alphabetic literacy. It also engages a broader archive in its effort to document the interactions between the products of such literacy and those who produce and consume them.

39

Market

Meredith L. McGill

References to "the market" abound in contemporary American cultural studies scholarship, but historians and critics who use this term are not always referring to the same thing. As an abstract noun, "market" can refer to the potential demand for a commodity or service, or to the actual state of trade at any one moment; it can refer to the trading network for a particular commodity, or, more generally, to the business of buying and selling. The phrases "market society" and "market culture" are frequently used to invoke the promises and constraints of a capitalist economy, even though the buying and selling of goods, often to distant consumers, is not specific to capitalism. Economic historians and political theorists have elaborated distinctions that can help us to use this term with greater precision: to distinguish stages in the historical development of the U.S. economy; and to attend to the uneven growth of markets for different kinds of goods.

From the early modern period through the nineteenth century, the dominant meaning of the word "market" was highly specific. Markets happened at a particular time and place; they involved groceries and other provisions, but were built around the sale of perishable goods such as meat. Butcher-turned-historian Thomas De Voe's *Market Book* (1862), for example, details which butchers occupied which stalls in the public markets of the major Eastern seaboard cities. The

kinds of barter and commerce—and the social mixing—that occurred in such markets are ancient in origin and remarkably persistent as cultural practices (Agnew 1986; Stallybrass and White 1986). When scholars of the nineteenth-century United States use the term "market," however, they are usually thinking of the shift from marketplaces to a market economy—the articulation of local and regional markets into a national trade system. Economic historians have a number of ways of judging when the coordination of local markets has occurred: when prices fluctuate in sync with one another, and when they converge, that is, when the inter-regional practice of buying in cheap markets and selling in expensive ones works to narrow the price differentials that fuel such trading (Rothenberg 1992). Other threshold conditions of a market system include the establishment of a competitive market for labor and the removal of geographic, social, and cultural impediments to the mobility of goods and labor. In the United States, a national trade system linking geographically distant and diverse regions was in place by the 1850s, but it was not until the final decades of the nineteenth century, when the Supreme Court began routinely to use the Constitution's "commerce clause" to overturn state and local regulation of interstate trade, that a truly national market was created (Bensel 2000).

Historians and theorists disagree as to when and how markets have made a difference in Western societies. Karl Polanyi (1944/2001) regards the nineteenth-century attempt to set up a self-regulating market—one subject neither to government regulations nor to the interventions of individuals—as the crucial pivot point between an economy that was embedded in social relations and one that turned social relations to market ends. Polanyi identifies the separation of economic relations from government superintendence and the exposure of individual workers to a competitive and often ruthless market for their labor as the most consequential legacies of what he called "The Great Transformation." By contrast, C. B. Macpherson (1962) locates the shift from a status society to a simple market society as early as the seventeenth century. In a customary or status society, neither land nor labor could be sold freely, while in a simple market society workers began to be bound by contracts rather than by their position in a social hierarchy rooted in relationships to the land. For Macpherson, the shift to a "possessive market society" characteristic of mature capitalism depended on an emerging consensus that all individuals maintained the right to sell their labor, a right that outstripped land as the primary locus of property and the engine of capitalist expansion (Haskell and Teichgraber 1996).

Part of what makes "the market" a tricky concept is that its character shifts depending on one's vantage point. From the perspective of government agencies and private organizations seeking to regulate corporate behavior, the market is aligned with the private sphere and is often depicted as dangerously independent of public oversight. And yet, from the perspective of women seeking economic independence or merely to work for wages outside the home, or from the perspective of emancipated slaves seeking to

loosen their ties to the land, the market is aligned with the public sphere and is cast as a site of potential liberation. Bruce Robbins (1993, xiv) has suggested that "the capitalist economy, which figures as both private (for liberals) and public (for feminists)" is "a crucial place both where the public/private opposition breaks down, and where it demonstrates its resistance as well."

Some differences in scholars' usage of the term can be traced to the transfer from history to literary and cultural studies of the idea of a "Market Revolution," a term popularized by Charles Sellers (1991). Sellers focuses on the social and cultural effects of economic change in order to forge a closer relationship between political history and economic history, recasting the period that had been known as the "Age of Jackson" or the "Second Party System" in explicitly economic terms. Sellers argues that in the antebellum United States, the shift from subsistence farming to a market economy was at every stage politically contested—in debates over centralized banking, national transportation networks, and tariff rates, as well as in the struggle over slavery. Literary and cultural critics, on the other hand, have tended to treat the "Market Revolution" as inexorable and apolitical, something that happened more or less in a single stroke, leaving only aftershocks for criticism to trace. The resulting emphasis on the market as an all-encompassing set of forces has obscured the differences between and among markets that developed at different rates in different regions, offering different sets of constraints and opportunities. After all, to note that there is a "market" for a particular good or service doesn't begin to describe how that market works, or what it is like to be subject to or subjects of that market. For instance, the market for literature in the United States was shaped by a host of local, institutional, and state forces; it was uneven in its development and uncertain in its reach, differed markedly by genre and format, and was complicated by the persistence of barter, exchange, patronage, gift economies, gentlemanly publishing, vanity publishing, and the substantial publishing operations of religious and charitable organizations. While cultural critics often use "market" as a synonym for "audience," the purchasers of books may not read them, and readers, such as those who read this book in a library, may not be purchasers.

Scholars as different as Fernand Braudel (1982–84) and J. K. Gibson-Graham (1996) have questioned the comprehensiveness of the reach of market culture at any one point in time. Braudel distinguishes market behavior, which he considers to be universal, from the historically specific development of monopoly capitalism, which he regards as a subversion of the ideals of market-exchange. Gibson-Graham provocatively argues that left-wing critics of capitalism have exaggerated its power by popularizing the image of a unified, totalizing market-system. Gibson-Graham details a range of anticapitalist and noncapitalist economic practices, such as self-employment, domestic labor, and producer cooperatives, which resist the logic of capitalism, even as they overlap with and depend on the market system. Both scholars enjoin us not to assume that the dominant economic system

absorbs and subsumes all forms of social and economic activity.

Along these lines, critics frequently use the term "market" as part of a compound noun, referring to the condition of trade with respect to a single commodity: book market, slave market, marriage market, stock market. Critical attention to the differences between and among multiple markets could reorient American cultural studies, encouraging us to consider different histories, rates of nationalization, and patterns of local and regional resistance. Attention to the specificity of markets might also help us to think about the ways in which a focus on the market-in-general has obscured a history of markets that is centrally shaped by race and gender. The print market provides an early instance of the general sense of the word. With the exception of publishers' trade sales, books and periodicals were not sold at a particular time and place but were made available at multiple sites and, for much of the nineteenth century, circulated chiefly through the mails.

By contrast, the dominant nineteenth-century image of a market localized in time and space came to be the slave market—a spectacular commodification of human labor that was, paradoxically, bound up with a critique of labor-as-commodity. Slaveholders frequently defended the slave system through passionate criticism of the degradations to which wage-laborers were subject in British and Northern factories. In order to sustain this critique, slaveowners needed to deflect attention from horrific scenes of buying and selling slaves to the supposedly more favorable labor conditions on the plantation (W. Johnson 1999). And yet the centrality of the slave market to the spread of the slave system should complicate the idea that the establishment of a market for labor could in any simple sense mark the threshold of a market system. The origin of the very notion of economy in household management similarly calls out for an account of how the idea of the market was wrenched away from contexts that included or privileged women. Scholars of nineteenth-century U.S. culture such as Gillian Brown (1990), Amy Dru Stanley (1996), and Lori Merish (2000) have detailed the centrality of gender to the legitimation and inner workings of an emergent market society, while Wendy Gamber (1997) has called our attention to the thriving millinery and dressmaking trades, which employed hundreds of thousands of women but which are frequently overlooked in male-centered definitions of what counts as commercial enterprise.

There is much to be gained by considering how the market-in-general—the abstraction of value, mobility of labor, and regional integration necessary for economic development on a national scale—has shaped U.S. society, transforming modes of sociality and fostering ideals of self-regulation and economic rationality. But there is also much to be gained by attending to the historical specificity of markets and the processes by which they are transformed into what is typically imagined today to be a single economic system, synonymous with capitalism. The *Oxford English Dictionary* identifies the understanding of the singular noun "market" as "the operation of supply and demand in the competitive free market," and the understanding

of "market forces" as independent economic factors, as extremely recent coinages—1970 for the former and 1942 for the latter. As we strive to understand the changing relations between economic conditions and U.S. culture, we should be careful not to project backwards a vision of the saturation and global reach of a market economy that many take to be characteristic of the twenty-first century.

40

Marriage
Elizabeth Freeman

Marriage seems to be an ordinary fact of life, not a contested concept. In U.S. culture, however, the term "marriage" has pointed to two simultaneous but incompatible functions. As a component of U.S. kinship law, marriage sanctions particular sexual alliances, from which property relations are determined. It thereby defines a sphere of protected sexual and economic interests, whose exterior is marked by sexual "deviants." Yet as an aspect of modern emotional life in the United States, marriage is the ideological linchpin of intimacy—the most elevated form of chosen interpersonal relationship. At the core of political debate and much critical debate in American cultural studies is whether marriage is a matter of love or law, a means of securing social stability or of realizing individual freedom and emotional satisfaction. These have become national questions; marriage seems so tied to collective national identity and democratic practices that many U.S. Americans view it as an expression of patriotism. This linkage is more than rhetorical. As well as structuring sexuality and gender, marriage law undergirds U.S. citizenship, because it is implicated in the property relations, racial hierarchy, immigration policy, and colonialist projects that have determined national membership.

Historically, the institution of marriage has been regulated by both church and state, a merging partly responsible for its contradictory meanings. Christian scriptures stipulate that marriage makes a man and a woman into "one flesh." But Christian marriage also takes place within a larger, communal body of Christ whose members are united by spiritual bonds rather than the property relations of aristocratic families. Protestants, in giving governments control over marriage in the mid-sixteenth century, elevated the couple as the primary social and economic unit. The burden of caretaking shifted from Christian communities, aristocratic *paterfamilias*, and the government, and onto spouses and parents. Here, legal issues (the loss of institutionalized provisions for the economically distressed) were reconfigured into emotional ones (family feelings). Western European popular culture eventually solidified this ideological triumph of love over law and property. The literary genre of the sentimental novel, emerging in the eighteenth century, secularized the Christian image of a couple embedded in and figuring a community bound by love, rather than terrorized by hierarchical class relations or, later, legal interference.

In England and its American colonies, the conflicting functions of marriage became implicated in questions of nationhood beginning with a clash in Enlightenment political theory. Following Sir Robert Filmer (1680), the male-headed, hierarchical Puritan household was considered an arm of the government. Later colonial and Revolutionary-era thinkers, however, adhered more closely to Locke's doctrine that the private "voluntary compact" between a man and a woman historically preceded and provided the basis for democratic relations in the public sphere, while remaining separate from it (Locke 1690/1988; Norton 1996). This ideal of consensual, private marriage suffused Revolutionary rhetoric in the eighteenth century (Fliegelman 1982). Thus the founders of the United States saw marriage as a template for the ideal society, in which a people freely consented to leadership rather than submitting to a hierarchy (Cott 2000). Intimacy, as they imagined it, would mirror kinship; love would meet law and even prefigure it. Correspondingly, marriages in the new republic were seen as rehearsals for or reenactments of a proper citizenship grounded in family feelings (Kerber 1986).

One problem with this use of marriage as a figure for liberal democracy was that marriage has long structured the asymmetrical power relations that constitute gender. The unwritten spousal contract, most visible in nuptial vows and suits for divorce or separation, assigned economic support and physical protection to men. In exchange, women's duties included sexual intercourse, childbirth, housework, and childrearing. Thus the term "marriage" also implied patriarchy, for men controlled the economic and physical well-being of their wives and children. It implied domesticity for women, who exercised their power in the home only. But this contract was not actually drawn between two legal individuals. Following the common laws of England even after the Revolution, U.S. women who married were *femes coverts*, with no legal existence independent from that of their husbands. Women could not own separate property, keep their earnings, sign contracts, or vote to change this system. In these and other practices, men and women were considered as one, and the one was the husband. Debates in American cultural studies about marriage were prefigured by early republican writers who analogized coverture and political tyranny. "Remember the Ladies," wrote Abigail Adams (1776) to her husband, "Do not put such unlimited power in the hands of the Husbands. Remember all men would be tyrants if they could."

Analogies between marriage and other forms of political inequality continued in the abolitionist era and beyond, as white feminists equated wifehood with slavery (Sánchez-Eppler 1993). Until the 1970s, the cultural expectation of husbandly economic support in exchange for wifely domestic support removed middle-class women from the workforce and provided uncompensated labor for working men and, thereby, for the institutions that employed them. As feminists would eventually argue, marriage creates domestic labor, the unpaid work of women who process raw materials for workers' consumption and socialize children for the workforce (Delphy 1977). Socialists argued that

marriage further bolsters the system of capitalism by keeping profits in the private family (Engels 1884/1972). It turns wealth into a matter of inheritance rather than lifetime accumulation, preventing redistribution to a larger public and thereby enforcing work for pay among the propertyless class. Yet the Protestant legacy has meant that marriage is also viewed as an individual solution to poverty, far preferable, for conservatives, to a welfare state. In 2003, for instance, the U.S. Congress passed a bill (H.R. 4) mandating that every state receiving welfare funds establish objectives for promoting marriage.

Still, to speak of marriage as a form of slavery, or even as an essential feature of market capitalism, fails to address its racial politics. Marriage law served as a means of securing white dominance. Slaves could not marry; free black people were legally forbidden to marry whites in many states from the 1660s to 1967; and rights to inheritance were denied to the black partners of whites and their children (Saks 1988). One effect of this history was that many African Americans saw the right to marry as fundamental to achieving full citizenship. After the failure of Reconstruction, black fiction writers often used the sentimental marriage plot to allegorize the civil justice they had been denied (Tate 1992). But not all African Americans have taken marriage to be a sign of or path to freedom. When in 1865 the Freedman's Bureau insisted that all former slave unions be legitimated by license or ceremony, some freedpeople, especially women, declined to register their unions (K. Franke 1999). A century later, when the infamous report on the black family by

Daniel Patrick Moynihan (1965) appeared, it blamed the social woes of African Americans in part on "matriarchal" households where unmarried women were the primary or only breadwinners. This interpretation of African Americans' kinship structures racialized, gendered, and sexualized poverty, setting the stage for the welfare reforms of the 1980s and beyond.

The racial politics of marriage have also inflected its role in colonial projects within the United States, as well as in the nation's immigration law. By legitimizing, promoting, and protecting the monogamous heterosexual relationships of its citizens and automatically extending citizenship to those born within them, nation-states make national belonging seem a matter of nature and not law. Marriage legitimates birthright, which trumps mere residence as a means of access to citizenship (Stevens 1999). Thus European settlers in the colonies persecuted Native Americans in part because their kinship systems and sexual practices sometimes included polygamy, easy divorce, and premarital sex. During the period of American Indian removal, the government allocated plots of land using Anglo, not Indian, kinship as a grid. Once the federal government took full control over immigration in 1891, marriage became a means of excluding racialized groups from entry or permanent resident status in the United States. Asians and Muslims, for instance, were often excluded under laws barring polygamists and prostitutes from entry. Since the lifting of racial quotas, immigrants have had an easier time entering the United States as family members than as laborers. The laws currently linking marriage explic-

itly to citizenship, known as family reunification laws, have their precedent in a 1907 statute mandating that the nationality of an American woman follow the nationality of her husband (Cott 2000). Although it was eventually repealed in the 1930s, this law provided a blueprint for the preferential treatment of foreign spouses over other immigrants. Lesbian and gay international couples, however, are denied this benefit.

While for the federal government marriage provides the very architecture of citizenship, the individual states actually have jurisdiction over marriage. Thus federal law has only rarely intervened positively to define marriage or to prohibit particular kinds of marriage between free people. The first of these interventions occurred in 1862, when Abraham Lincoln signed the Morrill Act prohibiting polygamy in the U.S. territories. In 1890, the Mormons were forced to give up polygamy as a condition of statehood for Utah. The next federal intervention was the Defense of Marriage Act, signed by Bill Clinton in 1996. George W. Bush has followed suit with a campaign for a constitutional amendment prohibiting same-sex marriage. An arguably theocratic state reemerged with these official enforcements of Christian, monogamous, heterosexual marriage. Even as a national lesbian and gay movement has promoted gay marriage, U.S. voters and government officials have moved furiously to prevent it.

The power of marriage as a guarantor of gender identity and sexual hierarchy, a paradigm of democratic consent, an island of economic security, a mechanism for racial solidarity, and the scaffolding of citizenship itself explains the passion of these debates (Duggan 2004a). Despite the constitutional separation of church and state, the Protestant model of marriage has historically been a prerequisite for belonging to "America." Merely allowing same-sex couples this privilege will not change that. The critical tasks ahead include continuing to ask what other hierarchical institutions marriage serves or is implicated in. At the same time, we must look beyond marriage and couplehood by working to democratize support for the diverse household structures and emotional bonds that organize people's lives.

41

Mestizo/a

Curtis Marez

The terms "mestizo" (masculine) and "mestiza" (feminine) come from sixteenth-century Portuguese and Spanish, but over the past few hundred years they have been incorporated into U.S. English. In general, mestizo/a refers to racial and cultural mixing among Europeans, Indians, and Africans. As nouns, "mestizo" and "mestiza" refer to a mixed man and woman, respectively, but the word may also be used as an adjective, as in "the mestiza writer" or "a mestizo nation." The process of such mixing is called "mestizaje." These words have long and complex histories in diverse parts of the world, including Asia and the Americas, but

their most prominent usages in American cultural studies scholarship have referred to the Mexico/U.S. borderlands. In that context, the meanings of "mestizo" have been intimately shaped by dominant and oppositional political movements.

The earliest known appearance of "mestizo" is in a Portuguese dictionary from the 1560s, where it is treated as a synonym for "mulatto." Subsequent texts emphasize a broad set of mixtures, including different kinds of animals and humans. In response to the long Moorish presence in Spain, "mestizo" was used to describe the offspring of Christian and non-Christian parents, as well as Spanish Catholics who had become acculturated Arabs. Like "hybrid," the early uses of "mestizo" referred to "almost any kind of mixture, of wild and tame, of citizen and non-citizen, of resident and traveler" (Forbes 1992, 125).

With the expansion of overseas empires, new uses of the term developed to describe and govern subjected peoples. In mid-sixteenth-century India, Portuguese speakers used "mestizo/a" to describe people who were half Asian and half Portuguese; around the same time, Jesuits in Brazil employed it in reference to the mixed population. Spanish colonizers used the word in the Philippines and in Spanish America, at first to signify mixtures of religion, class, local origin, and culture, but over time its meanings shifted toward racialism and caste. Starting in the mid-sixteenth century, "mestizo" was increasingly distinguished from "mulatto." Over the next hundred years, the semantic line between the two terms would harden, so that in Spanish colonial usage "mulatto" came to mean

African and Indian mixes whereas "mestizo" came to mean part Spanish and part Indian.

The earliest English citation recorded in the *Oxford English Dictionary* (*OED*) is from Richard Hakluyt's *Principall Navigations, Voiages, and Discoveries of the English Nation* (1583). Here and in subsequent entries from the seventeenth to the nineteenth centuries, English-language authors use "mestizo" to indicate intermarriages between Europeans and non-Europeans in the Portuguese and Spanish colonial worlds. The *OED* neglects, however, influential examples from the U.S.-Mexico War (1846–48). While the Spanish (and subsequent Mexican) political system was built on the incorporation and manipulation of mestizaje, mid-nineteenth-century commentators indicate that the U.S. empire was instead built on segregation. Opponents of the annexation of Mexico argued that it would harm U.S. democracy to incorporate a "mongrel" race such as the Mexicans. One newspaper editor warned that Mexico was "a sickening mixture, consisting of . . . a conglomeration of Negroes and Rancheros, Mestizos and Indians," while in Congress one Representative argued that it would be impossible to assimilate "the mongrel, miserable population of Mexico— the Mexicans, Indians, Mulattoes, (and) Mestizos" (quoted in Horsman 1981, 239, 242). Although pro-war forces won out and the United States invaded Mexico and took large portions of its land, the racism of the anti-annexation side continued to influence attitudes and policies directed at Mexican peoples in the United States, often serving as an excuse for discrimination and exploitation. By the 1920s, an influential

eugenics movement attempted to clothe such racism in the prestige of science, arguing that, as a mongrel race, Mexican mestizos threatened the nation with racial degeneration. So widespread had the negative meanings of the word become that in 1934, Fox Studios named one of its western film villains "El Mestizo." Although such frankly racist sentiments are uncommon in mainstream venues today, "mestizo" remains current on white-supremacist websites as a pejorative synonym for "Mexican."

In the first third of the twentieth century, another current of meanings emerged in Mexico, where intellectuals, artists, and politicians used "mestizaje" to represent the postrevolutionary nation. Mestizos were a significant force in the revolution, and subsequent Mexican governments promoted their images as symbols of national unity. Critics often cite José Vasconcelos's influential study *The Cosmic Race* (1925/1997), in which the Mexican minister of education outlined his theory that, far from being a form of racial degeneration, mestizaje was a means of progress. According to Vasconcelos, whereas the United States had insisted on racial purity, the Spanish empire had incorporated beneficial forms of racial mixing. He concluded that mestizaje had the potential to produce a universal culture that could overcome divisions and combine the best of world cultures. After the revolution, nationalist mestizaje was popularized in film and other media, particularly in the figure of Cantinflas, the popular Mexican actor who specialized in comic underdog roles about the mixture of the rural and the urban. One frequent critique of official Mexican uses of the term, however, is that they symbolically incorporate mestizos while leaving actual mestizos on the margins of society. The nationalist focus on mixture further tends to "disappear" Indian peoples. Similar claims could be made concerning Africans.

This brief etymology raises questions about the relationships among mestizos, Indians, and Africans in the Americas. As Jack Forbes (1992) suggests, in Spanish *mestizo* reflected a relatively new hierarchy with whites on top, Africans and Indians at the bottom, and mestizos/as in the middle. Mestizos/as were stigmatized by the Spanish, but because they were closer to "whiteness" they were often afforded rights and privileges denied to Indians and Africans. By contrast, some mid-nineteenth-century Anglo-Americans placed mestizos/as closer to Indians and Africans, while others argued that Mexico's mixed population made it an essentially Indian country. This ambivalence is also central to contemporary debates. Does mestizo/a identity stabilize hierarchies by partly "whitening" mixed people and dividing them from people of color? Or does it produce possibilities for oppositional coalitions by pushing mixed people closer to oppressed Indians and Africans?

During the late 1960s and early 1970s, writers and activists associated with the Chicano movement revised Mexican concepts in order to construct their own form of nationalism that was opposed to U.S. nationalism and imperialism. Insisting on the word "Chicano" to distinguish their political positions from those of prior generations, who sometimes identified as "Spanish" or "Mexican American," members of the

Chicano movement also used the term "mestizo" to guard against assimilationist identity constructions that denigrated indigenous histories and cultures (Valdez 1972). Instead, mestizaje was promoted as a source of pride and progressive political possibilities. Although some members of the movement based their political identities on essentialist models of racial mixing, others recalled earlier histories where the term signified cultural mixing. "Mestizo" and "mestizaje" were often employed to describe instances of cultural hybridity, as in the combination of indigenous and European rituals and belief systems, hybrid historical memories, and mixed European and indigenous iconographies.

In some cases, this version of mestizaje led Chicanos/as to seek coalitions with African Americans and Native Americans, but in others it led to an exclusionary nationalism in which Chicano political claims trumped those of other groups. This is particularly true with regard to Native Americans. "Mestizo" perspectives sometimes led Chicanos/as to make claims to a native or indigenous status that partly displaced Native American claims. This problem is not unique to the United States; concepts of mestizaje have created political conflicts between Latin American mestizos/as and indigenous peoples, and between mestizos/as and members of the African diaspora (Hale 1994; Rosa 1996; Beck and Mijeski 2000).

A related criticism of the Chicano movement is that its theory of mestizaje was masculinist and heterosexist, since its prototypical subject was imagined as decidedly male and straight. Feminists criticized the movement's elision of gender, but such arguments gained critical mass only in the 1980s, notably with the publication of Gloria Anzaldúa's *Borderlands/La Frontera: The New Mestiza* (1987/99). Combining the racial and cultural meanings of the term, Anzaldúa used "mestiza" as a metaphor for the kinds of borderland subjectivities produced by multiple discourses and practices of gender, sexuality, race, class, nationalism, and imperialism. Not only is *Borderlands/La Frontera* a powerful rejoinder to Chicano movement sexism and homophobia, but it also articulates a version of mestizaje that has served as the basis for coalition-building among women of color and others. Whereas historically "mestiza" has been used either pejoratively or, more recently, as a neutral descriptor (as in the fields of history and anthropology), Anzaldúa affirms mestiza consciousness as a potentially critical, activist identity informed by material histories of oppression (Alarcón 1996).

Although debates continue regarding the limits and possibilities of Anzaldúa's theories, her use of "mestiza" raises questions about the relationship between hybridity and power. Since the 1980s, cultural critics have increasingly used "mestizaje" to describe not racial but cultural differences. Although such an emphasis avoids the sorts of racism described above, the concept risks becoming a free-floating signifier, abstracted from the material histories that have produced mixed peoples. Moreover, cultural mestizaje may dovetail with the reifications of contemporary capitalism (Hames-Garcia 2000). In addition to the significant number of scholarly books that use the term in titles, "mestizo" is also the name of a commercial film, a popular music group, a paperback western novel, a café, and an Internet-based company that sells Mexican crafts. The Spanish translation of the sixth Harry Potter book, *Harry Potter and the Half-Blood Prince*, is entitled *Harry Potter y el Principe Mestizo*. And near the end of *The Motorcycle Diaries* (2004), the fair-skinned actor who plays Che Guevara makes a toast to the "mestizo race."

Finally, mestizo has become a privileged term for thinking about the future. It is often used in titles that project near-future mixtures, as in such books as *Mestizo: The History, Culture and Politics of the Mexican and the Chicano, the Emerging Mestizo-Americans* (Vento 2002), *Mestizo America: The Country of the Future* (Ospina 2000), and *The Future Is Mestizo* (Elizondo 2000). There the term signifies looming demographic transformations and cultural hybridities that are already beginning to overtake the present. In some versions, the coming mestizaje is positive and utopian, as in the "Mestizo Christianity" in which, recalling Vasconcelos, theologians argue that mesitzos/as bear the future hope of God's plans for humanity. In other cases, it recalls earlier uses that suggest a dystopian future. A recent public policy report called *The Changing Face of the San Fernando Valley* (Kotkin and Ozuna 2002), for instance, includes a chapter entitled "The Mestizo Valley." "Once virtually all-white, and overwhelmingly native born," the report claims, "the San Fernando Valley has become increasingly a mixed area—mestizo in Spanish—that challenges many of the traditional assumptions still held about the region." Recent work by Harvard political scientist Samuel P. Huntington projects such concerns nationally, arguing that immigration poses a threat to "the Anglo-Protestant values that built the American dream" (Huntington 2004a, 1). Well known for his influential theory of the clash of civilizations between Christian and Islamic cultures, Huntington's newest research translates the biological racism of the U.S.-Mexico War period into cultural racism by suggesting that Mexican Catholic values are inferior. In these ways, different articulations of mestizo draw upon different historical tendencies, including the dystopian futurology of Anglo-American racism and the utopian futurology of the post-Mexican revolutionary era and the Chicano movement.

42

Modern

Chandan Reddy

"Modern" is among the most difficult words in our critical vocabulary either to define or to abandon. Within different disciplinary contexts, both the origins and the features of the modern are differently inscribed. Philosophy locates the onset of the modern in the eighteenth-century secularization of knowledge about the human and material world, while history and political science periodize it alongside the generalization of the sovereign nation-state after the Treaty of Westphalia in 1648 and the emergence of the citi-

zen-subject after the French Revolution of 1789. For economics the modern began with the emergence of capitalist market economies following the British Industrial Revolution, whereas literary studies traces it to the invention of the printing press and the gradual universalization of schooling and literacy. The hallmarks of modernity as defined by these intellectual traditions include the development of free labor, universalist notions of culture, and abstract notions of equality. As 85 percent of the globe's land mass was forcibly submitted to colonial rule, Western intellectuals and their publics, enthralled by the birth of "modernity," promoted "progress" by fixating on these features as the endpoint of colonial development. It was now, as one British poet wrote on the eve of the U.S. colonization of the Philippines in 1899, "the white man's burden" to shine the light of modernity globally (Kipling 1899).

Derived from the Latin terms *modernus* and *modo* (meaning, respectively, "of today" and "recently"), "modern" first entered the English language around the twelfth century as a term to denote a newness that required legitimation in contrast to classical antiquity. Yet it was only with the rise of the European Enlightenment in the mid-eighteenth century that "modern" took on "the sense of a qualitative claim about the newness of the times, in the sense of their being 'completely other, even better than what has gone before'" (Koselleck 1985; Osborne 1995, 10). By the nineteenth century, the modern possessed an epochal character, promising a *qualitative* transformation from the past, now itself understood as comprised of discrete epochs with distinct features. Shaped by its relation to other terms such as "progress," "development," "freedom," "revolution," "society," and "civilization," modern was no longer a mere temporal descriptor. Instead, it signified a "newness" previously unavailable in human consciousness and societies, a distinctive orientation of thought toward the future rather than tradition, and a uniquely "scientific" worldview that located Europe as a coherent geography and temporal center of global history (T. Mitchell 2000). Largely through the force of British and European colonialism, the term was no longer contrasted with "antiquity," but instead with "backwardness," a category that encompassed both "older civilizations" in decline and "primitive societies" frozen in an earlier moment of human history. Whole societies, peoples, and art forms were now classifiable as primitive, degenerate, or modern, with the latter positioned at the leading edge of historical time and serving as the measure of human perfectibility.

By the mid-nineteenth century, the keyword "modern" thus began to function much as it does today, connoting something both temporal ("that which is most recent" within the context of developmental linear time) and spatial (the grouping of otherwise diverse phenomena into a single category or class). Modern peoples, practices, and objects are said to share a qualitative uniqueness that merits the reflexive practices by which modern societies interpret their particular historicity as representative of universal human progress. By this logic, to designate a thing, practice, place, or person as "modern" is to point to the signs by which reflexive acts of interpretation identify the modern condition (Habermas 1987). Virginia Woolf's (1986) famous modernist declaration, "On or about December 1910, human character changed," exemplifies how these meanings overlap: the use of a date to mark both a unique, irreversible event in chronological calendar time and a specific temporalized event, qualitatively new, bearing upon universal "human experience." As a representative statement of a broad aesthetic movement, it also conveys the sense of artistic modernism as centrally preoccupied with new *practices of representation*, a critical aspect of the reflexive scrutiny necessary for the modern age.

Emerging out of the same historical conjuncture as artistic modernism, the discipline of sociology describes the modern as coincident with the development of Western industrial capitalist societies. For mainstream sociologists, the defining features of modernity are mass citizenship, official bureaucracy, a national division of labor, long-term capital accumulation, the separation of social spheres, organized leisure, rational individualism, secularization, and a state monopoly on violence across a geographically bounded society. Identifying these features has enabled sociologists since the mid-twentieth century to study societies comparatively, recommending "modernization" to those areas of the globe that, lacking these features at the social and institutional levels, were characterized as socio-economically "backward." Modernity thus became a regulative ideal with multiple empirical coordinates, the presence or absence of which could be verified by specialists in particular "area studies." In the 1950s, the economist and political scientist W. W. Rostow distinguished between "traditional" and "modern societies," describing the latter as societies whose economies could "take off," or, in other words, could experience continuous long-term growth through processes "internal" to their separate national economies (N. Gilman 2003). As U.S. Cold War anti-communism extended to the newly decolonized world through various modernization strategies, Rostow's take-off model legitimated overt and covert interventionist wars and development policies in Asia and Latin America, coding them as acts that protected economies and societies from the perverting drives of communism (Escobar 1995; Saldaña-Portillo 2003). The irony that the task of "modernizing" non-Western economies sanctioned U.S. neocolonial interventions did little to undermine the theory's popularity or effectiveness in mapping a world of closed national economies in different stages of universal economic development, each "protected" by the benevolence of U.S. policies of modernization.

For some researchers and scholars today, the category of the "postmodern" names a break with the modern occasioned by the emergence of finance capital; a global division of labor across transnational communities; a decline of liberal freedom; the expansion of the prison-military-industrial complex; a loss of "nature"; an explosion of digital technologies and other simulacra; and an increasingly racialized, gendered, and sexualized cultural politics (Harvey 1989; Soja 1989; Baudrillard 1994). These theorists of postmodernism historicize ruptures in modernity as an effect of an advanced or late capitalism, naming postmodernity as the condition of late capitalism and postmodernism as its dominant cultural logic (Jameson 1991). In doing so they repeat a modernist impulse, namely, the desire for a knowable social totality graspable by a unitary epistemological subject. In response, postcolonial scholars have stressed that the postmodern critique of linear development ought to offer the opportunity for a radical displacement of "Western modernity" and the knowledge regimes that create and sanction our ignorance of the complex local histories that mediate modern processes (Spivak 1988). They see in the postmodernist stress on crisis, particularly of form and meaning, the disavowed recognition of the breakdown of unified Western histories and epistemological categories for regulating discrepant postcolonial modernities (Chakrabarty 2000).

To understand the origins and significance of this more thoroughgoing critique of modernity, we need to situate it as an engagement with the political economy of global Euro-American colonialism. Haunted by the racialized social practices that enabled metropolitan prosperity, the category of the modern has abetted the mischaracterization of that prosperity as universal progress, thus displacing the contemporaneity of colonial social formations from its account of the modern and temporalizing the peripheries of the world system as non-modern (Amin 1976). In this context, earlier conceptions of the "modern" should be seen as the effect of practices of intellectual abstraction that seek to extricate the West from the actual strategies and relations of accumulation that organized its domination of the world economy, including the violence, destruction, and privation that accompany its prosperity (Benjamin 1968). The social formations that have emerged out of practices of continental genocide (A. Franke 1998), slavery (E. Williams 1944), territorial colonialism (Chandra 1980), and imperialism (Du Bois 1995) have rarely been understood as modern. Instead, the term has named the practices and concepts through which Euro-American societies narrate their originality as the universal development and futurity of all human societies, occluding the global social relations, divisions of labor, and market economies through which they were built. Epistemologies of race and gender have mediated knowledge of these social forces, inventing the "West," not as a set of differentiating practices within a world economy or global modernity, but rather as a closed European historical space moving through linear time (Said 1978).

A different view of the modern can be found in the work of contemporary interdisciplinary scholars, particularly in the fields of historical sociology, postcolonial anthropology, and cultural studies. Here, the term indexes an attempt to understand the *multiple* modernities that have been produced through worldwide capitalism and that cannot be reduced to or understood through a universal norm, such as the nation-state. In American studies scholarship influenced by this research, explorations of racial, gender, and sexual formations that exceed the nation form have produced important critiques of the epistemologies that organize dominant and normative conceptions of U.S.

modernity (C. Robinson 1983; Ferguson 2004; Singh 2004). Some of this scholarship has found in the "female African slave," the "Asian coolie," and the "undocumented diasporic worker" the standpoint through which alternative, non-national modernities might be explored (Anzaldúa 1987; Camp 2003; Jung 2006). Some of it has stressed the ways in which U.S. modernity (and postmodernity) represses the intra- and international "regional" modernities of racialized working peoples, appraising these alternative *late* modern geographies as disjunctive social spaces that undo the nation's capacity to unify historical difference (Bonus 2000; Agarwal and Sivaramakrisnan 2003). And some scholarship has located *late* modernity in the standpoint of the perverse, privileging non-normative forms of sexual and gender embodiment that normative modern subjects persistently repudiate as pathology and atavism (Eng 2001; Shah 2001; Manalansan 2003; Gopinath 2005). In each instance, these critical studies of U.S. late modernities have interrogated the epistemologies through which we have come to know ourselves as modern; the racial, gendered, and sexual genealogies constitutive of these epistemologies; and the ethical and political implications of acknowledging the social relations and histories that these epistemologies have generated as our "non-modern" shadow.

To situate these various interventions within the context of late modernity is to suggest that our task today may be to ruminate collectively on the erasures, gaps, and incompletions that are a necessary part of any endeavor to tell the story of our modernity. But it is also to note that the conditions for these endeavors are not locatable, as they are for many postmodernists, exclusively in transformations to the structure of capital or in the break-up of the nation-state. They are equally to be found in the demographic transformation of the university through anti-racist struggle, in postcolonial migrations, and in the internationalization of the disciplines that have enabled a "return of the repressed" within modern epistemologies (Gulbenkian Commission 1996; Hong 2006). For scholars attentive to these shifts, modernity poses a question one cannot fully answer, since no single perspective or location can survey the social totality and each paradigm of thought must be critically scrutinized for what it encourages us to let go, forget, or disperse as historical detritus. The resulting research cannot seek merely to create a more inclusive "American modernity" by applying modern disciplinary knowledge to otherwise neglected social identities and histories. Rather, it needs to situate the formations of modern knowledge within global histories of contact, collaboration, conflict, and dislocation, examining in each instance how the category of the modern has distorted those global histories, producing unity out of hybridity and development out of displacement. These modernist misrepresentations are reproduced in the contemporary norms by which we feel and know ourselves to be modern subjects. But they also appear in the inability of modern knowledge to attend to "non-modern" social practices and formations. In the contradictions of our late modernity, these emerging practices and formations offer the opening for a differ-

ent politics of knowledge, what one scholar has called the "politics of our *lack* of knowledge" (Lowe 2006) about modern societies, their colonial histories, institutional forms, and possible futures.

43

Nation

Alys Eve Weinbaum

"Nation" has been in use in the English language since the fourteenth century when it was first deployed to designate groups and populations. Although the concept of "race" was not well defined in this period, the *Oxford English Dictionary* (*OED*) retrospectively refers to such groups and populations as "racial" in character. In the modern period, the *OED* continues, the meaning of "nation" came to refer to large aggregates of people closely associated through a combination of additional factors, including common language, politics, culture, history, and occupation of the same territory. Although it appears that an initial racial connection among nationals was later supplanted by a widened range of associating factors, the early understanding of "nation" as based in race and "common descent" remains central to discussions of the term to this day, either as a retrospective imposition of the sort orchestrated by the *OED* or as a "natural" grounding. An important contribution of American cultural studies has been to interrogate race as description, metaphor, and/or synecdoche for nation, and to insist that an uncritical conflation of race and nation constitutes a pressing political and theoretical problem. Indeed, as numerous scholars argue, ideas of race and racist ideologies continue to subtend the expression of nationalism in the United States, which is unsurprising given that the founding and consolidation of the nation was pursued as a project of racial nationalism that arrogated full belonging (if not citizenship) to whites, or, in nineteenth-century parlance, to those of Anglo-Saxon descent.

Beginning in the late eighteenth century, when nation first accrued consistent political usage and "national" became a routine noun used to designate individual subjects, the constitution of political units (nation-states) comprised of so-called nationals began to center around identification of the factors that would ideally cohere large aggregates and bestow belonging on individual members of such groups. During the nineteenth century, generally referred to as the century of modern nationalism, principles of inclusion and exclusion were hotly debated by political pundits favoring immigration restriction or curtailment and various population-control measures that, over time, profoundly shaped the racial, ethnic, and class composition of nations by designating those who could rightfully belong and by circumscribing that belonging through restriction on the reproductive pool and designation of the progeny of "mixed" unions as "illegitimate" or "foreign." Such nineteenth-century debates exposed nation-formation as deeply ideological—as involving processes of self-definition and self-consolidation as often dependent on the embrace as on the persecution of differences, especially those construed as racial in character.

Even as nationalization centers on the construction of a people, it also raises questions of land and territory. In the case of modern settler nations such as the United States, South Africa, and Israel, nationalization has depended upon the transformation of a territory into a "homeland," on the defeat, enslavement, and genocidal destruction of "natives," and on the subsequent expropriation of land from those already inhabiting it. In this sense, nation-building and imperialism ought to be seen as closely and historically allied. As Seamus Deane (1990, 360) eloquently explains, "Nationalism's opposition to imperialism is . . . nothing more than a continuation of imperialism by other means." Imperialism arises contemporaneously with modern nationalism because the two forms of power have needed each other. The ideology of racial, cultural, and often moral superiority that is used to justify imperialism is also always at least in part national and vice versa. Like imperialism, nation-building is an ideological and material project that involves continuing reorganization of space, bodies, and identities. It is at once individual and collective, internally and externally oriented, destructive and productive, and all too often brutally violent.

Although philosophers and political scientists writing in the transatlantic context tend to agree on the range of factors that may be used to identify nations and the nationals belonging to them, they continue to argue over the nature of the elusive glue that binds individuals into nations. In his famous lecture "What Is a Nation?," first delivered at the Sorbonne and often regarded as the gambit that inaugurated contemporary debate, Ernest Renan (1882/1990) suggests that language, culture, and territory are not in and of themselves enough to constitute a nation. Rather, to all these must be added a common substance capable of binding disparate individuals into a people. And yet, paradoxically, this substance is far too ephemeral to be readily or decisively distilled. Approximating religious faith or spirituality but not reducible to either, nationalism, Renan suggests, is nothing more or less than an inchoate feeling, albeit an extremely consequential one. By contrast with citizenship, a set of political and civil rights guaranteed to nationals based on their legal belonging within the nation, "nation-ness" and feelings of national belonging are far harder to pin down.

This vexing question of what binds nationals to one another has led contemporary theorists to argue that nations are fictions given solidity through political and juridical processes that transform them into material practices, including population control and eugenic containment, immigration restriction and curtailment, and full-scale genocide. As a materialized fiction, national belonging may thus be understood as what Raymond Williams (1977) has labeled, in a different context, a "structure of feeling": an emergent sentiment not easily articulated, but so deeply and fully inhabited by individuals and collectivities that it appears to them as primordial, inevitable, and enduring. Thus on the one side (commonly denoted as uncritically nationalist, often jingoistic) we find the

nation discussed as a "natural" formation. On the other side (which holds itself above nationalism, or opposes it in the form, for instance, of socialist internationalism or Enlightenment cosmopolitanism), we find the nation posited as a harmful construction. In this latter view, nationalism is seen as fomenting dangerously partisan solidarities, and the nation as a fiction that is made to cohere through ideological pressures that masquerade as "natural" but are in fact self-interested, self-consolidating, and ultimately driven by capitalist and imperialist imperatives. As world-systems theorists such as Immanuel Wallerstein (2004) argue, nations can be regarded as racialized economic and political units that compete within a world marketplace comprised of other similar units. As the globe divided into core and periphery, into regions comprised of those who labor and those who exploit such labor, nations at the core often rationalized their economic exploitation of those of the periphery by racializing it.

Although individuals may move from one nation to another, thus losing or being forced by law to forego one form of citizenship for another, feelings of national belonging cannot be forcibly stripped away. Indeed, such feelings are often willfully carried with individuals and groups as they migrate. In the United States, the bipartite, sometimes hyphenated, identities of some nationals—Italian Americans, Irish Americans, Polish Americans—express such national retention or carryover. In these instances, which must be contextualized within a framework of voluntary migration, the designations "Italian," "Irish" and "Polish" indicate a desire to retain a previous national identity now regarded as cultural or ethnic. In other instances, self-constituting invocations of national identity have been transformed into a critique of dominant nationalism, or into an alternative imagination of nation, as with the forms of insurgent Third World nationalism examined by the theorist of decolonization Frantz Fanon (1963). In such instances, the new or invented nationalism competes either to exist alongside or to displace the dominant national identity, which is viewed as a violent imposition. In the Americas, this is perhaps most evident in movements for Native sovereignty that work to build tribal nations, or in the form of Chicano nationalism that claims Aztlán as both a mythical homeland and a name for the portion of Mexico taken by the United States after the U.S.-Mexico War of 1846–48.

In the case of modern diasporas, we witness yet another form of oppositional nationalism, one occasioned by forced displacement and shared oppression. In those instances in which a homeland no longer exists or has never existed, or in which a diasporic people seek to constitute a new nation unconstrained by the dictates of geography, ideas of nation and national belonging come into sharp focus. Consider the black nationalism that had its heyday in the United States and the decolonizing world in the 1970s, or Queer Nation, an activist organization that gained prominence in the United States during the 1980s and early 1990s. Although very different in political orientation, both movements appropriated the idea of the nation to contest dominant forms of nationalism and to reveal the constitutive exclusions that enable national hegemony. Somewhat paradoxically, the imaginative creation of these collectivities revealed, even as it mimicked, the constructed nature of hegemonic nations formally recognized as political states.

This idea of hegemonic nations as ideologically constructed or "imagined communities" is most famously elaborated by Benedict Anderson who, in the early 1980s, theorized the emergence of the modern nation out of the nationalist revolutions that took place throughout the Americas in the late eighteenth and early nineteenth centuries. As Anderson (1983, 19) argues, nations are brought into being by peoples whose access to print culture enables collective imagination of involvement in a political and cultural project that extends back into a "immemorial past" and "glides into a limitless future." Anderson built his theory on modern European historiography (especially Eric Hobsbawm's work [1983]) that argued that nations produced themselves by inventing traditions that enabled them to constitute populations as historical and cultural entities meaningfully joined over time and in space. Anderson is also indebted to critical theorist Walter Benjamin (1968), who theorized the "homogeneous empty time" characteristic of modernity—a temporality that Anderson regards as necessary to national imagining and that he calibrates to a set of technological developments, principally the invention of the printing press and the tabloid newspaper. Together, print culture and the thinking of "nation time" that it enabled allowed people living in a given territory and speaking and reading a similar language to materialize connections to one another in a synchronic and cohesive manner that was previously unthinkable.

Numerous scholars of third world nationalisms have taken issue with Anderson's Eurocentric and teleological view of national development and have called attention to his overemphasis on print culture (thus exposing his theory's dependence on the application of European-style nationalism throughout the world, and on the presupposition of universal literacy as a requirement of national development). Yet others have used the idea of the nation as an "imagined community" to argue for the special relationship between nationalism and print culture, and nation and narration more generally. As postcolonial theorist Homi Bhabha (1990) avers in a formulation self-consciously indebted to both Renan and Anderson, "Nations, like narratives, lose their origins in the myths of time and only fully realize their horizons in the mind's eye. Such an image of the nation—or narration—might seem impossibly romantic and excessively metaphorical, but it is from . . . political thought and literary language that the nation emerges . . . in the west."

The idea that nations need narratives to exist—that they need to be narrated into being—has resonated for an entire generation of American cultural studies scholars. Their research suggests that elite and popular cultural texts, including public spectacle and performance, are and have been used to consolidate and contest various nationalist projects. Some of these scholars focus on texts manifestly intent on nation-building (e.g., the *Federalist Papers*) or on offering alternatives to hegemonic nationalism (e.g., W. E. B. Du Bois's *The Souls of Black Folk*), while others dwell on those that are less transparent in their ideological commitments, but that may be read against the grain to expose the processes through which nationalist sensibilities are generated and torn apart (e.g., Gertrude Stein's *The Making of Americans* and Americo Paredes's *George Washington Gómez*). Literary scholars working on U.S. culture from the Revolutionary War through the present have been at the forefront of such inquiry, focusing on canonized traditions and on texts authored by those who have been historically minoritized within the nation. Such writings frequently expose the ideologies of racism, sexism, and heterosexism that lie at the heart of U.S. nationalism (Berlant 1991, 1997; D. Nelson 1992, 1998; Wald 1995; Lowe 1996).

Central to this scholarship is an understanding that, in the United States and elsewhere, the relationship between nationalism and racism can be characterized as one of "historical reciprocity" (Balibar 1994) in that modern nationalism expresses itself as racial. With the centrality of this relationship in mind, researchers have focused on histories of Native American genocide, African American enslavement, and immigration to the United States over the last three centuries. As such work attests, westward expansion of the frontier in the eighteenth and nineteenth centuries was facilitated by racist ideologies that viewed Indians as "lesser breeds" whose removal or extermination was necessary to the establishment of Anglo-Saxon civilization (Horsman 1981; Hietala 1985;

Rogin 1996). Four hundred years of enslavement and disenfranchisement of Africans was the steep price paid for the creation of whiteness as a form of "personal status property" (C. Harris 1993) that functioned as a guarantor of national belonging and citizenship rights. After the Civil War and well into the twentieth century, the nativist and restrictionist policies toward immigrants from Southern and Eastern Europe and Asia allowed for further consolidation of the United States as a white nation whose population could be imagined as principally Anglo-Saxon, and thus as free of the taint of "foreign blood." As detailed case studies have demonstrated, ethnicized immigrant groups have shed the taint of their otherness through expressions of various forms of racism. Indeed, entrance into the national fold has invariably depended upon a group's ability to differentiate and distinguish itself as white and free (Roediger 1991; Allen 1994; Jacobson 1998). Central here are both internally directed racism responsible for keeping the national body "pure" by separating "true" nationals (free whites) from non-nationals (slaves and natives), and externally directed racism or xenophobia that clearly defines the nation's borders and keeps "undesirable" immigrant populations (those deemed "unassimilable") out.

Feminist and queer scholarship has further complicated our understanding of the dialectic between race and nation by demonstrating that men and women participate differently in nation-building and that reproductive heterosexuality plays a decisive role in the creation of nationalist ideologies, which are, in turn, deeply gendered and heteronormative. As such scholarship makes plain, it is misguided to study nations and nationalism without bringing to bear a theory of gender power and an understanding of the historically sedimented relationship of nation-building to reproductive politics (Parker et al. 1992; McClintock 1995; Caren Kaplan et al. 1999). Women commit themselves to and are either implicitly or explicitly implicated by others in the production of nations, nationals, and nationalism in a number of ways: as active participants in nationalist struggles for liberation; as mothers, the biological reproducers of subjects and national populations; as upholders of the boundaries of nations through restrictions on reproductive sexuality and the circumscription of marriage within ethnic and racial groups; as teachers and transmitters of national culture; and as symbolic signifiers of nations (Yuval-Davis and Anthias 1989).

Though often overlooked, the reproductive dimensions of the idea of "nation" are embedded within the term (derived as it is from the Latin root, *natio*, to be born). Likewise, the idea that nationals are literally reproduced has been naturalized and rendered invisible within many national cultures. In the United States, birth to a national is one of the principal bases upon which both national belonging and citizenship are granted (Stevens 1999). In practice, the idea that national populations are reproduced by racially "fit" or "superior" mothers has been used to justify a range of eugenic policies that allow some women to reproduce while restricting others. Nazi Germany is the most glaring example of such eugenic celebration of national motherhood and of the control of reproductive sexuality. However, it is too seldom acknowledged, particularly when the Nazi example is invoked, that the mainstream eugenics movement of the early part of the twentieth century emerged not in Europe but in the United States, where it was widely celebrated as a means to "strengthen" the national populace by "breeding out" so-called degenerate members of society, including immigrants, people of color, homosexuals, and the "feebleminded" (Ordover 2003).

The idea that nationals and nations are reproduced is not only or simply a material reality, but also an elaborate ideology positing that the essence of nationality is itself reproducible. Within this ideology, protection of the "naturalness" of heterosexual reproduction becomes central, as does the construction of women's wombs as repositories of racial identity (Weinbaum 2004). Buried within the ideology of national reproduction is a concept of the female body as the source from which nationals spring, and the related idea that national populations are racially homogeneous and can be maintained as such only if sexual unions that cross racial and ethnic lines are carefully monitored and even more carefully represented. Significantly, in the United States, it was not during the antebellum period that interracial sex was most forcefully legislated against and a mixed nation (a so-called miscege*nation*) vociferously denounced, but rather after the Civil War, Emancipation, and incorporation of African Americans as citizens. In other words, although master and slave sex was routine, it was only after black people began to be regarded as nationals and were granted at least some of the rights held by other (white) citizens that sexuality across racial lines was deemed threatening to the national body.

The continuous policing of reproductive sexuality characteristic of most forms of modern nationalism ought to lead us to the realization that just as nationalism is an ideology inextricably intertwined with racism, so too are racism and nationalism bound together with sexist and heterosexist reproductive imperatives. From this perspective, it becomes clear that in order to fully limn the idea of nation it is necessary to refocus the study of the keyword on discussions of the ideological and material processes that exploit existing race, gender, and sexual hierarchies in the production of nations, nationals, and feelings of national belonging. Such a reorientation ideally would begin with the idea that the "nation" is differently produced in each instantiation and historical conjuncture, and within the context of each raced, gendered, and sexualized social and political formation.

44

Naturalization

Priscilla Wald

"Naturalization" evolved as a keyword along with the modern conceptions of political belonging that we have come to associate with the nation. The term appeared first in Middle French to describe the conferral of the rights and privileges of a native-born subject on a foreigner. While the noun form dates from the late sixteenth century, the verb "naturalize" preceded it by a century. Usage of "naturalize" spread quickly throughout Western Europe in the sixteenth century, expanding to include the conversion of something foreign—words and phrases, beliefs and practices—into something familiar or native. With their roots in the Renaissance, "naturalize" and "naturalization" continue to register the concerns of the moment of their coinage: an emerging interest in social classification and taxonomy, an increasing emphasis on human agency and the potential to adapt sufficiently to a new environment to enable settlement, and a fascination with the interplay between the natural world and human experience.

A new word attests to the need for a new category. It is not surprising that "naturalization" debuted with the conferring of rights on the French in Scotland and the Scottish in France, since the intermarriage of the two royal families called for such accommodation. Nor is it an accident that its proliferation coincided with exploration and mercantilism. The movement of peoples, goods, and boundaries gave rise to the need for new models of belonging and new mechanisms of induction into emerging political and social communities. The terms "naturalization" and "naturalize" also signaled an interest in birthrights at a time when social hierarchies were tentatively but distinctly coming under new scrutiny.

The Latin *natio* (meaning "birth") is the root of "nature," "native," and "nation," and the interconnections among these terms have generated some of the most fundamental debates and discussions in statecraft and philosophy. They manifest an ongoing fascination with, and the relentless efforts to locate, the boundary between what is innate and what is learned. Raymond Williams (1985, 219) dubs *nature* "perhaps the most complex word in the language" and notes its various and sometimes almost contradictory meanings. It is at once what is most intrinsic and most external: the compelling force and the properties or features of the self and of the material world, that which precedes, exceeds, and informs culture. "Nature" operates according to its own laws, and the project of science, art, and philosophy is to discover, engage, and sometimes—at great risk—defy them.

"Naturalization" represents that defiance, as it heralds the possibility of adaptation and the promise of transformation. It implies an environment that can accommodate the introduction of a foreign element. While, as botanists and zoologists explain, the introduction of such an element might temporarily upset the equilibrium of an ecosystem, naturalization implies its restoration. In its original usage—as the conferral of political belonging—naturalization is not an occult process, is not meant to seem *natural*; it is squarely in the realm of civil law. Rituals and ceremonies—the performing of a prescribed oath, the pledging of allegiance to a flag—characteristically mark the conversion and call attention to the conventionality of the process.

This conventionality is perhaps nowhere more apparent than in the contradictory meanings of the word "native." Originally designating a person born in bondage or servitude, the term gradually came to refer to the more neutral fixity of one's birthplace before it again acquired a derogatory connotation, this time as an allusion to the indigenous population of an uncivilized (or "natural") place. The term was applied alternately to the native-born descendants of the colonizers, who automatically acquired the rights and privileges of citizenship, and the indigenous populations who preceded them and who were typically excluded from those rights, especially in "new world" territories settled by Europeans. A member of an indigenous tribe in the United States, for example, was a native, but not of a nation, as the Cherokee learned when they sought political representation through the U.S. Supreme Court in 1827, only to discover that they were neither citizens nor aliens, hence not entitled to legal personhood in the United States (Wald 1995). Eventually, the contradiction became unsustainable, and the 1924 Indian Citizenship Act conferred U.S. citizenship—which is to say nativity—on all non-citizen members of tribal nations "born within the territorial limits of the United States" (Michaels 1990; Maddox 1991).

As this example indicates, the origins of the United States in settler colonialism led to an especially fraught relationship between birthright and national citizenship. Naturalization was particularly important in this historical context since the survival of the nation depended upon its rapid population with citizens prepared to assume responsibility for its growth. Among the complaints leveled against the British monarch in the Declaration of Independence in order to justify colonial rebellion was that he had obstructed "the Laws of Naturalization of Foreigners; refusing to pass others to encourage their Migrations hither." Yet, the concept of a nation as a political entity rather than an aggregate of people distinguished by their common descent and heritage was still relatively new, and the original meaning of the term has haunted its subsequent incarnations. While national belonging was explicitly touted as a matter of affiliation rather than filiation, or consent rather than descent, the familial rhetoric that characterized the nation from the outset justified the earliest restrictions; not everyone was eligible for membership in the family (Sollors 1986; Lowe 1996; G. Brown 2001; Ordover 2003; Weinbaum 2004). The Naturalization Act of 1790 defined a potential citizen explicitly as "any free white person" and specified two years' residence in the territorial boundaries of the nation to qualify. These requirements underwent a rapid succession of revisions through the 1790s and into the early years of the new century amid debates about the ideal profile of the nation and its citizens and the nation's rapid ability to reproduce itself (R. Smith 1997; Jacobson 1998; Stevens 1999).

Subsequent debates about the qualifications for national citizenship waxed and waned with fluctuations in immigration and adventures in colonialism. Like earlier territorial annexations in the West and Southwest, global migrations that brought unprecedented numbers of immigrants, especially peasants from Southern and Eastern Europe, to the United States at the turn of the twentieth century spawned an obsession with political belonging (Higham 1963; Takaki 1989, 1993). The topic was extensively discussed and contested in the political speeches, editorials, and so-cial-scientific studies, as well as in the immigrant auto-biographies that proliferated during this period. These debates introduced a new element into the vocabulary of "naturalization," bringing the term "Americaniza-tion" into vogue, along with the language of rebirth and conversion to describe the assumption of citizen-ship. "Americanization" rhetorically replaced "na-ture" (descent) with "nation" (consent), but the substitution only underscored how fully "American" had become a birthright. The familial rhetoric, which intensified with the debates, undermined the distinction between citizenship and kinship, and nat-uralization was increasingly cast in the language of adoption.

A widely circulated 1894 speech by future president Theodore Roosevelt evinces this important shift. In-sisting that "Americanism" was a faith and not a birthright, Roosevelt welcomed the right kind of peo-ple with the appropriate attitude. Yet, those born into the fold could never renounce it any more than some-one could foreswear a biological kinship tie. No "American," he asserted, could ever become a "Euro-pean"; such a being "only ceases being American, and becomes nothing" (Roosevelt 1894, 22). This commit-ment to the possibility of naturalization despite an implicit belief in the fundamental biology of citizen-ship was not a contradiction for Roosevelt and others like him; rather, it was evidence of their profound faith in the transformative agency—the alchemy—of the state, which has the power to confer or withhold nativity.

An alternative biological model for national trans-formation was offered by Robert Park, an urban soci-ologist at the University of Chicago and one of the foremost early-twentieth-century theorists of ethnic-ity and Americanization. Park (1952) imported the concept of the ecosystem from zoology and botany to explain the processes of social change. He studied the interdependence—the biological and social intercon-nectedness—of human groups on a variety of scales, from the neighborhood to the nation, and argued that the transformation of these groups largely con-formed to the logic of an ecosystem in which the "in-vasion" of foreign elements resulted in a temporary imbalance followed by mutual transformation as the system returned inevitably to equilibrium. Park be-lieved that even the most enduring antipathies be-tween cultures and races would eventually erode and that interdependence would be followed by intermix-ture on a global scale. Naturalization was the first step in that process.

The danger of any biological model of social forma-tion is that it obscures the hierarchies implicit in that formation, thereby undermining the potential for crit-ical introspection and political change. In its current incarnation across the fields of American studies and cultural studies, the keyword "naturalization" names that danger, serving, somewhat colloquially, as a syn-onym for "biologization." In all of its usages, "natural-ization" evinces the alchemy of the state: the transformation of the many, if not into one, then at least into an intricate relatedness that hovers uncertainly between kinship and citizenship. In this modern concept of the nation, political affiliation (citizenship) and common descent (kinship) are interfused rather than sedimentary modes of belonging. Kinship, no less than citizenship, is a taxonomic construction that registers, even as it masks, social and political hierarchies. The interweaving of the two is evident in early-twentieth-century debates over topics ranging from eugenics to migration policy. As a primary mechanism of non-sexual state reproduction, naturalization thus offers an important site of inquiry for scholars who are committed to understanding the legacy of those debates in our contemporary moment (Weinbaum 2004). Naturalization laws and policies register change not only in the legal contours of political belonging, but also in the terms by which that belonging is articulated. Naturalization discloses, in these multiple senses, the science of the state.

45

Orientalism

Vijay Prashad

In 1849, Henry David Thoreau wrote, "Behold the difference between the Oriental and the Occidental. The former has nothing to do in this world; the latter is full of activity. The one looks in the sun till his eyes are put out; the other follows him prone in his westward course" (120). Thoreau's "Orientals" included the people of India and China, although his contemporaries often added the people of the Arab world. At the same time, Thoreau and other Boston Brahmins used the even more vaguely defined term "Occidental" to refer to Anglo-Protestant civilization (and only rarely included Catholics and non-Anglos). The point they made was simple: the world had to be sundered between East and West. The former once had a great history, but it had since descended into timelessness and stasis; the latter remained dynamic and cultivated wisdom. Thoreau, being a pacifist, forswore the values of conquest, but his confreres did not. They shared his revulsion toward the contemporary Orient and yet wanted to dominate it. He only wanted its knowledge.

A critical analysis of this Orientalist discourse is made easier because of the valuable work of such scholars as Anwar Abdel Malek (1963) and Edward Said (1978), as well as the field that is now known as postcolonial studies. This tradition lifted the commonplace category of Orientalism and filled it with analytical meaning. Before Abdel Malek and Said, the term referred to the academic study of all that lives in the lands outside Europe, the Americas, Sub-Saharan Africa, and Russia. Orientalists toiled away on the languages and cultures of regions of the world not often considered to be central to the activity of the U.S. and European academy. Said, in contrast, wrenched the term out of its disciplinary context and demonstrated how European and U.S. government bureaucrats, academics, cultural workers, and common sense defined and circumscribed knowledge about the "Orient."

The first step of Orientalist discourse is to sunder the world into a West and an East. Here the lonely academic and the public imperialist share a remarkable feat. Both collect vastly different areas of the world each into a zone called the "East," albeit the former for purposes of study, the latter for conquest and rule. The premise for both the academic and the imperialist is that these diverse regions can be assembled into a singular "Orient" and, in consequence, that their own lands can be seen as an equally singular "Occident." The second step is to impute values to these zones, with the West being productive, dynamic, adult, and masculine, while the East is slothful, static, childlike, and feminine. Once these two steps have been accomplished, it is easy to say that the West must have dominance over the East. Frequently, Orientalist discourse provided a useful justification for colonialism, as colonial rulers attempted with varying degrees of success to fashion real, living cultures into their image of the "Orient," while older historical traditions and the resistance of colonized peoples made such a divine act impossible.

As with any good theory, this early critique of Orientalism has its flaws. Some of these are conceptual, as pointed out by the literary critic Aijaz Ahmad. Said is unclear whether Orientalism is the ideology of colonialism or is rooted in the very psyche of European thought. If it is the latter, then Said's use of the term is an "Orientalism-in-reverse," in which the "West" has an inherently flawed understanding of the rest of the world (Ahmad 1992, 183). Additionally, Said underestimates the strong tradition within Arabic writing that draws ontological distinctions between East and West. The concept of Orientalism also suffers from an overly general application. It may aptly describe the English and French, though not the German, view of what they called the "Near" or "Middle East." Without alteration, however, it would not be of much use for understanding U.S. intellectual and political policy toward either Asia or the Middle East. Literary critics and historians have demonstrated that U.S. Orientalism was both heterogeneous and "far more mobile, flexible, and rich than the Orientalism binary would allow" (McAlister 2001, 270). While Thoreau shared a great deal with his English colleagues, he did not condone colonialism: "They may keep their rupees," he wrote of "Orientals"—he wanted only their wisdom (1958, 298). This was already a difference.

To fully understand U.S. Orientalism, we thus need to locate it within the context of the emergence of the U.S. empire as a truly global behemoth. U.S. imperialism was rooted in the wars against Amerindians, in the push westward after the Revolutionary War, in the Monroe Doctrine's implications for South and Central America, and in the war to supplant Spain in the Caribbean and the Philippines. Still, the United States remained a junior partner to the dynamic northwestern European empires (Dutch, English, French) until the close of World War II. Only during the Cold War did the United States become the political leader of the advanced capitalist states. At the same time, nationalist movements around the world and the horror of the Holocaust finally delegitimized formal racism on a global scale, producing the International Declaration of Human Rights in 1948, the many United Nations conventions against racial discrimination, and the intellectual work of the United Nations Education, Scientific and Cultural Organization (UNESCO). Whereas earlier forms of Orientalism could quite openly truck in racist stereotypes, the U.S. Orientalism of the era had to adjust to this assault on racism and direct colonial dominion.

U.S. domestic law eventually submitted to the dictates of international opinion and of the civil rights movement, overturning the Jim Crow laws of the South. Alongside the Civil Rights and Voting Rights acts came a 1965 revision of U.S. immigration law that finally allowed legal entry and naturalization to Asians (another complex category), who had either been barred or subjected to quotas for much of the twentieth century. The state claimed that its new immigration policy was designed to counter "Communist propaganda" about U.S. racism against Asians (Prashad 2000). U.S. pundits and policymakers welcomed highly skilled Asians, whose demographic advantages then became a foil for the indisputably wretched condition of most people of color. In 1966, *U.S. News & World Report* noted that the experience of Chinese Americans confirms "the old idea that people should depend on their own efforts—not a welfare check—in order to reach America's 'promised land.'" Asians worked hard to make it "at a time when it is being proposed that hundreds of billions of dollars be spent to uplift Negroes and other minorities." The sorting logic of this new U.S. immigration policy began to blur older categories of racist discourse. The

post–civil rights epoch inaugurated a discourse of colorblind racism, where the rhetorics of economic efficiency and cultural difference masked claims about racial inferiority. This shift is crucial to an understanding of U.S. Orientalism.

But just because the media began to praise Asians, in part by substituting the newer keyword "Asian" for the older keyword "Oriental," does not mean that Asians were sheltered from rebuke. The state allowed the racism nurtured by the long history of Orientalism to flourish in civil society, despite having disavowed it as public policy. The language and emotive charge of racism often drew its power from the ongoing U.S. wars in Asia. Beginning with the wars in the Philippines in the nineteenth century, the U.S. media and military pummeled the public and the troops with racist imagery of the Japanese (during World War II), the Koreans (during the Korean War), the Vietnamese (during the Vietnam War), and the Chinese (during the seemingly endless animosity toward Communist China). The examples are legion, from Douglas Macarthur's virulent comments about the Koreans ("give these yellow bastards what is coming to them") to the experience of Japanese American troops in Vietnam ("This is what the Viet Cong looks like, with slanted eyes," said a drill instructor as he pointed to a Japanese American recruit).

Today, U.S. Orientalism remains inherently ambiguous and heterogeneous—deeply committed to U.S. primacy and to multiculturalism. It posits that Asians are both required and repellent, both necessary to the economy (and as a weapon against other people of color) and a danger to society. Thoreau's views still resonate because it is commonplace to appreciate the culture of the ancient "East" and goods from the modern "East" and, at the same time, to be uneasy about the actual people who inhabit that entire region. Bindis and temporary tattoos are easier to accept than are those who wear bindis on a regular basis. If, however, those who would wear bindis choose not to, and simply work hard, they then become acceptable. That is the contradiction of U.S. Orientalism.

The analytical category "Orientalism" thus enables an analysis of the ambiguity of U.S. imperialism, which is driven by the twin goals of supremacy and liberation. The Iraqis and Afghans cannot liberate themselves, the logic goes, because they are supine, so the GIs must liberate them, especially Iraqi and Afghan women (Armstrong and Prashad 2005). So the U.S. army arrives as a force of liberation. At the same time, the army secures raw materials and creates markets for global corporations and for the dynamic of advanced capitalist states. The urge to liberate is as fundamental as the requirement to subordinate. What is forbidden in the Orientalism of our period is for the "native" to speak in its vital variety—and, because that voice is muted, the native might choose means that are unspeakable. That too is the price of Orientalism.

46
Performance
Susan Manning

In many studies of the arts, "performance" is defined as the set of artistic choices an actor, dancer, or musician makes in realizing a preexistent text—whether that text comprises a dramatic script, choreographic design, or musical score. Over the last few decades, however, some scholars in American cultural studies have redefined performance as a mode of cultural production composed of events bound in time and framed in space. Whereas the traditional usage of the noun "performance" implies an opposition to text, the new usage understands it as a framed event that may well deploy textual elements, but cannot be reduced to the realization of preexistent scripts or scores. Like other modes of cultural production, performance takes the form of diverse genres that emerge, alter, and disappear over time. Indian ceremonial, jubilee and Jonkonnu, melodrama, minstrelsy, vaudeville, world's fairs, modern dance, the Broadway musical: all are distinct genres of performance that have circulated within and without U.S. culture.

American cultural studies has adopted a new usage for the verb "perform" as well as for the noun "performance." "To perform" generally means to carry out, to complete, or to accomplish as well as to act in a play, execute a dance step, or play a musical instrument. In its new usage, the connotation of the verb shifts from the achievement of an action to the embodiment of an identity. This usage derives from theories in the social sciences and humanities. Kenneth Burke's *The Philosophy of Literary Form* (1957), Erving Goffman's *The Presentation of Self in Everyday Life* (1959), Victor Turner's *The Ritual Process* (1969), and Edward Hall's *The Hidden Dimension* (1969) all conceptualize social structure and communication in terms of theatrical imagery. Individuals take on roles in scenarios and, verbally and nonverbally, perform their identities for others in the scene. Adapting this language of theatricality, scholars today talk about how social actors perform race, ethnicity, gender, sexuality, class, profession, region, and nationality. This usage of "perform"—and its synonyms such as stage, rehearse, dramatize, enact—implies a process whereby physical bodies accrue social identities. It also underscores how some bodies become legible as "masculine" or "black" or "mainstream," while other bodies become legible as "feminine" or "white" or "marginal."

Taken together, the new usages for the noun and verb constitute the field of performance studies and propose two interrelated critical projects for the field of American cultural studies. Consider the example of performance at the turn of the twentieth century in U.S. culture. As Lawrence Levine (1988) has demonstrated, the hierarchy of high and low culture emerged during this period. Levine's paradigmatic example is Shakespeare. Through most of the nineteenth century, Shakespeare's plays appeared regularly on U.S. stages, both as full-blown productions, often starring visiting British actors, and as subject matter for farcical afterpieces, burlesque, and even blackface minstrelsy. The-

aters during the antebellum period drew spectators from the immigrant working class as well as from established elites, and in these public spaces workers and business owners shared their pleasure and familiarity with Shakespeare. Toward the end of the century, however, Shakespeare migrated from cross-class venues to a newly created realm of high culture, as elites created distinctive venues—the art museum, the symphony hall, the independent theater—separate from the changing spaces for popular culture—the dance hall, the amusement park, the sports stadium. Attending one venue rather than another became a way for people to assert—to perform—their class identities in an era of mass urbanization, industrialization, and immigration.

Strikingly, the cross-class theater of the antebellum era was for men only. Although actresses appeared onstage, only a few women ventured into the theater as spectators, and these women carried the social stigma of "public women," or prostitutes, whatever their actual livelihood. Only after the Civil War, as theaters split along class lines, did women begin to attend in significant numbers. In fact, one hallmark of the newly respectable theater was its accessibility to white, middle-class female patrons, made possible in part by changing codes for audience behavior. Earlier, male spectators had engaged in rowdy behavior, becoming as much a part of the show as the stage action. But after the Civil War innovations in stage design and lighting accompanied new protocols for quietly attentive spectatorship. Thus middle-class female theatergoers extended the domestic ideology of the first half of the nineteenth century into the public space of the theater, even as they challenged the strictures of that ideology by venturing out into the city. White, middle-class women's attendance at theaters performed changing conceptions of gender during an era when women first entered universities and the professions and began to organize for the vote.

The division between high and low culture carried racialized connotations as well. In fact, the terms "highbrow" and "lowbrow" derived from late-nineteenth-century phrenology, which differentiated "civilized" from "primitive" races according to the shape and size of the human cranium. Thus the new arena of high culture highlighted its connection with European culture and dismissed performance genres influenced by non-European cultures, most especially jazz music and jazz dance. Originating within African American subcultures during the early decades of the twentieth century, jazz soon attained a broad popularity among the urban working class and white middle class. Although high culture routinely borrowed the inflections of jazz, it disavowed the influence, even while the new technologies of recorded sound commodified jazz as a national sound. These dynamics continued to shape U.S. performance—and racial identities—for decades to come.

This brief case study demonstrates a type of inquiry made possible by new definitions of "performance" as a noun and "perform" as a verb. However, such cross-genre inquiry is not yet widespread in American cultural studies, most probably because it requires scholars to look across the disciplinary histories of dance, music, theater, popular entertainment, and exhibition. Doing so enriches our explorations because we then can trace the complex relations between expressive forms, individual identities, and social formations. The potential for cross-genre inquiry in performance studies is not limited to U.S. cultures or even to the cultures of the Americas, but holds across diverse national and regional boundaries.

Far more widespread in American cultural studies is scholarship that redefines the verb "perform." It has become commonplace for scholars to discuss the "performance" of race, gender, class, and so on. These scholars are indebted to the theory of performativity that feminist philosopher Judith Butler derived from philosopher of language J. L. Austin (Butler 1990; Austin 1962). Attempting to understand gender as a socially constructed rather than biologically inherent quality, Butler described it as a "stylized repetition of acts," a set of "bodily gestures, movements, and styles" that signal masculinity or femininity, corporeal signs endlessly repeated and subtly modified over time (139–40). Following Butler's lead, scholars proposed that other axes of social identity and difference operate in similar ways.

The widespread acceptance of theories of performativity has come under critique from several angles. From one perspective, these theories do not give sufficient weight to material determinants of social identity. This holds especially true for subordinate racial and class positions. To describe middle-class status as the performance of consumer choice makes more sense than to describe the strata of the impoverished as a performance. A performance of what? one might ask. Using the term "performance" in this context implies an unimpeded agency that belies the realities of economic inequality and systematic discrimination.

From another perspective, theories of performativity do not sufficiently account for the varying dynamics of everyday life and framed events. This holds especially true for cases of impersonation across race and gender, both onstage and offstage. Scholars have used such cases to illustrate their theories of performativity, but in so doing they typically blur and confuse the distinction between theater and life. Butler, for example, has advanced a controversial interpretation of drag balls staged in Harlem by African American and Latino men, as documented in Jennie Livingston's film *Paris Is Burning*, arguing that the performers' citation of social norms of femininity ultimately reinforce those norms (Butler 1993). More sustained ethnographic research reveals a radically different set of meanings for the participants in the drag balls, whose offstage lives of homelessness, sex work, and subsistence wages counter their glamorous onstage personae (Jackson 2002). Butler's misreading in part results from her overemphasis on gender and her underestimation of race and class as categories for analysis.

That Butler relied on a film documentary to draw conclusions about a performance event is also telling. To borrow Raymond Williams's (1982) terminology, performance has become a residual cultural form over the last hundred years, displaced first by film and radio, then by sound recording and television, and now by digital technologies. In retrospect, the emergence of the hierarchy of high and low anticipated the eclipse of performance and the rise of media as dominant cultural forms. This shift cannot be disentangled from contemporary usage of the noun "performance" and the verb "perform." The language of theatricality deployed by Burke, Goffman, Turner, and Hall in the 1950s and 1960s reflects the increasing mediatizing of culture evident during those decades, and the momentum has only intensified since then. Hence the seeming irony of our preoccupation with performance at precisely the cultural moment when encounters with live bodies bound in time and framed in space have become increasingly rare occurrences. Our fascination with physicality and embodiment reveals the underside of our mediatized age. Through its multiple intersections with American cultural studies, the interdisciplinary terrain of performance studies reflects an intellectual and institutional response to a larger shift toward media culture over the last century.

47

Property

Grace Kyungwon Hong

Property is as central to discussions of culture as culture is to discussions of property. Property not only references the things that are owned, as in common usage, but also a social system in which the right and ability to own are protected by the state. Property is commonly discussed as a universal state of being, and the U.S. nation-state is predicated on the notion that all citizens have equal rights to property. Yet in U.S. history, property relations have grown out of and secured class, racial, and gender hierarchies. The keyword "property" thus indexes a contradiction between the ostensibly universal endowment of the right to property for all U.S. citizens and the uneven actualization of that right through forms of racial and gender dispossession. U.S. culture is a crucial site where this contradiction is managed, troubled, and destabilized. Diverse cultural artifacts and practices disavow this contradiction, even as they serve as sites where the histories of the propertyless can be articulated.

Rather than merely referring to things that are owned, property is better understood as describing a set of *social relations*. In other words, ownership describes not only the relationship between oneself and the thing one owns, but also a system in which the state protects one's right to own something by ensuring that no one else does. Ownership of something entails the ability to do with it what one wills, thus suggesting that the will of others does not impinge upon one's ability to express one's will. When John Locke famously declared that "every man has *property* in his own *person*" (Locke 1980, 19), he named property as a system that produces a subject defined through its ability to own, a subject that political theorist C. B. Macpherson (1962) called the "possessive individual." This subject is defined by its ability not simply to own, but, first and foremost, to own itself. This right to property is guaranteed by the state; in-

deed, for Locke, this is the central role of the state: "*Political power*, then, I take to be a *right* of making laws with penalties of death, and consequently all less penalties, for the regulating and preserving of property" (Macpherson 1962, 8). The state does not merely allow for property relations; rather, the protection of property interests is the justification for the state's existence.

There is another fundamental contradiction embedded in this definition of property. No one can truly exercise will freely, as one person's expression of will is always the infringement of another's, and so the state privileges the will of some at the expense of others. This is a tension at the heart of what political theorists refer to as the liberal or liberal-democratic state. Karl Marx (1978, 34), one of the best-known of those theorists, notes in "On the Jewish Question" that membership in the political sphere of the liberal state requires the shedding of individual particularity for the "unreal universality" of the abstract citizen. However, representation through abstract citizenship does not mean that individuals in society somehow relinquish their self-interestedness. The state instead becomes the guarantor of those interests, albeit unequally, through being the guarantor of private property. Because the abstract citizen is also the propertied subject, the state must profess equality while also functioning as the guarantor of the unequal property relations occasioned by capitalist modes of production.

Recent American cultural studies scholarship has extended Marx's discussion of this *class* contradiction to note that claims of universality through citizenship are contradicted by racialized and gendered difference as well. The possessive individual is not universal, but is defined over and against these racial differences. Perhaps the most iconic example is that of chattel slavery. Orlando Patterson (1982), for instance, describes the enslaved person as existing in a condition of "social death," a condition that can be understood as the dialectical opposite of the possessive individual. If property becomes the basis for freedom, defined as the ability to exercise one's will in the absence of the influence of others, this definition of freedom needs an antithesis—enslavement, in this case. Yet because liberal societies are based on conceptions of equivalence and horizontal comradeship, these societies' material and ideological dependence on inequality and hierarchy must be erased. Enslavement, as an undeniably unequal condition, must be disavowed as freedom's historical antithesis.

Even after the formal abolition of enslavement in the United States, the legacy of possessive individualism and its erased corollary, social death, continues to structure racialized citizenship. As legal scholars have noted, property and whiteness are mutually constitutive categories. They delineate the history through which "courts established whiteness as a prerequisite to the exercise of enforceable property rights," thus ensuring that "it was solely through being white that property could be acquired and secured under law" (C. Harris 1993, 1724). But the law did more than establish whiteness as a prerequisite to ownership of property. It also established whiteness itself as property

that "white people" own. Citing precedents in which law has "protected even the expectation of rights as actual legal property" (Powell, cited in C. Harris 1993, 1729), Harris contends that in this type of racist society white privilege becomes an expectation that is then reified as property by law.

This analysis of property has implications beyond a strictly legal domain. If we think of property as the condition in which the state protects one's right to ownership equally, we must extend the definition of "dispossession" to mean the unequal inclusion of racialized subjects in the liberal state. While the normative citizen is theoretically able to forego private particularities for public universality, this process is not universally applicable in practice. In the United States, property relations have been constituted by myriad forms of racialized dispossession, many of which have been reinforced through the protection of white bourgeois domesticity. Gendered forms of slave labor in the U.S. South, for instance, provided the material and ideological conditions of possibility for the Cult of True Womanhood (Carby 1987), while the recruitment and exploitation of itinerant male laborers, such as Chinese and Filipino "bachelors" along the U.S. West Coast, created non-normative forms of belonging against which a proper and moral white domesticity could be articulated (Shah 2001). In the early twentieth century, new forms of consumerism emerged that reworked notions of domestic propriety by establishing the domestic sphere as a place where consumer goods were utilized in a proper manner; this too was defined against racialized excesses (Glickman

1997). In the mid-twentieth century, de jure segregation as well as de facto practices such as racist home-lending policies and restrictive covenants brought about racialized dispossession through the mechanisms of suburban home ownership and privatized domesticity (Lipsitz 1995; Oliver and Shapiro 1995). This genealogy explains why Rod Ferguson (2004) posits "queer of color critique" as the most telling intervention into the contradictions of capitalist relations within U.S. liberal democracy.

"Property" as a keyword thus marks the history of the U.S. liberal-democratic state that, in maintaining a conception of citizenship as the universal protection of property rights, must erase the ways in which those relations depend on racialized and gendered forms of dispossession. In this way, property is also an epistemology, or way of knowing; it allows for knowledge of nationalist narratives of subject formation, and disallows knowledge that attests to the ways in which propertied subjectivity is not universal. Alternative epistemologies, though occluded, rendered deviant, or erased by nationalist narratives, do emerge, often embedded in cultural forms and practices. While many definitions of culture emphasize the imaginative transcendence of the concerns of everyday life, the material histories of the propertyless emerge through culture differently. The imaginative function of literature and culture, in those instances, can reveal and intervene in the racial and gender structure of the property system. Investigations into the intersection of property and culture might productively take into consideration histories of race and gender that belie the ostensible universality of propertied citizenship, lest such studies reproduce the mystifying effects of national culture. Further, we might look to culture for ways of articulating notions of self and community that do not buy into the universalizing tendency of possessive individualism and national belonging.

48

Public

Bruce Robbins

According to the *Oxford English Dictionary*, "public" originated from the Latin *populus*, or "people," apparently under the influence of the word *pubes*, or "adult men." The term's considerable authority, based on its claim to represent the social whole, has continued to bump up against evidence that large classes of people have been omitted from it, as women and children are omitted from *pubes*. In American studies, relevant debates have focused on the continuing applicability of this ancient notion within a specialized modern division of labor where no one has knowledge of the whole (Dewey 1927; Lippman 1927); on whether the apparent decline of public life (as in Robert Putnam's "bowling alone" thesis [2000]) might reflect the larger percentage of U.S. women now doing paid rather than voluntary work; on whether "public spaces" in the past were ever really democratically accessible to all; and on how open or universal the goals, values, and membership of so-called "identity politics" movements ought to be. Recent critics, skeptical that such a thing as a social whole exists except at the level of ideology, have sometimes implied the desirability of removing the word from circulation. If there has been no moratorium, this is in part because current usage also acknowledges a need for the term's appeal against state despotism, a key motive for its rise in the eighteenth century, and against the free market economy, in which many see a newer, decentralized despotism.

Recoiling from the singular, putatively comprehensive usage (*the* public), cultural studies has undertaken to recognize the existence of multiple publics, especially among excluded or marginalized groups. Examples include Oskar Negt and Alexander Kluge's (1993) hypothesis of a proletarian public sphere, as well as the publics formed by political organizing, sexual role-playing, and diasporic affiliation on the Internet. These objects of ethnographic and sociological attention are often described as "counter-publics." The coinage is perhaps premature, for oppositionality remains to be demonstrated; to be smaller than or separate from *X* is not necessarily to oppose *X*. Nor can it be assumed that what is countered is the normative force of public-ness itself. To speak of an excluded group as a "public" is again to claim representation of a social whole (though a smaller one), and thus to invoke an authority that can be disputed on similar grounds. The multiplication of publics (the plural still causes distress to my computer's spell-checker) offers no escape from the term's onerous but alluring authority.

Empirical questions of who is and isn't included in a given public—a necessary component of cultural studies projects and one that always threatens to unsettle the term's authority—thus cannot overthrow it completely. Normativity seems to be hard-wired into usage. As Michael Warner (2002) suggests, speech is public only when it is addressed, beyond any already-existing group of members, to an indefinite number of strangers. As a result, the public is always open to the charge of being merely a wishful fiction, but by the same token it is immune to merely empirical verification, perpetually in excess of any delimited membership. This excessiveness, which is honored far beyond those responding to the works of Jürgen Habermas (1999), helps explain the term's tolerance for near-redundancy. "Public" can be added as an adjective to a noun that would already seem to *be* public. The events of September 11, 2001, Judith Butler (2004a) writes, "led public intellectuals to waver in their public commitment to principles of justice." There is no such thing as a *private* intellectual; "intellectual" already implies a concern for more than the (presumed) privacy of academic, field-specific knowledge. Similarly, a commitment that was kept secret would hardly deserve to be called a (true) commitment. Yet usage supports the supplement, which exhorts intellectuals and commitments to become, by strenuous effort, more fully and passionately that which they already are.

In addition to the distracting discrepancy between empirical reference and normative exhortation, "public" lends itself to other sorts of confusion. As a singular noun, it hesitates between social wholes of different scale and nature: between a collective organized as a body and an unorganized, unselfconscious aggregate; between the opinions of the empirically existing members and their conjectural long-term interest or welfare; between the inhabitants of a nation, and—in a sense that has recently returned from obsolescence—the world at large, all of humankind. If the public is what *pertains* to the social whole, other important ambiguities result from the distinct relations to that whole hidden away in *pertain*: that which is *potentially accessible* to the community, that which is *already visible to* and *viewed by* the community, that which *belongs to* or *is controlled by* the community, that which *affects* or is *of significance to* the community, that which is *authorized by* the community, and that which is done *in the service* or *on behalf of* the community.

In this context "community," which seems indispensable to the definition of "public," also provides an important contrast to it. Like "culture," another contiguous and overlapping term, "community" seems less tolerant of universal ethical principles, warmer to its members, and more hostile to strangers and self-estrangement. Public's referential indefiniteness leaves it more open, if also cooler and more abstract. But both "community" and "culture" also have senses that are closer to "public."

Related ambiguities result from a sliding set of oppositions between "public" and the diverse meanings of "private," a term that derives from the Latin *privatus*, or "withdrawn from public life." Shades of differ-

ence in "private" correspond to comparable differences in "public"; for example, the demand for citizen participation (which is asserted against private apathy) differs from the demand for scrutiny and debate (which is asserted against governmental restriction of access). Along with capitalist globalization and the revolution in digital technology, another major factor influencing usage of both terms has been the drive for gender equality. Here the clear movement has been toward an expansion of sites and occasions deemed public. For men, both the family and the workplace had seemed to belong to the domain of privacy, hence deserving protection from state interference. The women's movement refused this public/private distinction, redescribing the family as a domain of patriarchal injustice that must be opened up to public scrutiny and rectified by means of state action. With women adding salaried work outside the home to their unpaid work within it, the workplace too has been added to the public. Yet feminists have also questioned the seeming limitlessness of this enlargement. To what extent should sex be subject to scrutiny and regulation? As Jean Cohen (2002) notes, issues like reproductive rights, gays in the military, and sexual harassment in the workplace seem to demand a reworking, rather than an abolition, of the public/private distinction.

"Private" has come to signify both the domain of capitalist economics and the domain of personal freedom and domestic intimacy. To allow the deeply cherished emotions associated with intimacy to extend to the world market is to bestow a handsome gift of friendly propaganda upon defenders of large corporations and international finance. Any demand for public regulation of the economy thus becomes an unwanted and unwarranted intrusion into one's most personal space. Relevant cultural studies projects include the critical analysis of intellectual property, copyright law, file-sharing, and digital sampling, all of which investigate the fate of public access to cultural products and scientific knowledge, incursions into the public domain by private ownership, and movements to restore public rights (open access) to research results produced with the help of public funding.

But capitalism's effects on usage of "public" and "private" have been paradoxical. On the one hand, capitalism is associated with privatization and the shrinkage of the public. On the other, market-fueled digitalization is celebrated for democratically multiplying the shapes, rhythms, and vectors of publicness, and for allowing people to socialize with minimal interference from their spatially tethered and symbolically coded bodies or from the usual gatekeepers controlling for social status and professional expertise. (The same divide structures debates in architecture and urban studies over the fate of public space.) Yet digital technologies are also blamed for overextending the domain of the public. The degree of invisible nonstop surveillance made possible by new techniques of data retrieval, ranging from information on buying habits collected by retailers and marketers to governmental assaults on privacy and civil liberties, has intensified the term's further connotation of shaming exposure.

Like "private," "public" derives ideological force from the confusing of distinct senses and situations. The term switches between what is owned, decided upon, and managed by the community and what is merely observed by and relevant to the community—that is, between the public as active participant (modeled on the organized political group) and the public as passive spectator (modeled on the theatrical audience and reading public). "Public" thus can imply that the active, participatory aspects of politics are present within the more passive, aestheticized context of spectatorship. This switch encourages a tendency to inflate the degree and significance of agency available in the act of cultural consumption—the suggestion, say, that shopping and striking are comparable practices. Yet this ambiguity also raises such productive questions as how distinct the two sorts of publicness are and what role theatricality and symbolism can play within politics. The same ambiguity drives media research into how, when, and whether what is public in the minimal sense of *visibility* (celebrity, publicity) translates into what is public in a weightier sense like *sociability* or *organized political will* (activism, collaboration).

A closely related distinction helps clarify the ever-more-interesting issue of the public's *scale*. The word has been used most frequently about various collectivities up to the scale of the nation, but not about international or multinational entities. This fits its association with zones of actual conversation and self-consciously shared destiny, which have historically been limited. Yet there is increasing consensus among students of both American studies and cultural studies that this limitation is intellectually and politically unacceptable. The concept of the public as a zone of causal connectedness—those actions relevant to or significant for the welfare of a given group, whether or not the group is in conversation with itself or with the begetters of the actions—is much vaster. In the era of the world market, not to speak of official and unofficial violence across borders, this zone has become increasingly international. Thus the restrictively national scale of public (in the sense of conversation and control) is seen to be stretching, and at the same time to need *further* stretching. Enlarging the scale of international attention, conversation, and opinion so as to match the scale of international causal connectedness—that is, bringing these two senses of public into congruence with each other—means resetting the boundaries of the relevant moral community so that those likely to be affected by a course of action, wherever they live, are among those invited to debate it. The United Nations, so-called Non-Governmental Organizations, transnational television stations like CNN and Al-Jazeera, and the Internet are among the socio-technical institutions whose impact on the possible constituting of a global public now ought to be under hopeful and suspicious examination.

49

Queer

Siobhan B. Somerville

"Queer" causes confusion, perhaps because two of its current meanings seem to be at odds. In both popular and academic usage in the United States, "queer" is sometimes used interchangeably with the terms "gay" and "lesbian" or occasionally "transgender" and "bisexual." In this sense, it is understood as an umbrella term that refers to a range of sexual identities that are "not straight." But in some political and theoretical contexts, "queer" is used in a seemingly contradictory way: as a term that calls into question the stability of any categories of identity based on sexual orientation. In this second sense, "queer" is a *critique* of the tendency to organize political or theoretical questions around sexual orientation per se. To "queer" becomes a way to denaturalize categories such as "lesbian" and "gay" (not to mention "straight" and "heterosexual"), revealing them as socially and historically constructed identities that have often worked to establish and police the line between the "normal" and the "abnormal."

Fittingly, the word "queer" itself has refused to leave a clear trace of its own origins; its etymology is unknown. It may have been derived from the German word *quer* or the Middle High German *twer*, which meant "cross," "oblique," "squint," "perverse," or "wrongheaded," but these origins have been contested. The *Oxford English Dictionary* notes that, while "queer" seems to have entered English in the sixteenth century, there are few examples of the word before 1700. From that time until the mid-twentieth century, "queer" tended to refer to anything "strange," "odd," or "peculiar," with additional negative connotations that suggested something "bad," "worthless," or even "counterfeit." In the late eighteenth and early nineteenth centuries, the word "queer" began to be used also as a verb, meaning "to quiz or ridicule," "to puzzle," "to cheat," or "to spoil." During this time, the adjectival form also began to refer to a condition that was "not normal," "out of sorts," "giddy, faint, or ill."

By the first two decades of the twentieth century, "queer" became linked to sexual practice and identity in the United States, particularly in urban sexual cultures. During the 1910s and 1920s in New York City, for example, men who called themselves "queer" used the term to refer to their sexual interest in other men (Chauncey 1994). Contemporaneous literary works by African American writers such as Nella Larsen (1929) and Jean Toomer (1923/1969) suggest that the term could also carry racialized meanings, particularly in the context of mixed-race identities that exposed the instability of divisions between "black" and "white." But it was not until the 1940s that "queer" began to be used in mainstream U.S. culture primarily to refer to "sexual perverts" or "homosexuals," most often in a pejorative, stigmatizing way, a usage that reached its height during the Cold War era and that continues to some extent today. In the early twenty-first century, "queer" remains a volatile term; the *American Heritage Dictionary* even appends a warning label advising that the use of "queer" by "heterosexuals is often considered offensive" and therefore "extreme caution must be taken concerning [its] use when one is not a member of the group." The term has also carried specific class connotations in some periods and contexts. On the one hand, as one participant in a recent online forum put it, "'Queer' is a rebellion against those posh middle-class business owners who want to define gaydom as being their right to enjoy all the privileges denied them just cos they like cock" (Isambard 2004). On the other hand, these class connotations are unstable. "If I have to pick an identity label in the English language," wrote poet and critic Gloria Anzaldúa, "I pick 'dyke' or 'queer,' though these working-class words . . . have been taken over by white middle-class lesbian theorists in the academy" (1998, 263–64).

The use of "queer" in academic and political contexts beginning in the late 1980s represented an attempt to reclaim this stigmatizing word and to defy those who have wielded it as a weapon. This usage is often traced to the context of AIDS activism that responded to the epidemic's devastating toll on gay men in U.S. urban areas during the 1980s and 1990s. An outgrowth of ACT UP (AIDS Coalition To Unleash Power), a powerful AIDS activist group, Queer Nation became one of the most visible sites of a new politics that was "meant to be confrontational—opposed to gay assimilationists and straight oppressors while inclusive of people who have been marginalized by anyone in power" (Escoffier and Bérubé 1991, 14–16). Queer political groups have not always achieved this goal of inclusiveness in practice, but they have sought to transform the homophobic ideologies of dominant

U.S. culture, as well as strategies used by existing lesbian and gay rights movements, many of which have tended to construct lesbian and gay people as a viable "minority" group and to appeal to liberal rights of privacy and formal equality (Duggan 1992).

The more recent movement to gain the legal right to same-sex marriage demonstrates some of the salient differences between a lesbian/gay rights approach and a queer activist strategy. While advocates for same-sex marriage argue that lesbians and gay men should not be excluded from the privileges of marriage accorded to straight couples, many queer activists and theorists question why marriage and the nuclear family should be the sites of legal and social privilege in the first place. Because same-sex marriage would leave intact a structure that disadvantages those who either cannot or choose not to marry (regardless of their sexual orientation), a more ethical project, queer activists argue, would seek to detach material and social privileges from the institution of marriage altogether (Ettelbrick 1989; Duggan 2004b).

Sometimes in conversation with these activist efforts and sometimes not, queer theory emerged as an academic field during the late 1980s and early 1990s. Drawing on the work of Michel Foucault, scholars who are now referred to as queer theorists argued that sexuality, especially the binary system of "homosexual" and "heterosexual" orientations, is a relatively modern production. As Foucault (1978) argued, although illicit acts between two people of the same sex had long been punishable through legal and religious sanctions, these practices did not necessarily define individuals as "homosexual" until the late nineteenth century. While historians have disagreed about the precise periods and historical contexts in which the notion of sexual identity emerged, Foucault's insistence that sexuality "must not be thought of as a kind of natural given" has been transformative, yielding an understanding of sexuality not as a psychic or physical drive, but as a "set of effects produced in bodies, behavior, and social relations by a certain deployment" of power (127). Moving away from the underlying assumptions of identity politics and its tendency to locate stable sexual subjects, queer theory has focused on the very process of sexual subject formation. If much of the early work in lesbian and gay studies tended to be organized around an opposition of homosexuality and heterosexuality, the primary axis of queer studies shifted toward the distinction between normative and non-normative sexualities as they have been produced in a range of historical and cultural contexts.

For this reason, a key concept in queer theory is the notion of "heteronormativity," a term that refers to "the institutions, structures of understanding, and practical orientations that make heterosexuality seem not only coherent—that is, organized as a sexuality— but also privileged" (Berlant and Warner 1998, 548 n. 2). Heteronormativity, it is important to stress, is not the same thing as heterosexuality (though the two are not entirely separable); indeed, various forms of heterosexuality (adultery, polygamy, and interracial marriage, among others) have historically been proscribed rather than privileged (Rubin 1984; C. Cohen 1997; Burgett 2005). Rather, heteronormativity is a form of power that exerts its effects on both gay and straight individuals, often through unspoken practices and institutional structures.

Because queer critique has the potential to destabilize the ground upon which any particular claim to identity can be made (though, importantly, not destroying or abandoning identity categories altogether), a significant body of queer scholarship has warned against anchoring the field primarily or exclusively to questions of sexuality. Instead, these scholars have argued, we should dislodge "the status of sexual orientation itself as the authentic and centrally governing category of queer practice, thus freeing up queer theory as a way of reconceiving not just the sexual, but the social in general" (Harper et al. 1997). In local, national, and transnational contexts, such a formulation allows us to contest constructions of certain issues as "sexual" and others as "non-sexual," a distinction that has often been deployed by U.S. neoconservatives and neoliberals alike to separate "lesbian and gay" movements from a whole range of interconnected struggles for social justice.

The field of queer studies has increasingly challenged this tendency by using "intersectional" approaches that begin from the assumption that sexuality cannot be separated from other categories of identity and social status. Whereas some early queer theorists found it necessary to insist upon understanding sexuality as a distinct category of analysis, one that could not be fully accounted for by feminist theories of gender, it is now clear that sexuality and gender can never be completely isolated from one another (Rubin

1984; Sedgwick 1990). Indeed, Judith Butler (1990, 5) has shown that our very notions of sexual difference (male/female) are an effect of a "heterosexual matrix." A significant body of scholarship, largely generated out of questions raised by transgender identity and politics, has insisted on the pressing need to revisit and scrutinize the relationships among sex, gender, and sexuality, with an emphasis on recalibrating theories of performativity in light of materialist accounts of gender (Stone 1991; Prosser 1998).

If queer theory's project is characterized, in part, as an attempt to challenge identity categories that are presented as stable, transhistorical, or authentic, then critiques of naturalized racial categories are also crucial to its antinormative project. As a number of critics have shown, heteronormativity derives much of its power from the ways in which it (often silently) shores up as well as depends on naturalized categories of racial difference in contexts ranging from sexology and psychoanalysis to fiction and cinema (Somerville 2000; Eng 2001). Heteronormativity itself must be understood, then, as a racialized concept since "[racially] marginal group members, lacking power and privilege although engaged in heterosexual behavior, have often found themselves defined as outside the norms and values of dominant society" (C. Cohen 1997, 454). This insistence on putting questions of race at the center of queer approaches has been vigorously argued most recently in a body of scholarship identified as "queer of color critique" (Ferguson 2004).

At the same time that intersectional approaches have become more central to queer studies, the field has also increasingly turned to the specificities of nation-based models and the dynamics of globalization and imperialism. Scholars have begun to interrogate both the possibilities and the limitations of queer theory for understanding the movement of desires and identities within a transnational frame, as well as the necessity of attending to the relationship between the methods of queer theory and colonial structures of knowledge and power (Povinelli and Chauncey 1999; Manalansan 2003; Gopinath 2005). The resulting interest in the "nation" and its constitutive role in processes of racialization and sexualization has raised new questions about the ways that queer theory might usefully interrogate the nation's less charismatic companion—the state. Jacqueline Stevens (2004, 225), for instance, has envisioned queer theory and activism as a site for articulating "a revolution against all forms of state boundaries . . . the unhindered movement and full-fledged development of capacities regardless of one's birthplace or parentage."

If the origins of the term "queer" are elusive, its future horizons might be even more so. While the term itself has a contested and perhaps confusing history, one of the points of consensus among queer theorists has been that its parameters should not be prematurely (or ever) delimited (Sedgwick 1993; Berlant and Warner 1995). The field of queer studies is relatively young, but as it has made inroads in a number of different academic fields and debates, some critics have asserted that the term is no longer useful, that it has become passé, that it has lost its ability to create productive friction. Pointing to its seeming ubiquity in popular-cultural venues such as the recent television shows *Queer Eye for the Straight Guy* or *Queer as Folk*, others criticize the ways that the greater circulation of "queer" and its appropriation by the mainstream entertainment industries have emptied out its oppositional political potential. Whether we should be optimistic or pessimistic about the increasingly visibility of "queer" culture remains an open question. Meanwhile, scholars continue to carefully interrogate the shortcomings and the untapped possibilities of "queer" approaches to a range of diverse issues, such as migration (Luibhéid and Cantú 2005) or temporality (Edelman 2004; Halberstam 2005). Whatever the future uses and contradictions of "queer," it seems likely that the word will productively refuse to settle down, demanding critical reflection in order to be understood in its varied and specific cultural, political, and historical contexts.

50

Race

Roderick A. Ferguson

The study of race incorporates a set of wide-ranging analyses of freedom and power. The scope of those analyses has much to do with the broad application of racial difference to academic and popular notions of epistemology, community, identity, and the body. With regard to economic and political formations, race has shaped the meaning and profile of citizenship and labor. In relation to corporeality, race has rendered the body into a text upon which histories of racial differentiation, exclusion, and violence are inscribed. Analyzed in terms of subjectivity, race helps to locate the ways in which identities are constituted.

Many of these insights are the intellectual effects of anti-racist political struggles, particularly ones organized around national liberation and civil rights. In the United States, the minority movements of the 1950s and 1960s fundamentally changed the ways in which racial minorities thought about their identities and cultures and the ways that race worked within U.S. society (Omi and Winant 1994). In doing so, these movements intersected with sociological arguments that displaced notions of race as a strict biological inheritance and forced scholars to confront it as a category with broad political and economic implications. For the first time, there was mass mobilization around the deployment of the linguistic, historical, and artistic elements of minority cultures as a means of challenging racial oppression within the United States. Black, Chicano, and Asian American political and cultural groups emerged out of this context. In addition to cultural recovery, these groups argued for land redistribution, the end of police brutality, and community control over economic development. Race emerged out of these movements as an expression of cultural and political agency by marginalized groups. This was the notion of race that underwrote the ethnic studies movements of the 1960s and 1970s, including the student protests of 1968–69 that inaugurated the Division of Ethnic Studies at San Francisco State University. There and elsewhere, departments of Asian, Chicano, Native, and black studies worked to challenge race as a mode of exploitation within U.S. society in particular and Western nations more generally (Marable 2000).

At the same time, insights about the various meanings of race have also arisen out of movements that countered these largely nation-based forms of racial politics. As postcolonial and post-structuralist theorists have illustrated, race is more than a way of identifying and organizing political coalitions against forms of state repression and capitalist exploitation; it is also a category that sets the terms of belonging and exclusion within modern institutions. David Theo Goldberg (1993, 87) captures this tension nicely: "[Race] has established who can be imported and who exported, who are immigrants and who are indigenous, who may be property and who are citizens; and among the latter who get to vote and who do not, who are protected by the law and who are its objects, who are employable and who are not, who have access and privilege and who are (to be) marginalized." In other words, race both accounts for the logics by which institutions differentiate and classify, include and exclude, and names the processes by which people internalize those logics. Critical theorists of race like Goldberg have pointed out that ideals of political agency that rely on notions of race, including those derived from ethnic studies, have often bought into the same unspoken norms of racial regulation they elsewhere critiqued (Crenshaw 1995; Lowe 1996; Chuh 2003). Feminist and queer critiques of racial ideologies and discourses have complicated the matter further. As women of color and third-world feminists have argued since the mid- to late 1970s, civil rights and national liberation struggles shared important and largely unappreciated affiliations with the very racist regimes to which they were responding, affiliations concerning mutual investments in heterosexual and patriarchal forms of power (Clarke 1983; Combahee River Collective 1983; A. Davis 1997; Ferguson 2004).

One way of extending the interpretations by women of color and third-world feminists of the gendered and sexualized infrastructure of racial discourse is to attend to the ways in which that infrastructure was produced within a genealogy of morality. Morality, in this context, has a much broader definition and application than its more restricted modern understanding, which sees it largely in terms of gender and sexual restrictions. In classical social theory, morality refers to the social powers and privileges that come with political and civil enfranchisement, thus referencing a horizon of possibility rather than an ambit of restrictions and limitations. It was precisely this quality of morality—its promise of enlargement and endowment—that made conservative and liberatory demands for freedom into vehicles for all types of regulations. Morality was both the promise of freedom and the qualification of that promise through regulation. When women of color and third-world feminists troubled the gender and sexual footings of anti-racist social movements, they were actually struggling against the moral inheritance of those movements—

not simply the gender and sexual norms of those movements, but also the imperative to stipulate freedom through regulation. Thinking about race within that genealogy allows us to see how a critical interrogation of race must address the gender and sexual itineraries of both conservative and liberatory politics. It permits us to further tease out the unexpected affiliations that revolutionary and nationalist definitions of race share with liberal democratic and colonial deployments of race.

Several theorists have followed these leads by locating the procedures of racialization within the moral discourse of Western modernity. By doing so, they have interpreted modernity as an epistemological procedure that produces racial knowledge, a material formation that engenders the racial foundations of political economy, and a discursive formation that fosters racial subjects. Goldberg (1993, 14), for instance, situates our understanding of racial modernity within moral notions that constitute "personal and social identity." Take as an example Jean-Jacques Rousseau's linkage of race and morality in *The Social Contract*. According to Rousseau, man's transition from the state of nature to civil society effects a moral change in "him," one that delivers man to the morally constituted domain of civil society. In the state of nature, man is "governed by appetite alone"; in civil society, he is ruled by justice rather than instinct, and through this subjection ascends to freedom and rationality. Man thus becomes a moral being who is part of a civil order that gives his "actions the moral quality they previously lacked" (1762/1968, 64–65). Rousseau's formulation of morality as an entrance into freedoms that are both social and personal can help us to see the ways in which morality expresses a racialized genealogy that links emancipation and subjection.

Through the history of racial formations, we can outline these connections between emancipation and subjection. Indeed, that history reveals how a commitment to political ideals of freedom and liberty was often understood in explicitly racial terms and how it required forms of gender and sexual governance. In the Caribbean plantation economy, for instance, slaveholders and colonizers stood not only as symbols of whiteness and freedom but also of gender and sexual morality. The bodies of non-white Caribbean subjects—blacks, "coloureds," and indentured Indians—were unevenly constructed as outside of the parameters of gender and sexual propriety (M. Alexander 1994). In the nineteenth-century United States, black women's bodies were similarly constructed as the antithesis of true womanhood, a womanhood presumably embodied by white femininity. Responding to this construction became a simultaneously moral and political agenda for black feminists during and beyond this period. As historian Darlene Clark Hine (1989) has argued, African American clubwomen subscribed in the late nineteenth century to Victorian ideologies of gender and sexual propriety as a means of subverting negative stereotypes about black women's sexuality. In doing so, these clubwomen entered civil society by invoking forms of mastery and discipline, underlining and extending the connection between their relative freedom and the subjection of others.

In the early twentieth century this racialized genealogy shaped the emergence of sociology as a discipline that tried to assimilate U.S. residents and citizens to the presumably rational ideals of liberal democracy. That discipline worked to reconcile communities of color, particularly African Americans, to the gender and sexual regimes of morality in part by pressuring them into normative U.S. citizenship. For instance, W. E. B. Du Bois argued in 1900 for a partnership between the census (to track the social problems afflicting African American communities) and an emerging sociological profession (to lift African Americans from the moral residues of those problems) (Green and Driver 1978). U.S. sociology in the early to mid-twentieth century matured into a discipline that responded to the social changes of industrialization and migration by extending these moral prescriptions, including Gunnar Myrdal's famous recommendation that African Americans adhere to the gender and sexual ideals of heterosexual patriarchy as a means of achieving citizenship—a recommendation that used the "instability of the Negro family" to argue that Negro culture is a "distorted development, or a pathological condition, of the general American culture" (Myrdal 1944, 928; Ferguson 2005). By advocating the rational ideals of liberal democracy, sociology linked the political to the social morality of citizenship. In other words, a commitment to the political ideals of citizenship entailed a fidelity to the nuclear family, conjugal marriage, and heterosexual monogamy. Given this genealogy, a critical interrogation of race needs to locate the links between citizenship and gender and sexual regulation. By studying race through its emergence within this genealogy, we obtain an understanding of political agency as the extension of power and discover how political freedom is tied to gender and sexual subjection.

Apprehending political agency through its connections to gender and sexual subjection is also a way of understanding the anti-racist movements that decried regimes of race. Anti-colonial and anti-racist movements represented powerful challenges to racial regimes of colonial and liberal capitalist states. But they often did so without theorizing how those practices were constituted out of heterosexual and patriarchal relations. Anti-racist social movements within Africa, Asia, the Caribbean, and North America not infrequently became sites where women, especially, were subject to gender and sexual oppression and regulation. As Cynthia Enloe (1989, 44) notes, "nationalism typically has sprung from masculinized memory, masculinized humiliation and masculinized hope. Anger at being 'emasculated'—or turned into a 'nation of busboys'—has been presumed to be the natural fuel for igniting a nationalist movement." In the U.S. context, Angela Davis (1997) observes that the liberatory ideals of the civil rights and black power movements were constituted upon unexamined heterosexual and patriarchal norms. As anti-colonial and anti-racist movements figured liberation and freedom either as the acquisition of rights that would eventually empower racially marginalized men or as the decolonization of colonized spaces for those men, these movements produced freedom and liberation as the

extension of regimes of heterosexuality and patriarchy. As such, the anti-racist critiques developed in these settings could only apprehend part of race's genealogy as a social formation. Such analyses often failed to see how national liberation and rights-based action fostered new forms of power. Anti-racist and anti-colonial movements evinced a moral commitment to liberation and rights that did not necessarily entail a commitment to dismantling gender and sexual hierarchies.

In contrast, women of color and third-world feminist formations directly addressed freedom's connection to gender and sexual regulation. In doing so, these formations provided what is referred to today as an "intersectional" model for a more complete consideration of the moral genealogy of racial projects. The Combahee River Collective (1983, 277), for instance, argued in its organizational statement: "We need to articulate the real class situation of persons who are not merely raceless, sexless workers, but for whom racial and sexual oppression are significant determinants in their working/economic lives." Emerging from the failures and contradictions of national liberation and civil rights, this statement calls for a theory and practice of freedom that link differences of gender, sexuality, and class within specific epistemological and material formations. Subsequent work on the history of women of color and third-world feminisms illustrates how the regulatory architecture of emancipatory projects resulted in postcolonial state formations that rearticulated the moral agendas of colonial regimes (M. Alexander 1994). Hence, postcolonial states represented the dawn of dubious forms of neo-colonial freedom that depended on economic subordination to advanced capitalist states whose claims to universal freedoms were undermined by internal processes of exclusion at the level of gender and sexuality. Those processes, as M. Jacqui Alexander (1991) points out, eventuated in much regulatory activity, including the criminalization of lesbianism in the Caribbean.

In the United States, the gendered and sexual legacies of civil rights have powerfully illustrated the ways in which rights-based projects extended (and continue to extend) regimes of gender and sexual normativity. We might understand the critical cultural and political practices of queers of color as inheriting women of color feminism's critical assessment of liberation and emancipation. Groups such as Other Countries, Gay Men of African Descent, and the Audre Lorde Project have pointed to the historical and material limits of universal gay identity and the limited assumptions about freedom that such an identity presumes. The contemporary gay and lesbian movement has been organized along the axes of participation in the military, access to marriage and adoption, and protection from hate crimes, an agenda that has also been a means of fostering a universal gay identity (Spade and Willse 2000). In doing so, this mainstream movement has revealed itself as excluding the interests of queers marginalized by some intersectional combination of gender, race, or class. This analysis points to the ways in which hegemonic queer cultures presume the rationality of gay visibility, a visibility ritualized through the coming-out process and institutionalized through gay rights agendas. The study of race as it is applied to queer formations demonstrates how the mainstream gay rights movement fosters forms of white privilege and displaces queers of color, particularly those marginalized by class and nationality. We might therefore say that today's racialized gay rights agendas emanate from the dialectic of freedom and unfreedom that arises out of an equally racialized genealogy of modern morality. Work by queer scholars who engage questions of racialized modernity intervenes into the study of race by observing how the array of nationalist and normative formations has expanded within the contexts of diaspora and contemporary globalization. As it has for at least three centuries, the study of race today names the different permutations of morality that continue to shape social formations according to freedom's relationship to unfreedom.

51

Reform

Susan M. Ryan

Embedded in the term "reform" is a tension between constraint and possibility. The prefix *re-* suggests familiarity, boundedness, and recursion, just as the root *form* denotes structure, whether institutional or ideological. And yet reform also conveys a sense of movement and potential. As Ralph Waldo Emerson writes in "Man the Reformer," reform entails "the conviction that there is an infinite worthiness in man which will appear at the call of worth" (1983, 146). This optimistic undercurrent requires that reformers not simply deride the existing order but propose alternatives— that they must, in short, *form* something. And, to the extent that the term calls for a realignment of established elements rather than obliterating what exists and starting over, reform can seem less alarming—but also more tepid—than radicalism, even as it suggests greater political engagement than either benevolence or charity.

That said, scholarly and critical work in American cultural studies has shown that reform as a nexus of social movements, including their various persuasive texts and performances, cannot be neatly distinguished from benevolence, charity, or, for that matter, radicalism. In the nineteenth century, when the term enjoyed especially wide circulation as a generic descriptor of individuals and movements, its meanings shifted, expanded, and contracted, often depending on the social and political commitments of the author. Most who called themselves reformers described their work as benevolent, even when they called for structural change rather than the direct dispensation of aid, while opponents of particular reform movements characterized their adherents as radicals committed to undermining the stability of the nation.

As these contestations over meaning suggest, reform proved to be a crucial element of identity construction in the United States in the nineteenth and early twentieth centuries. Some activists laid claim to the general title of "reformer" to indicate their investment in all manner of social progress, but others chose the less grandiose mode of aligning themselves with specific projects (including abolition, temperance, dietary reform, dress reform, and women's suffrage). Such articulations drew on and, in turn, shaped a thriving culture of reform, comprising books, pamphlets, and periodicals, many with broad geographical circulation; organizations with frequent meetings in established gathering places; and a distinct material culture, which became a staple of various groups' fundraising efforts. Unsurprisingly, this culture of reform also engendered resistance: as the nineteenth-century socialist Albert Brisbane (1846, 142) explained, his organization, "not wishing to take a name so much abused as that of 'Reformer,' . . . [chose] the simple name of Associationists."

Nathaniel Hawthorne's essay "Earth's Holocaust" (1844) dramatizes a predominant nineteenth-century critique of reformers—that their efforts to improve the world paid insufficient attention to the foundational task of changing the individual heart. But Hawthorne's lament disregards reformers' deep engagement with questions of individual perception and transformation. Nineteenth-century reformers drew on the work of such thinkers as Adam Smith, whose *Theory of Moral Sentiments* (1759/1966) articulated the perceptual processes by which one human being comes to feel sympathy for another. As this genealogy suggests, their appeals were calculated to change individuals' beliefs and commitments. Thus the history of reform has long been imbricated with the history of affect, with reformers relying quite successfully on rhetorical modes such as sentimentalism and sensationalism to energize their texts and interventions.

This link between reform and emotions has also troubled its advocates. Mid-nineteenth-century attempts to rationalize and bureaucratize charitable efforts, for example, followed in an Anglo-American tradition, associated with Thomas Malthus, of trying to counterbalance affective responses to suffering, which, it was feared, might lead to unwise giving. Later in the century, as reformers sought to professionalize social service work, they drew on the emerging "scientific" fields of sociology and criminology in order to categorize and comprehend the immigrants, delinquents, and prisoners they hoped to change. Yet emotion could not be so easily banished from reformist projects. Jacob Riis's New York photographs are apt examples; some of his images purport to document urban squalor with a quasi-scientific detachment, but others represent sleeping children or an immigrant madonna with an unabashed affective potency.

Many of those seeking leftward social change in the late twentieth and twenty-first centuries have distanced themselves from the term "reform," preferring labels like "activism," "progressivism," and "protest." While the openness of the term "reform" to ridicule (as a marker of humorlessness or of unreflective zeal) has a long history—consider the use of the reformer Miss Ophelia as comic relief even in Harriet Beecher Stowe's earnestly reformist novel *Uncle Tom's Cabin*—its current status can be gauged by the broad discomfort that greets terms such as "reform school," where it

suggests archaic and unsavory methods of correction. Perhaps more salient for those who now avoid the term is its currency among political conservatives, who have launched neoliberal attacks on the social safety net under the names of welfare reform, education reform, and tax reform. But it would be inaccurate to call this a cooptation, as if "reform" at some point in U.S. history belonged exclusively to the left. On the contrary, conservative elements have suffused even the most ostensibly progressive reform movements in every era. And movements primarily associated with social and political conservatives are hardly peculiar to our own times.

"Reform" has more currency among contemporary scholars of U.S. culture, for whom the term still engages questions of identity construction. The history of reform has provided a field through which to interrogate definitions of gender, nation, race, faith, and empire, insofar as reformers have sought to redefine these social and ideological structures, even as they wrote and spoke from positions within them. More problematically, the study of reform is a site where contemporary values collide with and to some degree skew our understandings of the past. Scholarship on the subject is rife with examples of the search for pure heroes and the impulse to debunk the apparently pure, as scholars filter their interpretations of reformist rhetoric (and of reformers' biographies) through their own conceptions of what it might mean to improve society.

The study of reform is not, however, solely a means of anatomizing scholars' own political aspirations and failures. Indeed, a significant development within American cultural studies is the push to get beyond meditations, however well informed, on such issues as whether reform movements and their proponents were good or bad. One of the most promising avenues builds on the field's increasingly expansive definitions of aesthetics, within which reform's strategies of persuasion can be analyzed alongside—and can reshape our conceptions of—other modes of assessing value. Scholarship on reform will necessarily continue to engage narrow questions of political efficacy and moral credibility. But the relevance of such work to the field rests on its ability to illuminate a broader range of concerns as well. The energies animating and regulating reformist projects go to the heart of the representation and deployment of such key concepts as interiority and emotion, persuasion and coercion.

52

Region

Sandra A. Zagarell

The keyword "region" may seem self-evidently place-based, both culturally and economically. But this commonplace understanding of regions as natural effects of a stable geography misses a central paradox; historical processes of modernization have created "places" that then appear to preexist or be peripheral to the modern. The *American Heritage Dictionary* defines a region as a large segment of a surface or space, especially on the earth, or a specified district or territory; it thus registers, albeit implicitly, that regions are relational—a region is part of something beyond itself. Only the fourth definition, "an area of interest or activity, a sphere," recognizes human involvement in the creation of regions and thereby suggests that they are not simply effects of natural geography. Considered historically, regions have been created and re-created in conjunction with the unfolding of global capitalism, the ceaseless movement of populations, the consolidation of nation-states and uneven economic and cultural development. At the same time, individual regions' particularities distinguish them from one another, and regions may set conditions on or otherwise complicate the large-scale forces that generate them.

To engage this paradox requires an explanation of how the term has been institutionalized. That regions are place-defined and fixed is a pervasive assumption in the United States, embedded in the local historical societies sponsored by innumerable villages, towns, and cities throughout the nation; in the promotion of regional cuisines and lifestyles (e.g., *Southern Living*); and in the heritage tourism that is so widely embraced as a source of income that the website of the Vermont Arts Council advertises a "Cultural Heritage Tourism Toolkit." The assumption also informs the centers for regional studies that have proliferated in recent decades, including the 1999 National Endowment for the Humanities initiative to launch ten regional humanities centers devoted to developing a "sense of place" that would underwrite the study of regional "history, people, [and] cultures." For over a century, scholarship on U.S. culture, too, has presumed place as a given and viewed it as the most important component of various regionalisms. In canonical accounts, "regions" emerged when areas that had been "sections" of the federated nation—rural New England, the South, the West and Midwest—were integrated into a unified postbellum industrial capitalist, democratic nation. While history and political economy informed these accounts, regions have been conceived in accordance with a spatial metaphor—as physically, culturally, and economically distant from a presumed national center.

More recent work in American cultural studies is now illuminating the paradoxes that constitute regions. Research on the postbellum regionalism that first constructed U.S. regions has articulated persisting factors. Feminist critics and others have established regionalist literature's complicated engagement with identity in the context of late-nineteenth-century global developments—massive movement of populations, changes in gender and the family, urbanization, industrialization, and African American emancipation. Taken as a whole, the work of scholars such as Judith Fetterley and Marjorie Pryse (2003), Stephanie Foote (2001, 2003), Kate McCullough (1999), Amy Kaplan (1991), and Carrie Tirado Bramen (2000) highlights many paradoxical features of postbellum regionalism. Among these are the celebration of differences in race and ethnicity, gender and sexuality; the unsettling of white dominance; the nostalgic casting of certain regions as preserves of a racially and culturally homogeneous national heritage; and the accommodation of resistance to forces of economic consolidation. Focusing on the same cultural movement, Richard Brodhead (1993) and June Howard (1994) have clarified the roles played by the converging forces of corporate production, expanded consumption, and the consolidation of class distinctions. Brodhead has shown the relationship among regionalism, capitalism, and class, emphasizing the interarticulation between the publishing and tourist industries and stressing the social distinction that urban readers affirmed through the consumption of regionalism. Howard counterbalances this uninflected cosmopolitanism by emphasizing regionalism's immersion in local cultures and traditions as well.

American cultural studies has also been instrumental to conceptualizing the relationships between the local and the large-scale that shape specific regions and their cultural representations. Dona Brown's *Inventing New England* (1995) and the visually focused *Picturing New England,* edited by William H. Truettner and Roger B. Stein (1999), consider the history of that region's place in the nation's culture and politics as an ongoing process that involved frequent retoolings of its historical foundation, evinced by production of cultural commodities—mementos, works of visual art and literature, furniture, decorative objects. Audrey Goodman's *Translating the Southwest* (2002) takes a similar approach to that region, considering it as something brought into being by industrial advances such as railroads, even as it was figured in photographs, literature, and ethnographic writing as a non-modern environment with non-modern inhabitants.

Recent cultural production has been especially successful at representing specific regions' transformations and paradoxical character. Jane Smiley's Iowa-based *A Thousand Acres* (1991) explores the intersection of Reagan-era economics and environmental degradation with cherished traditions of land ownership and farming and the often injurious dynamics of the patriarchal family. Southwestern fiction and film make apparent that the Southwest, though commonly regarded only as a region of the United States, has never ceased to be part of larger transnational networks of peoples, cultures, and economies. Leslie Marmon Silko's *Almanac of the Dead* (1991) meditates fiercely on the complicated movements of and alliances among various racial and ethnic populations across the U.S. Southwest and into Central and South America. Films like Gregory Nava's *El Norte* (1983), John Sayles's *Lone Star* (1996), and Steven Soderbergh's *Traffic* (2000) explore the tangled genealogies, migrating populations, and legal and illegal economies that make the border that separates the southwestern United States from countries to the south at once an intensely policed national divide and a porous boundary that continues to reshape regions across nations.

All of this contemporary work also suggests that regions are changing rapidly. Continuing population shifts, the extraordinary national and international mobility underwritten by automobiles and air travel, the reconstitution of cities and suburbs, the growth of exurbia, the continuing depredation of rural areas, the omnipresence of franchises, electronic media, and wireless communication: these effects of modernization are altering not only particular places but the role of place in creating regions. Subnational regions exist alongside supranational economic and political alliances, including the North American Free Trade Agreement and the World Trade Organization, which are further cutting across nations and transforming economies and populations. These macro-forces, in turn, encourage new forms of cultural, creative, and political activity. For instance, the individual and collaborative performances of artist-activist Guillermo Gómez-Peña mix installation art, radio, poetry, journalism, performance, and video as they explode presumptions about the discreteness of the United States and of the Southwest as a region within it. As American cultural studies attends to the ongoing changes in regions and in related expressive work, it will also need to keep in sight the paradoxes that continue to constitute both.

53

Religion

Janet R. Jakobsen

The keyword "religion" names that which is not secular, is associated with the sacred rather than the profane, and is aligned with dogma rather than reason. This series of oppositions draws together a wide range of practices across cultures that may not have much in common with one another. The conflation of various practices under the sign of religion has its origins in the thought of Enlightenment writers such as David Hume, for whom religion named the universal experience that marked the unity of human beings, even as it served to distinguish among humans on the basis of their different religions (Baird 2000). The simultaneous attribution of similarity and difference established the terms through which the Enlightenment could conceive of all persons as equal while also legitimating the treatment of some persons as inferior. In the process, even practices that had no reference to a god, like Buddhism, were assimilated to a category of religion organized around the Protestant concept of "faith." The use of this Protestant heuristic can be seen today in U.S. public discourse, where the most common way of speaking of multiple religious groups is to refer to "faiths" (as in the Jewish "faith," despite the fact that most forms of Judaism prioritize practice over "faith").

Working from Protestantism as the model of religion implied that other practices must either conform to this model or suffer by the comparison. At different stages in colonial history, for example, the peoples of southern Africa were treated as if they had no religion, a religion like the ancient roots of Christianity, or a fundamentally different species of the genus religion. At each stage, the European understanding of southern African religion enabled particular forms of colonial interaction. In the final stage, when colonial rule was consolidated, southern Africans were seen as essentially like European Christians in that they "had" a religion, but also essentially different in their partic-

ular religion. This religious difference was the key to the institutionalization of unequal treatment (Chidester 1996).

The Enlightenment idea of religion has remained powerful from the colonial past through the postcolonial present, as the keyword "religion" continues to mobilize a broad range of politics along the lines of race, nation, gender, and sexuality. U.S. racial categories grew out of what was originally a religious distinction between Christians and "strangers," a categorization that differentiated between Christian indentured servants and African slaves (Sweet 2003). But as Africans converted to Christianity, this distinction shifted toward a racial category, while a refusal to convert, as was the case with some Native Americans, was also increasingly taken as a marker of an inherent difference (Murphree 2004). In this view, only those who were truly *un*reasonable would refuse to see the light of Christianity, and racial difference was invoked to buttress such a profound difference. This intertwining of religious and racial identities continues to be evident in U.S. public life, as exemplified by the frequent presumption that Arabs must be Muslim and Muslims must be Arab.

The linkage of race and religion also implies a politics of gender and nation. As Minoo Moallem (2005) has argued, a racialized idea of Islam contributes to the discourse of "fundamentalism" that distinguishes "the West" from Islam and undergirds both Iranian nationalism and the formulation of U.S. strategic interests. Gender signifiers are a crucial site for reifying this distinction. Particularly since the Iranian revolution in

1979, "a turning point in . . . the representation of Islamic fundamentalism outside of Iran" (6), Muslim "fundamentalists" have been repeatedly portrayed through a masculinity that is "irrational, morally inferior and barbaric" and a femininity that is "passive, victimized, and submissive" (8). In contrast, the West is understood as secular and appropriately religious, a state of affairs signaled by the presumed freedom of Western women in comparison to their Muslim counterparts.

The intertwining of religion and secularism is part and parcel of prevalent mythologies of "Americanness." The apparently contradictory positioning of the United States as a simultaneously secular *and* Christian country is based in a familiar narrative of national origin, in which religion—here again a mostly Protestant Christianity—plays a leading role. This dominant narrative, taught in virtually every U.S. public school, includes the settlement of the continent by the New England pilgrims in search of religious freedom, the institution of religious freedom in the First Amendment to the Constitution, the separation of church and state that was the basis of a putatively free and secular public sphere, and the rise of religious pluralism with successive waves of immigration. It is also possible, though certainly less common, to relate this narrative in a way that acknowledges the implication of religion in the violent underside of the establishment of the nation-state. This counter-narrative includes forced conversions, the destruction of indigenous cultures and societies, the use of the Bible to legitimate slavery, and the role of Christian missionary activity in U.S. imperialism throughout the world.

But even if the standard narrative is amended to include the history of colonial and imperial violence, the Enlightenment development of the sui generis concept of religion still implies a binary contrast with secularism that is both historically untenable and politically dangerous. This duality has been central to the ideology currently used by the Bush Administration to justify the "war on terrorism" as a struggle for secular freedom against the religious fanaticism of radical Islam. But as neoconservative pundit Andrew Sullivan (2001) claimed in a *New York Times Magazine* article entitled "This *Is* a Religious War," the United States is freer and more secular because it is the product of a specifically Christian history. Sullivan's claim is that the nation's simultaneously Christian and secular status justifies U.S. violence as supportive of tolerance, in contrast with the threat and irrationality of "Islamic civilization." For the Bush Administration, this threat apparently extends beyond the religious fanaticism that supposedly fuels "terrorism" to a secular government like that in Iraq, provided that Iraqi secularism can be associated with "Islamic civilization," while U.S. secularism is based on a more tolerant Christianity (Jakobsen 2004).

The idea of religious fanaticism or "fundamentalism" is crucial to this set of associations. Like the category of religion, "fundamentalism" is a term that originally developed in the context of Protestantism, specifically in a 1920s conflict within U.S. Protestantism over the literal interpretation of the Bible.

In dueling pamphlets ("The Fundamentals" and "Will the Fundamentalists Win?"), fundamentalists were positioned as those who threatened liberal Protestants (Marsden 1980). Though the term has been extended to refer to forms of conservative religion for which biblical literalism is not a relevant issue, the sense of threat imputed to fundamentalism at its origins is maintained and even magnified when applied to other religions. The term "fundamentalism," like Hume's category of religion, does the work of positing some "religions" as reasonable and others as threatening.

When the category of religion is deployed in this manner, particularly when it is used to legitimate violence, secularism becomes an appealing alternative, but such a turn to the secular will not provide a simple escape. This is because the Enlightenment terms with which we still live render religion and secularism mutually constitutive. Although the Enlightenment narrative posits a reason that eventually overcomes religion (and thus liberates humanity from the bonds of dogma), religion and reason have remained intertwined throughout modernity. In his influential *Genealogies of Religion*, Talal Asad (1993) shows how Western reason does not simply overcome religious belief, but is genealogically dependent upon religious thinking. In particular, he reads medieval legal history to show how moves that are usually interpreted as the progressive rationalization of law over and against religious superstition are actually redefinitions of a rationality that is specifically religious. Asad undertakes this argument to show that Western rationalization is not necessarily freer from religion than is the reason of predominantly Muslim societies.

To see how religion and secularism are historically and conceptually intertwined is to understand why those who are "secular" are no more necessarily progressive than those who are "religious." Many major social justice and peace movements throughout the world—from Catholic base communities fighting poverty in Latin America, to the peaceful resistance of Tibetan Buddhism, to the civil rights movements of the United States—have religious roots. Secularism cannot save the world from colonial, racist, and sexist uses of religion because secularism is constitutive of and constituted by those very instantiations of religion. Religion has not faded away in modernity; rather, it is a constitutive category of the modern age. The question for anyone who would use "religion" as a term of analysis in American cultural studies is neither to distinguish the religious from the secular nor to ask "What is religion?" but to consider how the use of the term affects social relations and practices. Perhaps through such consideration our understanding of both the keyword "religion" and the myriad ways in which it constitutes social relations might change.

54

Science

Laura Briggs

To speak of "science" is to deploy a deceptively simple word whose use confers the mantle of authority. As Raymond Williams (1976, 276–80) and the *Oxford English Dictionary* tell us, the word came into English from the Latin *scientia*, meaning simply "knowledge." In the fourteenth century, it was distinguished from *conscience*, with science signifying theoretical knowledge, as opposed to knowing something with conviction and passion. In the seventeenth century, it began to denote that which was learned through theoretical—as opposed to practical—knowledge. Already, the term "science" made hierarchical distinctions in kinds of learning, favoring the abstract and the dispassionate. In the nineteenth century, "science" came to distinguish the experimental from the metaphysical, that which was *known* as truth as opposed to *asserted*. In its current configurations, this struggle over which kinds of knowledge should be accorded the higher status of being known as "science" is carried out through adjectives; the word, with no modifier, most often refers to the "natural sciences" or "hard sciences," and less often the "medical sciences," but seldom the "social sciences" and never to work in the arts and humanities. Science is not *a* knowledge, then, but *the* knowledge, that which speaks truthfully about the real.

We can see this insistence on science as that which speaks about the "real" in the way the term was de-

ployed against cultural studies scholars in the hoax that became the crowning event of "the science wars." The hoax began when in 1996 the editors of *Social Text* unwittingly accepted an article submitted by physicist Alan Sokal (1996a,b). After the issue came out, Sokal revealed that the article was a "joke," and he generated much attention from the national media by pointing out that a cultural studies journal had published something full of nonsensical claims, such as the assertion that *pi* is not a constant. The substance of his brief against cultural studies was that as a physicist, he spoke on behalf of the *real* world, which he felt needed defense against the nihilism and relativism of cultural studies' focus on "social constructions." Stanley Fish (1996, A23), in his elegant rebuttal in the *New York Times*, quoted Sokal as saying, "There is a world; its properties are not merely social constructions; facts and evidence do matter. What sane person would contend otherwise?" To this taunt, Fish replied, "Exactly! Professor Sokal's question should alert us to the improbability of the scenario he conjures up: Scholars of impeccable credentials making statements no sane person could credit." Fish went on to make two points: when cultural studies scholars call something a "social construction" they are not opposing it to the "real world," because things can be both real and socially constructed; when natural scientists develop their procedures and test the reliability of their accounts, they are said to be right or wrong only in relation with each other—yet disease and gravity are real enough. Although Sokal undoubtedly won the round, primarily by invoking a P. T. Barnum tradition of fraud and trickery to reveal that we can all be duped, the procedure by which he did so was as old as the fourteenth century: by claiming to speak on behalf of the real.

Behind this hoax lies a longer history. Science became an object of study for both cultural studies and American studies in relation to historical and political struggles over sex, race, and reproduction. In the 1970s, it became conventional for feminists to clear space for their politics with regard to "biology-is-destiny" arguments by explaining that there were two things in play: sex, which referred to biology, and gender, which was a social system open to criticism and change. Pursuing this logic further, some began to ask: Do we have to agree that women's *sex* is what they say it is—flaky hormones, weak anatomy? As Judith Butler wrote, "Perhaps this construct called 'sex' is as culturally constructed as gender; indeed, perhaps it was always already gender" (1990, 7). Feminist scientists like Anne Fausto-Sterling challenged the basis in the natural sciences for suggesting that women could not hold some jobs (from police work to the presidency); that they were unfit for higher education, at least in math and science; and that menstrual cycles made them dangerously unreliable (Fausto-Sterling 1985; Hubbard 1979). Others like Evelyn Fox Keller went further, arguing that the epistemology of the natural sciences was intrinsically dominative, and hence patriarchal and militaristic (Keller 1985; Griffin 1978).

At about the same time, another battle was being fought over race, ostensibly over IQ, but more generally about African Americans and public school deseg-regation, admission to higher education, equality of opportunity in good jobs, and civil rights. Physicist Arthur Jensen wrote a *Harvard Educational Review* article in 1969 arguing that black children's lower IQs meant they could never achieve equal success in school alongside white children. It generated furious rebuttal, captured most enduringly in biologist Stephen Jay Gould's *Mismeasure of Man* (1981), and launched a parallel study of the social and natural science of race. (This entire controversy was reproduced almost without change two decades later, in response to *The Bell Curve* [1994], Richard Herrnstein and Charles Murray's nasty polemic against welfare reform and affirmative action, replete with charts and graphs about African Americans' supposedly lower intelligence.) Another contemporaneous struggle that cast science into question concerned the sterilization of African American, Latina, and Native American women, often under the aegis of eugenics laws. Civil rights and feminist groups opposed these sterilizations through lawsuits, Senate hearings, and public fights to stop new legislation from being enacted (J. Nelson 2003).

These struggles intersected with the analysis of science by scholars of sexuality influenced by Michel Foucault's genealogy of late nineteenth-century European sexology—what he referred to as the long history of *scientia sexualis*. Jennifer Terry (1999) has shown how sexology migrated from Europe to the United States, where it functioned simultaneously to contain, define, and make possible queer identities and practices. More recently, scholarship has explored the role of science in pathologizing transgender identities (as mental illness), while also literally incarnating them through the surgeries and hormones that offer the option of remaking transgendered bodies (Bornstein 1994; Halberstam 1998, 2005; Butler 2004).

Gyan Prakash and others have argued that natural science was first and foremost a colonial imposition that took the place of alternative, indigenous sciences (Prakash 1999; Fanon 1967). Other scholars have shown how science made colonialism imaginable and reasonable to imperial countries. Sander Gilman (1986), for example, has recounted the story of the "Hottentot Venus" (Sara, or Sartjie, Baartman) to illustrate the way nineteenth-century science conflated the "objective" with the pornographic and the colonial, constructing geographical, raced, sexed, and gendered "others." Baartman was a Khoi-San woman "collected" by British natural historians off the Cape of Good Hope in 1810. (Some years later, Charles Darwin on the *Beagle* witnessed the repatriation of several people collected from Tierra del Fuego and commented, "Viewing such men, one can hardly make one's self believe that they are fellow-creatures, and inhabitants of the same world" [Darwin 1909]). Baartman was "exhibited" in Picadilly and Paris, where her large buttocks and much-speculated-upon genitalia were the subject of unending "scientific" curiosity; after her early death, Baartman was dissected and exhibited in the Musée de l'Homme in Paris until 2002, when her remains were repatriated to South Africa (Gould 1982).

Contemporaneous with Baartman and the *Beagle* were other, similar scientific exploits. The science of craniometry compared skull sizes, particularly of different races, presuming to measure racial intelligence; pelviometry identified "race pelves," looking for smaller pelvic openings that supposedly corresponded to smaller crania in offspring in the "lower" races; phrenology identified criminality (particularly in the lower classes) from head shape; polygeny, the theory of multiple, separate "creations" of the world by God, provided a religiously heretical account (favored by many U.S. slaveholders) in which the "lower races" were separate, inferior species (Gould 1981; Briggs 2000).

A few decades later, after Darwin's *Origin of Species* had taken the world by storm, evolution provided a new grammar of difference for humans as well, from Social Darwinism to eugenics. Evolution, and the notion that some people were further along its track than others, provided ways of explaining why women should not vote; why immigration should be restricted (disease provided a parallel account of the supposed "threat" immigrants posed); why "overcivilization" and "degeneration" were dangerous; and how homosexuals, professional women, labor union men, and even children were like primitives (Newman 1999; Stern 1999a; Shah 2001;). The coming of "modern" science and the end of formal imperialism did not inaugurate a distinct change. Warwick Anderson has shown that reports of the supposedly unsanitary practices of "natives" were vital to the U.S. imperial project in the Philippines in the early twentieth century (W. Anderson 1995). Further, as old-style colonialism collapsed in much of the world in the post-1945 period, science and technology emerged as dominant languages of an emergent international development bureaucracy focused on population control and agriculture.

Perhaps ironically, the late twentieth century was a period in which resistance to the hegemony of science could take shape in relationship to calls for more and better science. Donna Haraway (1991) argued that we are all "cyborgs," and that the utopian, back-to-nature fantasies of radical feminists and others do not make sense in a world where virtually all forms of power, authority, economy, and family are shaped in relationship to science. AIDS activists embraced the terms of public health and science but contested the organization of AIDS research, struggling to shift the content of public health education, the quantity of funding overall, the kind of research conducted, and the conduct of clinical trials (Patton 1985, 1996; Epstein 1996; Treichler 1999). In the 1970s, women's health activists transformed doctor-patient relationships and, ultimately, scientific research on women by putting information in women's hands through *Our Bodies, Ourselves* (Boston Women's Health Book Collective 1973, 1976, 1996). At the same time, in the post–Cold War university, advocates for higher education have debated how to deal with the ripple effects of the sharp decline in government (often military) funding

for research in the natural sciences, and its replacement with corporate money—and with it, corporate organization and labor management styles—as well as an undervaluing of non-scientific and non-professional education and research (C. Nelson 1997).

In the early twenty-first century, scholars are beginning to argue that the emergent challenge for cultural studies of science is no longer to insist that science is open to critique because of its hegemonic agendas, but rather to develop procedures to defend the "reality" of scientific claims about such things as global warming, environmental degradation, evolution, the effectiveness of condoms in preventing the spread of HIV, and the putative tie between abortions and breast cancer (Latour 2004). As these and other well-established scientific claims come increasingly under attack by industry, right-wing religious groups, and anti-sex, anti-feminist, and homophobic conservatives in government, "social construction" has come to seem a tool that can be used effectively against many of the same groups it was developed to defend. As Haraway has been arguing for many years, perhaps what we need are simply more modest claims for science, acknowledging that it is not *the* knowledge but *a* knowledge, avoiding the hubris of the "god's-eye view," but nevertheless taking seriously the value of replicable, evidence-based claims.

55

Secularism

Michael Warner

"Secularism" is a late coinage in English, dating from the 1850s, when it was adopted by reformers who regarded the church and capital as the joint enemies of the worker (Holyoake 1854). But because the word is used by cultural critics in many antithetical senses, it occasions great confusion. The United States is sometimes held to be the model of secular democracy, and sometimes the most religious of all major modern democracies. Can both be true?

The root "secular" derives from the Latin for "the age"; in the Christian tradition the secular is the temporal or the worldly. The spiritual/secular opposition is fundamental, but Christian attitudes toward the secular have ranged from hostility to fervent immersion, and have seldom been simple. It was at one time possible, for example, to speak of "secular clergy," by which was meant ordinary parish priests, as opposed to the religious of the monastic orders.

Protestantism heightened the contrast, and Puritans especially differentiated spiritual and secular functions as part of their critique of the established church. Thus they relegated marriage to secular authorities and avoided the ecclesiastical courts. But they did not imagine the secular to be outside of Christianity, let alone outside of the abstract category "religion." Religion, as Wilfred Cantwell Smith pointed out in his classic *The Meaning and End of Religion*

(1964), had until recently the sense of piety rather than of any category of belief-systems and institutions. Only in the late eighteenth century could Christianity and Islam be seen as tokens of the same type. So although the new secularism of the Puritans may have fed the growth of the autonomous state, the aim was to purify rather than relativize religion.

Secularism refers sometimes to social conditions that can be embraced by the religious and nonreligious alike. Disestablishment is the most obvious of these; it was an idea developed largely by Baptists and other dissenters, at a time when virtually no one in North America expressed open antagonism to religion (Hamburger 2002). Somewhat more broadly, secularism refers to the idea that the complex set of social transformations called "secularization" can be embraced as a good thing. This idea, too, can be held for religious or nonreligious reasons; there are many Christian theologians who regard the conditions of secularization as restoring to Christianity a purity that it had lost through the corruption of institutional power and temporal preoccupations. For them, the litmus issues that are widely thought to indicate religious conviction—opposition to abortion, gay marriage, or evolution—are temporal concerns corrupting religion.

Secularism can also refer to atheism or freethought, though the term was coined largely to give the sense of a substantive ethical vision rather than the merely negative sense of infidelity or nonbelief. "Freethought" is a continuous tradition in Anglo-American culture, dating from the second half of the seventeenth century, though it was more vilified than evidenced in North America. Some versions of freethought are religious in many senses of the term. Most emphasize reason as the guide to religious truth. The earliest proponents of freethought in North America include Ethan Allen, Thomas Paine, and Elihu Palmer; all were deists, and Paine vigorously denounced atheism (Morais 1934). Their innovation was to make freethought a popular rather than elite cause. Nineteenth-century freethought had even more radical aspirations and was frequently elaborated as part of other movements, especially labor, feminism, antislavery, and pacifism. Among its greatest exponents were Frances Wright, Robert Ingersoll, and Ernestine Rose.

More radically still, secularism sometimes refers to an active quest for the elimination of religion, a quest that can be tied to projects as different as positivism, structuralism, or the post-Nietzschean move to expunge Christian moralism and redemptive theology from the culture. Despite the prominence of these antihumanist versions of secular thought, "secular humanism" emerged in the twentieth century as the target of fundamentalists, who often identify it with science, mass culture, liberal jurisprudence, and many other phenomena that may or may not be tied to humanist or other views of the secular.

More rarely, secularism can be embraced as a kind of spiritual worldliness in a way that is distinguished from Christianity, or the theological, but not necessarily from religion per se. William Connolly's *Why I Am Not a Secularist* (2000), despite the irony of its title, advocates a nontheist worldliness that—in contrast to what he regards as liberal statist secularism—would not be sharply distinguished from religious subjectivities or practices. It can be argued that some of the Transcendentalists—Ralph Waldo Emerson and, even more so, Henry David Thoreau and Walt Whitman—represent this kind of secularism as well.

Connolly joins several other recent scholars—Charles Taylor (2002, 2004), Talal Asad (1993, 2003), Leigh Schmidt (2000)—in seeing secularism not as the absence of religion, or as an antagonist to religion, but as a specific cultural formation in its own right, with its own sensibilities, rituals, constructions of knowledge, and ethical projects. Schmidt, for example, has documented a reeducation of the senses connected with the eighteenth-century critique of revelation. Secular culture in this sense remains comparatively understudied, possibly because—as Asad argues—one of its features is the consolidation of "religion" as an object of social-scientific knowledge in a way that takes for granted the secular character of explanation itself.

Secularism is often associated with the Enlightenment and with rationalism, but neither of these intellectual movements took hold in British America in the way that is often assumed by critics whose view of the Enlightenment is based on the French version. The deist movement that was so notable in England after the 1690s made only an indirect impact in the colonies before the Revolution. (Benjamin Franklin is one exception, and even he supported evangelical movements and clergy, largely on pragmatic grounds.) The anticlericism that marked the French

Enlightenment was also conspicuously absent from the colonies. The American Enlightenment, indeed, was often led by clergy (May 1976).

In classic studies by Carl Schmitt (1986), Carl Becker (1932), M. H. Abrams (1971), and others, the Enlightenment is seen historically as transposing religious values into nontheological equivalents, the significance of which often depends on the religious background that has been suppressed. Thus progress is secularized providence, utopia is secularized heaven, and sovereignty is secularized omnipotence. Hans Blumenberg (1983), however, has countered that these stories mistakenly assume a theological origin and neglect the new context, function, and impulse of secular themes.

By the end of the eighteenth century, it had become possible to speak of religion in a comparative sense, defined principally by belief. This understanding still reigns as common sense in the United States, but it does not go without saying; many kinds of religious practice have little to do with belief or sincerity of conviction. The Protestant quest for saving faith no doubt lies behind this assumption, but so does the development of the denominational system, in which churches are no longer taken to be national or territorially comprehensive, as they had been in the long history of the Catholic, Anglican, and even Congregationalist systems. Instead, they began competing for voluntary adherents in overlapping territories. Being outside a particular church no longer meant being alienated from a fundamental institution of belonging and public culture, thus opening more space for the secular. Yet this same system marked the rise of evangelicalism and the aggressive promotion of religious faith to a public of strangers. This association is so strong that it makes sense to speak of an evangelical public sphere, developing first with the so-called Great Awakening and exploding after the 1790s. The way this combination of disestablishment and denominationalism created fertile conditions for religiosity is what struck Alexis de Tocqueville (1835/2004) so forcibly.

For many scholars of the sociology of religion (Berger 1963, 1969; Stark and Finke 1992, 2000; Swatos and Olson 2000), this pattern is seen as a "marketplace of religion." The metaphor is highly questionable, since the key features that define a market— including abstract value, price as a mechanism for coordinating supply and demand, territorial integration of regulation—are absent. This model also leads people to think of religion as a constant, and thus to overlook its transformation and construction.

Rodney Stark and Roger Finke have argued strongly that the marked and enduring religiosity of U.S. culture refutes what they call "the secularization thesis." In their view, the secularization thesis is the idea that modernity necessarily entails a decline of religious belief. They point out that religious adherence—at least as measured by church attendance—was much lower in the premodern middle ages than in the United States of the past two centuries. "To classify a nation as highly secularized when the large majority of its inhabitants believe in God is absurd," writes Stark (Swatos and Olson 2000).

But this view depends on an extremely reductive view of secularization. The more robust understanding of secularization is that a variety of social changes—bureaucratization, the rationalization and professionalization of authority, the rise of the state, the separation of the economy, urbanization, and empirical science—change the position of religious institutions in the social landscape (D. Martin 1969, 1978; Weber 1983; B. Wilson 1998). Clergy compete with other public intellectuals; other grounds of legitimacy and authority are available; and the society itself is understood to be distinct from a confessional body. This understanding of secularization does not necessarily predict a decline in belief. In fact, the understanding of religion as defined primarily in terms of subjective belief could be seen as *evidence* of this larger transformation. Thus it would not at all be absurd to say that U.S. society, marked by high levels of belief in God, is highly secularized precisely because mental and voluntary adherence is the principal way that religion is salient.

Charles Taylor (2004) has recently elaborated this point. Modern social imaginaries, in his view, are secular in several senses, though they also allow for new kinds of religiosity. They take the social to be an order of mutual benefit in which governments answer to essentially prepolitical ends (natural rights, happiness, flourishing), directly comprehending all constituents. Political and social life is increasingly understood in a secular temporality of simultaneous and directional activity, rather than in a higher time of origins or ritually realized eternity. Religion can exist, even thrive, under the conditions of modern social imaginaries, but it is newly enframed. One major change, in Taylor's view, is the widespread assumption that religious convictions, to be truly authentic, should be the result of an individual path toward spirituality. Thus what is often called the "privatization of religion" is not just a reduction or restriction, but involves new ethical imperatives and a backgrounded understanding of the social.

Working against this trend, however, are several new kinds of public religion, from the prophetic character of the African American church (Chappell 2004) to what Robert Bellah (1970, 1975) calls "civil religion," by which he means not just a veneration of the nation's founding, documents, and rituals of citizenship, but a faith in a deity that providentially superintends the nation. In many contexts, U.S. Americans speak of God in a way that is nominally ecumenical. Eisenhower is supposed to have remarked: "Our government makes no sense unless it is founded in a deeply felt religious faith—and I don't care what it is." George W. Bush similarly speaks of a nation "guided by faith" without specifying what that faith is in. This vagueness bespeaks secularism, in that it is thought to be multiconfessional and disestablished. But the divine is assumed to be personal and historical; a being that actively addresses individuals and nations and has specially appointed a world-historical mission for the United States. This political religion is secular in an important sense: its proof lies not in spiritual truth or a higher time but in the politics of the present. The Gettysburg Address is a classic example of this crypto-

Protestant secular providentialism (Tuveson 1968). This strain of redemptive nationalism explains why those who speak of America's God believe themselves to be in a mainstream of U.S. history against advocates of church-state separation—who nevertheless also see themselves as in the mainline of Constitutionalism.

Among the greatest challenges in thinking about secularism is that although the term acquired its significance from the development of Christian culture, it was globalized in the period of the European empires to apply to cultures where local religions did not have the same tradition of distinguishing themselves from the secular. Thus in many parts of the world, including the Islamic world, secularism and Christianity are often presented not as opposites but as twin faces of Western dominance. Some of the strongest critiques of secularism have come from post-colonial India (Bhargava 1998). Secularism might thus be seen as a mode of political organization closely connected with global capitalism, and it is ironic but not simply inconsistent that secular governance in other countries is promoted with missionary and even violent fervor by the most evangelical Christian wing of U.S. politicians.

The dialectic unfolding of these ironies is lost on common sense, which continues to hold as self-evident that secularism means governmental neutrality, that religion is a universal category of subjective belief, and that the two are locked in combat. These convictions distort any attempt in American studies, cultural studies, or elsewhere, to confront such ultimate questions as finitude, mortality, nature, fate, and commonality.

56
Sentiment
June Howard

The term "sentiment" marks the recognition that emotions are social and historical. Feelings seem personal and interior—yet it is often easy to see that they are structured and shared. "Sentiment," "sentimental," and "sentimentality" are used at moments when the entanglement of the subjective and the public is implicitly or explicitly acknowledged. This entanglement makes them vexed and value-laden categories. They have a complex range of uses in everyday language, and have been the focus of much debate in American cultural studies.

Discussions of sentiment always depend upon concepts of emotion—itself a poorly understood phenomenon. When I am moved, the experience is anchored in my body: tears come to my eyes or my heart beats faster, my skin flushes or my stomach roils. These physiological responses are emotion's most intimate aspect, and at the same time its least individual, because they are common to all humans and in some cases can be observed in other animals. Sensations become emotions, however, only as they are played out in the theater of the brain. They come into being through, and their meaning is mediated by, language and memory. We can understand emotions as "embodied thoughts" (M. Rosaldo 1984). This makes sense, but it also might lead us to ask whether there can be *disembodied* thoughts. Arguably all human cognition must be oriented by the sense of an implicated self. Indeed, neurologists tell us that individuals with brain injuries that impair emotions also have trouble making sensible choices; they apparently cannot understand what is at stake in their decisions (Damasio 1994). Emotion appears to be fundamental to all mental life, infused in all thought.

Thus definitions of sentiment that equate it with emotion, as opposed to reason, will not take us very far. Although criticism has paid far less attention to the affective than to the intellectual dimensions of reading, our responses to literature are always emotional. So are our responses to music, to advertisements, to newspaper stories and political speeches. Since these emotions are themselves mediated by language and culture, the observation that sentiments are conventionalized, socially organized emotions cannot be a ground for dismissing them as inauthentic. These are common views, in both everyday speech and scholarship, but they derive from a map of the mind in which emotion preexists thought and remains separate from it, rather than being intricately and indispensably part of culture. They also neglect the specific history of the sentimental.

"Sentiment" is a very old word in English (the *Oxford English Dictionary* cites examples from Chaucer). Its longer derivatives "sentimental" and "sentimentality," on the other hand, entered the language in the mid-eighteenth century, at a moment when a great deal of attention was being paid to the moral and social function of emotion. Philosophers such as Francis

Hutcheson and Adam Smith found the source of benevolence in sympathy for others, and the authors of novels of "sensibility" portrayed their characters' intense emotional responsiveness as admirable and morally improving (Todd 1986). What was at stake in these philosophical and literary works was the shared and structured nature of feelings—their ability to link individuals in a chain of sympathy, and the view that they could and should be cultivated. In the process, they were creating a quite comprehensive system of beliefs and values, blending an account of mental life—what we would now call psychology—with epistemology and ethics. In this conceptual system, the process of identification—how an individual puts himself or herself in someone else's place and claims knowledge of what that other person is thinking and feeling—establishes the grounds for virtuous behavior and a humane social order.

Scholars of literature and culture have often been skeptical of the link between these works and sentimentality in the United States, opposing U.S. to European traditions in the exceptionalist mode typical of much American studies research. More recently, however, conversations about sensibility, sympathy, and sentiment have become thoroughly transatlantic (Fliegelman 1993; Barnes 1997; Ellison 1999). Racialized and gendered performances of emotional affiliation are important in Anglo-American thought, whether we examine the Declaration of Independence, William Hill Brown's *The Power of Sympathy* (published in 1789 and often called the first American novel), or Harriet Beecher Stowe's *Uncle Tom's Cabin*

(1852). In the latter, the narrator implicates the reader in a series of common experiences and bodily sensations, and offers this famous injunction to oppose slavery emotionally: "There is one thing that every individual can do,—they can see to it that *they feel right*. An atmosphere of sympathetic influence encircles every human being; and the man or woman who *feels* strongly, healthily and justly, on the great interests of humanity, is a constant benefactor to the human race" (1852/1981, 385). The influence of moral philosophy is clearly visible in a text that is probably the single most influential work of sentimental fiction.

The popular novels published by women writers of the antebellum period, such as *Uncle Tom's Cabin*, Susan Warner's *Wide, Wide World* (1850), and Maria Cummins's *The Lamplighter* (1854), have been classic locations for discussions of sentimentality in American cultural studies (Douglas 1977; Tompkins 1985; S. Samuels 1992). They are indeed frequently characterized by a focus on sympathy and an ethic of human connectedness, and by affiliation with a domestic ideology that locates these values in the home. Recent scholarship has shown not only the transatlantic nature of this tradition, but also its permeation of other discourses, including writing by and about men (Chapman and Hendler 1999). Didactic domestic novels are closely linked to the vast literature of the temperance movement and to anti-slavery writing, and sentimental conventions are unevenly visible in poetry, art, and music. For the mid-nineteenth century, in fact, one can speak broadly of a middle-class sentimental culture that included such matters as dress and etiquette (Halttunen 1982), imputing moral significance to fashion and manners.

In this constellation of attitudes and practices—which Raymond Williams might have called a "structure of feeling"—the home is imagined as a haven hedged off from the values of the marketplace and the state. Sympathy and benevolence are effective within a zone protected from the corrosive realities of economics and politics. One irony of this scenario is that it requires us to forget the everyday experience of family relations, which frequently entail negotiations over money and power. Another is that private homes of this sort can only be maintained by a constant flow of commodities to be consumed behind their doors. They rely on the labor of those who produce those commodities, and often on the labor of domestic servants who may even (especially before the twentieth century) reside within them. And they are the constant focus of public discourses and of government regulation and support, from sermons about the family to twentieth-century tax subsidies for home ownership. Sentimentality, by our day, is thoroughly intertwined with domestic ideology. It continues to proclaim the distinctive power of the private, while implicitly demonstrating the inseparability of the public and the private—or, we might say, the personal and the political—both at the level of individual psychology and in our cognitive maps of society (June Howard 2001).

The power of sentiment thus stems from the permeability of the very boundaries that sentimental culture strives to defend and secure (Burgett 1998;

Hendler 2001). Sentimental fictions are publications—by definition, public—but they address the reader intimately; these market-mediated stories circulate right through the heart and the home. In sentimental culture, in fact, virtually any commodity can be animated with personal meaning. Objects selected for purchase are considered expressions of taste and personality, and become the furniture and armature of a domestic world. That world has been considered women's sphere; the associations between women and consumption, and women and emotion, arrived together. None of this of course implies that these feelings are inauthentic—any more than a sentiment expressed by purchasing and sending a greeting card is necessarily insincere. But historicizing them points out that the notion that they are insulated from the economic is a wish rather than a truth. We also recognize the link between objects and feelings in everyday usage when we say that something that has been (usually) bought and (always) used and valued has "sentimental value."

Feeling right and having the right kind of home came to be fundamental to the life-world of the U.S. middle classes and to their broad-ranging claims to authority (Ryan 1981; Blumin 1989). The "disciplinary intimacy" that Richard Brodhead (1993) finds in sentimental literature carries social order deep into the self, as authorities are obeyed because they are loved and their laws internalized. The cultivated and virtuous seem to legitimize their privilege by deserving it; sometimes the less fortunate are depicted as lacking proper feelings and proper homes, as appropriate ob-

jects of sympathy, but also as less worthy citizens and perhaps even less fully human. This applies most often to racialized others—Indians, African Americans, sometimes the Irish and (later) other immigrant groups. But the sentimental has also been appropriated by subordinated speakers; its politics are variable and complex (L. Romero 1997).

Most prominently, recent scholarship has shown that the values associated with sentimentality are integral to the ideologies of colonialism and imperialism. What Laura Wexler (2000) has called "tender violence" justified brutal interventions in the family relations of indigenous people on the grounds that they had the wrong kind of families. Amy Kaplan (2002) has argued that "manifest domesticity" justified national expansion and U.S. imperialism, as the spaces of the home and the nation were rhetorically identified in the contrast between "domestic" and "foreign." The twenty-first century trope of "homeland security" is a contemporary deployment of this version of sentimentality. To point that out neither invalidates nor supports the formulation; emotion has an entirely legitimate role in politics (Marcus 2002). But doing so can offer a perspective from which to analyze such appeals; the sentimental entails a call to think critically about flushes of feeling that arise over the boundary between "in here" and "out there."

It seems unlikely that the controversies over sentimentality will be resolved by scholarly argument. The stigmatizing sense of "sentimental" entered the language very soon after the word itself. After the mid-nineteenth century, hostility to sentimentality hardened and became more organized, especially through the misleading opposition between self-consciously literary texts and feminized didactic works. Realist writers, for instance, incorporated many elements of the sentimental, even as they defined their movement against it (W. Morgan 2004); later, modernists were still more dismissive. In literary history during the twentieth century, the sentimental tradition was more and more thoroughly erased—until feminist scholars insisted that it was worthy of attention. Since that time both literary and cultural history have been rewritten. But American cultural studies continues to oscillate between affirming the sentimental as an expression of women's values and denouncing it as oppressive. Both of these perspectives have merit, and current scholarship is integrating them in a more fully historicized and critical view. But the term will remain charged and complex so long as our maps of the self and the world are divided between public and private, reason and emotion. The sentimental is a hinge that swings between the social and the subjective—reminding us, if we are willing to listen, that they are always connected.

57
Sex
Bruce Burgett

In common usage, the keyword "sex" names something an individual either is or has. It refers to both the material foundation (male or female) of binary gender difference (masculine or feminine), and the real and imagined acts that ground various sexual identities (homosexual, heterosexual, fetishist, sadomasochist, and so on). The *Oxford English Dictionary* (*OED*) dates the first sense of "sex" as male or female from the fourteenth century, though it also notes a more pluralized usage from the sixteenth century ("so are all sexes and sorts of people called upon"), a singular usage from the same period ("I am called The Squire of Dames, or the Servant of the Sex"), and a further revision in the early nineteenth century ("the third sex"). In contrast, the *OED* dates the second sense of the term from the mid- to late-nineteenth century, when "sexual" ("Berlin is outbidding Paris in its sexual immorality") and "sexuality" ("Precocious sexuality . . . interferes with normal mental growth") began to reference a discrete domain of physical and mental acts isolated from other corporeal appetites, imaginative practices, and forms of social relation. Coincident with these developments was the emergence of terms such as "heterosexual" and "homosexual" that name and police specifically "sexual" orientations and preferences, as well as the largely medical or scientific usage of the verb "to sex," meaning to identify a plant or animal as male or female ("The . . . barbarous phrase 'collecting a specimen' and then of 'sexing' it").

The last of these mutations in the term's etymology reveals the growing belief in the late nineteenth century that sex and sexual identities were discrete and deadly serious matters best overseen by scientific, clerical, and juridical authorities, including well-known "sexologists" ranging from Sigmund Freud to Alfred Kinsey (Irvine 1990; Terry 1999). Yet the specific usage chosen by the *OED* editors also documents a critical response to those new forms of power, one that satirized the labeling practices of civil authorities as "barbaric." As Raymond Williams pointed out when he added "sex" to his revised edition of *Keywords* in 1983, the early twentieth century marked a continued boom in the production of terms and terminology, nearly all of which carried both positive and negative valences: "sexy" and "sex appeal," "sex repression" and "sex expression," "undersexed" and "oversexed." It is significant that Williams's revision itself coincided with the entry of feminist politics and methodologies into the institution that many regard as the origin of cultural studies as a field—the Centre for Contemporary Cultural Studies at the University of Birmingham. Williams's short entry concluded with phrases coined within the Anglo-American feminisms of the 1960s and 70s: "sexism" and "sexist" (terms he saw as derived from "racism" and "racist"), "sex-objects" and "gender." But his focus on the first meaning of "sex" (male or female) led him to neglect the more promiscuous politics of the contemporary "sexual revolu-

tion." Centre director Stuart Hall (1991, 282) commented in a retrospective history that feminism had, in the late 1970s, "interrupted, made an unseemly noise, seized the time, crapped on the table of cultural studies." Had he been writing a few years later, he might (or might not) have added that lesbian-gay and queer activism had done the same.

As indicated by this lacuna, the keyword "sex" continues to draw much of its force from its dual referent. In academic research, nearly as frequently as in popular discourse, mainstream scholars still wed "sex" (male or female) to "sexuality" (homo- or hetero-), applying what feminist philosopher Judith Butler (1990) famously called a "heterosexual matrix" across a wide array of disciplinary and interdisciplinary research fields, often by relying implicitly on the concept of biological reproduction. A more critical approach also assumes that "sex" is the real-life referent for studies of both gender and sexuality, but then shifts its attention away from questions concerning the physical foundations of sex and toward a focus on the relations of power that have organized historically variable constructions of gender and sexuality. This social-constructivist form of analysis draws its force in large part from the feminist insistence that "gender," understood as a cultural or social system, can be neither reduced to nor deduced from "sex," understood as a biological destiny that, with rare exceptions, makes men "masculine" and women "feminine." It also profits from the related move within "sex-positive" strains of feminism and, more recently, queer theory to suggest that the critical study of sex and sexuality has no more intimate relation to the study of gender than it to does to that of any other system of cultural or social classification (Rubin 1984; Sedgwick 1990). The result has been the development of a new and paradoxical common sense: Sex tends to be treated today as a stable category of analysis, even as it is said to require scrutiny for the ways in which it intersects with other axes of social recognition and power, including gender, race, class, religion, region, and ability, among many others (Harper et al. 1997).

Take as a representative example of this paradox a passage from one of the most canonical (and useful) surveys of the history of sexuality written about the United States: John D'Emilio and Estelle Freedman's *Intimate Matters: A History of Sexuality in America* (1988, 1997). Appearing in the context of a discussion of nineteenth-century same-sex romantic friendships, the passage begins with the assertion that "the overlap of the romantic, erotic, and physical has made it difficult to define these relationships, especially in light of the way sexual meanings have changed in the twentieth century," and includes a criticism of more conventional historians who have responded to this difficulty by assuming that such relationships were devoid of "sex" (121). D'Emilio and Freedman then raise the related and apparently more vexing question of what counts as "sex," opening a new paragraph with the following assertion: "However difficult it may be to know whether sexual—that is, genital—relations characterized particular same-sex friendships, it is clear that the meaning of same-sex love gradually changed over the course of the nineteenth century"

(122). Typical of much social-constructivist historiography, this epistemological compromise is notable in two ways: It draws on and confirms the key insight of constructivist research on the history of sexuality by insisting that the social and cultural meanings of "sex" vary over time and place; however, it fails to apply that insight to a critical analysis of the foundational categories of "sex" and "sexual," both of which are equated in the passage with the "genital." What is the difference, a skeptical reader might ask, between a history of sexuality and a history of genitality, either in "America" or elsewhere?

One answer to this question comes from a strand of research influenced by the writings of the French philosopher and historian Michel Foucault. In the first volume of *The History of Sexuality* (1976, 1978) and later interviews (2006), Foucault extended the logic of the constructivist critique by historicizing not just the diverse *meanings* of sex and sexuality, but also the *categories* themselves. His history concerned not real-life things called "sex" and "sexuality," but the ways those concepts have come to structure contemporary thinking about political relations among bodies, sensations, appetites, and pleasures. This approach broke decisively with academic research in historical and sociological fields built on the empiricist assumption that "sex" and its related terms named things in the world that could be counted, quantified, and archived. It also broke with the tendency in psychology and political theory to treat sex as a physical drive that encounters power primarily through mechanisms of repression or liberation. Some of the resulting work produced by Foucault and his many followers displayed a penchant for periodization, quibbling over the precise historical moment when a given term ("sex," "sexual," "sexuality," "homosexuality," "heterosexuality") came into common usage. But more important was the shift in the way research questions and conversations about sex were formulated and shaped. No longer concerned primarily with mapping the many varieties of human sexual expression or contributing to the related debates about how sex could be best liberated or repressed, this newer research asked a more fundamental question: When, where, and in what specific contexts has sex been abstracted from the relations of power within which some corporeal practices, social formations, and political ideologies become "sexualized" and others do not?

The novelty of this critical turn in the study of sex and sexuality has often been overstated, as Gayle Rubin (2002) has pointed out in a careful reconstruction of the earlier groundbreaking work of scholars in the fields of interactionist sociology, cultural anthropology, social history, and even minority forms of sexology. But it is undeniable that the rapid and wide dissemination of Foucault's writings both inside and outside of academic circles galvanized a new critical consensus that began to coalesce in the 1990s under the rubrics of queer theory and, in its more institutionalized form, queer studies. Across the fields of American studies and cultural studies, this research has produced work on a broad range of historical sites, social movements, policy initiatives, legal debates, and aesthetic forms: Oral historians and ethnographers

have traced the ways in which the question of what did and did not count as a sexual practice or identity shaped the lives of men in the rural south and across the Filipino diaspora (John Howard 2001; Manalansan 2003); social and cultural historians have detailed the intersections of emergent constructions of sex as an isolable danger, the racialization of underclass and migrant labor populations, and the promotion of top-down health and welfare policies (Patton 1996; Shah 2001); historians of science have excavated the contested origins of sex as a core concept in the biological and natural sciences (Schiebinger 1989; Laqueur 1990; Fausto-Sterling 2000); cultural and social critics have discussed the deployment of the concept of sex as a strategic means of undermining egalitarian urban planning and democratic public space (Mumford 1997; Berlant and Warner 1998; Delany 2001); legal and literary theorists have archived and critiqued the ways in which sex figures into immigration policy, military recruitment, and cultural canon formation (Halley 1999; Luibhéid 2002; Ferguson 2004).

Given the scope of this new research, one danger today may be that sex is being asked to do too much critical and conceptual work (Eng, Halberstam, and Muñoz 2005). Such a worry opens onto a more political version of the question that has restructured much of the recent historiography: How, to what ends, and in what specific contexts have scholars and activists generated the intellectual abstractions and disciplinary frameworks that allow for the treatment of sex as an entity that stands on its own? An answer to this question would need to take into account several heterogeneous developments in the later half of the twentieth century: the mid-century naturalization of "sex" as the core of identity formation and psychological development; the late-century move to isolate "sex" as a category of analysis located at the center of lesbian-gay and queer studies; the more recent rise of a gay neoconservatism that insists on bracketing the politics of sexuality from a wider social justice agenda; the many vernacular discourses and dissident practices that have clustered around sex and sexuality throughout the period (Duggan 2004b; Burgett 2005). These diverse intellectual, political, and social formations are neither reducible to a core ideology nor elements of a linear history. But they do suggest that one challenge for future work organized around the keyword "sex" may be to produce research that is more episodic than sequential, more local (and trans-local) than national. Such scholarship needs to focus both on those moments and places where "sex" becomes available as an isolable way of thinking about and experiencing oneself and one's relations to others, and on those moments and places where "it" does not. The corresponding task, which may call for even greater inventiveness and creativity, involves the archiving and cultivation of alternative vocabularies for thinking and talking about bodies, pleasures, and the political relations between and among them.

58
Slavery
Walter Johnson

"Slavery has never been represented, slavery never can be represented," said the novelist, antislavery lecturer, and former slave William Wells Brown in 1847 (18). Brown referred, in the first instance, to the world-making violence of the system of kidnapping, dispossession, and labor extraction that emerged in the fifteenth century and persisted almost to the dawn of the twentieth. But he referred in the second instance to a sort of epistemological violence, a murderous, forcible forgetting of the history of slavery. Only slavery's victims—if it is possible to use the word "only" in the context of so many millions of stolen lives—might have truly told the story he wanted to tell. Brown reminds us that we approach the history of slavery by way of whispers and shadows, where truth has often been hidden in half truth in order to be saved away for the future. We approach it, that is to say, across a field of argument in which the history of slavery has often been conscripted to the economic, political, and imperial purposes that have hidden inside the word "freedom."

Over the four centuries of Atlantic slavery, millions of Africans and their descendants were turned into profits, fancies, sensations, and possessions of New World whites. The vast majority of the enslaved were agricultural workers whose lives were devoted to the production of staple crops (sugar, tobacco, indigo, coffee, and cotton). Their labor provided the agricultural base of European mercantile capitalism and much of the surplus capital that, by the late eighteenth century, was being invested in the development of European industry. North America was alone among New World slave societies in having a self-reproducing slave population. Elsewhere, particularly in the Caribbean and Brazil, the murderous character of the slaveholding regime (the life expectancy of Africans put to work cultivating sugar in the Americas was seven years from the time they stepped ashore) meant that slaveholders depended upon the Atlantic slave trade as a replacement for biological reproduction.

The history of New World slavery was characterized by daily resistance on the part of the enslaved, terrific brutality on the part of the enslaving, and frequent military conflict between the two. Daily forms of resistance took the form of everything from mouthing off and shamming sickness to flight, arson, and assault. The slaveholders' violent responses, which seem at first to emblematize the license of unchecked power, upon closer inspection reveal the brittleness of their control; mastery had constantly to be—could only be—shored up through brutality. Everyday forms of resistance helped slaves come to trust one another enough to plan a hemisphere-wide series of insurgencies—some on a very small scale, some mobilizing thousands at a time—which varied widely in their ideology and aspiration, but which continually presented the possibility that the "Atlantic World" might be remade as a "Black Atlantic" (James 1938; Genovese

1979; Stuckey 1987; G. Hall 1992; Gilroy 1993; da Costa 1994; Sidbury 1997; Berlin 1998; W. Johnson 2002; Dubois 2004; J. Morgan 2004). Indeed, the military and diplomatic history of the New World was distilled in the alembic of black revolt. From the Maroon Wars in Jamaica to the Haitian Revolution to the American Revolution, the Civil War, and the Cuban Revolution, armed and insurgent blacks (and the almost unspeakable threat they represented to white leaders) decisively shaped the course of European and American history.

The foundational role of African and African American labor and resistance in the history of European imperialism and the economic growth of the Atlantic economy was reflected in the institution's role in shaping Atlantic culture. Institutions of law and governance, structures and styles of authority, religious faith and medical knowledge, cultural forms ranging from popular amusements to sentimental novels and autobiographies: all of these emergent forms of European modernity bore the stamp (often forcibly obscured) of slavery. So, too, did the ongoing identification of blackness with the condition of dispossession, and the disposition to insurgency.

The long nineteenth century, beginning with the Haitian Revolution in 1792 and culminating with the legislative emancipation in Brazil in 1888, marked the passing of slavery from the governing institutional solution to problems of labor, empire, and difference, to a residual social form (persisting to this day, it should be said) with tremendous discursive power. The end began with the idea that the opposite of slavery was neither redemption (as the Christian emphasis on sin as a form of slavery would have it) nor mastery (as the idea of history as a sort of race war would have it), but "freedom." The emergent antislavery version of enslavement was one that tried to demonstrate the ways in which slavery deformed the course of right and history by specifying its evils: its epochal barbarities and quotidian tortures; its corruptive tyranny and degrading license; its economic and moral backwardness; its un-freedom. And over the course of the nineteenth century this new view increasingly contested a proslavery argument that slavery itself represented the unfolding course of "freedom": the alignment of social institutions with natural (racial) history; the propagation of the earth for the benefit of its masters; the temporal manifestation of an institution that was both ancient in provenance and providential in design. Beginning with the Haitian Revolution, it was the antislavery argument about slavery that won: African American slavery came to be seen as the antithesis of "freedom."

Though it referred over the course of that century-long argument to a condition that was historically specific to black people, the term "slavery" came to serve as a sort of switchboard through which arguments over the character of "freedom" could be routed and defined: the archaic pendant to the emergent future. By using the word "slavery" to describe institutions ranging from wage labor and marriage to prostitution and peonage, nineteenth-century reformers sought to extend the moral force of the argument against African American slavery to other sorts of so-

cial relations. Their efforts were generally met with an insistence that "slavery" was a condition that was (or had been) unique to African Americans, who were, with emancipation, presumed to be experiencing "freedom."

The framing of slavery as archaic and freedom as emergent has a complex history in Western political economy. In both Smithian and Marxian thought, slavery remained an almost wholly unthought backdrop to the unfolding history of capitalism in Europe. For Adam Smith, slavery was destined to fall away before the superior capacity of wage labor to motivate workers through their own self-interest; the inferior motivation of bonded labor was in the Smithian tradition taken as a given rather than recognized (and theorized) as the result of the resistance of enslaved people (Oakes 2003). For Karl Marx, slavery was a moment in the history of primitive accumulation—the initial process of dispossession out of which capitalist social relations were subsequently built. It was the past to the present of "capitalism" (understood here as that system of social relations characterized by "free" labor and the factory mode of production) with which he was primarily concerned (Marx 1867/1976, 1: 667–712; W. Johnson 2004). To this day, much of the scholarship on slavery done in each of these traditions—so radically opposed in so many other ways—shares the common metanarrative shape of outlining a "transition" from slavery to capitalism.

Even as it provided the term with enormous critical potential, the marking of "slavery" as an archaism, destined to be superceded by the emergent history of freedom, made the term (and the history of the millions of martyrs it contains) useful to those who defined freedom in terms of national belonging or economic license. In this usage, as found in nineteenth-century reform and political economy, the relationship between slavery and freedom is figured as one of temporal supercession. The United States is no longer figured as a place where the contest between the two is to be fought out, but as a place where it has been uniformly and once-and-for-all completed. As George W. Bush put it in his 2001 inaugural address, the history of the United States is "the story of a slaveholding society that became a servant of freedom." Through their struggle against injustice, he later explained, "the very people traded into slavery helped to set America free" (Bush 2001, 2003). In the historical vision expressed by (but certainly not limited to) Bush's addresses, the history of slavery has been turned into a cliché, a set of images that have been emptied of any authentic historical meaning through their sheer repetition in connection with their supposed extinction at the hands of "freedom." The history of slavery in this usage exists in a state of civil servitude to the idea of "American freedom."

A countercurrent within mostly Marxist and black radical thought—notably W. E. B. Du Bois (1935), C. L. R. James (1938), Eric Williams (1944), Stuart Hall (2002), Sidney Mintz (1985), David Brion Davis (1975), and Cedric Robinson (2000)—has insistently contested the temporal framing of the relationship of slavery to freedom as one of linear progress. By insisting upon the place of slavery in the history of European and American capitalism—upon the way that the palpable experiences of freedom in Europe and the Americas and the narrowness of an idea of freedom defined as the ability to work for a wage both depended upon slavery—they have framed the relationship between the two terms as being one of dynamic simultaneity. They have, that is to say, insistently pointed out practices of servitude at the heart of the history of freedom, a set of insights that gives new and subversive meaning to Bush's phrase "servant of freedom."

The idea of the simultaneous coproduction of slavery and freedom lies at the heart of the case for reparations for slavery. This ongoing case has a history in the United States that dates to Reconstruction, and it represents a powerful (if also powerfully stigmatized by the intellectual and cultural mainstream) refiguration of the relationship of capitalism, slavery, freedom, past, and present. By reworking the history of the exploitation of Africans in the Americas—by whatever means, under whatever mode of production, mystified by whatever Western category of analysis—as a single extended and ongoing moment of time, the heterodox historiography of reparations calls upon us to recognize slavery not as an element of the national (or hemispheric) past but of the global present.

59

Society

Glenn Hendler

"Society" is a keyword used in both academia and everyday life to refer to forms of human collectivity and association. These forms may be organizations with specific agendas (the American Society for the Prevention of Cruelty to Animals; the Society for Creative Anachronism) or they may be delimited by an ascribed characteristic such as national affiliation or social class (American society; high society). High school students discuss society in social studies classes; colleges offer majors in sociology; and many universities organize their faculties into social science, natural science, and arts and humanities divisions. In political discourse, "civil society" is distinct from the state, yet "social welfare" programs are often portrayed as an expansion of state power, if not an avatar of "socialism." We "socialize" freely with others, but we are also "socialized" into normative patterns of behavior shaped by larger legal and political institutions. Debutantes and queers both "come out" into society, though the former do so as budding "socialites," while the latter become part of a subcultural "social formation" organized through implicit and explicit sexual norms.

What these complex and contradictory usages have in common is their reference to a structure, a principle or set of principles that organize human diversity into identifiable collectivities. As Raymond Williams (1983, 291) notes, "society" thus names a generalization ("the body of institutions and relationships within which a relatively large group of people live") and an abstraction ("the condition in which such institutions and relationships are formed"). Crucial to both of these meanings is an attempt to think through and beyond the idea that the individual is the sole agent and object of action. This mode of thought rubs up against the long tradition in the United States of construing society as a static entity that represses or limits the individual, as in Ralph Waldo Emerson's (1841/1990, 151) claim that "Society everywhere is in conspiracy against the manhood of every one of its members." Emerson here represents society as an impersonal structure that produces "conformity" by enforcing conventional "names and customs" on the otherwise free (white and male) individual. This commonsense notion greatly simplifies the processes though which individualities and subjectivities are formed. One of the tasks of any research that takes society as its object is to recognize that the dynamic of "individual" and "society" is fraught with complexity. Such work starts from the premise that individual agency is socially constructed even as the world is made and transformed through individual and collective social action.

This dynamic has been latent in the term throughout its etymology. "Society" and "social" both derive from a Latin word for companionship or fellowship, a connotation that persists most clearly when one speaks of "socializing" with friends. Writers have long commented on human association, casting collectivity in terms of the *polis*, the body politic, or the commonwealth, to name only three of the more familiar terms. But it was only in the eighteenth century that thinkers began to study society systematically. This new focus on the social as an object of analysis can be traced to the French, Scottish, and American Enlightenments, particularly in the works of *philosophes* such as Voltaire and the Baron de Montesquieu; "Common Sense" philosophers David Hume, Adam Ferguson, and Adam Smith; and Anglo-American political radicals such as Thomas Jefferson, Thomas Paine, and William Godwin. In the early nineteenth century, these theorizations of society were increasingly mapped onto concrete populations, institutions, and activities by classical sociologists such as Henri de Saint-Simon and August Comte. Saint-Simon proposed that "man" could be understood using a methodology modeled on the natural sciences and called "social physiology," while it remained for Comte to name the "science" of "sociology," to systematize the predetermined stages through which all societies developed, and to draw an analogy between societies' development and that of organic, usually human, bodies. Comte argued that the sociologist, like the physical or natural scientist, could produce knowledge about society that would allow technocratic elites to maintain social order while simultaneously advancing human progress (Hall and Gieben 1992; Gulbenkian Commission 1996; Wallerstein 2001).

The question remained to what purpose such social knowledge would be put. Comte's technocratic leanings prefigured the increasing prevalence of positivistic research methods across the social sciences. Positivism treated social actions and relations as taking place within a relatively stable system or field organized through predictable laws. Aided by increasingly complex forms of statistical analysis, the pursuit of these laws often resulted in normalizing forms of knowledge since exceptions to social patterns could be treated as deviations from the norm, in both the moral and the statistical sense (Poovey 1998). Although the term "statistic" shares an etymology with "state," both governmental and nongovernmental organizations quickly learned to deploy statistically generated social facts to support their arguments and legitimate their existence (P. Cohen 1982). For instance, in 1855 New York's city government hired William Sanger to produce a statistical study of prostitution (Stansell 1986). Temperance and antislavery activists similarly relied on statistics and social analysis to bolster their claims, thus emerging as the first of many "social movements" that saw society itself as a system that required transformation. In each of these cases, the production of social facts served to constitute widespread practices—vagrancy, prostitution, drinking—not as individual moral failings, but as social problems. As deviations from social norms, such activities became sites both of governmental and (quasi-governmental) intervention and of political struggle among diverse social agents and movements (Foucault 1991).

Even as these positivist forms of social knowledge were being instrumentalized by various state and nonstate political organizations in the late nineteenth and early twentieth centuries, sociology was gaining institutional status as an academic discipline. Herbert Spencer, the leading purveyor of "Social Darwinism" (another extension of an organic metaphor into society, this time analogizing the history of societies and races to the evolution of species), published *The Study of Sociology* in 1894. Among the earliest practitioners of sociology in the United States were Lester Frank Ward and William Graham Sumner, both of whom were influenced by Spencer. The first course with "sociology" in the title was taught at the University of Kansas in 1890, and the first Sociology Department was initiated at the University of Chicago in 1892. Emile Durkheim and Max Weber were leading figures in a similar institutionalization at European universities. Sociology developed an extra-academic presence as well. Opened in 1913, the Ford Motor Company's "sociological department" provided aid to the company's poorest workers, though only after requiring regular "home visits" to ensure that a worker's domestic life was "worthy" of support and that the mostly immigrant workforce was being properly "Americanized." Here again sociology normalizes social behavior, this time by linking normativity to productivity.

The analysis of society was nowhere limited to one particular discipline or methodology. Nor did many of the major social theorists of the nineteenth and twentieth centuries consider themselves sociologists. Variants on the word "society" appear today in the names of several disciplines and subdisciplines that cut across the boundaries of sociology as a field, including social history, social psychology, social work, and social theory. At the same time, the overarching rubric of the "social sciences" suggests that society remains a meta-category capable of organizing the study of markets

(economics), governments (political science), and individuals (psychology) into a conceptual and institutional singularity. Of course, these objects of study are not really discrete things: An economic theory that ignored the importance of the state in constructing and maintaining markets would be impoverished at best, as would a theory of the individual that neglected the roles of markets and governments in shaping human agency. For this reason, much energy in the past few decades of social theory has gone toward critiquing conceptions of society as a totalized system, wholly structured and determined by a subsystem—the economy, for instance—that is treated as if it were external to the social. One influential thread of this critique has taken place in the languages of structuralism, post-structuralism, and deconstruction, including Ernesto Laclau's argument about "the impossibility of society" (1990, 89–92) and Cornelius Castoriadis's claim that society is "not a thing, not a subject, and not an idea" but an "imaginary institution" (1997, 207).

Many similar critiques of society as a concept derive from debates on the left, which range from intellectual tendencies described as neo- and post-Marxist to welfare-state policy analysts and grassroots community organizers. But they also resonate with attacks from the opposite end of the political spectrum, such as British Prime Minister Margaret Thatcher's (1987) famous and often-repeated claim that "there is no such thing as society." The similarities between this type of statement—predominant in the United States at least since Ronald Reagan's presidency—and neo-Marxist arguments for "the impossibility of society" are largely superficial. Theorists like Laclau and Castoriadis take aim at reductive understandings of social causation in which an economic "base" (conceived of in Marxism not as a "market," but as a "mode of production") provides the foundation for any explanation for "superstructural" social and cultural phenomena. In contrast, the neoconservative position mobilizes a reductive understanding of the market as an isolable, self-regulating subsystem to argue against the extension of state power into social realms where "politics" does not belong. As such, neoconservatism is a theory of society in the classic sense: It argues for a particular way of differentiating various social realms and justifies its differentiation by claiming that each realm operates by identifiable laws. To quote Thatcher again, while society does not exist, "[t]here are individual men and women and there are families and no government can do anything except through people and people look to themselves first." In this formulation, the social is reduced to individual and familial interactions, implicitly governed by the market. The family here joins the list of naturalized figures—the body, the market, or the evolution of a species—that stand in for the entire social field (Barrett and McIntosh 1982).

Like "public," "community," "civilization," and other keywords that point to collective human experience, "society" is often described as being in decline. What is different about this declension narrative is that "society" has real enemies, people and political tendencies that work explicitly against the more radical and progressive tendencies inscribed within the concept. The notion of society is also diminished in the social sciences themselves to the degree that they premise their investigations on rational choice theory, the assumption that society is best understood as an aggregate of individuals intent upon maximizing their interests. A strong argument can be made that the ascendancy of neoconservative politics and neoliberal economic policy in the United States and elsewhere is a response to a decrease in the persuasiveness and affective force of major categories of collectivity such as nation and class, and a concomitant reduction of the sense of solidarity that such "social imaginaries" could at least potentially produce (C. Taylor 2004). In such a context, Thatcher's claim that individuals and families are the only bases for human association can come to seem depressingly plausible, and even inevitable. This is also the context in which some progressive social movements have narrowed their political ambitions by portraying normative forms of collectivity and association such as marriage and the nuclear family as the best and only means of effecting social change (Warner 1999; Duggan 2004b).

In American studies and cultural studies, "society" is currently a much less lively and debated keyword than "culture." This represents a shift from the early history of these fields, each of which originally emerged as an attempt to cross the boundary dividing the social sciences from the humanities and to resist deterministic and totalizing understandings of the social. One of the questions American studies was designed to answer concerned the vexed opposition between the "individual" and "society," and one early sign of the field's legitimacy was the extent to which this opposition subtended high-level scholarly projects, more middlebrow arguments, and even high school and college curricula. Foundational and field-defining texts determinedly placed "society" on a par with "culture" as key terms. Williams's original *Keywords* bore as its subtitle *A Vocabulary of Culture and Society* and had its inception as an appendix to his *Culture and Society, 1790–1950.* Even texts instrumental in the American studies turn toward issues of subjectivity still identified the "social" as a causative force, as is evident in the title of Peter Berger and Thomas Luckmann's *Social Construction of Reality* (1966). Though they privileged "culture" as worthy of analysis—as a corrective to an excessively mechanistic Marxism, and as definitional of their object and method of study—their emphasis on culture was nearly always a means of accessing the more difficult but fundamental subject of society.

The most promising recent tendencies in American cultural studies approach the question of the social in terms that work to avoid the risk of determinism and totalization embedded in the concept. Instead of studying "society" as an object, they tend to view the social as a process. Stuart Hall (Hall and Gieben 1992, 7) has argued that "modern societies [have] a distinctive shape and form, making them not simply 'societies' (a loose ensemble of social activities) but social formations (societies with a definite structure and a well-defined set of social relations)." One aspect of that structure is the differentiation into distinct realms—the economy, politics, and culture—that the modernist social sciences have both documented and

reified. Yet rather than naturalizing these realms as objects of analysis, the notion of social formation is meant to keep in mind "both the activities of emergence, and their outcomes or results: both process and structure" (ibid.). This analytic development has its counterpart in American cultural studies scholarship that treats crucial social categories as historical formations: sexual formations, class formations, and, most influentially, racial formations. Avoiding the tendency to view race "as an essence, as something fixed, concrete, and objective," as well as the "opposite temptation to imagine race as a mere illusion" or ideology, Michael Omi and Howard Winant (1994, 54–55) define racial formation as "the sociohistorical process by which racial categories are created, inhabited, transformed, and destroyed." Only a mode of analysis that can keep these elements in play as a dynamic process can address the questions of structure and agency raised by the concept of society.

Beyond academia, some of the most successful political movements since the end of the Cold War are reviving the concept of society as the basis of a critique of capitalist globalization and neoliberalism. The reemergence of the socialist left in Latin America has included the electoral victories of the Movement Toward Socialism Party in Bolivia and Hugo Chavez's "new socialism of the twenty-first century" in Venezuela. Both countries seem to be undergoing more than political change; the introduction of subaltern indigenous perspectives into the political process is also producing significant shifts in national and transnational social imaginaries (Aronson 2006). And among the most intriguing deployments of "society" as a keyword has been by the World Social Forum, a transnational organization founded to counter the World Trade Organization (WTO) and other forces of neoliberalism. While its agenda is misleadingly short-handed as "anti-globalization," its very name declares its intent to globalize not capital but society itself. This claim raises important questions about the concept of society: Are there models of a global civil society that avoid subsuming all forms of association and collectivity under the rubrics either of the state (as in Soviet-style communism) or of the market (as in WTO-supported attempts to impose a particular model of "civil society" onto diverse social formations (Cohen and Arato 1992; Walzer 1995; Keane 2003)? Are there alternative social formations and imaginaries implicit in transnational movements working against sweatshop labor or the militarization of international borders? These are all simultaneously political questions about what these alternative notions of society would look like in practice and research questions in which the definition of "society" is both the site and stakes of debate.

60
South
Matthew Pratt Guterl

To use the keyword "South" is to invoke, above all else, the importance of place and history. "South" is an imagined location, an inherently unstable unit of space, and yet most people in the United States feel they know exactly where it is: just below the Mason-Dixon line and just above the Gulf of Mexico. One needs only a compass and an atlas to find it. But the phrase "South" defies such directional certainty; it has multiple meanings, competing positions, and different personalities. "South," of course, is not the same thing, or place, or concept, as "*the* South," or "Souths," or even "southern." Recent American cultural studies scholarship seeks to understand the purpose and meaning of this much-anticipated place—envisioning "South" and its variants, wherever and whenever they are invoked, as situational ideals, as political statements, as self-referential terms, as frustratingly mobile, sometimes overlapping spots on a map. Each "South" is the creation of a particular historical moment, though the idea of it lingers on powerfully, sometimes clashing and sometimes harmoniously blending with newer meanings of the term.

For a long while, there was only one "South" in the popular imagination, drawn from the critiques of H. L. Mencken and W. J. Cash and the dreams of *Gone with the Wind* and the Nashville Agrarians. Specifically, there was "*the* South"—a region defined against "the

North," and captured by the melancholy prose of William Faulkner, by moonlight and magnolias, by the rattle of the air conditioner and the creak of the front porch, or by rumors of black rape and fantasies of white racial supremacy. This particular South was assumed to be sexualized, tropical, and horribly violent; it was the low-slung id to the North's preening superego. It was, most of all, a melodramatic confusion of the antebellum slaveholding South and the South of Jim Crow, featuring Bull Connor's wild dogs and water hoses, and bloodied young black men and women, all battling for their lives in a location whose borders were presumed to be unchanged from the days of the old Confederate States of America. In the 1950s and 1960s—when this place seemed most monolithic and uniform, when its rejection of racial equality seemed like one great shout—it was an easy habit to imagine it as a singular place, as *"the* South," or, more explicitly, as the *only* South. In the wake of the racial revolution, it was just as simple for those who loathed the imposition of federal authority, and who saw parallels between Reconstruction and the civil rights movement, to resurrect a vision of the Old South that owed far more to Margaret Mitchell than to John C. Calhoun.

What, then, was the difference between the Old South (defined by slavery) and "the New South" (defined by "free labor," new technologies, "the Lost Cause," and industrial manufacturing)? Generations of scholars—most famously, W. E. B. Du Bois and C. Vann Woodward—narrated the political significance of that New South, emphasizing the role of the region in national politics and its repeated efforts to control "the Negro." But the worst abuses of Jim Crow emphasized for much of the U.S. public a kind of yearning for slavery and "docile" labor, and a certain perpetual indebtedness to the Old South. The New South, to borrow from Du Bois, seemed always to be "looking backward" at the Old South, resulting in a peculiar brand of conservatism that made it possible for the Confederate battle flag to reemerge as a symbol of resistance to civil rights, and for the end of Jim Crow to be labeled a "second Reconstruction." This somewhat synchronic "South" is still with us, flourishing in movies like *Mississippi Burning*, in the novels of John Grisham, in "River Road" tours from New Orleans to Baton Rogue, and in journalistic travel accounts like Tony Horowitz's *Confederates in the Attic* (1999).

Of course, even within the borders of the former Confederacy, there was never a universal "South." There was "the Southern South," as Albert Bushnell Hart once put it, otherwise known as "the deep South," though it was never exactly clear where this region-within-a-region began. There was also the Gulf South, defined by the port cities of Galveston, New Orleans, Mobile, and Charleston, as much connected to Havana as to New York. At different moments in history, the outer rim of the former slaveholding galaxy—Louisiana, Texas, and Florida—were culturally and geopolitically confusing, sometimes French or Spanish and not English, sometimes Catholic and not Baptist, sometimes brown and not white. The entire southwestern United States seems, at times, to have functioned as a hard-worn threshold between Mexico,

California, and the Old South. Indeed, one of the most striking features of the region is not its permanence and uniformity but its repeated exchange (the larger southern expanse has changed hands, or been "sold" or "taken," more often than any other part of the United States) and its memories of a past life as somewhere and something else.

In national popular culture, "the South" has long stood as a universal marker of rural poverty and racist attitudes. In the nineteenth and twentieth centuries, the region was portrayed as the home of slack-jawed, poorly bred, and half-civilized whites. When Democratic campaign advisor James Carville defined the state of Pennsylvania by its cities, Pittsburgh and Philadelphia, "with Alabama in between," the reference was to the section's intellectual and financial impoverishment and, by extension, its presumed social conservatism. By this logic, there are "Souths" all over the United States: in Montana, where white supremacist groups are indebted to the slaveholding era's enthusiasm for unrepentant white supremacy; in New York City's Howard Beach neighborhood, where it is dangerous to be black, even if one is just walking along on the sidewalk; and in Appalachia, where the deepest poverty exists. We lose some vital meaning of the word if we assume that "South" is always in *the* South, or that it is subaltern in some way—always poor, always racist, always oppressed by its opposite, "the North." "South" is, in fact, the most politically significant orientation in the United States. We gain some crucial understanding of this if we imagine it to be a sort of situational location, as much a temporary

mood or state of life as it is a state of mind, a political philosophy, or place of business. One need only follow the ebb and flow of President George W. Bush's Texas twang—here one day and gone the next—to understand that "the southern strategy" refers not simply to the nationwide electoral tactic devised by the apparatchiks of the Republican Party, and described by Dan Carter and Thomas Frank, among others, but also to a certain kind of cognitive style that strikes a particular racial, political, and socio-economic chord for much of the United States.

"South," though, cannot be contained by national borders any more than it is defined by the Mason-Dixon line. The movements of capital and labor have reshuffled the human population since the 1960s, bringing migrant Central American laborers to the same southern cities in the United States that were once national signifiers of the civil rights conflict. Atlanta and Houston are home to expanding communities from Mexico, Panama, the Dominican Republic, Guatemala, and El Salvador. Nashville, Mobile, and other mid-sized southern cities are, in some ways, newer versions of New Orleans and Charleston, marked by polylingual, transnational, and economic connections to a "global South" running from Southeast Asia to Africa to Latin America. None of this is new. There were powerful links between the southern reaches of the nineteenth-century United States and the Atlantic world; the region was in many ways tightly bound to the Caribbean, with its traditions of human bondage and cash-crop agriculture, and it served as a cultural and economic outlier of the republic. These connections were strong enough to foster expatriate communities after the Civil War at nearly every longitude and latitude, most famously in Brazil, where the "stars and bars" are still flown. The best of the recent work on this subject—for instance, that of Jon Smith (2004), Deborah Cohn (1999), Tara McPherson (2003), and Kirsten Silva Gruesz (2002)—examines and carefully historicizes the extraordinary personal, intellectual, cultural, and economic links between the bottom half of the United States and the wider southern hemisphere.

But *that* South—the United States South—was never (and is not today) a part of what we call the "global South," that band of subaltern states that lacks not resources, manpower, or ingenuity, but only capital advantage in the world economy. From the geopolitical and financial perspectives of Venezuela, Sumatra, or Kenya, the State of Mississippi—with its limitless borrowing capacity, its safe roads and reliable shipping firms, its blue jeans, clean water, and quality healthcare—looks a lot like the state of Minnesota. In fact, to limit a discussion of "South" to the former North American hotbed of secession, slavery, and segregation is to reproduce this same system of advantage, ignoring the more than half of the world's population who actually live *south* of the United States and allowing the borders of that country to block off a comparative consideration of regional identity. It is a great irony that "*the* South" is technically, locationally southern in just one, rather limited context: within the borders of the United States. It is an even greater irony that any region of the United States, no

matter how poorly treated, should develop its own parallel subaltern critique of "Northern capital," emphasizing dispossession and disadvantage at the hands of supposedly meddling, self-righteous outsiders, and romanticizing the past over the present. Many "Souths," then, in very different locations define themselves against a wealthier and healthier "North," with its strong-armed "Yankee imperialists," and its troublesome chauvinism. This does not mean, however, that we should simply point our fingers at Mississippi or Louisiana, noting their own imperial appetites, following their gaze southward. The great challenge of the future is not just to write about the dominant role played by "the South" in the Caribbean, in Central America, or South America, but also to consider the people, cultures, and institutions of those "other" places as equal partners in the making of hemispheric and world history, literature, music, and art, and to weigh as well the role of this more accurately named "South" in shaping the United States.

61

State

Paul Thomas

Gore Vidal (2004) recently observed that we no longer live in a state; we live in a Homeland. The Cold War is over, but the U.S. national security state (supposedly called forth by the Cold War) is alive and well, fortified—now that the State Department is no longer sufficient—by its Department of Homeland Security. The rhetorical sleight-of-hand involved in this transposition of "state" into "Homeland" is not without precedent, and the 2001 Patriot Act is but the latest incident in a long history of state-sponsored countersubversion that long predated the Cold War (Rogin 1987). Euphemisms for "state" ("Motherland," "Fatherland," *la patrie*) have long abounded, and so has the unwieldy and often inaccurate composite "nation-state." Note also the substitution of "nation" for "state" in names such as United *Nations* and the Inter-*national* Monetary Fund.

The centrality of the state to the sphere of political activity seems self-evident to some. Prominent contemporary political theorist Quentin Skinner (1978), taking his cue from the writings of Max Weber, regards the very use of the word state as a confirmation of his thesis that the state—as legitimate monopolizer of the means of violence—is foundational to what he calls "modernity." Political science as a discipline has long tried to substitute for "state" some semantically equivalent term such as "governmental process" or "political system." Such attempts are invariably ruses; they merely underscore the status of "state" as a keyword that both defines the field of political science and characterizes various positions within that field (Bartelson 2001).

It is not enough simply to cut through such subterfuge. States do exist, and they matter. They appear as unitary entities when seen from the outside looking in; their claims to sovereignty have no counterpart in the international or inter-state sphere. At the same time, viewed from the inside looking out, they are distinct from civil society. Karl Marx claimed that the state "is based on the unhampered development of bourgeois society, on the free movement of private interest"; "it is not the state that holds together the atoms of civil society . . . in reality, the state is held together by social life" (Marx and Engels 1975, 4:113). Here and elsewhere, Marx critiques the modern state not because he rejects the need for community to which the state lays claim, but because the alienation of the state from civil society means that it cannot deliver on its promise of human freedom.

Marx's question remains powerful today: How can something singular, the state, be based on or held together by something as fragmentary and divided as civil society? This is where cultural studies (American or otherwise) and political science can fruitfully collaborate. The play of private interests in civil society generates political and cultural divisions (such as class, race, and gender) among its human constituents. The state and its official culture must then reunite, or claim to reunite, people by transcending, but not obliterating, these same divisions. The state, that is to say, must *represent* what its citizens and subjects have in common, an identity or equivalence. But this equivalence, in any radically unequal society—and *all* known societies are radically unequal—can only be formal, not substantive (Lloyd and Thomas 1995, 1998).

Take as one example the nineteenth-century struggles for extension of the electoral franchise in Britain and the United States. These struggles introduced a developmental narrative intended to produce an equivalence (political citizenship), which then would become a *potential* category. The conservative argument against extension of the franchise, an argument that carried the day for a long time, was *cultural.* It involved the claim that women, the poor, and others to be excluded were insufficiently formed, ethically incomplete beings, unprepared or unfit to exercise the faculty of disinterested judgment that representation and citizenship required. Matthew Arnold (1869/1965, 5:134–35) put it in a nutshell: "culture suggests the idea of the state." Once democracy became practicable only as *representative* democracy, Marx's famous judgment on the nineteenth-century French peasantry ("they cannot represent themselves . . . they must be represented") becomes pregnant indeed (1954, 106). People are to be made worthy of the state or excluded from it; the state is not to be made worthy of them, as in radical participatory theories like those of Jean-Jacques Rousseau and Thomas Paine.

This conjuring trick, this substitution of cultural and political representation for participation, took hold elsewhere, not least in twentieth-century struggles for national liberation from colonial hegemony. And its shelf-life has been remarkable. States make universalist claims, but popular participation in the state is always and everywhere limited (Thomas 2001). These limitations may be horizontal: How much participation is enjoined by those who are to participate? Casting ballots in periodic elections is a common answer. They may also be vertical: Who, among those who can or could participate, may or will participate?

Citizens, as opposed to "undocumented aliens," is a familiar answer. Either way, the basic tension remains. Political representation, which theoretically unites, takes place apart from, and outside, the sphere of civil society, which divides in practice.

What then is a state, so circumscribed, supposed to do? Hegel in 1821 rebutted the easy answer: It protects property and preserves the peace. States, he observed, tax their citizens and wage wars (Hegel 1821/1962, 209–10). Still, the diverse claims of citizenship remain. Personal rights, which include freedom of speech, assembly, and religion, are distinct from political rights, which center around participation in the state. Both are distinct from what T. H. Marshall (1965) called rights of "social citizenship," including guaranteed education, full employment, decent housing, and free medical care. The latter category of social rights, the warp and woof of the twentieth-century "welfare state," is essential if citizenship and participation in the state are to be meaningful, not merely formal or rhetorical. However, recent phenomena such as the emergence of the "Homeland" should remind us that citizenship in the state was a formal phenomenon all along, and that attempts to give it substance in the form of social citizenship—which, by contrast with social democracies like those in Western Europe, has never counted for much in the United States—can readily be short-circuited from above, in a way that affects neither a burgeoning military budget nor the interplay of personal or political rights.

In contrast to social citizenship, personal and political rights can then be fetishized as though they were ends in themselves. This helps to explain why conservative writers like Friedrich Hayek and Milton Friedman, along with their neoconservative and neoliberal progeny, stridently denounce the use of state power to promote the claims of social citizenship, why they do so in the name of "liberty" or "democracy," and why they have been more influential to date in the United States than anywhere else. It also helps to explain why foreign wars prosecuted by the U.S. state, from the nineteenth century to the present, have claimed to advance the frontiers of democracy and have clothed themselves in the mantle of elections as though these were ends in themselves. This ruse leaves the substance of democracy at home and abroad (education, employment, housing, medicine) not to the state, but to the vagaries of the market. We are evidently not yet done with conjuring tricks.

62

War

Susan Jeffords

"Tug of war." "Cold War." "World War II." "Make love, not war." "*War Games*." "War on poverty." "Prisoner of war." "*War of the Worlds*." "Iraq War." "War on drugs." "Antiwar." "All's fair in love and war." It is difficult today to open a newspaper or magazine, turn on a television, or go to a movie theater anywhere in the United States without encountering a verbal or a visual reference to "war." Whether through reports of

wars around the globe; declarations of "war on" a variety of social issues, from AIDS to poverty to crime; reportedly cheaper costs brought on by price wars (in airline ticket fares, gasoline, or fast food); or descriptions of sporting events ("throwing a bomb," "blitzing," "sudden-death")—references to "war" permeate U.S. culture. The semantic origins of the word—the Indo-European root *wers*, meaning to confuse or mix up—may say more about contemporary usages than anything else. The ways in which "war" is used as a term in U.S. culture can themselves be complex and confusing.

Dictionary definitions of "war" highlight two primary meanings: a state of open, armed, often prolonged conflict between nations, states, or parties; and a condition of active antagonism or contention. Prior to the 1960s and 1970s, discussions of war in U.S. culture focused primarily on the first definition and were largely grounded in the fields of history and political science. Such analyses were wide-ranging in their focus, ranging from examinations of military operations to debates about geopolitics to biographies of key figures to readings of the poetry and art that depicted warfare. Because of the key role that war played in the founding and early history of the United States, it was difficult to discuss what it meant to be "American" without in some way referencing the Revolutionary War, the Civil War, or the wars of U.S. expansion into the West. Other wars were casually forgotten: the U.S.-Mexico War and the lengthy guerrilla war in the Philippines. World War II established the United States as a dominant military and economic force, while also serving as an iconographic image of a "good war," one that was taken to affirm the moral foundations of U.S. warfare. With the advent of the Vietnam War and the accompanying antiwar activism on college campuses, analyses of warfare became more widely infused with the kinds of social dimensions that characterized the antiwar movement and were brought to the foreground by feminist and civil rights critiques. In particular, scholars began to look more carefully at issues facing women and men of color in war and military service.

The second half of the twentieth century also saw increasing use of "war" to refer to more than direct military encounters. One of the most prominent among these was the use of "Cold War" to name the ongoing tensions between the United States and the Soviet Union (the term was first coined by George Orwell in his 1945 essay "You and the Atom Bomb"). While the Cold War referred largely to nonmilitary encounters between what came to be called the two "superpower" nations, it was also characterized by proxy wars around the world in which often devastating battles were fought. From the U.S. point of view, the Korean and Vietnam Wars were among the most significant of these, but citizens of Nicaragua, the Dominican Republic, and Afghanistan, among many others, would surely have different perspectives.

Most prominently, the "war on poverty" solidified the use of the popular terminology of "war" to refer to an entirely nonmilitary government action. President Lyndon Johnson surprised the nation in his 1964 State of the Union address by declaring: "This administration today, here and now, declares unconditional war on poverty in America." While many still debate the effectiveness and the legacy of Johnson's commitment to eradicate poverty, there is little question about the impact of his use of the terminology of warfare to refer to a domestic, nonmilitary problem. Although it had been common to refer to competition between corporations as war—as in the 1860s struggle between Daniel Drew and Cornelius Vanderbilt for controlling interest in the stock of the Erie Railroad—Johnson's deployment of the term solidified the use of an explicit vocabulary of war to refer to a broad social issue. Since that time, we have had the "war on drugs" announced by President Nixon in 1971, the "war against crime" declared by Bill Clinton in June of 1994, and, most recently, George W. Bush's "war on terror."

Outside of the arena of national policy, perhaps the most influential nonmilitary use of "war" in recent decades has been in what came to be called "the culture wars." Most prominent in the 1980s and 1990s, the "culture wars" referred to a broad debate between conservative and liberal voices in U.S. culture. Cutting across political, religious, and social issues ranging from abortion to gay parenting, the "culture wars" often focused on education as the key vehicle for the transmission of these values. When a 1989 task force appointed by the New York commissioner on education proposed revisions to the state curriculum to include multicultural components, a battle ensued over what counted as legitimate history. This debate reached national prominence following the 1994 publication by the History Standards Project of guidelines for K-12 history instruction, which, among other emphases, stressed an awareness of the multicultural aspects of U.S. history. The National Endowment for the Arts came under particular scrutiny as a result of contributing funding to several controversial art exhibits, most prominent among them Robert Mapplethorpe's photographs at the Contemporary Arts Center in Cincinnati in 1990, and the work of artist Andres Serrano, whose *Piss Christ* was condemned on the floor of the Senate in 1989. The tensions that underlay the "culture wars" continue today in the polarized debates over social issues and moral values.

Any discussion of the use of "war" as a term in U.S. culture must also recognize the plethora of words that surround it. Even when "war" itself is not used, its resonant vocabularies are ubiquitous and often create oppositional or binary structures that disable nuanced and critical thinking about complex issues. Whether in sports, politics, corporate takeovers, relationships, or television ratings, the language of "war" permeates U.S. culture: battle, conflict, combat, hostility, collateral damage, attack, surgical strike, victory, soldier, enemy, and so on. One of the clearest indications of the pervasiveness of this vocabulary is its commonplace acceptance in everyday usage, with few people even recognizing the references to "war" in using such terms.

While individual wars have been discussed in the study of U.S. culture (Slotkin 1992), and critics such as George Lakoff (1991) have written eloquently about the rhetoric of war, many cultural studies scholars have chosen to focus on "militarism" rather than "war," largely because the former refers to the complex set of social, political, economic, and cultural activities and institutions that support a society that engages in warfare. Analyses of militarism allow, for example, discussions of race, gender, and sexuality that go beyond the question of the demographics of military service and lead instead to analyses of the racialized images of U.S. enemies (Dower 1986), the influence of U.S. military bases upon structures of gender in other countries (Enloe 1989), and the constructions of masculinity that underlay the Cold War (Dean 2001). As U.S. military engagements around the world stray further from the traditional definitions of war (even as they recycle the rhetoric of war), cultural analyses of war and militarism should continue to critique the complex ways in which "war" extends beyond the battlefield and into the day-to-day operations of U.S. culture.

63

West

Krista Comer

One power of the keyword "west" is its ability to conflate the geopolitical entity and physical topography currently referred to as "the American West" with matters of identity, style, and cultural belonging. "Western-ness" is highly mobile. If the term typically invokes conventional forms of masculinity, a good deal of its social force and moral credibility owes to a suppressed but sustained dialogue with that "other" West: "Western civilization." Together these connotations map flexible investments in both masculine in-dividualism, including "wild western" bohemianism, and Western civilization's grandest claims. Since the late eighteenth century, Western forms of cultural be-longing and style have been mobilized in the United States in defense of nation, home, white supremacy, and empire.

To secure western-ness as a badge of identity requires the performance of a recognized regional vernacular. Such performances proliferate in contem-porary culture through any number of everyday be-haviors: the consumption of commodities associated with western spaces; western speech idioms; rigorous outdoor activities; the western types produced by liter-ary westerns, popular westerns, and film, as well as painting, photography, and music. Individuals and whole communities might reside in the official social space called today's American West while not claiming themselves or their communal ways as "western" (in-habitants of Indian country would be one generalized example). Similarly, people outside western geopoliti-cal domains might—through the enactment of a vari-ety of everyday regionalisms—construct identities in relation to the values and practices of things called "western."

In U.S. contexts, it is only in the twentieth century that the geographical referents for the West have sta-bilized to mean that region west of the Mississippi, or more precisely, beyond the ninety-eighth meridian. Given the perception of California as different from, or sometimes even "west of the West," its regional sta-tus remains vexed. Many older usages of the word re-veal its Teutonic, Aryan historical character. According to the *Oxford English Dictionary*, "West" occurs in Old English only as an adverb, coming into use later as noun and adjective. Two additional figurative senses of the word are significant. One, as early as 1400, is to die, perish, disappear; and this meaning, one can spec-ulate, owes to the worry in the premodern period that sailing far enough west would put one in danger of falling off the earth's edge. The other, gaining from the mid-nineteenth century on, is the slippage between "west" and certain European American nations. If the keyword has functioned as a social logic distinguish-ing U.S. empire from its competitors, it does so be-cause the project of settling the "west" of the Americas invoked parallel projects undertaken in the name of civilizing, Christianizing, and modernizing "non-Western" peoples.

West also retains in its connotations the early peril of going west, what Joan Didion (1968) has called a U.S. preoccupation with the cautionary tale. For every injunction to "Go West, young man, go West"—made famous in the 1850s by the journalist and western pro-moter Horace Greeley—one finds counter-injunctions like those in Caroline Kirkland's *A New Home: Who'll Follow?* (1839), which is replete with accounts of fron-tier violence against settler women. Clearly, Richard Slotkin's famous "regeneration through violence" the-sis did not describe a form of regeneration open to everyone (1973).

In the early nineteenth century, U.S. usages of the word "west" leaned heavily on the discourse of West-ern civilization. They became more fully nationalized only after the U.S.-Mexican and Spanish-U.S. wars ended Mexico's and Spain's competing claims in the territories, and even more so after "Indian relocation" settled other major threats to nationalist consolidation. By the late nineteenth century, "the West" had come to mean the "frontier" or "wild West," now "won" by virtue of bravery, pluck, adaptability, wilderness skills, and faith in common people invigorated and reborn by the western trek. This vocabulary circulated internationally, especially in Europe, in dime novels, visual culture (sketches, exploration photography), travel guides, performance theater (Buffalo Bill's "Wild West Show"), publicity for tourist sites (Alamo, Grand Canyon), and science (paleontology). As the century closed, Western vocabularies indexed the triumph of civilized white masculinity over "savagery"; at the same time, figures like Teddy Roosevelt produced the idea that "manly men" of the United States should extend their mandate beyond U.S. borders. A sickly northeastern boy but avid reader of dime novels, Roosevelt's masculine vigor was recuperated and articulated as nationalist vision though Western cultural embrace, ultimately taking him and his Rough Riders up San Juan Hill and into Panama (Bederman 1995).

This underside of the keyword has always been visible in the wide range of cultural forms designed to represent "the West." Western adventure stories often signal not just victory but also trauma: about the West's lawlessness, misogyny, and racism; about attempts to master animals and nature. Consider *Joaquin Murieta*, the 1851 sensational tale about a Mexican man driven to banditry and sadistic cruelty by Anglo incursions upon his mining claim in the gold fields of California. Authored by Yellow Bird, a mixed-blood Cherokee who wrote under the name John Rollin Ridge, this story is as much an allegory of the mistreatment of Cherokees as it is a folkloric vindication of Mexicans who avenge legalized white terror. The novel also implicitly critiques the hypocrisy enabled by quasi-romantic figures of bohemian civility like James Fenimore Cooper's Natty Bumppo. Even the key figure in U.S. western landscape painting, Frederic Remington, makes visible cautions similar to those of Yellow Bird in his depictions of the hunt and other rituals of masculine self-realization. As Stephen Tatum (2004, 218) argues, Remington's major paintings demonstrate a "beautiful but terribly brittle pathos," a recognition that power and mastery never run in one direction.

These countervocabularies and counterhistories have never seen global circulation on a scale remotely comparable to what popular rhetorics enjoy. Indeed, the West's persistent association with American exceptionalism, a classic case study of which is offered in Frederick Jackson Turner's frontier thesis (1893), has conditioned the reception of these countervocabularies. For Turner, the West had been "won," "free land" had run out, the frontier had closed, and thus the great adventure of the Old West had concluded. Turner looked backward with imperial nostalgia and forward with concern. Without land, the nation's democratic spirit would falter (F. Robinson 1997). Like Roosevelt, Turner found hope in the vision that "American energy will continually demand a wider field for its exercise" (quoted in Dippie 1991, 115).

Although there were some dissenters, the Turner thesis governed western historiography for over fifty years. The major break came in the mid-1980s with the appearance of a "new western history." This multiracial, feminist, environmentalist, urban-embracing, and anti-imperial academic project astonished even its own spokespeople by becoming an overnight media sensation (Limerick 1991, 61). In retrospect, it is clearer that in the wake of the Cold War, the West would need a popular reevaluation, given its persistent symbolic power to convey ideas about U.S. uniqueness, that is, its exceptional and providentially blessed status. For much of the late 1980s to the mid-1990s, the keywords of this new western history—"conquest" (as opposed to "frontier") and "realism" (as opposed to "myth")—dominated definitions of "the West" in public life, perhaps most tellingly at the Smithsonian Museum's 1991 exhibition *The West as America*. Conservative pundits and politicians turned the exhibition into a controversy, denouncing its alternative readings of historical photographs, paintings, and other visual artifacts. One sign of the new western history's success is that sign-in books record that the Smithsonian's visitors approved of the exhibition's themes of conquest by a margin of two-to-one.

The sea change in "western" meanings registered by the new western history's public reception forced a range of contemporary critical projects to the fore. The most obvious was contemporary literary regionalism, whose vocabularies of western-ness echoed the anxieties of nineteenth-century writers while also formulating alternative community logics in the wake of trauma. In a U.S. version of what the Birmingham School of Cultural Studies called the "empire writing back," N. Scott Momaday's *House Made of Dawn* (1968), Gloria Anzaldúa's *Borderlands/La Frontera* (1987), Maxine Hong Kingston's *China Men* (1989), and the poetic works of Wanda Coleman all created new historical and geographical knowledges of the West. Re-examination of earlier twentieth-century literary production also made it clear that relatively canonical authors such as Willa Cather had the company of writers such as Sui Sin Far, D'Arcy McNickle, Americo Paredes, Carlos Bulosan, and María Cristina Mena. No less crucial was the emergence of related critical projects in which literary and cultural critics remapped the West in ways that neither reproduced conservative nationalisms and masculine authority nor reinscribed notions of Western authenticity (including de facto defenses of Western civilized values). Importing materials from borderlands studies, urban studies, immigration history, critical Asian studies, feminist studies, race studies, and cultural geography, and drawing from postcolonial reconfigurations of area studies as well as indigenous reconfigurations of postcoloniality, a new critical regionalism has for a decade been under construction. Some of its most celebrated practitioners—Mike Davis (1990), José David Saldívar (1997), José Limon (1999), Lisa Lowe (1996), Gerald Vizenor (1999)—have not claimed the designation "western studies," no doubt because their subject matter (urban studies, Los Angeles, Asian immigration, border issues, post-Indian simulation) has itself been historically policed by the keyword's dominant meanings.

Such tensions suggest the complicated politics and suspicions the term elicits. At present in American cultural studies, at least two competing strains of "western" connotation operate. The dominant one at this moment in global history invokes traditional myth and iconography: that of righteous imperial mandate. President Bush's everyday western regionalisms—his retreat to Crawford Ranch, his invocation of the mythical line at the Alamo to separate cowards from heroes in the "war on terror," his posting of old-western "wanted" lists after 9/11—has renarrated "western" to justify multiple U.S. wars in defense of the values of "Western civilization." At the traditional inaugural luncheon following Bush's 2001 swearing-in ceremonies, the presidential menu—quail, braised turnips, beets, and rutabagas—explicitly mimicked the meals of Teddy Roosevelt and the Lewis and Clark expeditions. Renewing the nationalist masculine individualism of earlier periods by remembering the rough-and-tumble nineteenth-century frontier "adventure," the President's performance of "wild western" ritual moves the keyword in twenty-first century directions.

The second connotation—and the one that is most promising for future work—indexes an emergent critical regionalism or postnational West. In attempts to understand and theorize the phenomenon we call "globalization," critical regionalism offers some of the most advanced work on the topic of place and the forms local-global interactions take in various political, economic, and cultural sites. The recent move of the American Studies Association's official journal

American Quarterly to Los Angeles from its previous institutional home in Washington, D.C., signals the organization's attempt to reconfigure the field—by way of attention to theorizing space, place, and culture—in directions of a critical post-exceptionalist American studies. Revisionist renderings of what variously is called the "glocal" or "transregional" will thus be on the horizon of American cultural studies for some time, which means that "the West"—in its multiple invocations—necessarily must be at the center of multiple field debates. This raises the most difficult and productive challenge: to critique the keyword while refusing to vacate a dialogue with it, because to concede the term would be to permit its most regressive political and social effects. The kinds of interdisciplinary conversations such a refusal requires must bring attention to the keyword as a site of global domination, but also as one that has produced a powerful countervocabulary.

64

White

Pamela Perry

For U.S. census purposes, "white" is currently defined as "a person having origins in any of the original peoples of Europe, the Middle East or North Africa." *Webster's Dictionary* differs somewhat, defining it as "being a member of a group or race characterized by light pigmentation of the skin." Scholarship in American studies, cultural studies, and critical versions of "whiteness studies" has deconstructed and redeployed "white" in ways that have taken its meanings far beyond geographical origin and skin color. Specifically, scholars have examined the social-historical meanings of "white" identity and revealed its mutable, socially constructed, and ideological character. Others have adopted the keyword to codify the various processes and practices that systematically reproduce white racial dominance. Most prevalent across this research are the conceptualizations of "white" as a "norm," a "performance," and a "privilege."

From as early as the 1800s, African American writers and scholars critically debated what "white" meant, but most (white) European Americans did not (Roediger 1999). W. E. B. Du Bois, James Baldwin, C. L. R. James, Richard Wright, bell hooks, Toni Morrison, Cheryl Harris, and many others have argued that "white" is an ideology of domination that confers privilege, and that it commits psychological and physical violence against people of color. Those deemed "white" might receive a "public and psychological wage" of status and privilege (Du Bois 1965, 700), but the "price of the ticket" is self-delusion and moral decrepitude (Baldwin 1985).

Until the early 1970s, the dominant academic literature on "race" did not engage whiteness in the same way. It tended to focus on blacks and other subordinated peoples as the occasion of the "race problem" and to limit inquiry about white complicity in racial inequality to studies of individual prejudice. The structures and institutions that privileged whites as a whole were not examined, and white people were frequently unmarked in the literature, often referred to simply as "the people," "Americans," or the "dominant group." This absence of "white" as descriptor and construct may best be explained by Richard Dyer's luminous comment, "white power secures its dominance by seeming not to be anything in particular" (1988, 44).

Critical versions of what is now called "whiteness studies" emerged with the mission of particularizing, making visible, and assessing "whiteness"—the constellation of identities, processes, and practices that systematically privilege white people and reproduce white domination. Whiteness studies arose, in large part, as a response to the black power movement. This movement's emphasis on the institutional character of racism gave rise to an antiracist politics, both in the academy and in social-justice activism, where white antiracists learned they needed to think self-reflectively about white privilege. While whiteness scholars currently cross national perspectives and span the arts, humanities, social sciences, and legal studies, they have tended to agree on the codifications of "white" as a socially and historically constructed identity, a cluster of racialized norms and performances, and a set of privileges.

"White" as a nonessential, socially constructed identity has been vividly illuminated in historical studies. Likely drawing on the religious symbolism of "light" versus "dark"— purity versus contamination, saintliness versus heathenism (Dyer 1997)—"white" arose as a putatively "biological" and "scientific" term that replaced "Christian" as religious justifications for colonial slavery gave way to liberal and secular rationalizations of inequality (Jordan 1969). Although the universalistic tenets of secular democracy proclaimed the "equality of all men," this mandate was sidestepped by basing the characteristics of "universal" humanity on Western European male interests, values, lifestyles, and religious beliefs, and by declaring "dark" peoples as not quite human (Goldberg 1993; Balibar 1994; Dyer 1997).

The term "white" emerged in the Americas as early as the first European settlements and, though continually shifting in meaning, became embedded in national and class identities. It first distinguished "civilized" and "hard-working" Europeans from "savage" and "lazy" Indians (Roediger 1991); then it asserted the moral superiority of "whites" over heathen "black" Africans (Fredrickson 1981). As the demographics and politics of the new nation changed, so did the meanings of "whiteness" and the conditions under which one could claim it. The U.S. Naturalization Act of 1790 limited naturalized citizenship to "free white persons." Although "white" was considered a scientific category, the courts varyingly adjudicated the whiteness of plaintiffs on nonscientific grounds. Asian Indians, for example, were considered "Caucasian," but in the famous case of *United States v. Thind* (1923) were denied "white" status because their skin color belied "common knowledge" of what "white" was (Haney-Lopez 1996). Working-class Irish, Italians, and Poles were allowed to naturalize on the basis of being "Caucasian," but were not fully accepted as "white," and thus were relegated to an inferior so-cial status. To take advantage of the political and economic opportunities of whiteness, some working-class ethnics became "white" by taking on the racial ideologies of whiteness and distinguishing themselves as a "free" (white) labor force from "bounded" (black) African slaves (Baldwin 1985; Saxton 1990; Roediger 1991; Allen 1994; Jacobson 1998).

With respect to contemporary forms of identity and practice, "whiteness" remains a norm widely acknowledged within and outside the academy. In mainstream U.S. culture today, as in the past, the interests and values of white people are positioned as unmarked universals by which difference, deficit, truth, and justice are determined. The normative character of whiteness is well illustrated in ethnographic studies that reveal that, when asked, most whites will say that they have no racial identity, culture, or advantages as whites; they are just "normal" (Frankenberg 1993; Perry 2002). This mindset reproduces white dominance by blaming people of color for failing to meet normative standards. Some whites also see themselves as the new "victims" of race-based policies, thereby overlooking their participation in racial inequality and responsibility for redressing it (Gallagher 1997).

When it intersects with U.S. legal, political, and educational institutions, this unofficial understanding of whiteness as an implicit norm produces official ideologies of "color-blindness," race neutrality, and meritocracy. Colorblind ideology asserts that race no longer matters in legal, political, and economic institutions; they are "race neutral." The historical accumulation of white privilege and the persistence of personal and institutional racisms are thus ignored (Bonilla-Silva 2003). Furthermore, "race-neutral" practices are often expressions of normative whiteness. To the extent that whites see themselves as "raceless" and "normal," they perceive their expectations, styles, and types of knowledge to be neutral. Hence, norms assumed to be universal privilege those most comfortably versed in them, namely whites. This dynamic is part of the racial character of meritocracy.

In an effort to counteract this dynamic, some scholars have conceived of whiteness as "performance." Those who can "naturally" perform the somatic, moral, and cultural norms of whiteness are white and benefit from racialized institutional arrangements. White performativity is more than an expression of whiteness, however; it is also constitutive of it. From the performances of antebellum white minstrels (Roediger 1991; Lott 1993) and white characters in literature and film (Dyer 1988; Morrison 1993; Vera and Gordon 2003), to the sanctions and rewards placed upon stylistic and behavioral acts in everyday interactions (Hartigan 1999; Dolby 2000), performances of whiteness mark boundaries of inclusion and exclusion and provide the grounds on which white people learn what being "white" means and where they stand in the racial hierarchy. The conceptualization of "white" as performance also helps illuminate class, gender, and sexual hierarchies within whiteness. The term "white trash," for example, objectifies and sanctions poor whites for not performing the proper class decorums of whiteness (Hartigan 1997).

"White privilege" is another area of interest for whiteness scholars and activists. White performativity confers many privileges, including the explicit and implicit granting of certain rights to white people. As legal scholar Cheryl Harris has argued, whiteness has long been a "legally recognized [metaphysical] property interest" (1993, 1708). Until passage of the Civil Rights Act in 1964, U.S. law conferred upon whites (propertied males, especially, but also white women and workers) singular access to full human and civil rights and protected white identity, privilege, and property. Today, "colorblind" law and the disproportional wealth that whites have accrued from a long-term "possessive investment in whiteness" provide ongoing benefits to whites (better schools, toxic-free neighborhoods, excellent credit). Historically, these privileges were solidified even in progressive public policies like those of the New Deal, which specifically advantaged white workers and homebuyers (Lipsitz 1995).

In sum, "white" as a keyword in American cultural studies has expanded contemporary understandings of race and racial inequality by turning a critical eye to white supremacy and its systemic reproduction through identity, norms, performance, and privilege. However, some potential dangers lurk around current critical usages of *white* as a keyword. One is that it may be so overdefined as to render it useless (Kolchin 2002; Andersen 2003). More foreboding is the tendency of whiteness studies to reassert white power and privilege and re-center white authority. As an example, some antiracist strategies springing from whiteness studies, such as "white abolitionism"—which encourages whites to "defect" from the white race (Ignatiev and Garvey 1996)—tend to foreground white people and whiteness in activist work, thus losing sight of the critical and very powerful roles people of color play in coalitions and struggles for justice and equality.

While it is true that oppositional identities and politics that do not transcend norm-exception dichotomies risk recentering and revalidating whiteness as a norm, it is also true that "white" will remain an important analytical construct as long as racial exclusion and oppression remain salient in U.S. domestic and world affairs. Shifting demographics in the United States and increasing migrations of people on a global scale have already begun to destabilize white cultural and political hegemonies in the United States and abroad. Given this global context, the continued deconstruction of normative whiteness will remain essential to the creation of truly liberatory identities, knowledges, and collaborative strategies aimed at social and political transformation. Whether this ongoing work will open possibilities for progressive change or be met with retrenchments of white identity and privilege will be critical subjects for future research and activism.

Works Cited

Abdel Malek, Anwar. "Orientalism en Crise." *Diogenes* 44 (Winter 1963): 107–8.

Abrams, M. H. *Natural Supernaturalism: Tradition and Revolution in Romantic Literature.* New York: W. W. Norton, 1971.

Abu-Lughod, Lila. "Writing Against Culture." In *Recapturing Anthropology: Working in the Present*, edited by Richard G. Fox, 137–162. Santa Fe, NM: School of American Research Press, 1991.

Adamic, Louis. *From Many Lands.* New York: Harper, 1940.

———. *Nation of Nations.* New York: Harper, 1945.

Adams, Abigail. "Letter to John Adams. Braintree, MA, 31 March Rep." 1776. In *The Feminist Papers: From Adams to de Beauvoir*, edited by Alice Rossi, 11–12. Boston: Northeastern University Press, 1988.

Adams, Rachel. *Sideshow U.S.A.: Freaks and the American Cultural Imagination.* Chicago: University of Chicago Press, 2001.

Adorno, Theodore. *Aesthetic Theory.* Translated by C. Lenhardt. Edited by Gretel Adorno and Rolf Tiedemann. London: Routledge and Kegan Paul, 1984.

Agamben, Giorgio. *The Coming Community.* Translated by Michael Hardt. Minneapolis: University of Minnesota Press, 1993.

Agarwal, Arun, and K. Sivaramakrisnan. *Regional Modernities: The Cultural Politics of Development in India.* Palo Alto, CA: Stanford University Press, 2003.

Agnew, Jean-Christophe. *Worlds Apart: The Market and the Theater in Anglo-American Thought, 1550–1750.* New York: Cambridge University Press, 1986.

Ahmad, Aijaz. *In Theory: Classes, Nations, Literature.* London: Verso, 1992.

Alarcón, Norma. "Anzaldúa's *Frontera*: Inscribing Gynetics." In *Displacement, Diaspora, and Geographies of Identity*, edited by Smadar Lavie and Ted Sweedenburg, 41–54. Durham, NC: Duke University Press, 1996.

"Alcatraz Reclaimed." *Newsletter of the Indian Tribes of All Nations.* January 1970. Reprinted in The Council on Interracial Books for Children, *Chronicles of American Indian Protest.* Greenwich, CT: Fawcett Publications, 1971.

Alcoff, Linda Martín. "Who's Afraid of Identity Politics?" In *Reclaiming Identity: Realist Theory and the Predicament of Postmodernism*, edited by Paula M. L. Moya and Hames-García, 312–44. Berkeley: University of California Press, 2000.

Alexander, J. Robert. *The Right Opposition: The Lovestoneites and the International Communist Opposition of the 1930s.* Westport, CT: Greenwood, 1981.

Alexander, M. Jacqui. "Redrafting Morality: The Postcolonial State and the Sexual Offences Bill of Trinidad and Tobago." In *Third World Women and the Politics of Feminism*, edited by Chandra Talpade Mohanty, Ann Russo, and Lourdes Torres. Bloomington and Indianapolis: Indiana University Press, 1991.

———. "Not Just Any Body Can Be a Citizen." *Feminist Review* 48 (1994): 5–23.

Allen, Theodore. *The Invention of the White Race*, vol. 1: *Racial Oppression and Social Control.* London: Verso, 1994.

Amariglio, J., and A. Callari. "Marxian Value Theory and the Problem of the Subject: The Role of Commodity Fetishism." *Fetishism as Cultural Discourse*, edited by E. Apter and W. Pietz, 186–216. Ithaca, NY: Cornell University Press, 1993.

Works Cited

Amin, Samir. *Unequal Development: An Essay on the Social Formations of Peripheral Capitalism.* Translated by Brian Pearce. New York: Monthly Review Press, 1976.

———. *Capitalism in the Age of Globalization: The Management of Contemporary Society.* London: Zed, 1997.

Amory, Hugh, and David D. Hall. *The Colonial Book in the Atlantic World.* Cambridge: Cambridge University Press, 2000.

Amott, Teresa, and Julie Matthaei. *Race, Gender and Work: A Multi-Cultural Economic History of Women in the United States,* rev. ed. Boston: South End Press, 1996.

Andersen, Margaret. "Whitewashing Race: A Critical Perspective on Whiteness." In *White Out: The Continuing Significance of Racism,* edited by Ashley Doane and Eduardo Bonilla-Silva, 21–34. New York: Routledge, 2003.

Anderson, Benedict. *Imagined Communities: Reflections on the Origin and Spread of Nationalism.* London: Verso, 1983; rev. ed., 1991.

Anderson, Warwick. "Excremental Colonialism: Public Health and the Poetics of Pollution." *Critical Inquiry* 21, no. 3 (1995): 640–69.

Anzaldúa, Gloria. *Borderlands/La Frontera: The New Mestiza.* San Francisco: Spinsters/Aunt Lute, 1987; rev. ed., New York: Aunt Lute Books, 1999.

———. "To(o) Queer the Writer—Loca, escritora y chicana." In *Living Chicana Theory,* edited by Carla Trujillo, 263–76. Berkeley: University of California Press, 1998.

Aparicio, Frances R. "Latino Cultural Studies." In *Critical Latin American and Latino Studies,* edited by Juan Poblete, 3–31. Minneapolis: University of Minnesota Press, 2003.

Apess, William. *On Our Own Ground: The Complete Writings of William Apess, a Pequot.* Edited by Barry O'Connell. Amherst: University of Massachusetts Press, 1992.

Appadurai, Arjun. *Modernity at Large: Cultural Dimensions of Globalization.* Minneapolis: University of Minnesota Press, 1996.

———, ed. *The Social Life of Things: Commodities in Cultural Perspective.* New York: Cambridge University Press, 1986.

Armstrong, Elisabeth, and Vijay Prashad. "Solidarity: War Rites and Women's Rights." *CR: The Centennial Review* 5, no. 1 (2005): 213–53.

Arnold, Matthew. *Culture and Anarchy.* 1869. Reprinted in *The Complete Prose Works of Matthew Arnold,* vol. 5, edited by R. H. Super. Ann Arbor: University of Michigan Press, 1965.

———. *Culture and Anarchy.* 1869. Reprint, edited by J. Dover Wilson. Cambridge: Cambridge University Press, 1971.

Aronson, Ronald. "The Left Needs More Socialism." *The Nation* 282, no. 15 (April 17, 2006): 28–30.

Asad, Talal. *Genealogies of Religion: Discipline and Reasons of Power in Christianity and Islam.* Baltimore: Johns Hopkins University Press, 1993.

———. *Formations of the Secular: Christianity, Islam, Modernity.* Stanford: Stanford University Press, 2003.

Asch, Adrienne, and Michelle Fine, eds. *Women with Disabilities: Essays in Psychology, Culture and Politics.* Health, Society and Policy Series. Philadelphia: Temple University Press, 1988.

Asch, Adrienne, and Erik Parens, eds. *Prenatal Testing and Disability Rights.* Hastings Center Studies in Ethics. Washington, D.C.: Georgetown University Press, 2000.

Ashcroft, Bill, Gareth Griffiths, and Helen Tiffin. *The Empire Writes Back: Theory and Practice in Post-Colonial Literatures.* London: Routledge, 1989.

Asher, R. E., and J. M. Y. Simpson, eds. *The Encyclopedia of Language and Linguistics.* 10 vols. New York: Pergamon Press, 1994.

Austin, J. L. *How to Do Things with Words.* Cambridge, MA: Harvard University Press, 1962.

Baird, Robert. "Late Secularism." *Social Text* 64 (2000): 123–36.

Baldwin, James. *The Price of the Ticket: Collected Nonfiction 1948–85.* New York: St. Martins / Marek, 1985.

Balibar, Etienne. *Masses, Classes, Ideas: Studies on Politics and Philosophy before and after Marx*. New York: Routledge, 1994.

Bamberger, Bill, and Cathy N. Davidson. *Closing: The Life and Death of an American Factory*. New York: W. W. Norton, 1999.

Barnes, Elizabeth. *States of Sympathy: Seduction and Democracy in the American Novel*. New York: Columbia University Press, 1997.

Barrett, Michèle, and Mary McIntosh. *The Anti-Social Family*. London: Verso, 1982.

Bartelson, Jens. *The Critique of the State*. Cambridge: Cambridge University Press, 2001.

Battiste, Marie. "Print Culture and Decolonizing the University: Indigenizing the Page: Part 1." In *The Future of the Page*, edited by Peter Stoicheff and Andrew Taylor, 111–23. Toronto: University of Toronto Press, 2004.

Baudrillard, Jean. *Simulacra and Simulation*. Translated by Sheila Faria Glaser. Ann Arbor: University of Michigan Press, 1994.

Baynton, Douglas. *Forbidden Signs: American Culture and the Campaign against Sign Language*. Chicago: University of Chicago Press, 1998.

Beck, Scott H., and Kenneth J. Mijeski. "Indigena Self-Identity in Ecuador and the Rejection of Mestizaje." *Latin American Research Review* 35, no. 1 (2000): 119–37.

Becker, Carl. *The Heavenly City of the Eighteenth-Century Philosophers*. New Haven: Yale University Press, 1932.

Bederman, Gail. *Manliness and Civilization: A Cultural History of Gender and Race in the United States, 1880–1917*. Chicago: University of Chicago Press, 1995.

Beecher, Catherine. *A Treatise on Domestic Economy for the Use of Young Ladies at Home and at School*. Boston: Marsh, Capen, Lyon, and Webb, 1841.

Beecher, Catherine, and Harriet Beecher Stowe. *The American Woman's Home; or, Principles of Domestic Science*. New York: J. B. Ford, 1869.

Bell, Daniel. *The End of Ideology: On the Exhaustion of Political Ideas in the Fifties*. Glencoe, IL: Free Press, 1960.

Bellah, Robert. *Beyond Belief: Essays on Religion in a Post-Traditional World*. Berkeley: University of California Press, 1970.

———. *The Broken Covenant: American Civil Religion in Time of Trial*. New York: Seabury Press, 1975.

Bellah, Robert, et al. *Habits of the Heart: Individualism and Commitment in American Life*. New York: Harper and Row, 1985.

Bender, Thomas. *Community and Social Change in America*. Baltimore: Johns Hopkins University Press, 1978.

Benedict, Ruth. *Patterns of Culture*. Boston: Houghton Mifflin, 1934.

Benjamin, Walter. *Illuminations: Essays and Reflections*. Edited by Hannah Arendt. Translated by Harry Zohn. New York: Schocken Books, 1968.

Bennett, Tony. *The Birth of the Museum: History, Theory, and Politics*. London: Routledge, 1995.

Bennett, Tony, Lawrence Grossberg, and Meaghan Morris, eds. *New Keywords: A Revised Vocabulary of Culture and Society*. Oxford: Blackwell, 2005.

Ben-Sasson, Haim Hillel. "Galut," s.v., *Encyclopaedia Judaica*, vol. 7, edited by Cecil Roth and Geoffrey Wigoder, 275–94. Jerusalem: Encyclopaedia Judaica, n.d.

Bensel, Richard Franklin. *The Political Economy of American Industrialization, 1877–1900*. New York: Cambridge University Press, 2000.

Bercovitch, Sacvan, and Myra Jehlen, eds. *Ideology and Classic American Literature*. Cambridge: Cambridge University Press, 1986.

Berestein, Leslie. "Border Desert Nearing Grim Record." *San Diego Union-Tribune*. August 10, 2005, A3.

Berger, Peter. "A Market Model for the Analysis of Ecumenicity." *Social Research* 30, no. 1 (Spring 1963): 77–93.

———. *The Sacred Canopy*. Garden City, NY: Doubleday, 1969.

Works Cited

Berger, Peter, and Thomas Luckmann. *The Social Construction of Reality*. New York: Doubleday, 1966.

Berlant, Lauren. *The Anatomy of National Fantasy: Hawthorne, Utopia, and Everyday Life*. Chicago: University of Chicago Press, 1991.

———. *The Queen of America Goes to Washington City: Essays on Sex and Citizenship*. Durham, NC: Duke University Press, 1997.

———. "Uncle Sam Needs a Wife: Citizenship and Denegation." In *Materializing Democracy: Toward a Revitalized Cultural Politics*, edited by Dana D. Nelson and Russ Castronovo, 144–74. Durham, N.C.: Duke University Press, 2002.

Berlant, Lauren, and Michael Warner. "What Does Queer Theory Teach Us About X?" *PMLA* 110, no. 3 (1995): 343–349.

———. "Sex in Public." *Critical Inquiry* 24, no. 2 (Winter 1998): 547–66.

———. *Intimacy*. Chicago: University of Chicago Press, 2000.

Berle, Adolf A., and Gardiner C. Means. *The Modern Corporation and Private Property*. New York: Macmillan, 1932.

Berlin, Ira. *Many Thousands Gone: The First Two Centuries of Slavery in North America*. Cambridge, MA: Harvard University Press, 1998.

Berlin, Ira, et al., eds. *Freedom: A Documentary History of Emancipation, 1861–1867*, series 1, vol. 3, *The Wartime Genesis of Free Labor*. New York: Cambridge University Press, 1990.

Bernal, Martin. "Greece: Aryan or Mediterranean? Two Contending Historiographical Models." In *Enduring Western Civilization: The Constructions of the Concept of Western Civilization and Its "Others,"* edited by Silvia Federici, 3–11. Westport, CT: Praeger, 1995.

Bhabha, Homi K. "Introduction: Narrating the Nation." In *Nation and Narration*, edited by Homi Bhabha, 1–7. New York: Routledge, 1990.

———. *The Location of Culture*. New York: Routledge, 1994.

Bhagwati, Jagdish. *Free Trade Today*. Princeton: Princeton University Press, 2003.

Bhargava, Rajeev, ed. *Secularism and Its Critics*. Delhi: Oxford University Press, 1998.

Bierce, Ambrose. *Devil's Dictionary*. New York: Albert and Charles Boni, 1911.

Birkerts, Sven. *The Gutenberg Elegies: The Fate of Reading in an Electronic Age*. New York: Fawcett Columbine, 1994.

Black, Edwin. *War against the Weak: Eugenics and America's Campaign to Create a Master Race*. Berkeley, CA: Four Walls Eight Windows, 2003.

Blackstone, William. *Commentaries on the Laws of England*, vol. 1, *1765–69*. Chicago: University of Chicago Press, 1979.

Blumenberg, Hans. *The Legitimacy of the Modern Age*. Translated by Robert M. Wallace. Cambridge, MA: MIT Press, 1983.

Blumin, Stuart M., et al. *The Emergence of the Middle Class: Social Experience in the American City, 1760–1900*. New York: Cambridge University Press, 1989.

Blyden, Edward W. *Christianity, Islam and the Negro Race*. Edinburgh: Edinburgh University Press, 1967.

Boas, Franz. *The Mind of Primitive Man*. New York: Macmillan, 1911.

———. *Anthropology and Modern Life*. New York: W. W. Norton, 1928.

———. *Race, Language, and Culture*. New York: Macmillan, 1940.

Bogues, Anthony. *Black Heretics, Black Prophets: Radical Political Intellectuals*. New York: Routledge, 2003.

Bolton, Herbert Eugene. *The Spanish Borderlands: A Chronicle of Old Florida and the Southwest*. New Haven: Yale University Press, 1921.

Bonilla-Silva, Eduardo. *Racism without Racists*. Lanham, MD: Rowman and Littlefield, 2003.

Bonus, Rick. *Locating Filipino Americans: Ethnicity and Cul-*

tural Politics of Space. Philadelphia: Temple University Press, 2000.

Boris, Eileen. "Beyond Dichotomy: Recent Books in North American Women's Labor History." *Journal of Women's History* 4, no. 3 (1993): 162–79.

Bornstein, Kate. *Gender Outlaw: On Men, Women, and the Rest of Us.* New York: Routledge, 1994.

Bosniak, Linda. "The Citizenship of Aliens." *Social Text* 56 (1998): 29–35.

Boston Women's Health Book Collective. *Our Bodies, Ourselves.* New York: Simon and Schuster, 1973; revised 1976, 1996.

Bourdieu, Pierre. *Distinction: A Social Critique of the Judgment of Taste.* Cambridge, MA: Harvard University Press, 1987.

Bourne, Randolph. "Trans-National America." *Atlantic Monthly* 118 (July 1916): 86–97.

Bowlby, Rachel. "Domestication." In *Feminism Beside Itself,* edited by Diane Elam and Robyn Wiegman, 71–92. New York: Routledge, 1995.

Boyarin, Jonathan, and Daniel Boyarin. *Powers of Diaspora: Two Essays on the Relevance of Jewish Culture.* Minneapolis: University of Minnesota Press, 2002.

Boydston, Jeanne. *Home and Work: Housework, Wages and the Ideology of Labor in the Early Republic.* New York: Oxford University Press, 1990.

Brady, Mary Pat. "The Fungibility of Borders." *Nepantla: Views from South* 1, no. 1 (2000): 171–90.

Bramen, Carrie Tirado. *The Uses of Variety: Modern Americanism and the Quest for National Distinctiveness.* Cambridge, MA: Harvard University Press, 2001.

Braudel, Fernand. *Civilization and Capitalism, Fifteenth to Eighteenth Century.* 3 vols. New York: Harper and Row, 1982–84.

Braxton, Joanne, ed. *The Collected Poetry of Paul Laurence Dunbar.* Charlottesville: University of Virginia Press, 1993.

Brennan, Denise. *What's Love Got to Do with It? Transnational Desires and Sex Tourism in the Dominican Republic.* Durham, NC: Duke University Press, 2004.

Briggs, Laura. "The Race of Hysteria: 'Overcivilization' and the 'Savage' Woman in Late Nineteenth-Century Obstetrics and Gynecology." *American Quarterly* 52, no. 2 (June 2000): 246–73.

Brisbane, Albert. "The American Associationists." *United States Magazine, and Democratic Review*, February 1846, p. 142.

Brodhead, Richard. *Cultures of Letters: Scenes of Reading and Writing in Nineteenth-Century America.* Chicago: University of Chicago Press, 1993.

Brodkin, Karen. *How Jews Became White Folks and What That Says about America.* New Brunswick, NJ: Rutgers University Press, 1998.

Brown, Dona. *Inventing New England: Regional Tourism in the Nineteenth Century.* Washington, D.C.: Smithsonian Institution Press, 1995.

Brown, Gillian. *Domestic Individualism: Imagining Self in Nineteenth-Century America.* Berkeley: University of California Press, 1990.

———. *The Consent of the Governed: The Lockean Legacy in Early American Culture.* Cambridge, MA: Harvard University Press, 2001.

Brown, Wendy. *States of Injury: Power and Freedom in Late Modernity.* Princeton: Princeton University Press, 1995.

———. "Neo-Liberalism and the End of Liberal-Democracy." *Theory and Event* 7, no. 1 (2003).

Brown, William Wells. "Lecture." In *Four Fugitive Slave Narratives,* 81–98. Reading, MA: Addison-Wesley, 1969.

Bruce, Steve, and David Voas. "The Resilience of the Nation-State: Religion and Politics in the Modern Era." *Sociology* 38, no. 5 (2004): 1025–34.

Buck-Morss, Susan. "Aesthetics and Anaesthetics: Walter Benjamin's Artwork Essay Reconsidered." *October* 62 (1992): 3–41.

Buell, Lawrence. *The Environmental Imagination: Thoreau, Nature Writing, and the Formation of American Culture*. Cambridge, MA: Harvard University Press, 1995.

Bullard, Robert D. "Confronting Environmental Racism in the Twenty-First Century." In *The Colors of Nature: Culture, Identity, and the Natural World*, edited by Alison H. Deming and Lauret E. Savoy, 90–97. Minneapolis: Milkweed, 2002.

Burch, Susan. *Signs of Resistance: American Deaf Cultural History, 1900 to World War II*. New York: New York University Press, 2004.

Burgett, Bruce. *Sentimental Bodies: Sex, Gender, and Citizenship in the Early Republic*. Princeton: Princeton University Press, 1998.

———. "On the Mormon Question: Race, Sex, and Polygamy in the 1850s and the 1990s." *American Quarterly* 57, no. 1 (March 2005): 75–102.

Burke, Kenneth. *The Philosophy of Literary Form*. New York: Vintage Books, 1957.

Bush, George W. "Inaugural Address," January 21, 2001, archived at http://www.whitehouse.gov/news/inaugural-address.html.

———. "Remarks by the President on Goree Island, Senegal," July 8, 2003, archived at http://usinfo.state.gov/gi/Archive/2003/Jul/08-193733.html.

Butler, Judith. *Gender Trouble: Feminism and the Subversion of Identity*. New York: Routledge, 1990.

———. *Bodies That Matter: On the Discursive Limits of "Sex."* New York: Routledge, 1993.

———. *Antigone's Claim*. New York: Columbia University Press, 2000.

———. *Precarious Life: The Powers of Mourning and Violence*. London: Verso, 2004a.

———. *Undoing Gender*. New York: Routledge, 2004b.

Butler, Kim. "Defining Diaspora, Refining a Discourse." *Diaspora* 10, no. 2 (2001): 189–219.

Callon, Michel. *The Laws of the Markets*. Oxford: Blackwell, 1998.

Cameron, Sharon. *Choosing Not Choosing: Dickinson's Fascicles*. Chicago: University of Chicago Press, 1992.

Camp, Stephanie. *Closer to Home: Enslaved Women and Everyday Resistance in the Plantation South*. Chapel Hill: University of North Carolina Press, 2003.

Campbell, James. *Songs of Zion: The African Methodist Episcopal Church in the United States and South Africa*. Chapel Hill: University of North Carolina Press, 1995.

Carby, Hazel. *Reconstructing Womanhood: The Emergence of the Afro-American Woman Novelist*. New York: Oxford University Press, 1987.

Carey, Henry Charles. *The Past, the Present, and the Future*. New York: Augustus M. Kelley, 1967.

Carlson, Elof Axel. *The Unfit: A History of a Bad Idea*. Cold Harbor, NY: Cold Spring Harbor Laboratory Press, 2001.

Carmichael, Stokely, and Charles Hamilton. *Black Power: The Politics of Liberation in America*. New York: Vintage, 1967.

Castells, Manuel. "La ciudad de la nueva economía." *La factoría* 12 (July–August 2000a), http://www.lafactoriaweb.com/articulos/castells12.htm.

———. *The Rise of Network Society*. Oxford: Blackwell, 2000b.

Castiglia, Christopher. "Abolition's Racial Interiors and the Making of White Civic Depth." *American Literary History* 14 (2002): 32–59.

Castoriadis, Cornelius. "The Social Imaginary and the Institution." *The Castoriadis Reader*, edited by David Ames Curtis, 196–217. Oxford: Blackwell, 1987.

Caves, R. *Creative Industries: Contracts between Arts and Commerce*. Cambridge, MA: Harvard University Press, 2000.

Chakrabarty, Dipesh. *Provincializing Europe: Postcolonial Thought and Historical Difference*. Princeton: Princeton University Press, 2000.

Chamfort, Sébastien-Roch-Nicolas. *Products of the Perfected*

Civilization. Translated by W. S. Merwin. San Francisco: North Point Press, 1984.

Chan, Jeffrey Paul, and Frank Chin. "Racist Love." In *Seeing through Schuck*, edited by Richard Kostelanetz, 65–79. New York: Ballantine, 1972.

Chandra, Bipan. "Colonialism, Stages of Colonialism, and the Colonial State." *Journal of Contemporary South Asia* 10, no. 3 (1980): 272–85.

Chapman, Mary, and Glenn Hendler, eds. *Sentimental Men: Masculinity and the Politics of Affect in American Culture*. Berkeley: University of California Press, 1999.

Chappell, David. *A Stone of Hope: Prophetic Religion and the Death of Jim Crow*. Chapel Hill: University of North Carolina Press, 2004.

Charles, Ray. "America the Beautiful." *A Message from the People . . . by the People . . . and for the People*. Los Angeles: Tangerine Records, 1972.

Chase, Richard. *Quest for Myth*. Baton Rouge: Louisian State University Press, 1949.

Chauncey, George. *Gay New York: Gender, Urban Culture, and the Making of the Gay Male World, 1890–1940*. New York: Basic Books, 1994.

Chevigny, Bell Gale, and Gari Laguardia, eds. *Reinventing the Americas: Comparative Studies of Literature of the United States and Spanish America*. New York: Cambridge University Press, 1986.

Chidester, David. *Savage Systems: Colonialism and Comparative Religion in Southern Africa*. Charlottesville: University of Virginia Press, 1996.

Chomsky, Noam. "The Non-Election of 2004." *Z Magazine*, January 2005, 31–35.

Chomsky, Noam, and Edward S. Herman. *The Washington Connection and Third World Fascism*. Boston: South End Press, 1979.

Christiansen, John, and Sharon Barnartt. *Deaf President Now! The 1988 Revolution at Gallaudet University*. Washington, D.C.: Gallaudet University Press, 2002.

Chuh, Kandice. *Imagine Otherwise: On Asian Americanist Critique*. Durham, NC: Duke University Press, 2003.

Clarke, Cheryl. "The Failure to Transform: Homophobia in the Black Community." In Combahee River Collective, *Home Girls: A Black Feminist Anthology*, edited by Barbara Smith, 197–208. New York: Kitchen Table / Women of Color Press, 1983.

Clifford, James. *Routes: Travel and Translation in the Late Twentieth Century*. Cambridge, MA: Harvard University Press, 1997.

———. "Taking Identity Politics Seriously: 'The Contradictory, Stony Ground . . .'" In *Without Guarantees: in Honor of Stuart Hall*, edited by Paul Gilroy, Lawrence Grossberg, and Angela McRobbie, 94–112. New York; Verso, 2000.

Clifford, James, and George Marcus, eds. *Writing Culture: The Poetics and Politics of Ethnography*. Berkeley: University of California Press, 1986.

Cohen, Cathy J. "Punks, Bulldaggers, and Welfare Queens: The Radical Potential of Queer Politics?" *GLQ* 3 (1997): 437–65.

Cohen, Jean L. *Regulating Intimacy: A New Legal Paradigm*. Princeton: Princeton University Press, 2002.

Cohen, Jean L., and Andrew Arato. *Civil Society and Political Theory*. Cambridge, MA: MIT Press, 1992.

Cohen, Lizabeth. *A Consumer's Republic: The Politics of Mass Consumption in Postwar America*. New York: Alfred A. Knopf, 2003.

Cohen, Patricia Cline. *A Calculating People: The Spread of Numeracy in Early America*. Chicago: University of Chicago Press, 1982.

Cohn, Deborah N. *History and Memory in the Two Souths: Recent Southern and Spanish American Fiction*. Nashville: Vanderbilt University Press, 1999.

Collingwood, R. G. *The New Leviathan*. New York: Crowell, 1971.

Combahee River Collective. *Home Girls: A Black Feminist An-*

thology. Edited by Barbara Smith. New York: Kitchen Table / Women of Color Press, 1983.

Condorcet, Jean-Antoine-Nicolas de Caritat, Marquis de. *Sketch for a Historical Picture of the Progress of the Human Mind*. 1793. London: Weidenfeld and Nicolson, 1955.

Commager, Henry Steele, ed. *America in Perspective: The United States through Foreign Eyes*. New York: Random House, 1947.

Connolly, William. *Why I Am Not a Secularist*. Minneapolis: University of Minnesota Press, 2000.

Coontz, Stephanie. *The Social Origins of Private Life: A History of American Families, 1600–1900*. New York: Verso, 1988.

Cooper, Anna Julia. *A Voice From the South*. Xenia, OH: Aldine Printing House, 1892.

Corker, Mairian. "Sensing Disability." *Hypatia* 16, no. 4 (2001): 34–52.

Cott, Nancy. *Public Vows: A History of Marriage and the Nation*. Cambridge, MA: Harvard University Press, 2000.

Creed, Gerald, ed. *The Seductions of Community*. Santa Fe, NM: SAR Press, 2006.

Crenshaw, Kimberlé Williams. "Mapping the Margins: Intersectionality, Identity Politics, and Violence Against Women of Color." In *Critical Race Theory: The Key Writings That Formed the Movement*, edited by Kimberlé Crenshaw, Neil Gotanda, Gary Peller, and Kendall Thomas, 357–83. New York: The New Press, 1995.

Cronin, Ann. *Advertising and Consumer Citizenship: Gender, Images, and Rights*. London: Routledge, 2000.

Cronon, William, ed. *Uncommon Ground: Toward Reinventing Nature*. New York: W. W. Norton, 1995.

Crozier, Michael, and Samuel Huntington, et al. *The Crisis of Democracy: Report on the Governability of Democracies to the Trilateral Commission*. New York: New York University Press, 1975.

Cruikshank, Barbara. "The Will to Empower: Technologies of Citizenship and the War on Poverty." *Socialist Review* 23, no. 4 (1994): 29–55.

Da Costa, Emilia Viotti. *Crowns of Glory, Tears of Blood: The Demerara Slave Rebellion of 1823*. New York: Columbia University Press, 1994.

Dahlberg, Lincoln. "Democracy via Cyberspace: Mapping the Rhetorics and Practices of Three Prominent Camps." *New Media and Society* 3, no. 2 (2001): 157–77.

Damasio, Antonio R. *Descartes' Error: Emotion, Reason and the Human Brain*. New York: G. P. Putnam's Sons, 1994.

Darwin, Charles. *The Voyage of the Beagle*. Harvard Classics, vol. 29. New York: P. F. Collier, 1909.

Davidson, Cathy N. *Revolution and the Word: The Rise of the Novel in America*. New York: Oxford University Press, 1986; expanded ed., 2004.

Davidson, Cathy N., and Jessamyn Hatcher, eds. *No More Separate Spheres!* Durham, NC: Duke University Press, 2002.

Davies, W. D. *The Territorial Dimension of Judaism*. Berkeley: University of California Press, 1982.

Davis, Angela. *Women, Race, and Class*. New York: Vintage, 1983.

———. Interview with Lisa Lowe. "Reflections on Race, Class, and Gender in the USA." In *The Politics of Culture in the Shadow of Capital*, edited by Lisa Lowe and David Lloyd, 303–23. Durham, NC: Duke University Press, 1997.

Davis, David Brion. *The Problem of Slavery in the Age of Revolution, 1770–1823*. Ithaca, NY: Cornell University Press, 1975.

Davis, Lennard. *Enforcing Normalcy: Disability, Deafness, and the Body*. New York: Verso, 1995.

Davis, Mike. *City of Quartz: Excavating the Future in Los Angeles*. London: Verso, 1990.

Dean, Robert. *Imperial Brotherhood: Gender and the Making of Cold War Foreign Policy*. Amherst: University of Massachusetts Press, 2001.

Deane, Seamus. "Imperialism/Nationalism." In *Critical Terms for Literary Study*, edited by Frank Lentricchia and Thomas McLaughlin, 354–68. Chicago: University of Chicago Press, 1990.

de Kock, Leon. "Sitting for the Civilization Test: The Making(s) of a Civil Imaginary in Colonial South Africa." *Poetics Today* 22, no. 2 (2001): 391–412.

Delany, Samuel R. *Return to Nevèrÿon*. Middletown, CT: Wesleyan University Press, 1994.

———. *Times Square Red, Times Square Blue*, rev. ed. New York: New York University Press, 2001.

Deleuze, Gilles, and Félix Guattari. *Anti-Oedipus: Capitalism and Schizophrenia*. Minneapolis: University of Minnesota Press, 1983.

Delgado Bernal, Dolores. "Using a Chicana Feminist Epistemology in Educational Research." *Harvard Educational Review* 68, no. 4 (1998): 555–82.

Deloria, Philip. *Playing Indian*. New Haven: Yale University Press, 1998.

Delphy, Christine. *The Main Enemy: A Materialist Analysis of Women's Oppression*. London: Women's Resources and Research Centre Publications, 1977.

D'Emilio, John, and Estelle Freedman. *Intimate Matters: A History of Sexuality in America*, 2d ed. Chicago: University of Chicago Press, 1997.

Denning, Michael. *Culture in the Age of Three Worlds*. London: Verso, 2004.

De Voe, Thomas. *The Market Book*. New York: Printed for the author, 1862.

Dewey, John. *The Public and Its Problems*. New York: Henry Holt, 1927.

———. *Art as Experience*. New York: Perigree, 1980.

Di Chiro, Giovanna. "Nature as Community: The Convergence of Environment and Social Justice." In *Uncommon Ground: Rethinking the Human Place in Nature*, edited by William Cronon, 298–320. New York: W. W. Norton, 1996.

Didion, Joan. *Slouching Towards Bethlehem*. New York: Pocket, 1968.

di Leonardo, Micaela. *Exotics at Home: Anthropologies, Otherness, and American Modernity*. Chicago: University of Chicago Press, 1998.

Dionne, E. J., Jr., ed. *Community Works*. Washington, D.C.: Brookings Institution Press, 1998.

Dippie, Brian W. "American Wests: Historiographical Perspectives." In *Trails: Toward a New Western History*, edited by Patricia Nelson Limerick, Clyde A. Milner II, and Charles E. Rankin, 112–38. Lawrence: University of Kansas Press, 1991.

Dolby, Nadine. "The Shifting Ground of Race: The Role of Taste in Youth's Production of Identities." *Race, Ethnicity, and Education* 3, no. 1 (2000): 7–23.

Douglas, Ann. *The Feminization of American Culture*. New York: Alfred A. Knopf, 1977.

Dowd, Douglas Fitzgerald. *The Twisted Dream: Capitalist Development in the United States Since 1776*, 2d ed. Cambridge, MA: Winthrop, 1977.

Dower, John. *War without Mercy: Race and Power in the Pacific War*. New York: Pantheon, 1986.

Drucker, Johanna. *The Century of Artists' Books*. New York: Granary, 1995.

Duboff, Richard B. *Accumulation and Power: An Economic History of the United States*. Armonk, NY: M. E. Sharpe, 1989.

Dubois, Laurent. *Avengers of the New World: The Story of the Haitian Revolution*. Cambridge, MA: Harvard University Press, 2004.

Du Bois, W. E. B. *The Souls of Black Folk*. 1903. Reprinted in *W. E. B. Du Bois: Writings*, edited by Nathan Huggins. New York: Library of America, 1986.

———. *Black Reconstruction in America*. New York: Russell and Russell, 1935; reprint, 1965.

———. "The African Roots of the War." In *W. E. B. Du Bois: A Reader*, edited by David Levering Lewis, 642–51. New York: Henry Holt, 1995.

DuCille, Ann. *The Coupling Convention: Sex, Text, and Tradition in Black Women's Fiction*. New York: Oxford University Press, 1993.

Duggan, Lisa. "Making It Perfectly Queer." *Socialist Review* 22 (1992): 11–31.

———. "Holy Matrimony!" *The Nation Online*, February 26, 2004a (March 15, 2004 print edition), http://www.thenation.com/doc.mhtml?i=20040315&c=1&s=duggan.

———. *The Twilight of Equality: Neoliberalism, Cultural Politics, and the Attack on Democracy*. Boston: Beacon Press, 2004b.

Dunn, Christopher. *Brutality Garden*. Chapel Hill: University of North Carolina Press, 2001.

Durkheim, Émile, and Marcel Mauss. "Note on the Notion of Civilization." Translated by Benjamin Nelson. *Social Research* 38 (1971): 808–13. Originally published in *L'Anée Sociologique* 12 (1913): 46–50.

Dyer, Richard. "White." *Screen* 29, no. 4 (1988): 44–64.

———. *White*. New York: Routledge, 1997.

Eade, J. *Living the Global City: Globalization as a Local Process*. London: Routledge, 1997.

Eagleton, Terry. *The Ideology of the Aesthetic*. Oxford: Blackwell, 1990.

———. *The Idea of Culture*. Malden, MA: Blackwell, 2000.

Edelman, Lee. *No Future: Queer Theory and the Death Drive*. Durham, NC: Duke University Press, 2004.

Edmondson, Locksley. "Black America as a Mobilizing Diaspora: Some International Implications." In *Modern Diasporas in International Politics*, edited by Gabriel Sheffer, 164–211. London: Croon Helm, 1986.

Edmundson, Mark. *Why Read?* New York: Bloomsbury, 2004.

Edwards, Brent Hayes. "The Uses of *Diaspora*." *Social Text* 66 (2001): 45–73.

———. *The Practice of Diaspora: Literature, Translation, and the Rise of Black Internationalism*. Cambridge, MA: Harvard University Press, 2003a.

———. "The Shadow of Shadows." *Positions* 11, no. 1 (2003b): 11–49.

Elias, Norbert. *Über den Prozess der Zivilisation*. 1969. Reprint, Munich: Franke Verlag Bern, 1969.

Eliot, T. S. "Notes Towards the Definition of Culture." In *Christianity and Culture*. New York: Harcourt, Brace & World, 1949.

Elizondo, Virgilio. *The Future Is Mestizo: Life Where Culture Meets*. Denver: University Press of Colorado, 2000.

Ellison, Julie. *Cato's Tears and the Making of Anglo-American Emotion*. Chicago: University of Chicago Press, 1999.

"El Plan Espiritual de Aztlán." *El Grito del Norte* 2, no. 9 (July 6, 1969). Reprinted in *Aztlan: An Anthology of Mexican American Literature*, edited by Louis Valdez and Stan Steiner. New York: Vintage, 1972.

Emerson, Ralph Waldo. "The American Scholar." 1837. Reprinted in *Selected Lectures and Poems*, edited by Robert D. Richardson, Jr., 82–100. New York: Bantam, 1990.

———. "Self-Reliance." 1841. Reprinted in *Selected Essays, Lectures, and Poems*, edited by Robert D. Richardson, Jr., 148–71. New York: Bantam, 1990.

———. "Art." In *Essays and Lectures*. New York: Library of America, 1983a.

———. "Man the Reformer." In *Essays and Lectures*, 135–50. New York: Library of America, 1983.

Eng, David. *Racial Castration: Managing Masculinity in Asian America*. Durham, NC: Duke University Press, 2001.

Eng, David, Judith Halberstam, and Jose Munoz. "Introduction: What's Queer about Queer Studies Now?" *Social Text* 84–85 (Fall/Winter 2005): 1–17.

Engels, Frederick. *The Origins of the Family, Private Property, and the State*. 1884. Reprint, New York: Pathfinder Press, 1972.

Enloe, Cynthia. *Bananas, Beaches, and Bases: Making Feminist Sense of International Politics*. London: Pandora; Berkley: University of California Press, 1989.

Epstein, Steven. *Impure Science: AIDS, Activism, and the Politics of Knowledge, Medicine and Society.* Berkeley: University of California Press, 1996.

Escobar, Arturo. *Encountering Development: The Making and Unmaking of the Third World.* Princeton: Princeton University Press, 1995.

Escoffier, Jeffrey, and Allan Bérubé. "Queer/Nation." *OUT/LOOK: National Lesbian and Gay Quarterly* 11 (1991): 14–16.

Ettelbrick, Paula. "Since When Is Marriage the Path to Liberation?" *OUT/LOOK: National Lesbian and Gay Quarterly* 2 (1989): 14–16.

Etzioni, Amitai. *The Spirit of Community: Rights, Responsibilities, and The Communitarian Agenda.* New York: Crown, 1993.

Falk, Richard. "The Making of Global Citizenship." In *The Condition of Citizenship*, edited by Bart Van Steenbergen, 127–40. London: Sage, 1994.

Fanon, Frantz. *The Wretched of the Earth.* Translated by Constance Farrington. New York: Grove Press, 1963.

———. *A Dying Colonialism.* New York: Grove Press, 1967.

Fanuzzi, Robert. *Abolition's Public Sphere.* Minneapolis: University of Minnesota Press, 2003.

Fausto-Sterling, Anne. *Myths of Gender: Biological Theories about Women and Men.* New York: Basic Books, 1985.

———. "The Five Sexes: Why Male and Female Are Not Enough." *The Sciences* (March–April 1993): 20–24.

———. *Sexing the Body: Gender Politics and the Construction of Sexuality.* New York: Basic Books, 2000.

Ferguson, Roderick A. "The Stratifications of Normativity." *Rhizomes* 10 (2005), http://www.rhizomes.net/issue10/ferguson.htm.

———. *Aberrations in Black: Toward a Queer of Color Critique.* Minneapolis: University of Minnesota Press, 2004.

Fetterley, Judith, and Marjorie Pryse. *Writing out of Place: Regionalism, Women, and American Literary Culture.* Urbana: University of Illinois Press, 2003.

Filmer, Sir Robert. *Patriarcha, or, the Natural Power of Kings.* London, 1680.

Fish, Stanley. "Professor Sokal's Bad Joke." *New York Times*, May 21, 1996, A23.

Fishkin, Shelley Fisher, and David Bradley, eds. *Sport of the Gods and Other Essential Writing by Paul Laurence Dunbar.* New York: Random House/Modern Library, 2005.

Fisk, Clinton B. *Plain Counsels for Freedmen: In Sixteen Brief Lectures.* Boston, 1866.

Fliegelman, Jay. *Prodigals and Pilgrims: The American Revolution against Patriarchal Authority, 1750–1800.* New York: Cambridge University Press, 1982.

———. *Declaring Independence: Jefferson, Natural Language, and the Culture of Performance.* Stanford, CA: Stanford University Press, 1993.

Florida, Richard. *The Rise of the Creative Class.* New York: Basic Books, 2002.

Foote, Stephanie. *Regional Fictions: Culture and Identity in Nineteenth-Century American Literature.* Madison: University of Wisconsin Press, 2001.

———. "The Cultural Work of American Regionalism." In *A Companion to the Regional Literatures of America*, edited by Charles L. Crow, 25–41. Malden, MA: Blackwell Pub, 2003.

Forbes, Jack D. *Africans and Native Americans: The Language of Race and the Evolution of Red-Black Peoples.* 2d ed. Urbana: University of Illinois Press, 1992.

Foster, Tom. " 'The Souls of Cyberfolk': Performativity, Virtual Embodiment, and Racial Histories." In *Cyberspace Textualities: Computer Technology and Literary Theory*, edited by Marie-Laure Ryan, 137–63. Bloomington: Indiana University Press, 1999.

Foucault, Michel. *Discipline and Punish: The Birth of the Prison.* Translated by Alan Sheridan. New York: Random House, 1975.

———. *The History of Sexuality*, vol. 1, *An Introduction*. Translated by Robert Hurley. New York: Random House, 1978.

———. "The Subject and Power." In Hubert L. Dreyfus and Paul Rabinow, *Michel Foucault: Beyond Structuralism and Hermeneutics*. Chicago: University of Chicago Press, 1982.

———. "Governmentality." In *The Foucault Effect: Studies in Governmentality*, edited by Graham Burchell, Colin Gordon, and Peter Miller, 87–104. Chicago: University of Chicago Press, 1991.

———. *Essential Works of Foucault, 1954–1984*, vol. 1, *Ethics*. New York: New Press, 2006.

Fowler, O. S. *Education and Self-Improvement*. New York: O. S. and L. N. Fowler, 1844.

Fox, Claire. *The Fence and the River: Culture and Politics at the U.S.-Mexico Border*. Minneapolis: University of Minnesota Press, 1999.

Fox, Richard. "The Breakdown of Culture." *Current Anthropology* 36 (1995): 1–2.

Franke, Andre Gunder. *ReOrient: Global Economy in the Asian Age*. Berkeley: University of California Press, 1998.

Franke, Katherine M. "Becoming a Citizen: Reconstruction-Era Regulation of African-American Marriages." *Yale Journal of Law and the Humanities* 11, no. 2 (1999): 251–309.

Frankenberg, Ruth. *White Women, Race Matters: The Social Construction of Whiteness*. Minneapolis: University of Minnesota Press, 1993.

Fredrickson, George. *White Supremacy: A Comparative Study in American and South African History*. Oxford: Oxford University Press, 1981.

Fregoso, Rosa Linda. *MeXicana Encounters: The Making of Social Identities on the Borderlands*. Berkeley: University of California Press: 2003

Freyre, Gilberto. *Casa Grande e Senzala: Formação da Familia sob o Regime da Familia Patriarcal*. Rio de Janeiro: José Olimpio, 1933. Published in English as *The Masters and the Slaves*. New York: Alfred A. Knopf, 1956.

Friedan, Betty. *The Feminine Mystique*. New York: Dell, 1963.

Friedman, Lawrence M. *American Law in the Twentieth Century*. New Haven: Yale University Press, 2002.

Friedman, Thomas L. *The Lexus and the Olive Tree: Understanding Globalization*. New York: Farrar, Strauss, Giroux, 2000.

———. *The World Is Flat: A Brief History of the Twenty-First Century*. New York: Farrar, Strauss, Giroux, 2005.

Fujitani, Takeshi, Geoffrey Wright, and Lisa Yoneyama, eds. *Perilous Memories: The Asian Pacific Wars*. Durham, NC: Duke University Press, 2001.

Fukuyama, Francis. *Trust: The Social Virtues and the Creation of Prosperity*. New York: The Free Press, 1995.

Gaines, Kevin K. *American Africans in Ghana: Black Expatriates and the Civil Rights Era*. Chapel Hill: University of North Carolina Press, 2006.

Gallagher, Charles. "White Racial Formation: Into the Twenty-First Century." In *Critical White Studies: Looking behind the Mirror*, edited by Richard Delgado and Jean Stefancic, 6–11. Philadelphia: Temple University Press, 1997.

Gamber, Wendy. *The Female Economy: The Millinery and Dressmaking Trades, 1860–1930*. Urbana: University of Illinois Press, 1997.

García Canclini, Néstor. *Hybrid Cultures*. Translated by Christopher Chippari and Silvia López. Minneapolis: University of Minnesota Press, 1995.

———. *Diferentes, desiguales y desconectados. Mapas de la interculturalidad*. Barcelona: Gedisa, 2004.

Geertz, Clifford. "Religion as a Cultural System." In *Reader in Comparative Religion: An Anthropological Approach*, 2d rev. and enlarged ed., edited by William Armand Lessa and Evon Zartman Vogt, 204–13. New York: Harper and Row, 1965.

Genovese, Eugene D. *From Revolution to Rebellion: Afro-American Slave Revolts in the Making of the Modern World*. Baton Rouge: Louisiana State University Press, 1979.

Georgacas, Demetrius J. "The Name *Asia* for the Continent: Its History and Origin." *Names* 17, no. 1 (1969): 1–90.

Gibson-Graham, J. K. *The End of Capitalism (as We Knew It): A Feminist Critique of Political Economy*. Cambridge, MA: Blackwell, 1996.

Gibson-Graham, J. K., Stephen Resnick, and Richard Wolff, eds. *Re/Presenting Class: Essays in Postmodern Marxism*. Durham, NC: Duke University Press, 2001.

Giles, Paul. *Transatlantic Insurrections: British Culture and the Formation of American Literature, 1730–1860*. Philadelphia: University of Pennsylvania Press, 2001.

———. "Transnationalism and Classic American Literature" *PMLA* 118, no. 1 (2003): 62–77.

Gilman, Nils. *Mandarins of the Future: Modernization Theory in Cold War America*. Baltimore: Johns Hopkins University Press, 2003.

Gilman, Sander. "Black Bodies, White Bodies: Toward an Iconography of Female Sexuality in Late Nineteenth Century Art, Medicine, and Literature." In *"Race," Writing, and Difference*, edited by Henry Louis Gates, Jr., 223–61. Chicago: University of Chicago Press, 1986.

———. *Picturing Health and Illness: Images of Identity and Difference*. Baltimore: Johns Hopkins University Press, 1995.

Gilmore, Grant. *The Death of Contract*. Columbus: Ohio State University Press, 1974.

Gilmore, Michael T. *American Romanticism and the Marketplace*. Chicago: University of Chicago Press, 1985.

Gilmore, R. W. "Globalisation and U.S. Prison Growth: From Military Keynesianism to Post-Keynesian Militarism." *Race and Class* 40, nos. 2–3 (1998): 171–88.

Gilroy, Paul. *"There Ain't No Black in the Union Jack": The Cultural Politics of Race and Nation*. Chicago: University of Chicago Press, 1987.

———. *The Black Atlantic: Modernity and Double Consciousness*. Cambridge, MA: Harvard University Press, 1993.

Ginsburg, Faye T. *Contested Lives: The Abortion Debate in an American Community*. Berkeley: University of California Press, 1998.

Glazer, Nathan. *Ethnic Dilemmas, 1964–1982*. Cambridge, MA: Harvard University Press, 1983.

Glenn, Evelyn Nakano. *Unequal Citizenship: How Race and Gender Shaped American Citizenship and Labor*. Cambridge, MA: Harvard University Press, 2004.

Glickman, Lawrence B. *A Living Wage: American Workers and the Making of Consumer Society*. Ithaca, NY: Cornell University Press, 1997.

Gobineau, Arthur. *The Inequality of Human Races*. 1853–55. Translated by Adrian Collins. New York: H. Fertig, 1967.

Goffman, Erving. *The Presentation of Self in Everyday Life*. Garden City, NY: Doubleday, 1959.

Goldberg, David Theo. *Racist Culture: Philosophy and the Politics of Meaning*. Cambridge, MA: Blackwell, 1993.

Goldberg, Jonathan. *Sodometries: Renaissance Texts, Modern Sexualities*. Stanford: Stanford University Press, 1992.

Gómez-Peña, Guillermo. *Border Brujo*. Videocassette recording. Cinewest Productions, 1990.

Goodman, Audrey. *Translating the Southwest: The Making of an Anglo Literary Region*. Tucson: University of Arizona Press, 2002.

Goodman, Paul. *Of One Blood: Abolitionism and the Origins of Racial Equality*. Berkeley: University of California Press, 1998.

Gopinath, Gayatri. *Impossible Desires: Queer Diasporas and South Asian Public Cultures*. Durham, NC: Duke University Press, 2005.

Gordley, James. *The Philosophical Origins of Modern Contract Doctrine*. New York: Clarendon Press, 1991.

Gordon, David M. *Fat and Mean: The Corporate Squeeze of Working Americans and the Myth of Managerial "Downsizing."* New York: Free Press, 1996.

Gordon, Edmund T. *Disparate Diasporas: Identity and Politics in an African Nicaraguan Community*. Austin: University of Texas Press, 1998.

Gould, Stephen Jay. *The Mismeasure of Man.* New York: W. W. Norton, 1981.

———. "The Hottentot Venus." *Natural History* 91, no. 10 (1982): 20–25.

Graeber, David. "The New Anarchists." *New Left Review* 13 (2002): 61–73.

Graff, Gerald. *Professing Literature: An Institutional History.* Chicago: University of Chicago Press, 1987.

Gramsci, Antonio. *Selections from the Prison Notebooks.* Edited and translated by Quintin Hoare and Geoffrey Nowell Smith. New York: International Publishers, 1971.

Grant, Madison. *The Passing of the Great Race, or, the Racial Basis of European History.* New York: Charles Scribner, 1916.

Green, Dan S., and Edwin D. Driver. *W. E. B. Du Bois: On Sociology and the Black Community.* Chicago: University of Chicago Press, 1978.

Griffin, Susan. *Woman and Nature: The Roaring inside Her.* New York: Harper and Row, 1978.

Gruen, Erich S. "Diaspora and Homeland." In *Diasporas and Exiles: Varities of Jewish Identity,* edited by Howard Wettstein, 18–46. Berkeley: University of California Press, 2002.

Gruesz, Kirsten Silva. *Ambassadors of Culture: The Transamerican Origins of Latino Writing.* Princeton: Princeton University Press, 2002.

Gulbenkian Commission. *Open the Social Sciences: Report of the Gulbenkian Commission on the Restructuring of the Social Sciences.* Edited by Immaneul Wallerstein et al. Palo Alto, CA: Stanford University Press, 1996.

Gupta, Akhil, and James Ferguson. "Beyond 'Culture': Space, Identity and the Politics of Difference." *Cultural Anthropology* 7, no. 1 (1992): 6–23.

Gustafson, Sandra M. *Eloquence Is Power: Oratory and Performance in Early America.* Chapel Hill: University of North Carolina Press, 2000.

Guterson, David. *Snow Falling on Cedars: A Novel.* New York: Vintage, 1995.

Gutiérrez-Jones, Carl. "Desiring B/orders." *diacritics* 25, no. 2 (1995): 99–112.

Gutman, Herbert G. *Work, Culture, and Society in Industrializing America.* New York: Vintage, 1976.

Habermas, Jürgen. *The Philosophical Discourse of Modernity: Twelve Lectures.* Translated by Frederick Lawrence. Cambridge: Polity Press, 1987.

———. *The Structural Transformation of the Public Sphere: An Inquiry into a Category of Bourgeois Society.* Translated by Thomas Burger. Cambridge, MA: MIT Press, 1999.

Halberstam, Judith. *Female Masculinity.* Durham, NC: Duke University Press, 1998.

———. *In a Queer Time and Place: Transgender Bodies, Subcultural Lives.* New York: New York University Press, 2005.

Hale, Charles R. "Between Che Guevara and the Pachamama: Mestizos, Indians, and Identity Politics in the Anti-Quincentenary Campaign." *Critique of Anthropology* 14, no. 1 (1994): 9–39.

Hall, David D. *Cultures of Print: Essays in the History of the Book.* Amherst: University of Massachusetts Press, 1996.

Hall, Edward. *The Hidden Dimension.* Garden City, NY: Doubleday, 1969.

Hall, Gwendolyn Midlo. *Africans in Colonial Louisiana: The Development of Afro-Creole Culture in the Eighteenth Century.* Baton Rouge: Louisiana State University Press, 1992.

Hall, Stuart. *Policing the Crisis: Mugging, the State and Law and Order.* New York: Holmes and Meier, 1978.

———. "Cultural Identity and Diaspora." In *Identity: Community, Culture, Difference,* edited by Jonathan Rutherford, 222–37. London: Lawrence and Wishart, 1990.

———. "Cultural Studies and Its Theoretical Legacies." In *Cultural Studies Reader,* edited by Lawrence Grossberg, Cary Nelson, and Paula Treichler, 277–94. New York: Routledge, 1991.

———. "Culture, Community, Nation." *Cultural Studies 7*, no. 3 (1993): 349–63.

———. "Race, Articulation, and Societies Structured in Dominance." In *Race Critical Theories: Text and Context*, edited by Philomena Essed and David Theo Goldberg, 38–68. Malden, MA: Blackwell, 2002.

Hall, Stuart, and Bram Gieben, eds. *Formations of Modernity*. Cambridge: Polity Press, 1992.

Halley, Janet E. *Don't: A Reader's Guide to the Military's Anti-Gay Policy*. Durham, NC: Duke University Press, 1999.

Halttunen, Karen. *Confidence Men and Painted Women: A Study of Middle-Class Culture in America, 1830–1870*. New Haven: Yale University Press, 1982.

Hamburger, Philip. *Separation of Church and State*. Cambridge, MA: Harvard University Press, 2002.

Hames-Garcia, Michael. "How to Tell a Mestizo from an Enchirito: Colonialism and National Culture in the Borderlands." *diacritics* 30, no. 4 (2000): 102–22.

Hammer, Michael, and James A. Champy. *Reengineering the Corporation: A Manifesto for Business Revolution*. New York: HarperCollins, 1993.

Hammonds, Evelynn. "Toward a Genealogy of Black Female Sexuality: The Problematic of Silence." In *Feminist Genealogies, Colonial Legacies, Democratic Futures*, edited by M. Jacqui Alexander and Chandra Talpade Mohanty, 170–82. New York: Routledge, 1997.

Hanchard, Michael. *Party/Politics: Horizons in Black Political Thought*. Oxford: Oxford University Press, 2006.

Haney-Lopez, Ian F. *White by Law: The Legal Construction of Race*. New York: New York University Press, 1996.

Hannerz, U. *Cultural Complexity: Studies in the Social Organization of Meaning*. New York: Columbia, 1992.

Haraway, Donna. *Simians, Cyborgs, and Women: The Re-Invention of Nature*. New York: Routledge, 1991.

Hardin, Garrett. "The Tragedy of the Commons." *Science* (new series) 162, no. 3859 (1968): 1243–48.

Harding, Susan. *The Book of Jerry Falwell: Fundamentalist Language and Politics*. Princeton: Princeton University Press. 2001.

Hardt, Michael, and Antonio Negri. *Empire*. Cambridge, MA: Harvard University Press, 2000.

Harper, Philip Brian. *Framing the Margins: The Social Logic of Postmodern Culture*. New York: Oxford University Press, 1994.

———. *Are We Not Men? Masculine Anxiety and the Problem of African-American Identity*. Oxford: Oxford University Press, 1996.

Harper, Phillip Brian, Anne McClintock, José Esteban Muñoz, and Trish Rosen. "Introduction." *Queer Transexions of Race, Nation, and Gender*, edited by Phillip Brian Harper et al. Special issue of *Social Text* 52–53 (Fall/Winter 1997): 1–4.

Harris, Cheryl. "Whiteness as Property." *Harvard Law Review* 106 (1993): 1707–91.

Harris, Laura. "The Subjunctive Poetics of C. L. R. James's *American Civilization*." Unpublished manuscript, 2005.

Harris, Marvin. *Cannibals and Kings: The Origins of Cultures*. New York: Random House, 1977.

Harrison, Lawrence E., and Samuel P. Huntingon, eds. *Culture Matters: How Values Shape Human Progress*. New York: Basic Books, 2000.

Hartigan John, Jr. "Objectifying 'Poor Whites' and 'White Trash' in Detroit." In *White Trash: Race and Class in America*, edited by Matt Wray and Annalee Newitz, 41–56. New York: Routledge, 1997.

———. *Racial Situations: Class Predicaments of Whiteness in Detroit*. Princeton: Princeton University Press, 1999.

Hartman, Saidiya. *Scenes of Subjection: Terror, Slavery, and Self-Making in Nineteenth-Century America*. New York: Oxford University Press, 1997.

Hartz, Louis. *The Liberal Tradition in America: An Interpretation of American Political Thought since the Revolution*. New York: Harcourt Brace, 1955.

Harvey, David. *The Condition of Postmodernity: An Enquiry*

into the Origins of Cultural Change. Oxford: Blackwell, 1989.

Haskell, Thomas. "Capitalism and the Origins of the Humanitarian Sensibility." *American Historical Review* 90, nos. 2–3 (1985): 339–61, 547–66.

Haskell, Thomas L., and Richard F. Teichgraeber III, eds. *The Culture of the Market: Historical Essays.* New York: Cambridge University Press, 1996.

Hawthorne, Nathaniel. "Earth's Holocaust." *Graham's Lady's and Gentleman's Magazine*. March 1844.

Hay, Denys. *Europe: The Emergence of an Idea*. Edinburgh: Edinburgh University Press, 1957.

Hebdige, Dick. *Subculture: The Meaning of Style*. London: Methuen, 1979.

Hegel, G. W. F. *The Philosophy of History*. 1837. Reprint; translated by J. Sibree. New York: Dover, 1956.

——. *Hegel's Philosophy of Right*. 1821. Translated, edited, and with an introduction by T. M. Knox. Oxford: Claredon Press/Galaxy Books, 1962; reprint, 1979.

Hendler, Glenn. *Public Sentiments: Structures of Feeling in Nineteenth-Century American Literature*. Chapel Hill: University of North Carolina Press, 2001.

Herder, Johann Gottfried von. "On the Change of Taste." 1766. Reprinted in *Herder: Philosophical Writings*, 247–56. Cambridge: Cambridge University Press, 2002.

Herrnstein, Richard J., and Charles Murray. *The Bell Curve: Intelligence and Class Structure in American Life*. New York: Free Press, 1994.

Hietala, Thomas R. *Manifest Design: Anxious Aggrandizement in Late Jacksonian America*. Ithaca, NY: Cornell University Press, 1985.

Higham, John. *Strangers in the Land: Patterns of American Nativism, 1860–1925*. New York: Atheneum, 1963.

Hine, Darlene Clark. "Rape and the Inner Lives of Black Women in the Middle West: Preliminary Thoughts on the Culture of Dissemblance." *Signs* 14, no. 4 (1989): 912–20.

Ho, Fred, ed. *Legacy to Liberation: Politics and Culture of Revolutionary Asian/Pacific America*. San Francisco: AK Press, 2000.

Hobsbawm, Eric. "Introduction: Inventing Tradition." In *The Invention of Tradition*, edited by Eric Hobsbawm and Terence Ranger, 1–14. Cambridge: Cambridge University Press, 1983.

——. *Nations and Nationalism since 1780: Programme, Myth, Reality*. Cambridge: Cambridge University Press, 1990.

Hofmeyr, Isabel. *The Portable Bunyan: A Transnational History of The Pilgrim's Progress*. Princeton: Princeton University Press, 2004.

Hogeland, Lisa Maria, and Mary Klages, et al. *The Aunt Lute Anthology of U.S. Women Writers*: vol. 1, *Seventeenth through Nineteenth Centuries*. San Francisco: Aunt Lute Books, 2004.

Holyoake, George J. *Secularism, the Philosophy of the People*. London, 1854.

Hong, Grace Kyungwon. *The Ruptures of American Capital: Women of Color Feminism and the Culture of Immigrant Labor*. Minneapolis: University of Minnesota Press, 2006.

Honig, Bonnie. "Immigrant America? How Foreignness 'Solves' Democracy's Problems." *Social Text 56* (1998): 1–27.

Hopfyl, Harro, and Martyn P. Thompson. "The History of the Contract as a Motif in Political Thought." *American Historical Review* 84, no. 4 (1979): 919–44.

Horowitz, Tony. *Confederates in the Attic: Dispatches from the Unfinished Civil War*. New York: Vintage, 1999.

Horsman, Reginald. *Race and Manifest Destiny: The Origins of American Racial Anglo-Saxonism*. Cambridge, MA: Harvard University Press, 1981.

Horwitz, Howard. "The Standard Oil Trust as Emersonian Hero." *Raritan* 6, no. 4 (1987): 97–119.

Howard, John. *Men Like That: A Southern Queer History*. Chicago: University of Chicago Press, 2001.

Howard, June. "Introduction: Sarah Orne Jewett and the Traffic in Words." In *New Essays on The Country of the Pointed Firs*, edited by June Howard. Cambridge: Cambridge University Press, 1994.

———. *Publishing the Family*. Durham, NC: Duke University Press, 2001.

Howe, Susan. *The Birth-mark: Unsettling the Wilderness in American Literary History*. Hanover, NH: Wesleyan University Press / University Press of New England, 1993.

Hubbard, Ruth, Mary Sue Henifin, and Barbara Fried. *Women Look at Biology Looking at Women: A Collection of Feminist Critiques*. Cambridge, MA: Schenkman, 1979.

Huntington, Samuel P. *The Clash of Civilizations and the Remaking of World Order*. New York: Simon and Schuster, 1996.

———. "The Hispanic Challenge." *Foreign Policy*, March/April, 2004a, http://www.foreignpolicy.com.

———. *Who Are We: The Challenges to America's National Identity*. New York: Simon and Schuster, 2004b.

Hurtado, Aida. "Relating to Privilege: Seduction and Rejection in the Subordination of White Women and Women of Color." *Signs* 14, no. 4 (1989): 833–55.

Ignatiev, Noel, and John Garvey, eds. *Race Traitor*. London: Routledge, 1996.

Irick, Robert L. *Ch'ing Policy toward the Coolie Trade, 1847–1878*. Taipei: Chinese Materials Center, 1982.

Irvine, Janice. *Disorders of Desire: Sex and Gender in Modern American Sexology*. Philadelphia: Temple University Press, 1990.

Isambard. "Would You Describe Yourself as Queer?" Online posting, May 22, 2004. Urban75 Forums, http://www.urban75.net/vbulletin/archive/index.php/t-76675.html.

Isenberg, Nancy. *Sex and Citizenship in Antebellum America*. Chapel Hill: Univeristy of North Carolina Press, 1998.

Jackson, Jonathan David. "The Social World of Voguing."

Journal for the Anthropological Study of Human Movement 12, no. 2 (2002): 26–42.

Jacobs, Harriet. *Incidents in the Life of a Slave Girl*. 1861. Edited by Nellie Y. McKay and Frances Smith Foster. New York: Norton, 2001.

Jacobson, Matthew Frye. *Whiteness of a Different Color: European Immigrants and the Alchemy of Race*. Cambridge, MA: Harvard University Press, 1998.

———. *Barbarian Virtues: The United States Encounters Foreign Peoples at Home and Abroad, 1876–1917*. New York: Hill and Wang, 2000.

Jakobsen, Janet R. "Is Secularism Less Violent than Religion?" In *Interventions: Activists and Academics Respond to Violence*, edited by Elizabeth A. Castelli and Janet R. Jakobsen, 53–67. New York: Palgrave/Macmillan, 2004.

James, C. L. R. *The Black Jacobins; Toussaint L'Ouverture and the San Domingo Revolution*. New York: Dial Press, 1938.

———. "Every Cook Can Govern: A Study of Democracy in Ancient Greece." In *The Future in the Present: Selected Writings*, 160–74. Westport, CT: Lawrence Hill, 1956.

Jameson, Fredric. *Postmodernism, or The Cultural Logic of Late Capitalism*. Durham, NC: Duke University Press, 1991.

———. "On 'Cultural Studies.' " *Social Text* 36 (1993): 17–52.

Jehlen, Myra, and Michael Warner. *The English Literatures of America, 1500–1800*. New York: Routledge, 1997.

Jefferson, Thomas. "Declaration of Independence." In *Writings*, 19–24. New York: Library of America, 1984a.

———. "Notes on the State of Virginia." In *Writings*, 123–325. New York: Library of America, 1984b.

Jensen, Arthur. "How Much Can We Boost IQ and Scholastic Achievement?" *Harvard Educational Review* 39 (1969): 1–123.

Johnson, Walter. *Soul by Soul: Life inside the Antebellum Slave Market*. Cambridge, MA: Harvard University Press, 1999.

———. "Time and Revolution in African America." In *Rethinking American History in a Global Age*, edited by

Thomas Bender. Berkeley: University of California Press, 2002.

———. "The Pedestal and the Veil: Re-Thinking the Capitalism/Slavery Question." *Journal of the Early Republic* 24 (2004): 299–308.

Jones, Gavin. *Strange Talk: The Politics of Dialect Literature in Gilded Age America*. Berkeley: University of California Press, 1999.

Jordan, Winthrop. *White over Black: American Attitudes toward the Negro 1550–1812*. Baltimore: Pelican Books, 1969.

Joseph, Miranda. *Against the Romance of Community*. Minneapolis: University of Minnesota Press, 2002.

———. "A Debt to Society." In *The Seductions of Community*, edited by Gerald Creed, 199–226. Santa Fe, NM: SAR Press, 2006.

Jung, Moon-Ho. *Coolies and Cane: Race, Labor, and Sugar Production in the Age of Emancipation*. Baltimore: Johns Hopkins University Press, 2006.

Justice, Daniel. *Kynship: The Way of Thorn and Thunder, Book One*. Neyaashiinigmiing, Nawash First Nation: Kegedonce Press, 2005.

Kagan, D., and F. Kagan. *While America Sleeps: Self-Delusion, Military Weakness, and the Threat to Peace Today*. New York: St. Martin's, 2000.

Kallen, Horace. "Democracy versus the Melting-Pot." *The Nation* 100, no. 2590 (February 18, 1915).

Kant, Immanuel. *The Critique of Judgment*. Translated by James Creed Meredith. London: Oxford University Press, 1952.

Kantorowicz, Ernst. *The King's Two Bodies*. Princeton: Princeton University Press, 1957.

Kanter, Rosabeth Moss. *When Giants Learn to Dance*. New York: Free Press, 1990.

Kaplan, Amy. "Nation, Region, Empire." In *The Columbia History of the American Novel*, edited by Emory Elliott et al. New York: Columbia University Press, 1991.

———. "'Left Alone with America': The Absence of Empire in the Study of American Culture." In *Cultures of United States Imperialism*, edited by Amy Kaplan and Donald Pease, 3–21. Durham, NC: Duke University Press, 1993.

———. "Manifest Domesticity." *American Literature* 70 (September 1998): 581–606.

———. *The Anarchy of Empire in the Making of U.S. Culture*. Cambridge, MA: Harvard University Press, 2002.

———. "Violent Belongings and the Questions of Empire Today." Presidential Address to the American Studies Association, Hartford, CT, October 17, 2003. *American Quarterly* 56, no.1 (March 2004): 1–18.

Kaplan, Amy, and Donald E. Pease, eds. *Cultures of United States Imperialism*. Durham, NC: Duke University Press, 1993.

Kaplan, Caren, et al. *Between Women and Nation: Nationalisms, Transnational Feminisms, and the State*. Durham, NC: Duke University Press, 1999.

Kaplan, Carla. *The Erotics of Talk: Women's Writing and Feminist Paradigms*. New York: Oxford University Press, 1996.

Kaplan, Morris. *Sexual Justice: Democratic Citizenship and the Politics of Desire*. New York: Routledge, 1997.

Keane, John. *Global Civil Society?* Cambridge: Cambridge University Press, 2003.

Keller, Evelyn Fox. *Reflections on Gender and Science*. New Haven: Yale University Press, 1985.

Kelley, Robin D.G. *Race Rebels: Culture, Politics, and the Black Working Class*. New York: Free Press, 1994.

Kempadoo Kamala, and Jo Doezema, eds. *Global Sex Workers: Rights, Resistance and Redefinition*. New York, Routledge, 1998.

Ken Burns's America. New York: PBS Home Video; Turner Home Entertainment, 1996.

Keohane R. O., and J. S. Nye. *Power and Independence*. Glenview, IL: Scott, Foresman, 1989.

Kerber, Linda K. *Women of the Republic: Intellect and Ideology in Revolutionary America*. New York: W. W. Norton, 1986;

reprint, Chapel Hill: University of North Carolina Press, 1980.

Kerber, Linda K., and Jane Sherron De Hart. *Women's America: Refocusing the Past*. 5th ed. New York: Oxford University Press, 2004.

Kernan, Alvin. *The Death of Literature*. New Haven: Yale University Press, 1990.

Kersten, Holger. "Using the Immigrant's Voice: Humor and Pathos in Nineteenth-Century 'Dutch' Dialect Texts." *Melus 21*, no. 4 (1996): 3–18.

———. "The Creative Potential of Dialect Writing in Later-Nineteenth-Century America." *Nineteenth-Century Literature* 55, no.1 (2000): 92–117.

Kessler, Suzanne J. *Lessons from the Intersexed*. New Brunswick, NJ: Rutgers University Press, 1998.

Kessler, Suzanne J., and Wendy McKenna. *Gender: An Ethnomethodological Approach*. Chicago: University of Chicago Press, 1990.

Kessler-Harris, Alice. *A Woman's Wage: Historical Meanings and Social Consequence*. Lexington: University of Kentucky Press, 1990.

Kim, Ahan. "Poll Finds Many Want Restrictions on Arab Americans." *Seattle Post-Intelligencer* 19 (2001).

Kingston, Maxine Hong. *China Men*. New York: Vintage, 1989.

Kipling, Rudyard. "The White Man's Burden." *McClure's Magazine* (February 1899): 240–41.

Kirkland, Caroline M. *A New Home—Who'll Follow? Or, Glimpses of Western Life*. 1839. Edited by Sandra A. Zagarell. New Brunswick, NJ: Rutgers University Press, 1990.

Kochhar-Lindgren, Kanta. *Hearing Difference: The Third Ear in Experimental, Deaf, and Multicultural Performance*. Washintgon, D.C.: Gallaudet University Press, 2006.

Kolchin, Peter. "Whiteness Studies: The New History of Race in America." *Journal of American History* 89 (2002): 154–74.

Kosselleck, Reinhart. *Futures Past: On the Semantics of Historical Time*. Translated by Keith Tribe. Cambridge, MA: MIT Press, 1985.

Kolodny, Annette. *The Lay of the Land: Metaphor as Experience and History in American Letters*. Chapel Hill: University of North Carolina Press, 1975.

Kotkin, Joel, and Erika Ozuna. "The Mestizo Valley." In *The Changing Face of the San Fernando Valley*. Davenport Institute Research Report. Malibu, CA: School of Public Policy, Pepperdine University, 2002.

Krapp, George Philip. *The English Language in America*. 2 vols. New York: The Century, 1925.

———. "The Psychology of Dialect Writing." *The Bookman* 63 (1926): 522–27.

Kroeber, Alfred Louis. "The Superorganic." *American Anthropologist* 19 (1917): 163–213.

Kroeber, Alfred Louis, and Clyde Kluckhohn. *Culture: A Critical Review of Concepts and Definitions*. New York: Vintage, 1952.

Krugman, Paul. *The Age of Diminished Expectations: U.S. Economic Policy in the 1990s*. Cambridge, MA: MIT Press, 1997.

Krugman, Paul, and Robin Wells. *Microeconomics*. New York: Worth Publishers, 2004.

Kuppers, Petra. *Disability and Contemporary Performance: Bodies on Edge*. New York: Routledge, 2003.

Lacey, Nicola. "Community in Legal Theory: Idea, Ideal or Ideology." *Studies in Law, Politics and Society* 15 (1996): 105–46.

Lacey, Nicola, and Lucia Zedner. "Discourses of Community in Criminal Justice." *Journal of Law and Society* 22, no. 3 (1995): 301–25.

Laclau, Ernesto. *New Reflections on the Revolution of Our Time*. London: Verso, 1990.

———, ed. *The Making of Political Identities*. London: Verso, 1994.

LaFeber, Walter. *The New Empire: An Interpretation of Ameri-*

can Expansion, 1860–1898. Ithaca, NY: Cornell University Press, 1963.

Lakoff, George. "Metaphor and War: The Metaphor System Used to Justify War in the Gulf." (1991), http://www.arieverhagen.nl/11-sept-01/Lakoff_1991.html

Landry, Charles. The Creative City: A Toolkit for Urban Innovators. London: Earthscan Publications, 2000.

Laqueur, Thomas. Making Sex: Body and Gender from the Greeks to Freud. Cambridge, MA: Harvard University Press, 1990.

Larsen, Nella. Passing. New York: Alfred A. Knopf, 1929.

Latour, Bruno. "Why Has Critique Run Out of Steam? From Matters of Fact to Matters of Concern." Critical Inquiry 30, no. 2 (2004): 225–48.

Lauter, Paul. "The Literatures of America: A Comparative Discipline." In Redefining American Literary History, edited by A. La Vonne Brown Ruoff and Jerry W. Ward, Jr., 9-34. New York: MLA Press, 1990.

Lears, Jackson. No Place of Grace: Antimodernism and the Transformation of American Culture, 1880–1920. New York: Pantheon, 1981.

Lederer, Richard M. Colonial American English: A Glossary. Essex, CT: Verbatim, 1985.

Lee, James Kyung-Jin. Urban Triage: Race and the Fictions of Multiculturalism. Minneapolis: Minnesota, 2004.

Lévi-Strauss, Claude. Cultural Anthropology. New York: Anchor Books, 1963.

———. The Elementary Structures of Kinship. Boston: Beacon Press, 1971.

Levine, Lawrence. Highbrow, Lowbrow: The Emergence of Cultural Hierarchy in America. Cambridge, MA: Harvard University Press, 1988.

Levine, Robert. Martin Delany, Frederick Douglass, and the Politics of Representative Identity. Chapel Hill: University of North Carolina Press, 1997.

Lewis, Earl. "To Turn as on a Pivot: Writing African Americans into a History of Overlapping Diasporas." American Historical Review 100 (June 1995): 765–87.

Lewis, Oscar. Five Families: Mexican Case Studies in the Culture of Poverty. New York: Basic Books, 1959.

Lewis, R.W.B. The American Adam: Innocence, Tradition and Tragedy in the Nineteenth Century. Chicago: University of Chicago Press, 1955.

Lewis, Victoria Ann, ed. Beyond Victims and Villains: Contemporary Plays by Disabled Playwrights. New York: Theatre Communications Group, 2005.

Lichtenstein, Nelson. State of the Union: A Century of American Labor. Princeton: Princeton University Press, 2002.

Limerick, Patricia Nelson. "The Trail to Santa Fe: The Unleashing of the Western Public Intellectual." In Trails: Toward a New Western History, edited by Patricia Nelson Limerick, Clyde A. Milner II, and Charles E. Rankin, 59–80. Lawrence: University of Kansas Press, 1991.

Limon, José. American Encounters: Greater Mexico, the United States, and the Erotics of Culture. Boston: Beacon, 1999.

Linton, Simi. Claiming Disability: Knowledge and Identity. Cultural Front Series. New York: New York University Press, 1998.

Lippmann, Walter. The Phantom Public. New York: Macmillan, 1927.

Lipset, Seymour. The First New Nation: The United States in Historical and Comparative Perspective. New York: Basic Books, 1963.

Lipsitz, George. "The Possessive Investment in Whiteness: Racialized Social Democracy and the 'White' Problem in American Studies." American Quarterly 47, no. 3 (1995): 369–87.

———. The Possessive Investment in Whiteness: How White People Profit from Identity Politics. Philadelphia: Temple University Press, 1998.

———. American Studies in a Moment of Danger. Minneapolis: University of Minnesota, 2001.

Lloyd, David, and Paul Thomas. "Culture and Society or 'Culture and the State'?" In *Cultural Materialism: On Raymond Williams*, edited by Christopher Prendergast, 268–304. Minneapolis: University of Minnesota Press, 1995.

———. *Culture and the State*. New York: Routledge, 1998.

Locke, John. *Second Treatise of Government*. Edited by C. B. Macpherson. Indianapolis: Hackett, 1980.

———. *Two Treatises of Government*. 1690. Edited with an Introduction by Peter Laslett. New York: Cambridge University Press, 1988.

London, Jack. *The People of the Abyss*. New York: Lawrence Hill, 1903.

Longmore, Paul. *Why I Burned My Book and Other Essays on Disability*. American Subjects. Philadelphia: Temple University Press, 2003.

Longmore, Paul, and Lauri Umansky, eds. *The New Disability History: American Perspectives*. History of Disability. New York: New York University Press, 2001.

Loraux, Nicole. *Mothers in Mourning*. Ithaca, NY: Cornell University Press, 1998.

Lott, Eric. *Love and Theft: Blackface Minstrelsy and the American Working Class*. New York: Oxford University Press, 1993.

Lowe, Lisa. *Immigrant Acts: On Asian American Cultural Politics*. Durham, NC: Duke University Press, 1996.

———. "The Intimacies of Four Continents." In *Haunted by Empire: Geographies of Intimacy in North American History*, edited by Ann Laura Stoler, 191–212. Durham, NC: Duke University Press, 2006.

Lowe, Lisa, and David Lloyd, eds. *The Politics of Culture in the Shadow of Capital*. Durham, NC: Duke University Press, 1997.

Luibhéid, Eithne. *Entry Denied: Controlling Sexuality at the Border*. Minneapolis: University of Minnesota Press, 2002.

Luibhéid, Eithne, and Lionel Cantú, eds. *Queer Migrations: Sexuality, U.S. Citizenship, and Border Crossings*. Minneapolis: University of Minnesota, 2005.

Lye, Colleen. *America's Asia: Racial Forms and American Literature, 1893–1945*. Princeton: Princeton University Press, 2004.

Lyman, Stanford M. *Civilization: Contents, Discontents, Malcontents, and Other Essays in Social Theory*. Fayetteville: University of Arkansas Press, 1990.

Macpherson, C. B. *The Political Theory of Possessive Individualism: Hobbes to Locke*. New York: Oxford University Press, 1962.

Maddox, Lucy. *Removals: Nineteenth-Century American Literature and the Politics of Indian Affairs*. New York: Oxford University Press, 1991.

Manalansan, Martin F. *Global Divas: Filipino Gay Men in the Diaspora*. Durham, NC: Duke University Press, 2003.

———. "Queer Intersections: Gender and Sexuality in Migration Studies." *International Migration Review* 40, no. 1 (Spring 2006): 224–49.

Mandel, Ernest. *Late Capitalism*, rev. ed. New York: Schocken Books, 1976.

Marable, Manning. "Introduction: Black Studies and the Racial Mountain." In *Dispatches from the Ebony Tower: Intellectuals Confront the African American Experience*, edited by Manning Marable, 1–30. New York: Columbia University Press, 2000.

Marchand, Ronald. *Creating the Corporate Soul: The Rise of Public Relations and Corporate Imagery in American Big Business*. Berkeley: University of California Press, 1998.

Marcus, George E. *The Sentimental Citizen: Emotion in Democratic Politics*. University Park: Pennsylvania State University Press, 2002.

Marcus, George E., and Michael Fischer. *Anthropology as Cultural Critique: An Experimental Moment in the Human Sciences*. Chicago: University of Chicago Press, 1986.

Marsden, George. *Fundamentalism and American Culture: The*

Works Cited

Shaping of Twentieth-Century Evangelicalism, 1879–1925.
New York: Oxford University Press, 1980.

Marshall, T. H. *Class, Citizenship and Social Development.*
New York: Doubleday Anchor, 1965.

Martí, José. "Our America." 1891. In *Selected Writings*, 288–95. New York: Penguin, 2002.

Martin, Biddy, and Chandra Mohanty. "Feminist Politics: What's Home Got to Do with It." In *Feminist Studies, Critical Studies*, edited by Teresa de Lauretis, 191–212. Bloomington: Indiana University Press, 1986.

Martin, David. *The Religious and the Secular.* London: RK-Press, 1969.

———. *A General Theory of Secularization.* New York: Harper and Row, 1978.

Marx, Karl. *Capital: A Critique of Political Economy.* 3 vols., 1867–94. Translated by Ben Fowkes and David Fernbach. New York: Vintage Books, 1976–81.

———. *The Eighteenth Brumaire of Louis Bonaparte.* Moscow: Progress Publishers, 1954.

———. "On the Jewish Question." In *The Marx-Engels Reader*, 2d ed., edited by Robert Tucker, 26–52. New York: W.W. Norton., 1978.

———. *Grundrisse.* New York: Penguin, 1993.

Marx, Karl, and Friedrich Engels. *The German Ideology.* 1845–46. Edited and with an Introduction by C. J. Arthur. New York: International Publishers, 1972.

———. "Manifesto of the Communist Party." 1848. In *Collected Works*, vol. 6., pp. 477–519. New York: International Publishers, 1976.

Marx, Leo. *The Machine in the Garden: Technology and the Pastoral Ideal in America.* New York: Oxford University Press, 1964.

Mathias, Charles M., Jr. "Ethnic Groups and Foreign Policy." *Foreign Affairs* 59, no. 5 (1981): 975–98.

Matory, J. Lorand. "The English Professors of Brazil: On the Diasporic Roots of the Yorùbá Nation." *Comparative Studies in Social History* 41, no. 1 (1999): 72–103.

Matthews, Glenna. *"Just a Housewife": The Rise and Fall of Domesticity in America.* New York: Oxford University Press, 1987.

Matthiessen, F. O. *American Renaissance: Art and Expression in the Age of Emerson and Whitman.* New York: Oxford University Press, 1941.

May, Henry F. *The Enlightenment in America.* New York: Oxford University Press, 1976.

McAlister, Melanie. *Epic Encounters: Culture, Media and U.S. Interests in the Middle East, 1945–2000.* Berkeley: University of California Press, 2001.

McCarthy, Kevin F., Elizabeth H. Ondaatje, Laura Zakaras, and Arthur C. Brooks. *Gifts of the Muse: Reframing the Debate about the Benefits of the Arts.* Santa Monica, CA: Rand, 2005.

McClintock, Anne. "Family Feuds: Gender, Nationalism and the Family." *Feminist Review* 44 (1993): 61–80.

———. *Imperial Leather: Race and Gender in the Colonial Contest.* Durham, NC: Duke University Press, 1995.

McCullough, Kate. *Regions of Identity: The Construction of America in Women's Fiction, 1885–1914.* Stanford: Stanford University Press, 1999.

McGann, Jerome. *Radiant Textuality: Literature after the World Wide Web.* New York: Palgrave Macmillan, 2001.

McGill, Meredith L. *American Literature and the Culture of Reprinting 1834–1853.* Philadelphia: University of Pennsylvania Press, 2003.

McPherson, Tara. *Reconstructing Dixie: Race, Gender, and Nostalgia in the Imagined South.* Durham, NC: Duke University Press, 2003.

Mead, Margaret. *Cooperation and Competition among Primitive Peoples.* New York: McGraw-Hill, 1937.

———. *And Keep Your Powder Dry: An Anthropologist Looks at America.* 1942. New York: Morrow Quill, 1965.

Mehta, Uday Singh. *Liberalism and Empire: A Study in Nineteenth-Century British Liberal Thought.* Chicago: University of Chicago Press, 1999.

Melville, Herman. *Moby-Dick; or, The Whale*. 1851. Edited by Harrison Hayford, Hershel Parker, and G. Thomas Tanselle. Evanston, IL: Northwestern University Press; Chicago: Newberry Library, 1971.

Merish, Lori. *Sentimental Materialism: Gender, Commodity Culture, and Nineteenth-Century American Literature*. Durham, NC: Duke University Press, 2000.

Meriwether, James H. *Proudly We Can Be Africans: Black Americans and Africa, 1935–1961*. Chapel Hill: University of North Carolina Press, 2002.

Michaels, Walter Benn. "Corporate Fiction." In *The Gold Standard and the Logic of Naturalism*, 181–213. Berkeley: University of California Press, 1987.

———. "The Vanishing American." *American Literary History* 2, no. 2 (1990): 220–41.

Mignolo, Walter. *Local Histories / Global Designs: Coloniality, Subaltern Knowledges, and Border Thinking*. Princeton: Princeton University Press, 2000.

Mill, John Stuart. *Three Essays*. New York: Oxford University Press, 1976.

Miller, Angela. The *Empire of the Eye: Landscape Representation and American Cultural Politics, 1825–1875*. Ithaca, NY: Cornell University Press, 1993.

Miller, Perry. *Errand into the Wilderness*. Cambridge, MA: Harvard University Press, 1960.

Miller, Toby. *The Well-Tempered Self: Citizenship, Culture, and the Postmodern Subject*. Baltimore: Johns Hopkins University Press, 1993.

———. "Introducing . . . Cultural Citizenship." *Social Text* 19, no. 4 (2001): 1–5.

Miller, Toby, et al. *Global Hollywood*. London: British Film Institute, 2001.

Mills, Charles. *The Racial Contract*. Ithaca, NY: Cornell University Press, 1997.

Mindt, Mark L. *Koda the Warrior*. Harvey, ND: Pony Gulch, 2005.

Mintz, Sidney. *Sweetness and Power: The Place of Sugar in Modern History*. New York: Viking, 1985.

Mishra, Vijay. "The Diasporic Imaginary: Theorizing the Indian Diaspora." *Textual Practice* 10, no. 3 (1996): 421–47.

"Mr. Otis's Speech at Fanevil Hall." *The Liberator*, September 5, 1835, 4.

Mitchell, David, and Sharon Snyder, eds. *The Body and Physical Difference: Discourses of Disability*. The Body, in Theory: Histories of Cultural Materialism. Ann Arbor: University of Michigan Press, 1997.

———. *Narrative Prosthesis: Disability and the Dependencies of Discourse*. Corporealities: Discourses of Disability. Ann Arbor: University of Michigan Press, 2001.

Mitchell, Timothy. "The Stage of Modernity." In *Questions of Modernity*, edited by Timothy Mitchell, 1–34. Minneapolis: University of Minnesota Press, 2000.

———. *Rule of Experts: Egypt, Techno-Politics, Modernity*. Berkeley: University of California Press, 2002.

———. "Economists and the Economy in the Twentieth Century." In *The Politics of Method in the Human Sciences: Positivism and Its Epistemological Others*, edited by George Steinmetz, 126–41. Durham, NC: Duke University Press, 2005.

Miyoshi, M. "A Borderless World? From Colonialism to-Transnationalism and the Decline of the Nation State." *Critical Inquiry* 19, no. 4 (1993): 726–51.

Moallem, Minoo. *Between Warrior Brother and Veiled Sister: Islamic Fundamentalism and the Cultural Politics of Patriarchy in Iran*. Berkeley: University of California Press, 2005.

Mohanty, Chandra T. *Feminism without Borders*. Durham, NC: Duke University Press, 2003.

Mohanty, Chandra T., and M. J. Alexander, eds. *Feminist Genealogies, Colonial Legacies, Democratic Futures*. New York: Routledge, 1997.

Mohanty, Chandra T., Anna Russo, and Lourdes Torres.

Third World Women and the Politics of Feminism. Indiana: Indiana University Press, 1991.

Momaday, N. Scott. *House Made of Dawn*. New York: Harper and Row, 1968.

Money, John, and Anke Ehrhardt. *Man and Woman, Boy and Girl: The Differentiation and Dimorphism of Gender Identity from Conception to Maturity*. Baltimore: Johns Hopkins University Press, 1972.

Montagu, Ashley. *Man's Most Dangerous Myth: The Fallacy of Race*. New York: Columbia University Press, 1942.

Moraga, Cherríe, and Gloria Anzaldúa. *This Bridge Called My Back: Writings by Radical Women of Color*. Watertown, MA: Persephone Press, 1981.

Morais, Herbert M. *Deism in Eighteenth-Century America*. New York: Columbia University Press, 1934.

Morgan, Jennifer L. *Laboring Women: Reproduction and Gender in New World Slavery*. Philadelphia: University of Pennsylvania Press, 2004.

Morgan, William. *Questionable Charity: Gender, Humanitarianism, and Complicity in U.S. Literary Realism*. Hanover: University Press of New Hampshire, 2004.

Morone, James A. *Hellfire Nation: The Politics of Sin in American History*. New Haven: Yale University Press, 2003.

Morrison, Toni. *Playing in the Dark: Whiteness in the Literary Imagination*. New York: Random House, 1993.

Moses, Wilson J. *Afrotopia: The Roots of Popular African American History*. Cambridge: Cambridge University Press, 1998.

Mouffe, Chantal. "Democratic Citizenship and the Political Community." In *Dimensions of Radical Democracy: Pluralism, Citizenship and Community*. Ed. Chantal Mouffe. London: Verso, 1992.

———. "Citizenship." In *The Encyclopedia of Democracy*, edited by Seymour Martin Lipset, vol. 1, pp. 217–21. Washington: Congressional Quarterly, 1995.

Moynihan, Daniel Patrick. *The Negro Family: The Case for National Action*. Washington, D.C.: U.S. Department of Labor, 1965.

Mumford, Kevin. *Interzones: Black/White Sex Districts in Chicago and New York in the Early Twentieth Century*. New York: Columbia University Press, 1997.

Muñoz, Jose. *Disidentifications: Queers of Color and the Performance of Politics*. Minneapolis: University of Minnesota Press, 1999.

Murphree, Daniel. "Race and Religion on the Periphery: Disappointment and Missionization in the Spanish Floridas, 1566–1763." In *Race, Nation, and Religion in the Americas*, edited by Henry Goldschmidt and Elizabeth McAlister, 35–59. New York: Oxford University Press, 2004.

Myrdal, Gunnar. *An American Dilemma: The Negro Problem and Modern Democracy*. New York: Harper and Brothers, 1944.

Nandy, Ashis. "Dialogue and the Diaspora: Conversation with Nikos Papastergiadis." *Third Text* 11 (1990): 99–108.

Nash, Gary B. *Race, Class, and Politics: Essays on Colonial and Revolutionary Society*. Urbana: University of Illinois Press, 1986.

Nash, Roderick. *Wilderness and the American Mind*. 3d ed. New Haven: Yale University Press, 1982.

Negt, Oskar, and Alexander Kluge. *Public Sphere and Experience: Toward an Analysis of the Bourgeois and Proletarian Public Sphere*. Translated by Peter Labanyi, Jamie Owen Daniel, and Assenka Oksiloff. Minneapolis: University of Minnesota Press, 1993.

Nelson, Benjamin. "Civilizational Complexes and Intercivilizational Encounters." *Sociological Analysis* 34 (1973): 79–105.

Nelson, Cary, ed. *Will Work for Food: Academic Labor in Crisis*. Minneapolis: University of Minnesota Press, 1997.

Nelson, Dana. *The Word in Black and White: Reading 'Race' in*

American Literature, 1638–1867. Oxford: Oxford University Press, 1992.

———. *National Manhood: Capitalist Citizenship and the Imagined Fraternity of White Men.* Durham, NC: Duke University Press, 1998.

Nelson, Jennifer. *Women of Color and the Reproductive Rights Movement.* New York: New York University Press, 2003.

Nevins, Joseph. *Operation Gatekeeper: The Rise of the Illegal Alien and the Making of the U.S.-Mexico Boundary.* New York: Routledge, 2002.

Newfield, Christopher. "Corporate Culture Wars." In *Corporate Futures: The Diffusion of the Culturally Sensitive Corporate Form*, edited by George E. Marcus, 23–62. Chicago: University of Chicago Press, 1998.

Newman, Louise. *White Women's Rights: The Racial Origins of Feminism in the United States.* New York: Oxford University Press, 1999.

New Social History Project. *Who Built America?* 2 vols. New York: Pantheon, 1989, 1992.

Newton, Esther. *Mother Camp: Female Impersonators in America.* Chicago: University of Chicago Press, 1972.

Ngai, Mae. *Impossible Subjects: Illegal Aliens and the Making of Modern America.* Princeton: Princeton University Press, 2004.

Noiriel, Gerárd. *La Tyrannie du National.* Paris: Calmann Levy, 1991.

North, Michael. *The Dialect of Modernism: Race, Language and Twentieth-Century Literature.* New York: Oxford University Press, 1994.

Norton, Mary Beth. *Founding Mothers and Fathers: Gendered Power and the Formation of American Society.* New York: Alfred A. Knopf, 1996.

Oakes, James. "The Peculiar Fate of the Bourgeois Critique of Slavery." *In Slavery and the American South*, edited by Winthrop Jordan, 29–48. Jackson: University of Mississippi Press, 2003.

Oliver, Melvin, and Thomas Shapiro. *Black Wealth, White Wealth: A New Perspective on Racial Inequality.* New York: Routledge, 1995.

Omi, Michael, and Howard Winant. *Racial Formation in the United States: From the 1960s to the 1990s.* 2d ed. New York: Routledge, 1994.

Ong, Aihwa. "Cultural Citizenship as Subject Making: Immigrants Negotiate Racial and Cultural Boundaries in the United States." *Current Anthropology* 37, no. 5 (1996): 737–62.

Ordover, Nancy. *American Eugenics: Race, Queer Anatomy, and the Science of Nationalism.* Minneapolis: University of Minnesota Press, 2003.

Ortiz, Fernando. *El engaño de las razas.* Havana: Editorial Páginas, 1946.

Osborne, Peter. *The Politics of Time: Modernity and Avant-Garde.* New York: Verso, 1995.

Ospina, William. *Mestizo America: The Country of the Future.* New York: Villegas Editores, 2000.

Paine, Thomas. *Common Sense and Other Political Writings.* Indianapolis: Bobbs-Merrill, 1953.

Paranjape, Makarand. "Theorising Postcolonial Difference: Culture, Nation, Civilization." *SPAN: Journal of the South Pacific Association for Commonwealth Literature and Language Studies* 47 (1998): 1–17.

Paredes, Américo. *With His Pistol in His Hand: A Border Ballad and Its Hero.* Austin: University of Texas Press, 1958.

Park, Robert Ezra. *Race and Culture: The Collected Papers of Robert Ezra Park.* Edited by Everett C. Hughes et al. Glencoe, IL: Free Press, 1950.

———. *Human Communities: The City and Human Ecology.* Glencoe, IL: Free Press, 1952.

Parker, Andrew, et al. *Nationalism and Sexualities.* New York: Routledge, 1992.

Parker, Theodore. *Sermons on War.* 1863. Reprint, edited by Frances P. Cobbe. New York: Garland Publishing, 1973.

Parreñas, Rhacel Salazar. *Servants of Globalization: Women,*

Migration and Domestic Work. Stanford: Stanford University Press, 2001.

Pateman, Carole. *The Sexual Contract.* Stanford: Stanford University Press, 1988.

Patterson, Orlando. *Slavery and Social Death: A Comparative Study.* Cambridge, MA: Harvard University Press, 1982.

Patton, Cindy. *Sex and Germs: The Politics of AIDS.* Boston: South End Press, 1985.

———. *Fatal Advice: How Safe-Sex Education Went Wrong.* Series Q. Durham, NC: Duke University Press, 1996.

Payne, Daniel G. *Voices in the Wilderness: American Nature Writing and Environmental Politics.* Hanover, NH: University Press of New England, 1996.

Pease, Donald E. "New Perspectives on U.S. Culture and Imperialism." In *Cultures of United States Imperialism*, edited by Amy Kaplan and Donald E. Pease, 22–37. Durham, NC: Duke University Press, 1993.

Peiss, Kathy. *Cheap Amusements: Working Women and Leisure in Turn-of-the-Century New York.* Philadelphia: Temple University Press, 1986.

Perry, Pamela. *Shades of White: White Kids and Racial Identities in High School.* Durham, NC: Duke University Press, 2002.

Phillips, Kevin. *Wealth and Democracy: A Political History of the American Rich.* New York: Broadway Books, 2002.

Piore, Michael, and Charles F. Sabel. *The Second Industrial Divide: Possibilities for Prosperity.* New York: Basic Books, 1984.

Plummer, Brenda Gayle. *Rising Wind: Black Americans and Foreign Affairs, 1935–1960.* Chapel Hill: University of North Carolina Press, 1996.

Polanyi, Karl. *The Great Transformation.* New York: Farrar and Rinehart, 1944. Reprint, Boston: Beacon Press, 2001.

Pollin, R. *Contours of Descent: U.S. Economic Fractures and the Landscape of Global Austerity.* London: Verso, 2003.

Poovey, Mary. *A History of the Modern Fact: Problems of Knowledge in the Sciences of Wealth and Society.* Chicago: University of Chicago Press, 1998.

Porter, James I. "Foreword." In *The Body and Physical Difference: Discourses of Disability in the Humanities*, edited by David T. Mitchell and Sharon Snyder, xiii–xiv. Ann Arbor: University of Michigan Press, 1997.

Poster, Mark. "CyberDemocracy: Internet and the Public Sphere" (1999). Accessed July 14, 2005, http://www.hnet.uci.edu/mposter/writings/democ.html.

Povinelli, Elizabeth A., and George Chauncey, eds. "Thinking Sexuality Transnationally: An Introduction." *GLQ* 5, no. 4 (1999): 439–50.

Prakash, Gyan. *Another Reason: Science and the Imagination of Modern India.* Princeton: Princeton University Press, 1999.

Prashad, Vijay. *Karma of Brown Folk.* Minneapolis: University of Minnesota Press, 2000.

———. *Everybody Was Kung Fu Fighting: Afro-Asian Connections and the Myth of Cultural Purity.* Boston: Beacon Press, 2001.

Prince, Mary. *The History of Mary Prince.* Edited by Sara Salih. New York: Penguin, 2000.

Prosser, Jay. *Second Skins: The Body Narratives of Transsexuality.* New York: Columbia University Press, 1998.

Putnam, Robert D. "The Prosperous Community." *American Prospect* 13 (1993): 35–42.

———. *Bowling Alone: The Collapse and Revival of American Community.* New York: Simon and Schuster, 2000.

Raboteau, Albert. *Slave Religion: The "Invisible Institution" in the Antebellum South.* New York: Oxford University Press, 1978.

Radway, Jan. "What's in a Name?" In *The Futures of American Studies*, edited by Donald Pease and Robyn Wiegman, 45–75. Durham, NC: Duke University Press, 2002.

Rafael, Vicente. *Contracting Colonialism: Translation and Christian Conversion in Tagalog Society under Early Spanish Rule.* Ithaca, NY: Cornell University Press, 1988.

Rancière, Jacques. *Disagreement: Politics and Philosophy*. Minneapolis: University of Minnesota Press, 1998.

Ransom, John Crowe. "Forms and Citizens." In *The World's Body*. Baton Rouge: Louisiana State University Press, 1965.

Raphael, Ray. *A People's History of the American Revolution*. New York: The New Press, 2001.

Reed, T. V. *The Art of Protest: Culture and Activism from the Civil Rights Movement to the Streets of Seattle*. Minneapolis: University of Minnesota Press, 2005.

———. "Theory and Method in American/Cultural Studies: A Bibliographic Essay," http://www.wsu.edu/%Eamerstu/tm/bib.html.

Renan, Ernest. "What Is a Nation?" 1882. In *Nation and Narration*, edited by Homi K. Bhabha, 8–22. London: Routledge, 1990.

Reynolds, David S. *Beneath the American Renaissance: The Subversive Imagination in the Age of Emerson and Melville*. Cambridge, MA: Harvard University Press, 1989.

———. *John Brown, Abolitionist: The Man Who Killed Slavery, Sparked the Civil War, and Seeded Civil Rights*. New York: Alfred A. Knopf, 2005.

Resnick, S. A., and R. D. Wolff. *Knowledge and Class: A Marxian Critique of Political Economy*. Chicago: University of Chicago Press, 1987.

Rich, Adrienne. "Sources: IV." In *Your Native Land, Your Life*. New York: W. W. Norton, 1986.

Rifkin, Jeremy. *The Age of Access: The New Culture of Hypercapitalism, Where All of Life Is a Paid-for Experience*. New York: Jeremy P. Tarcher/ Putnam, 2000.

Robbins, Bruce, ed. *The Phantom Public Sphere*. Minneapolis: University of Minnesota Press, 1993.

Roberts, Dorothy. *Killing the Black Body: Race, Reproduction, and the Meaning of Liberty*. New York: Vintage, 1998.

Robinson, Cedric J. *Black Marxism: The Making of the Black Radical Tradition*. 1983. Reprint, Chapel Hill: University of North Carolina Press, 2000.

Robinson, Forrest G. "Clio Bereft of Calliope: Literature and the New Western History." In *The New Western History: The Territory Ahead*, edited by Forrest G. Robinson, 61–98. Tucson: University of Arizona Press, 1997.

Roediger, David R. *The Wages of Whiteness: Race and the Making of the American Working Class*. London: Verso, 1991, 1999.

———. *Toward the Abolition of Whiteness: Essays on Race, Politics, and Working Class History*. London: Verso, 1994.

Rogin, Michael. *Ronald Reagan, the Movie, and Other Episodes in Political Demonology*. Berkeley: University of California Press, 1987.

———. *Black Face, White Noise: Jewish Immigrants in the Hollywood Melting Pot*. Berkeley: University of California Press, 1996.

Romero, Lora. *Home Fronts: Domesticity and Its Critics in the Antebellum United States*. Durham, NC: Duke University Press, 1997.

Romero, Mary. *Maid in the U.S.A*. New York: Routledge, 1992.

Roosevelt, Theodore. "True Americanism." *The Forum* (April 1894): 15–31.

Rosa, Andrew Juan. "El Que No Tiene Dingo, Tiene Mandingo: The Inadequacy of the 'Mestizo' as a Theoretical Construct in the Field of Latin American Studies—The Problem and Solution." *Journal of Black Studies* 27, no. 2 (1996): 278–91.

Rosaldo, Michelle Z. "Toward an Anthropology of Self and Feeling." In *Culture Theory: Essays on Mind, Self and Emotion*, edited by Richard A. Shweder and Robert A. LeVine, 137–57. New York: Cambridge University Press, 1984.

Rosaldo, Renato. "Cultural Citizenship, Inequality, and Multiculturalism." In *Race, Identity, and Citizenship: A Reader*, edited by Roldofo D. Torres, Louis F. Miron, and Jonathan Xavier Inda, 253–61. Oxford: Blackwell, 1999.

Rose, Nikolas. *The Powers of Freedom*. Cambridge: Cambridge University Press, 1999.

Rosenberg, Samuel. *American Economic Development since 1945*. New York: Palgrave, 2003.

Ross, Andrew. *No Sweat: Fashion, Free Trade, and the Rights of Garment Workers*. New York: Verso, 1997.

Rossi, Alice S., ed. *The Feminist Papers: From Adams to de Beauvoir*. New York: Columbia University Press, 1973.

Rothenberg, Winifred Barr. *From Market-Places to a Market Economy: The Transformation of Rural Massachusetts, 1750–1850*. Chicago: University of Chicago Press, 1992.

Rousseau, Jean-Jacques. *A Discourse on Inequality*. 1754. Translated by Maurice Cranston. New York: Penguin, 1984.

———. *The Social Contract*. 1762. Translated by Maurice Cranston. London: Penguin Books, 1968.

Rowe, John Carlos, ed. *Post-Nationalist American Studies*. Berkeley: University of California Press, 2000.

Roy, William G. *Socializing Capital: The Rise of the Large Industrial Corporation in America*. Princeton: Princeton University Press, 1997.

Rubin, Gayle. "The Traffic in Women: Notes on the 'Political Economy' of Sex." In *Toward an Anthropology of Women*, edited by Rayna R. Reiter, 157–210. New York: Monthly Review Press, 1975.

———. "Thinking Sex: Notes for a Radical Theory of the Politics of Sexuality." In *Pleasure and Danger: Exploring Female Sexuality*, edited by Carole S. Vance, 267–319. Boston: Routledge and Kegan Paul, 1984.

———. "Studying Sexual Subcultures: Excavating the Ethnography of Gay Communities in Urban North America." In *Out in Theory: The Emergence of Lesbian and Gay Anthropology*, edited by Ellen Lewin and William L. Leap, 17–67. Chicago: University of Illinois Press, 2002.

Ruccio, David F. "Globalization and Imperialism." *Rethinking Marxism* 15 (2003.): 75–94.

Ruccio, David F., and J. K. Gibson-Graham. "'After' Development: Reimagining Economy and Class." In *Re/presenting Class: Essays in Postmodern Political Economy*, edited by J. K. Gibson-Graham, Stephen Resnick, and Richard D. Wolff, 158–81. Durham, NC: Duke University Press, 2001.

Russ, Joanna. "Speculations: The Subjunctivity of Science Fiction." In *To Write Like a Woman: Essays in Feminism and Science Fiction*, 15–25. Bloomington: Indiana University Press, 1995.

Ryan, Mary P. *Womanhood in American from Colonial Times to the Present*. New York: New Viewpoints, 1975.

———. *Cradle of the Middle Class: The Family in Oneida County, New York, 1790–1865*. New York: Cambridge University Press, 1981.

Rybczynski, Witold. *Home: A Short History of an Idea*. London: Longman, 1988.

Safran, William. "Diasporas in Modern Societies: Myths of Homeland and Return." *Diaspora* 1, no. 1 (1991): 83–99.

Said, Edward. *Orientalism*. New York: Vintage, 1978.

———. *Culture and Imperialism*. New York: Random House, 1993.

Sakai, Naoki. "'You Asians': On the Historical Role of the West and Asia Binary." *South Atlantic Quarterly* 99, no. 4 (2000): 789–817.

Saks, Eva. "Representing Miscegenation Law." *Raritan* 8 (1988): 39–69.

Saldaña-Portillo, María Josefina. "Who's the Indian in Aztlan?" In *Latin American Subaltern Studies Reader*, edited by Ileana Rodriguez, 402–23. Durham, NC: Duke University Press, 2001.

———. *The Revolutionary Imagination in the Americas and the Age of Development*. Durham, NC: Duke University Press, 2003.

Saldívar, José David. *Border Matters: Remapping American Cultural Studies*. Berkeley: University of California Press, 1997.

Samuels, Ellen. "Critical Divides: Judith Butler's Body Theory and the Question of Disability." *NWSA Journal* 14, no. 3 (2002): 58–76.

Samuels, Shirley. *Romances of the Republic: Women, the Family, and Violence in the Literature of the Early Republic*. New York: Oxford University Press, 1996.

Samuels, Shirley, ed. *The Culture of Sentiment: Race, Gender and Sentimentality in Nineteenth-Century America*. New York: Oxford University Press, 1992.

Samuelson, Paul A., and William D. Nordhaus. *Economics*. 18th ed. New York: McGraw-Hill / Irwin, 2004.

Sánchez-Eppler, Karen. "Bodily Bonds: The Intersecting Rhetorics of Feminism and Abolition." In *The Culture of Sentiment: Race, Gender, and Sentimentality in Nineteenth Century America*, edited by Shirley Samuels, 92–114. New York: Oxford University Press, 1992.

———. *Touching Liberty: Abolition, Feminism, and the Politics of the Body*. Berkeley: University of California Press, 1993.

Sandahl, Carrie, and Philip Auslander, eds. *Bodies in Commotion: Disability and Performance*. Corporalities: Discourses of Disability. Ann Arbor: University of Michigan Press, 2005.

Sanger, Margaret. *Family Limitation*. New York, 1914.

Santiago, Silviano. *Latin American Literature: The Space in Between by Silviano Santiano*. Translated by Stephen Moscov. Buffalo: Council on International Studies, SUNY Buffalo, 1971, 1973.

Sarmiento, Domingo Faustino. *Facundo: Civilization and Barbarism*. 1845. Translated by Kathleen Ross. Los Angeles: University of California Press, 2004.

Sassen, Saskia. *The Global City*. Princeton: Princeton University Press, 1991.

———. "Why Migration?" *Report on the Americas* 26, no. 1 (1992): 14–19.

———. *Globalization and Its Discontents: Essays on the New Mobility of People and Money*. New York: New Press, 1998.

Saxton, Alexander. *The Rise and Fall of the White Republic*. New York: Verso, 1990.

Schiebinger, Londa. *The Mind Has No Sex? Women in the Origins of Modern Science*. Cambridge, MA: Harvard University Press, 1989.

Schiller, Friedrich. *On the Aesthetic Education of Man, in a Series of Letters*. 1794. Edited and translated by Elizabeth M. Wilkinson and L.A. Willoughby. Oxford: Clarendon; New York: Oxford University Press, 1982.

———. *On the Aesthetic Education of Man in a Series of Letters*. Translated by Reginald Snell. New Haven: Yale University Press, 1954.

Schlesinger, Arthur M. Jr. *The Age of Jackson*. Boston: Little Brown, 1945.

———. *The Disuniting of America: Reflections on a Multicultural Society*. Rev. ed. New York: W. W. Norton, 1998.

Schmidt, Leigh Eric. *Hearing Things: Religion, Illusion, and the American Enlightenment*. Cambridge: Cambridge University Press, 2000.

Schmitt, Carl. *The Crisis of Parliamentary Democracy*. Cambridge, MA: MIT Press, 1985.

———. *Four Chapters on the Concept of Sovereignty*. Translated by George Schwab. Cambridge, MA: MIT Press, 1986.

Schwarz, Roberto. "Culture and Politics in Brazil, 1964–1969." 1970. Reprinted in *Misplaced Ideas: Essays on Brazilian Culture*. London: Verso, 1992.

Sedgwick, Eve. *Epistemology of the Closet*. Berkeley: University of California Press, 1990.

———. "Queer and Now." In *Tendencies*. Durham, NC: Duke University Press, 1993.

Sellers, Charles. *The Market Revolution: Jacksonian America, 1815–1846*. New York: Oxford University Press, 1991.

Sen, A. *Development as Freedom*. New York: Random House, 1999.

Shah, Nayan. *Contagious Divides: Epidemics and Race in San*

Works Cited

Francisco's Chinatown. Berkeley: University of California Press, 2001.

Shain, Yossi. "Ethnic Diaspora and U.S. Foreign Policy." *Political Science Quarterly* 109, no. 5 (1994–95): 811–42.

Shanley, Kathlryn W. "The Indians America Loves to Love and Read: American Indian Identity and Cultural Appropriation." *American Indian Quarterly* 21, no. 4 (1997): 675–702.

Sharpe, Jenny. "Is the United States Postcolonial? Transnationalism, Immigration, and Race." *Diaspora* 4, no. 2 (1995): 181–99.

Shell, Marc, ed. *American Babel: Literatures of the United States from Abnaki to Zuni*. Cambridge, MA: Harvard University Press, 2002.

Sidbury, James. *Ploughshares into Swords: Race, Rebellion, and Identity in Gabriel's Virginia, 1730–1810*. Cambridge: Cambridge University Press, 1997.

Siebers, Tobin. "Disability as Masquerade." *Literature and Medicine* 23, no. 1 (2004): 1–22.

Silko, Leslie Marmon. *Almanac of the Dead: A Novel*. New York: Simon and Schuster, 1991.

Silvers, Anita. *Disability, Difference, Discrimination*. New York: Rowman and Littlefield, 1998.

Sinclair, Upton. *The Jungle*. 1906. Reprint, introduction by James Barrett. Urbana: University of Illinois Press, 1988.

Singh, Nikhil. *Black Is a Country: Race and the Unfinished Struggle for Democracy*. Cambridge, MA: Harvard University Press, 2004.

Sinha, Mrinalinhi. *Colonial Masculinity: The 'Manly Englishman'and the 'Effeminate Bengali' in the Late Nineteenth Century*. Manchester: Manchester University Press, 1995.

Skinner, Quentin. *Foundations of Modern Political Thought*. 2 vols. Cambridge: Cambridge University Press, 1978.

Sklair, L. *The Sociology of the Global System*. Herfordshire, UK: Harvester Wheatsheaf, 1991.

Slotkin, Richard. *Regeneration through Violence: The Mythology of the American Frontier, 1600–1860*. Middletown, CT: Wesleyan University Press, 1973.

———. *The Fatal Environment: The Myth of the Frontier in the Age of Industrialization, 1800–1890*. Middletown, CT: Wesleyan University Press, 1985.

———. *Gunfighter Nation: The Myth of the Frontier in Twentieth-Century America*. New York: Atheneum, 1992.

Smiley, Jane. *A Thousand Acres*. New York: Alfred A. Knopf, 1991.

Smith, Adam. *The Theory of Moral Sentiments*. 1759. Reprint, New York: Augustus M. Kelley, 1966.

———. *An Inquiry into the Nature and Causes of the Wealth of Nations*. 1776. Reprint, edited by Edwin Canaan. New York: Modern Library, 1937.

Smith, David L. "Huck, Jim and American Racial Discourse." In *Satire or Evasion? Black Perspectives on "Huckleberry Finn,"* edited by James S. Leonard, Thomas A. Tenney, and Thadious M. Davis, 103–20. Durham, NC: Duke University Press, 1991.

Smith, Henry Nash. *Virgin Land: The American West as Symbol and Myth*. Cambridge, MA: Harvard University Press, 1950.

Smith, Jon, and Deborah N. Cohn. *Look Away! The U.S. South in New World Studies*. Durham, NC: Duke University Press, 2004.

Smith, Martha Nell. "Dickinson's Manuscripts." In *The Emily Dickinson Handbook*, edited by Gudrun Grabher et al. Amherst: University of Massachusetts Press, 1998.

Smith, Neil. *The Endgame of Globalization*. New York: Routlege, 2004.

Smith, Rogers M. *Civic Ideals: Conflicting Visions of Citizenship in U.S. History*. New Haven: Yale University Press, 1997.

Smith, Wilfred Cantwell. *The Meaning and End of Religion*. New York: New American Library, 1964.

Snyder, Sharon, and David T. Mitchell. "Re-engaging the

Body: Disability Studies and the Resistance to Embodiment." *Public Culture* 13, no. 3 (2001): 367–89.

Soja, Edward. *Postmodern Geographies: The Reassertion of Space in Postmodern Geographies*. London: Verso, 1989.

Sokal, Alan. "A Physicist Experiments with Cultural Studies." *Lingua Franca* 6, no. 4 (1996a): 62–64.

———. "Transgressing the Boundaries: Toward a Transformative Hermeneutics of Quantum Gravity." *Social Text* 46/47 (1996b): 217–52.

Solanas, Valerie. *The Scum Manifesto*. 1970. Reprint, with an introduction by Avital Ronell. New York: Verso, 2004.

Sollors, Werner. *Beyond Ethnicity: Consent and Descent in American Culture*. New York: Oxford University Press, 1986.

Sollors, Werner, ed. *Multilingual America: Transnationalism, Ethnicity, and the Languages of American Literature*. New York: New York University Press, 1998.

Somerville, Siobhan B. *Queering the Color Line: Race and the Invention of Homosexuality in American Culture*. Durham, NC: Duke University Press, 2000.

Sone, Monica. *Nisei Daughter*. 1953. Seattle: University of Washington Press, 1979.

Spade, Jane, and Craig Willse. "Confronting the Limits of Gay Hate Crimes Activism: a Radical Critique." *Chicano-Latino Law Review* 21 (2000): 38–52.

Spillers, Hortense. "Mama's Baby, Papa's Maybe: An American Grammar Book." *Diacritics* (Summer 1987): 65–81.

———. *Black, White, and in Color: Essays on American Literature and Culture*. Chicago: University of Chicago Press, 2003.

Spivak, Gayatri Chakravorty. "Can the Subaltern Speak?" In *Marxism and the Interpretation of Culture*, edited by Cary Nelson and Lawrence Grossberg. Urbana: University of Illinois Press, 1988.

———. *The Post-Colonial Critic: Interviews, Strategies, Dialogues*. Edited by Sarah Harasym. New York: Routledge, 1990.

———. "Scattered Speculations on the Question of Cultural Studies." In *Outside in the Teaching Machine*, 255–84. New York: Routledge, 1993.

———. *A Critique of Postcolonial Reason: Toward a History of the Vanishing Present*. Cambridge, MA: Harvard University Press, 1999.

Stacey, Judith. *Brave New Families: Stories of Domestic Upheaval in Late Twentieth Century America*. New York: Basic Books, 1990.

Stallybrass, Peter, and Allon White. *The Politics and Poetics of Transgression*. Ithaca, NY: Cornell University Press, 1986.

Stanley, Amy Dru. "Home Life and the Morality of the Market." In *The Market Revolution in America: Social, Political, and Religious Expressions, 1800–1880*, edited by Melvyn Stokes and Stephen Conway. Charlottesville: University Press of Virginia, 1996.

———. *From Bondage to Contract: Wage Labor, Marriage and the Market in the Age of Slave Emancipation*. New York: Cambridge University Press, 1998.

Stansell, Christine. *City of Women: Sex and Class in New York, 1789–1860*. New York: Alfred A. Knopf, 1986.

Stark, Rodney, and Roger Finke. *The Churching of America, 1776–1990: Winners and Losers in Our Religious Economy*. New Brunswick, NJ: Rutgers University Press, 1992.

———. *Acts of Faith: Explaining the Human Side of Religion*. Berkeley: University of California Press, 2000.

Starobinski, Jean. *1789: The Emblems of Reason*. Cambridge, MA: MIT Press, 1988.

Stephanson, Anders. *Manifest Destiny: American Expansion and the Empire of Right*. New York: Hill and Wang, 1995.

Sterling, Dorothy, ed. *The Trouble They Seen*. Garden City, NY: Doubleday, 1976.

Stern, Alexandra Minna. "Buildings, Boundaries and Blood: Medicalization and Nation-Building on the U.S.–Mexico Border, 1910–1930." *Hispanic American Historical Review* 79, no. 1 (1999a): 41–82.

———. "Secrets Under the Skin: New Historical Perspectives on

Disease, Deviation, and Citizenship." *Comparative Studies in Society and History* 41, no. 3 (July 1999b): 589–96.

Stevens, Jacqueline. *Reproducing the State*. Princeton: Princeton University Press, 1999.

———. "The Politics of LGBTQ Scholarship." *GLQ* 10, no. 2 (2004): 220–26.

Stiglitz, J. E. *Globalization and Its Discontents*. New York: W. W. Norton, 2002.

Stiglitz, Joseph E., and Carl E. Walsh. *Economics*. 3d ed. New York: W. W. Norton, 2002.

Stone, Sandy. "The 'Empire' Strikes Back: A Posttranssexual Manifesto." In *Body Guards: The Cultural Politics of Gender Ambiguity*, edited by Kristina Straub and Julia Epstein, 280–304. New York: Routledge, 1991.

Stowe, Harriet Beecher. *Uncle Tom's Cabin or, Life among the Lowly*. New York: Penguin, 1981.

Strackey, William. "True Reportory." In *A Voyage to Virginia in 1609: Two Narratives*, edited by Louis B. Wright. Charlottesville: University of Virginia Press, 1964.

Stuckey, Sterling. *Slave Culture: Nationalism and the Foundations of Black America*. New York: Oxford University Press, 1987.

Sudarkasa, Niara. "Interpreting the African Heritage in Afro-American Family Organization." In *Black Families*, edited by Harriett P. McAdoo, 37–53. Beverly Hills, CA: Sage, 1988.

Sudbury, J. *"Other Kinds of Dreams": Black Women's Organisations and the Politics of Transformation*. London: Routledge, 1998.

Sullivan, Andrew. "This *Is* a Religious War." *New York Times Magazine*, October 7, 2001: 44–53.

Sundquist, Eric. "Slavery, Revolution, and the American Renaissance." In *The American Renaissance Reconsidered*, 1–33. Baltimore: Johns Hopkins University Press, 1985.

Susman, Warren I. *Culture as History: The Transformation of American Society in the Twentieth Century*. New York: Pantheon, 1984.

Swatos, William H., Jr., and Daniel V. A. Olson, eds., *The Secularization Debate*. Lanham, MD: Rowman and Littlefield, 2000.

Sweet, John. *Bodies Politic: Renegotiating Race in the American North, 1730–1830*. Baltimore: Johns Hopkins University Press, 2003.

Takaki, Ronald. *Strangers from a Different Shore: A History of Asian Americans*. Boston: Little, Brown and Company, 1989.

———. *A Different Mirror: A History of Multicultural America*. Boston: Little, Brown, 1993.

Tarter, Jim. "Some Live More Downstream Than Others." In *The Environmental Justice Reader*, 213–28. Tucson: University of Arizona Press, 2002.

Tate, Claudia. *Domestic Allegories of Political Desire: The Black Heroine's Text at the Turn of the Century*. New York: Oxford University Press, 1992.

Tatum, Stephen. "Animal Calling/Calling Animal: Threshold Space in Frederic Remington's *Coming to the Call*." In *True West: Authenticity and the American West*, edited by William R. Handley and Nathaniel Lewis, 194–221. Lincoln: University of Nebraska Press, 2004.

Taylor, Charles. *Multiculturalism and "the Politics of Recognition."* Princeton: Princeton University Press, 1992.

———. *Varieties of Religion Today*. Cambridge, MA: Harvard University Press, 2002.

———. *Modern Social Imaginaries*. Durham, NC: Duke University Press, 2004.

Taylor, P. J. *Modernities: A Geohistorical Interpretation*. Minneapolis: Minnesota, 1999.

Terry, Jennifer. *An American Obsession: Science, Medicine, and Homosexuality in Modern Society*. Chicago: University of Chicago Press, 1999.

Thatcher, Margaret. Interview: "AIDS, Education, and the Year 2000." *Woman's Own*, October 31, 1987: 8–10.

Thomas, Paul. "Modalities of Consent." In *Beyond National-*

ism? edited by Fred Dallmayr and José Maria Rosales, 3–18. Lanham, MD, Lexington Books, 2001.

Thomas, William I., and Florian Znanieki. *The Polish Peasant in Europe and America*. 5 vols. Boston: Gorham, 1918–20.

Thompson, E. P. "The Long Revolution." *New Left Review* 9 (1961a): 24–33.

———. "The Long Revolution." *New Left Review* 10 (1961b): 34-39.

———. *The Making of the English Working Class*. New York: Vintage, 1963.

Thomson, Rosemarie Garland. *Extraordinary Bodies: Figuring Physical Disability in American Culture and Literature*. New York: Columbia University Press, 1997.

Thoreau, Henry David. *The Correspondence of Henry David Thoreau*, edited by W. Harding and C. Bode. New York: New York University Press, 1958.

———. *Reform Papers*, edited by Wendell Glick. Princeton: Princeton University Press, 1973.

———. "A Week on the Concord River and Merrimack" 1849. In *A Week, Walden, Maine Woods, Cape Cod*. New York: Library of America, 1985.

Tinker, Hugh. *A New System of Slavery: The Export of Indian Labour Overseas, 1830–1920*. London: Oxford University Press, 1974.

Tocqueville, Alexis de. *Democracy in America*. 1835. Reprint, translated by Arthur Goldhammer. New York: Library of America, 2004.

Todd, Janet. *Sensibility: An Introduction*. New York: Methuen, 1986

Tölölyan, Khachig. "Rethinking Diaspora(s): Stateless Power in the Transnational Moment." *Diaspora* 5, no. 1 (1996): 3–36.

Tompkins, Jane. *Sensational Designs: The Cultural Work of American Fiction 1790–1860*. New York: Oxford University Press, 1985.

Toomer, Jean. *Cane*. 1923; New York: Liveright, 1969.

Trachtenberg, Alan. *The Incorporation of America: Culture and Society in the Gilded Age*. New York: Farrar, Strauss, Giroux, 1982.

Treichler, Paula A. *How to Have Theory in an Epidemic: Cultural Chronicles of Aids*. Durham NC: Duke University Press, 1999.

Tribe, Keith. *Land, Labour and Economic Discourse*. London: Routledge and Kegan Paul, 1978.

Truettner, William, and Roger B. Stein, eds. *Picturing Old New England: Image and Memory*. Washington, DC: National Museum of American Art, Smithsonian Institution; New Haven: Yale University Press, 1999.

Turner, Bryan S. *Citizenship and Social Theory*. London: Dage, 1993.

Turner, Frederick Jackson. *The Frontier in American History*. 1893. Reprint, New York: Henry Holt, 1920.

Turner, Victor. *The Ritual Process: Structure and Anti-Structure*. Chicago: Aldine, 1969.

Tuveson, Ernest Lee. *Redeemer Nation: The Idea of America's Millennial Role*. Chicago: University of Chicago Press, 1968.

Twain, Mark. "A True Story, Repeated Word for Word As I Heard It." *Atlantic Monthly*, November 1874: 591–94.

———. *Adventures of Huckleberry Finn*. 1885. Reprint, Berkeley: University of California Press, 1985.

Tylor, Edward Burnett. *Primitive Culture: Researches into the Development of Mythology, Philosophy, Religion, Art, and Custom*. London: J. Murray, 1871.

Tyrell, Ian. "American Exceptionalism in an Age of International History." *American Historical Review* 96 (1991): 1031–55.

U.S. News and World Report. "Success Story of One Minority Group in the United States." December 26, 1966, 158–63.

Valdez, Luis. "La Plebe." In *Aztlan: An Anthology of Mexican American Literature*, edited by Luis Valdez and Stan Steiner. New York: Vintage Books, 1972.

Works Cited

Van Alstyne, Richard. *The Rising American Empire*. Oxford: Blackwell, 1960.

Van Wyck, Peter C. *Primitives in the Wilderness: Deep Ecology and the Missing Human Subject*. Albany: State University of New York Press, 1997.

Vasconcelos, José. *The Cosmic Race*. 1925. Translated by Didier T. Jaén. Baltimore: Johns Hopkins University Press, 1997.

Vento, Arnoldo Carlos. *Mestizo: The History, Culture and Politics of the Mexican and the Chicano, the Emerging Mestizo-Americans*. New York: University Press of America, 2002.

Venturelli, Shalini. *From the Information Economy to the Creative Economy: Moving Culture to the Center of International Public Policy*. Washington, DC: Center for Arts and Culture, 2001.

Vera, Hernán, and Andrew Gordon. *Screen Saviors: Hollywood Fictions of Whiteness*. New York: Rowman and Littlefield, 2003.

Vidal, Gore. "State of the Union, 2004." *The Nation*, September 13, 2004.

Villa, Pablo. *Ethnography at the Border*. Minneapolis: University of Minnesota Press, 2003.

Vizénor, Gerald, and A. Robert Lee. *Postindian Conversations*. Lincoln: University of Nebraska Press, 1999.

Von Eschen, Penny. *Race against Empire: Black Americans and Anticolonialism, 1937–1957*. Ithaca, NY: Cornell University Press, 1997.

———. *Satchmo Blows Up the World: Jazz Ambassadors Play the Cold War*. Cambridge, MA: Harvard University Press, 2004.

Wald, Priscilla. *Constituting Americans: Cultural Anxiety and Narrative Form*. Durham, NC: Duke University Press, 1995.

Walker, Alice. *The Color Purple: A Novel*. New York: Harcourt, Brace, Jovanovich, 1982.

Walker, David. *David Walker's Appeal, in Four Articles, Together with a Preamble, to the Coloured Citizens of the World, But in Particular, and Very Expressly, to Those of the United States of America*. New York: Hill and Wang, 1995.

Wallerstein, Immanuel. *The Modern World-System*. New York: Academic, 1976.

———. *Unthinking Social Science: The Limits of Nineteenth-Century Paradigms*. 2d ed.. Philadelphia: Temple University Press, 2001.

———. *World-Systems Theory: An Introduction*. Durham, NC: Duke University Press, 2004.

Walzer, Michael, ed. *Toward a Global Civil Society*. New York: Berghahn Books, 1995.

Warner, Michael. *The Letters of the Republic: Publication and the Public Sphere in Eighteenth-Century America*. Cambridge, MA: Harvard University Press, 1990.

———. *The Trouble with Normal: Sex, Politics, and the Ethics of Queer Life*. New York: Free Press, 1999.

———. "Publics and Counter-Publics." *Public Culture* 14, no. 1 (2002): 49–90.

Warner, W. Lloyd, and Leo Srole. *The Social Systems of American Ethnic Groups*. Chicago: University of Chicago, 1945.

Warren, Kenneth W. "Appeals for (Mis)recognition: Theorizing the Diaspora." In *Cultures of United States Imperialism*, edited by Amy Kaplan and Donald E. Pease, 392–406. Durham, NC: Duke University Press, 1993.

Watkins, Evan. *Everyday Exchanges: Marketwork and Capitalist Common Sense*. Stanford: Stanford University Press, 1998.

Wayne, Michael. "Post-Fordism, Monopoly Capitalism, and Hollywood's Media Industrial Complex." *International Journal of Cultural Studies* 6, no. 1 (2003): 82–103.

Weber, Max. *The Protestant Ethic and the Spirit of Capitalism*. 1905. Translated by Talcott Parsons. New York: Scribner's, 1958.

———. *Economy and Society: An Outline of Interpretive Sociology*. New York: Bedminster, 1968.